Media Issues

Media Issues

Point / Counterpoint

Jennifer D. Greer
Wm. David Sloan
Editors

VISION PRESS
Northport, Alabama

ACKNOWLEDGMENTS

We wish to thank Richard LeCompte, Joanne Sloan and Justin Blankenship for their assistance in reading the manuscript for this book. Their suggestions for both stylistic and substantive matters helped immeasurably.

Copyright © 2013, by Vision Press.

ALL RIGHTS RESERVED. No part of this publication may be reproduced, stored in a retrieval system, or transmitted in any form or by any means, electronic, mechanical, photocopy, recording, or otherwise, without the prior written permission of the publisher.

Vision Press
4195 Waldort Drive
P.O. Box 1106
Northport, Alabama 35476

ISBN 978-1-885219-45-9

Printed in the United States of America

Table of Contents

Table of Contents

MEDIA ISSUES

Point / Counterpoint

1 'Let Us Reason Together'

A 5-year-old boy set his bed on fire with a cigarette lighter. His 2-year-old sister died in the blaze. Investigators blamed the fire on the boy's TV habits. He'd been watching the MTV program *Beavis and Butt-head*, in which one of the characters proclaimed, "Fire is cool."

Since their attacks on the World Trade Center in 2001, terrorists have become skilled at manipulating the media. With the growth of inexpensive video equipment, they are able to furnish news organizations with prepared ready-for-television footage. Critics claim that modern technology has made it possible for them to manipulate the news media to their advantage.

While working at CBS, reporter Bernie Goldberg says, he began to recognize a pattern of liberal bias, but the "liberals in the newsroom" frowned upon discussing it. After he critiqued "liberal media bias," his colleagues viewed him as a traitor and a "right-wing ideologue" — even though he has a liberal record on most issues — because, he says, they think anyone who describes journalists as liberal must be a reactionary conservative.

When Jeff Greene lost his bid for a U.S. Senate seat from Florida, he sued the *St. Petersburg Times* and *Miami Herald*, accusing them of "a coordinated and agreed-upon plan to assassinate" his character. They had run stories about his dealings with a businessman who was later indicted for fraud and boxer Mike Tyson's allegations of illegal drug use and partying on Greene's yacht. Before the papers published the stories, Greene gave them evidence that the stories were false. His lawsuit involved the publication of information that some would consider private — personal business dealings, drug use and activities at a private party. Crtics claim that coverage of such matters deflects debate from important political issues.

These four incidents are just small snapshots of the many issues that the media face. On each of the four, one can find opposing views that are equally persuasive. The same is true of other issues as well. No one should think the issues the media confront today are simple. They are complex. They're not always easy to navigate. Therein is the purpose of this book. It is intended to serve as a primer on major media issues and as a guide to the variety of views on each one.

Most issues are complicated. In fact, any time an issue is controversial, you can be fairly certain that it has no easy answer. On any controversial issue, most of us will have views. We see things differently. As a simple example, look at the cover of this book. What do you see in it? Swirling liquid paint? An oil slick? A swordfish? The head of a wolf? A symbolic comment about media issues? A meaningless jumble? The more controversial an issue is, the stronger those views tend to be.

On important issues it becomes vital that we strive to understand opposing views and discuss them fairly. That principle has been accepted among thoughtful, educated people at least since the time of the Greek philosopher Aristotle (384 - 322 B.C.). He said that one of the most important aspects of making an argument is the speaker's credibility — and that one way to gain credibility is to present the opponent's arguments fairly. One of our earliest records of that principle of mature discussion is in the biblical book of Isaiah, which contains the well-known statement "Come, let us reason together." It was written about 700 B.C.

It's an old principle — and it still is one that should guide debate today. In fact, some people feel it is even more critical now. They note that our culture seems to be getting more politicized and polarized. Such a situation calls for respectful consideration of competing views. Controversial issues are not the place to dismiss points of view that disagree with our own. Meaningful discussion and debate require an understanding of the variety of viewpoints on issues.

This book's premise is that we can make the best judgments and decisions on issues only if we understand and appreciate various points of view. We must respect both sides in a debate, and we must be tolerant of opposing views and respectful of those who hold them.

That mindset, unfortunately, doesn't always guide discussions on media issues. We sometimes think in black-vs-white terms. Even among journalists trained for a field that traditionally has emphasized fairness and balance, differing viewpoints don't always get a fair hearing. Certain issues are particularly sensitive, and media professionals can be rigid about them. You will recognize a number of them as you read the chapters in this book. A good principle to follow in discussing any issue is to try to recognize our own "biases" and be particularly alert when they come into play. It is on issues about which we feel strongly that we need to assure that we think clearly and treat opposing views carefully.

That is the approach that you will find in this book. Each author, a specialist on the topic of a chapter, provides a balanced presentation of the main, differing viewpoints. The goal is to provide you with a knowledge of the best evidence and arguments that each side has to offer. After the chapter author introduces the topic, you will find the following material:

1. Origins of the issue

No issue suddenly pops up from nowhere. Every one has a background. Sometimes — as with objectivity, for example, the subject of Chapter 11 — people have debated the issue for a hundred years or more. With other issues, the debate may have begun in earnest within the last decade. Whether the history is short or long, knowing about the background will give you a better perspective on the issue.

2. Opposing sides

Each chapter devotes most of its space to the differing views on its issue. It summarizes the major works that opponents have written. This part of the chapter is the equivalent of an analytical literature review. The chapter authors don't take sides in the debate, and they try to treat each side fairly. This balanced approach is intended to give you a working knowledge of the arguments of each side, uncolored by the views of the chapter authors themselves.

3. Assessment

In judging the arguments of each side of an issue, we should go beyond mere opinion. Opinion needs to be supported by *evidence*. In the assessment section, the chapter author provides a short analysis of the evidence or supporting reasons that each side in the argument presents. The intent is to offer a reasoned judgment about the strengths and weaknesses of the evidence. The author then provides suggestions of what media professionals and students should be doing to resolve the issue.

4. Readings

Each chapter concludes with a list of recommended readings of works that deal with the issue. This list will point you to the most pertinent books and articles should you wish to investigate the issue further.

The chapters are arranged in a sequence that progresses logically from broad questions about the role of the media in society to issues of media performance in specific areas. Because this book's purpose is to examine arguments about how the media perform, the first chapter focuses on the issue of how to critique performance. It analyzes the question of whether media professionals do an adequate job of holding themselves accountable. Its discussion offers a number of insights that will prove valuable as you examine other issues covered in this book. From there, chapters range over major areas of concern, from the perceived influence of the media on attitudes, to the attitudes of people who work in the media, to the nature of media ownership, to media practices in their day-to-day operations. The essential concern that ties them all together is how well the media serve the society in which they exist.

This book has been designed to help you consider these issues and draw your own thoughtful conclusions. Indeed, as some of the chapter authors explain in their own suggested resolutions, the issues are so complex that there usually are no simple answers. In fact, the nature of the issues themselves suggests exactly the same thing. On any issue on which disputants of integrity and goodwill believe strongly in their own views, it is likely that a proper resolution would incorporate ideas from both, or all, sides. Thus, one should beware of disputants who are certain they are right and their opponents wrong. Examine cautiously any arguments that do not take into consideration the opposing views. Be wary of suggestions that seem simple or one-sided. Rarely in a democratic society such as ours is one side completely right and the other entirely wrong. The best answers usually lie in a middle ground rather than solely in one camp or the other. Thus, we encourage you to read these chapters critically, and we hope you will be able to take away a sense of the challenges that face today's media, as well as your own assessment of those challenges.

9 Media Self-Criticism

Jon Stewart watches the watchdogs. At least that's the conclusion of some media experts. The host of Comedy Central's *The Daily Show* spoofs the news, but he also keeps an eye on the journalists who gather it. His premise is simple: Journalists consider themselves watchdogs. They report on powerful institutions to hold them accountable. But who holds the news media accountable? Many groups and individuals evaluate the media from the outside, including academicians, bloggers and activists. This chapter looks inside the media to see how they criticize themselves — or fail to do so. Stewart might be an unlikely media critic, but he's among the most influential. Whether that is good or bad is part of an ongoing debate.

The debate about self-criticism raises a crucial issue: Do the news media do an adequate job of holding themselves accountable? To answer that question, it helps to make some distinctions. What is media self-criticism? Entertainment media have long been the subjects of critiques. For example, television, video games and movies frequently come under fire for showing too much sex or violence. People inside those fields, however, do not routinely criticize their work as a matter of self-improvement. Entertainment is subject to some regulation, but it is overwhelmingly market-driven. Public relations and advertising messages, which by nature are persuasive, often become targets for critics who might label them as deceptive. Advertising is subject to regulation, and many persuasive communicators police themselves through professional associations and codes of ethics. Much of this self-regulation is invisible to outsiders, however.

This chapter focuses on news media for several reasons. First, observers have noted journalism's importance for public life, from tracking the weather to supporting democracy. Second, journalists have a longstanding tradition of criticizing their vocation in an effort to improve it. Finally, new media technologies have expanded exponentially the number of people who can act as journalists. Anybody with a cell-phone camera potentially can scoop the mainstream media.

by Glen Feighery
University of Utah

The blurring of the lines between journalist and citizen is important to understanding news media accountability.

For now, it helps to note some basics. In their 2007 *Journal of Mass Media Ethics* article "Who Is a Journalist and Why Does it Matter?" Erik Ugland and Jennifer Henderson observed that journalists "gather and disseminate news ... deliberately, regularly, and conspicuously." Many also value truth, "independence, proportionality, comprehensiveness, and accountability."

What does self-criticism involve? German scholar Suzanne Fengler's 2003 *Journalism & Mass Communication Quarterly* article "Holding the News Media Accountable" stated that it includes "monitoring, investigating, and analyzing developments in journalism" to "expose mistakes, point toward potentially harmful developments and encourage attention to ethics." In *Critical Studies in Media Communication,* Tanni Haas went a step further. In his 2006 article "Mainstream News Media Self-Criticism," he urged "journalists to reflect on how their own and others' reporting is shaped" by economic pressures (advertising) and work pressures (deadlines and reporting conventions). Driving these concerns is the idea of accountability, that journalists should explain their actions to the public. Sandra Borden and Chad Tew's 2007 *Journal of Mass Media Ethics* article "The Role of Journalist and Performance of Journalism" defined accountability as being "responsive to demands for an explanation when journalists fail to give role-appropriate performances." The public expects three things, Borden and Tew contended. First, journalists should be gatekeepers, and only newsworthy information should pass through the gates. Second, journalists are expected to be accurate. Third, the public expects impartiality, which sometimes is called objectivity. That means reporters present all sides of a story without favoring one over another.

Origins of the Issue

Media self-criticism has deep roots. Historian John Ferré asserted that "press criticism began to be conceived in terms of ethics at the end of the 19th century," when people were concerned about sensationalism (graphic details of crimes and disasters) and dishonesty (false reports of atrocities during the Spanish-American war). As Ferré explained in his 2009 chapter "A Short History of Media Ethics in the United States" in *The Handbook of Mass Media Ethics*, these concerns spurred journalists to adopt tenets of professionalism, an early venture into self-criticism that tried to enhance journalism's stature. Journalists formed associations, including Sigma Delta Chi (later the Society of Professional Journalists) and the American Society of Newspaper Editors. By the 1920s, groups began adopting codes of ethics, which enshrined such values as accuracy, fairness and independence. In 1947, the Commission on Freedom of the Press, also known as the Hutchins Commission, published *A Free and Responsible Press*. It acknowledged the importance of freedom but was concerned that the news media were not sufficiently responsible. The Hutchins Commission had two major impacts: the development of social responsibility theory of journalism and the acceleration of self-criticism. The theory, Ferré observed, "valued both freedom from government interference and commitment to the public good." The power to reach tens of millions of people at once, the Hutchins Commission said, needed to be balanced by responsibility. Meanwhile, the commission urged "that the members of the press engage in vigorous mutual criticism."

Journalists' self-criticism also has intellectual roots. Ethicist Wendy Wyatt traced them in her 2007 book *Critical Conversations*. She started with the question of whether journalists should critique themselves at all. Some theorists argued that they should, because the news media have a responsibility to scrutinize themselves. Others, such as James Carey, believed that criticism should be culturally based. He argued that the public should understand how news is conceptualized (why certain items get through the gates) and how reports are shaped by conventions such as the inverted pyramid writing style (with the most important news at the top of an article). Contributions by Carey and others, Wyatt wrote, provided guidelines for how journalists would criticize themselves in the future.

No background of journalism self-criticism would be complete without considering autonomy. In "Fears of Corporate Colonization" in a 2002 issue of *Journalism Studies*, Tanni Haas and Linda Steiner observed that acting as watchdogs requires independence, which prevents conflicts of interest. Journalists cannot, for example, freelance for a company they report on. Most crucially, independence means not only freedom from external control but the ability to exercise vocational and individual control. Patrick Lee Plaisance and Joan Deppa argued in their 2009 article "Perceptions and Manifestations of Autonomy, Transparency and Harm" in *Journalism & Communication Monographs* that autonomy goes beyond the First Amendment's legal protections. It has ethical implications. They explained that "philosophers have long claimed that the concepts of autonomous agency and responsibility are two sides of the same coin." If journalists can determine their own destinies, they can choose what ethical duties they will accept. Many journalists have resisted attempts by outsiders to tell them what to do. In "Creating an Effective Newspaper Ombudsman" in a 2000 issue of the *Journal of Mass Media Ethics*, Christopher Meyers wrote, "Resistance is rooted in recognition that journalistic enterprises are importantly different than other self-regulating businesses and professions. They have different historical roots, justifications and social roles." This claim has passionate advocates. Right or wrong, autonomy is a key to understanding media self-criticism.

Do the media do an adequate job of criticizing themselves?

Journalism self-criticism takes many forms. Some critiques occur daily in individual newsrooms, while others address issues at a broad vocational level. Accountability is not the same as self-criticism, but it is a key component and a common thread running through all these measures. At the same time, a broad context of media ethics surrounds this subject. Although not synonymous with self-criticism, ethical behavior usually is the goal. Like the question of who is a journalist, questions about ethics are important to understanding accountability.

Media Do a Good Job

Journalists and scholars have identified several ways in which the media hold themselves accountable through self-criticism: corrections, ombudsmen, news councils, critics, journalism reviews, codes of ethics and satire.

Corrections are a mundane but integral way that journalists monitor their performance. "Although methods and policies vary across platforms, it is standard practice to acknowledge and correct errors quickly and prominently in the print, online and broadcast news industries," ethicist Michael Bugeja observed in his 2007 article "Making Whole: The Ethics of Correction" in the *Journal of Mass Media Ethics.* It has not always been that way. Former editor Robert J. Haiman pointed to "a difference between what the public thinks about corrections and what many journalists think about them." In 2000's *Best Practices for Newspaper Journalists*, he wrote that journalists tend to think that only "the most egregious factual errors need to be corrected now," but "the public sees it quite another way." Audiences want more corrections and clarifications, which make the news media more credible, Haiman concluded.

Neil Nemeth and Craig Sanders found a similar tension in their 2009 article "Number of Corrections Increase at Two National Newspapers" in *Newspaper Research Journal.* Like Haiman, they noticed contrasting opinions about corrections. Journalists worry that they will undermine credibility, but the public sees them as proof that the news media care about accuracy and accountability. Nemeth and Sanders suggested that corrections are an effective means of self-criticism because they foster dialogue between newspapers and their readers.

Journalist Mark Bowden, author of *Black Hawk Down*, agreed. His narrative about a bloody battle in Somalia was serialized online in the *Philadelphia Inquirer* before it became a book. "One critical way it improved the story was by giving readers all over the world a chance to instantly correct my mistakes," Bowden wrote in "Being Accountable Through a Digital Dialogue" in the 2010 book *The*

Ethical Journalist. "Readers who received an apology and thanks from me saw that they had contributed directly to the story's accuracy. This greatly enhanced the account's credibility."

Bugeja offered a final note about the value of corrections. He argued that the goal of corrections should not simply be avoiding legal culpability against potential libel suits. Instead, the practice of correcting mistakes should reflect a desire to make people whole — for example, to restore the reputation of someone harmed by an erroneous report. Such good intentions can put moral power behind an otherwise mechanical process of correcting the record, he wrote.

Another form of self-criticism has an unusual name: ombudsman. It stems from the Swedish tradition of appointing an official to hold government accountable to the people, and it gained popularity in the news media beginning in the 1960s. Ombudsmen also have been called reader advocates, reader representatives and public editors. Their numbers have remained low, with a peak of only about forty nationwide. In his 2003 book *News Ombudsmen in North America,* Neil Nemeth defined the position as "typically a senior editor equipped with the authority to investigate complaints and get answers." Among the duties are writing internal memos or taking corrective actions inside news organizations, writing columns that air grievances and assess journalists' performance, and simply listening to an unhappy member of the public.

Sometimes, these steps are enough to provide an effective means of accountability. In his "Creating an Effective Newspaper Ombudsman" article, Meyers noted supporters' arguments that ombudsmen can reduce libel actions, efficiently direct complaints to the right person and build good relationships with the public. Overall, he believes, ombudsmen can enjoy success if "they have real authority to reward and discipline" and if they are not "insiders" steeped in an organization's culture and ethos. For one-time National Public Radio ombudsman Jeffrey Dvorkin, the position is worthwhile in its own right. "It is an indication that a news organization is committed to good standards and practices in its journalism," he told *American Journalism Review* in 2005 in "The Ombudsman Puzzle."

Along with corrections and ombudsmen, media supporters point to press councils. Also called news councils, they are "non-governmental associations of journalists and non-journalists who hear, assess and resolve public complaints against news media," Erik Ugland wrote in 2008 in the periodical *Journalism.* His definition reflects what he called "a partnership between two distinct constituencies," but news councils can be considered a form of self-criticism because they include journalists engaged in a process of accountability. Councils are even rarer than ombudsmen, with only a handful in places such as Hawaii, Washington state, Southern California, Minnesota and New England. Consistent with journalists' autonomy, councils are informal. They lack enforcement power, and media can choose to participate or not. News councils occasionally publish opinions that explain whether complaints are justified and recommend what journalists might do better. For proponents, councils are a nonbinding, nonlitigious way to air grievances. They can do more than that, Southern California News Council executive Bill Babcock told *American Journalism Review* in 2006. Councils provide a platform from which to act as "a media evangelist" to tell the public that "we're here as another media accountability tool and not as media bashers." Overall, Patrick Lee Plaisance contended in "The Concept of Media Accountability Reconsidered," an article in the *Journal of Mass Media Ethics* in 2000, councils represent the "best balance between the free press needs of autonomy and the need for a formal way to ensure a responsible press."

News councils are group critics on a national or regional level. Individual critics also evaluate journalism from a broad perspective. These media critics, or media reporters, are often full-time staffers at publications such as the *New York Times*, the *Washington Post*, or the *New Yorker*. News outlets such as CNN, Fox News and National Public Radio perform a similar function with programs such as *Reliable Sources*, *NewsWatch* and *On the Media*. These critics and programs address topics such as controversial news coverage, journalism ethics and business pressures. One well-known media critic is Howard Kurtz, Washington bureau chief for The Daily Beast and *Newsweek*. He also hosts CNN's weekly *Reliable Sources* program and formerly covered the media for the *Washington Post*. Another is David Carr of the *New York Times*, who monitors the impact of media ownership on journalists' ability to cover news and remain independent.

Experts are divided about press critics' effectiveness. Among those who think it succeeds as a form of self-criticism is Arthur S. Hayes, who thinks journalists pay attention to some critics because they are insiders — people like themselves. In his 2008 book *Press Critics Are the Fifth Estate*, Hayes cited Ben Bagdikian, an early media critic, whom he deemed "difficult to summarily dismiss, largely because his ... achievements as a journalist are distinguished. He has newsroom 'cred.'" Similar to ombudsmen and news councils, full-time critics are few. Does that mean that media reporters will go the way of teletype operators? Not so fast, say Paul D'Angelo and Frank Esser. In "Metacoverage as an Accountability System," they argued at the 2009 International Communication Association conference that there is value to what they called metacoverage — coverage about news coverage. Unlike news councils, media reporters can address potentially large audiences and use publicity to improve journalists' practices and help self-regulate the profession.

Not all critics work for news organizations. Many write for journalism reviews — magazines that assess the work of the news media. The first, *Nieman Re-*

ports, started in 1947. It emerged as a direct result of the Hutchins Commission's call for "mutual criticism." Two others, *Columbia Journalism Review* and *American Journalism Review*, also monitor the profession on a national scale. They were founded in 1961 and 1977, respectively, bracketing a time when "movements ... were questioning mainstream institutions, including the press," wrote Kristie Bunton in a chapter in the 2000 book *Holding the Media Accountable*. She distinguished between media critics writing for the public and those writing for journalism reviews, whose "target audience is composed principally of journalists." They can be considered a form of media self-criticism because their contributors primarily are journalists writing for their peers.

Bunton was interested in the degree to which journalism reviews provide "an effective self-regulatory mechanism for a profession averse to external control." She offered three criteria. First, reviews should explain how journalists cover news. Second, they should criticize coverage, as *Columbia Journalism Review* does in its "Darts and Laurels" column. "Critical articles in a journalism review," Bunton wrote, "aim to point out violations of accepted professional norms, in the hope that identifying transgressors will prevent future transgressions." Third, journalism reviews should propose changes to practices and standards. This "reform content ... questions whether existing norms satisfy journalism's social obligations." When Bunton applied her criteria to a local journalism review, she found mixed results, perhaps because it "and its writers may have been too close to local news organizations." Still, Haas and Steiner acknowledged journalism reviews' potential to provide a forum "to debate the proper role and responsibility of journalism."

The controversies surrounding corrections, ombudsmen, councils, critics and reviews illustrate the challenges of oversight. Another approach to self-criticism is professionalism. "Basically, an occupation qualifies as a profession if it possesses certain idealized attributes," wrote Sandra Borden and Peggy Bowers in their chapter in *The Handbook of Mass Media Ethics*. They added that the definition is far more complex. They listed attributes such as "mastery of a complex body of knowledge; considerable discretion in how members define and perform their work; organization along collegial lines of authority; and a commitment to public service and common standards of excellence."

Journalism, Borden and Bowers argued, "usually gets left off the list of professions." Why? Even though journalists enjoy some discretion and are committed to public service, they often disagree about ethical priorities and cannot claim exclusive expertise in gathering and presenting news. Furthermore, "the term 'professional' is contested among journalists themselves" because it implies controls that most of them find unacceptable. Medicine and law have such standards for regulation such as credentials (an earned M.D. or J.D.), licensure by a state and formal sanctions encoded in law. These rules present a stark contrast with journalistic autonomy. When physicians or lawyers engage in ethical misconduct, they face possible punishments and can even lose their licenses. For journalists, such measures would "pose intolerable dangers to press freedoms under the First Amendment," Borden and Bowers concluded.

That does not mean that professionalism plays no role in journalists' self-criticism. As noted above, journalists began forming associations in the 1920s to improve their vocation. This activity reflects a professional orientation, ethicist Lou Hodges contended in the 2004 article "Accountability in the Professions: Accountability in Journalism" in the *Journal of Mass Media Ethics*. Journalism organizations resemble the American Medical Association and the American Bar Association. Unlike licensing agencies that can punish physicians and lawyers, these associations are "educational and inspirational," Hodges wrote. As forums for self-criticism, they serve as an additional means of accountability.

The influence of professionalism is also apparent in ethics codes. "To earn the trust of their clients and of society," Borden and Bowers wrote, "professionals voluntarily adopt codes of ethics that spell out their aspirations and minimal moral expectations." Journalism associations with ethics codes include the American Society of News Editors, the Radio-Television News Directors Association and the Online News Association. The best-known code is that of the Society of Professional Journalists. In his 2010 article "Coded Controversy" in *Quill* magazine, Casey Bukro, former chair of SPJ's Ethics Committee, recalled that after years of discussing punitive measures, the society went in another direction. SPJ approved what Bukro called a "green light" code of ethics that emphasizes four positive principles: "Seek Truth and Report It," "Minimize Harm," "Act Independently" and "Be Accountable."

One more form of media self-criticism reflects the blurry definitions of journalists seen so far. TV watchers have been familiar with comedy news since *Saturday Night Live* began doing spoof newscasts in the 1970s. More recent iterations have followed, and they have added a new function: comedy criticism. This is where Jon Stewart and another Comedy Central star, Stephen Colbert, come in. They do not provide criticism *of* journalism *by* journalists. Stewart acts like a news anchor, and Colbert impersonates a talk-show host. Nevertheless, numerous scholars have argued that they should be valued as critics — not because people might mistake them for journalists, but because they have something valuable to say.

In their 2007 article "The Role of Journalist and Performance of Journalism: Ethical Lessons from 'Fake' News (Seriously)," Sandra Borden and Chad Tew contended that the Comedy Central personalities "occupy a place on the line between internal and external criticism." They linked satire to traditional news, noting that "the starting premise of the fake news routine often begins with real journalism." This premise includes an acceptance of journalistic values such as gatekeeping, factuality and impartiality. When audiences see unedited film clips on *The Daily Show*, they laugh at a politician's entire statement that reveals his or her contradictions. But the public is also reminded of gatekeeping — how journalists make selective judgments and control what people see.

Factuality works in a similar way. *The Colbert Report* presents a pretend-conservative news-talk host who believes in "truthiness," in contrast with traditional fact-based reporting, which reflects the value of impartiality. Borden and Tew argued that such "absurd performances" reflect how neutrality leads journalists to "dutifully reproduce official pronouncements that distort or hide pertinent information." Thus, what appears to be balance can actually be a failure to act as a watchdog.

Rachel Smolkin further critiqued the power of humor in "What the Mainstream Media Can Learn from Jon Stewart" in *American Journalism Review* in 2007. "Much of the allure of Stewart's show lies in its brutal satire of the media," she wrote. "He exposes their gullibility. He derides their contrivances." On a broader level, Hayes' book *Press Critics Are the Fifth Estate* emphasized comedians' commitment to the public-service role of journalism. In the chapter "Press Criticism as a Laughing Matter," he concluded that "Stewart takes a centrist, populist and common-sense approach to his media criticism." Hayes added, "Stewart's critique of the news media seems to be grounded in the social responsibility concept of journalism." In 2010 Chad Painter and Louis Hodges also deemed satire effective. In their article "Mocking the News" in the *Journal of Mass Media Ethics* they wrote, "If Jon Stewart and *The Daily Show* is a watchdog on the Fourth Estate, then the show alerts its audience through laughter ... informed by ethical standards."

Media Don't Do a Good Job

The news media have several ways to criticize themselves. For many observers, however, these tactics do not add up to an effective means of accountability. They note weaknesses or flaws in these processes. As for corrections, scholars have argued that a good-faith desire to amend the record clashes with journalists' autonomy and sense of professionalism. That leads to resistance. In their 2009 article "Number of Corrections Increase at Two National Newspapers," Neil Nemeth and Craig Sanders highlighted this tension. They found that the public is quick to spot mistakes, but journalists "are reluctant to admit error or seek to understand how often they err." This disparity is driven in part by the fact that news judgments involve subjective decisions — what to include or exclude —

that members of the public later challenge. "Editors and reporters may be reluctant to speak to subjective errors for fear of leaving themselves open to readers and sources seeking another weapon to manipulate and control what is written about them." Because that represents an infringement on journalistic autonomy, it limits corrections' effectiveness as a means of self-criticism, Nemeth and Sanders suggested.

As for ombudsmen, some of the same scholars who found that they could sometimes be successful also discovered serious shortcomings. Of the ombudsmen studied by Neil Nemeth in his book, only one "engaged in regular, systematic, public criticism of the news organization. The reason for this sole exception seems clear: It's not a high priority for ombudsmen or their editors because it's too uncomfortable." This problem illustrates a clash between journalists' desire to preserve their autonomy and the fact that some ombudsmen are not fully independent of their organizations. If reader representatives wanted to work in another position in the same newsroom, Nemeth reasoned, they would have little incentive to hold their colleagues accountable. Doing so might put ombudsmen's careers in jeopardy. Furthermore, in several anecdotal situations Nemeth described, "the ombudsmen had little role to play in the resolution of these incidents because they had no power." These are not the only controversial aspects of the practice. Patrick Lee Plaisance dismissed it in "The Concept of Media Accountability," writing that "by the nature of the position," which potentially puts people in a conflict between their loyalties to the public versus their loyalties to their employer, "ombudsmen should not be considered a reliable function of journalistic accountability."

Christopher Meyers listed specific concerns in "Creating an Effective Newspaper Ombudsman": cost, the perception that reader representatives are "public relations ploys" and the fear that they create a barrier between the public and the journalists who need to hear directly from their audiences. "News media are broadly seen as arrogant, unresponsive and wielding far too much power, exactly the sorts of concerns that motivated external regulation in law [and] medicine," Meyers wrote. "Ombudsmen, to date, have not done much to improve this standing.... [I]f the public perceives ombudsmen as being mere public relations officers, there will be little confidence in their ability effectively to rein in journalistic excess."

Andrew R. Cline went a step further, applying Meyers' ideas to two high-profile ombudsmen, one at the *Washington Post* and the other at the *New York Times*. In a 2008 article in the *Journal of Mass Media Ethics*, Cline employed Meyers' criterion that the ombudsman must be independent of the news organization, not a promoter or defender of it. In the case of the *Post*, at least, he didn't see the independence needed to create a middle ground, "a space in which the concerns of journalists for adequately covering the news meets readers' subjective experiences of the news." A different orientation — a different ethos — is needed, Cline wrote. "If an ombudsman is to be a PR agent for the paper or the chief complaint department, it may be that the voice of journalistic authority fits these models best." To be an effective ombudsman, it takes a commitment to step away from that authority and act as a representative of the audience.

News councils also have their critics. Erik Ugland's article about the U.S. National News Council was complemented by David Pritchard's research into the Quebec Press Council in Canada. Pritchard's 2000 chapter in *Holding the Media Accountable* concluded that the Quebec council, like its U.S. counterpart, lacked clearly articulated ethical standards. Thus, it was difficult for journalists to know how their work would be judged, which fueled resistance to participation. Also, a lack of explicit standards deprived councils of opportunities to educate the public about journalism, as Southern California News Council executive Bill Babcock suggested in *American Journalism Review*. Instead, Ugland wrote, "the council's work provides grist for those who might question its legitimacy and its value as a model of authentic press-public collaboration."

Another persistent concern about councils has been the threat of government control. Because the National News Council sought to assess the accuracy and fairness of journalism, "it agitated a number of journalists who saw [this] as an affront to their autonomy and a step toward regulation," Ugland wrote. This fear contributed to the council's demise after only eleven years. "The council never established a place in the public's consciousness," Ugland said. "Its members and staff worked in relative obscurity, and its dissolution in 1984 received only a flicker of media coverage." Indeed, in his 2010 book *The Ethical Journalist*, former editor Gene Foreman noted that "The National News Council ... [died] without ever gaining significant support from the media." Since 1984, the United States has had no national council. Foreman observed that the regional news councils represent only "tepid stirrings of sentiment for such a body." Rowland Thompson, head of a newspaper association in Washington state, was quoted in the *American Journalism Review* article on news councils as saying individual papers are "tougher on ourselves" than a press council could be. This statement again highlights the importance that journalists place on autonomy and regulating themselves, and not letting another entity — even one that includes journalists — do it for them. Thompson also expressed concern that U.S. news councils could become like some international bodies that are "used to control ... news content" in countries that lack the United States' First Amendment protections for freedom of the press.

Experts also disagree over the effectiveness of media critics. Hayes' *Press Critics Are the Fifth Estate* hinted at one shortcoming, which is the same problem that others have with news councils: a lack of clear standards. He observed that some critics "have been merely influential, whatever that means." Hayes was echoing a 1989 critique from James B. Lemert. In *Criticizing the Media*, Lemert was bothered that media critics did not seem to have any established criteria for judging journalism. "Given the disarray and contradictions present among critics," he wrote, "it should be no surprise to find that many journalists may have trouble sorting workable ideas out of a confusing cacophony of critical voices." Tom Goldstein, former dean of journalism graduate schools at Columbia University and the University of California at Berkeley, agreed in his 1989 book *Killing the Messenger*. "Contemporary journalists have not shown any great appetite for self-analysis.... Only sporadically have they trained on themselves the same skepticism they routinely bring to bear on city councilmen, police chiefs, movie directors, football coaches and heads of state. They need to subject themselves to the same critical analysis they apply to others." Even when critics have done so, they have not been effective, Meyers argued in his article on ombudsmen. "The Howard Kurtzes and David Shaws [critics for the *Washington Post* and *Los Angeles Times*], for all their Pulitzer Prizes and public popularity have little to no effect on journalistic behavior," Meyers wrote. This is because "they have no authority and thus are easily dismissed, or even denigrated, by their newsroom colleagues."

Adding to this perception, Prof. Christopher Harper raised questions about the future of media critics. At the 2009 Media in Transition conference, he noted "that the number of media critics in the mainstream media and even the alternative press has declined significantly in recent years." Finally, in their 2007 *Atlantic Journal of Communication* article "Mock News and Democracy," Paul Brewer and Emily Marquardt found reason to suggest that metacoverage "may activate or foster cynicism about both politics and the news media."

Journalism reviews, like other means of self-criticism, also have their detractors. Prominent among them are Haas and Steiner, who raised fundamental questions in their *Journalism Studies* article about how the *Columbia Journalism Review* (CJR) and *American Journalism Review* (AJR) treated the civic journalism movement. The idea, also known as public journalism, aimed to reflect the public's priorities in news coverage. Haas and Steiner were sharply critical of the reviews. They found that instead of evaluating civic journalism on its merits, the two reviews "propped up [traditional] journalistic ideology" by scapegoating the still-growing movement." Haas and Steiner asserted that CJR and AJR treated civic journalism "as just another manifestation of the increasing profit orientation of the news media," a judgment based on accusations that civic journalism pandered to public tastes and thus was a ploy to increase audience size. "By devoting so much space to unsubstantiated allegations against public journalism,

CJR and AJR may ultimately have served not as agents of progressive social change, but rather as agents of social control, incapable of specifying what journalists should, and indeed can, do," Haas and Steiner wrote. They concluded that CJR and AJR's performance in this instance "raises questions about their status as vehicles for critical self-reflection."

Like other aspects of media self-criticism, professionalism and ethics codes have proved controversial. "Professional codes of ethics have become popular ... as demonstrations of accountability," Plaisance wrote in his *Journal of Mass Media Ethics* article. "However, reliance on codes generates significant suspicion that they are often used to merely put an ethics veneer over questionable behavior." Plaisance cited ethicist Clifford Christians, whose 1989 chapter on self-regulation in *Media Freedom and Accountability* described codes as providing "oratory" that sounds noble but does not lead to media accountability. Codes also clashed with journalists' sense of autonomy, wrote Casey Bukro of the Society of Professional Journalists' Ethics Committee. Before SPJ adopted its "positive" code, one version provided for sanctions against violators. This was not an effective means of holding journalists accountable, Bukro wrote in his *Quill* article, because it set off a firestorm of protest about the news media's independence. "SPJ was torn between a desire to lead journalism to a greater sensitivity toward ethical conduct and a fear that such efforts might lead to 'witch hunts' against journalists."

Meanwhile, some critics disagree that satire by people such as Jon Stewart is a powerful means of holding the news media accountable. Although Borden and Tew contended that comics Stewart and Colbert are idealists, not cynics, other scholars assert just the opposite. Paul Brewer and Emily Marquardt found evidence that *The Daily Show* helps audiences think critically about the media, but "one could see such content as likely to encourage cynicism about not only politics but also the news media themselves." In a 2007 *Critical Studies in Media Communication* article, "The Political Sins of Jon Stewart," Roderick Hart and Johanna Hartelius argued that "Stewart makes cynicism attractive" while dodging responsibility for improving journalism. Cynicism is not productive, the authors believe, because cynics operate in the realm of "observation, not participation, and see irony as the only stable source of pleasure." In their view, Stewart might critique the foibles of the news media, but he fails to specify what the media should do instead. "His discourses are both an art form and a style, a type of display more than a type of argument," Hart and Hartelius wrote. "As such, Stewart's performances become ends in themselves rather than ways of changing social or political realities." Moreover, Hart and Hartelius have little faith in Comedy Central's medium, television, which they called "cynicism's most reliable delivery system" and thus, by implication, a poor channel for self-criticism.

Another strident critic of satire as a form of media accountability is *New York Times* media critic David Carr. On the eve of the 2010 midterm Congressional elections, Stewart and Colbert held a "Rally to Restore Sanity" on the Mall in Washington, D.C. One of their goals — expressed in character and through direct commentary — was to demonstrate that the majority of Americans were moderate, but that the news media pandered to the extremes. The rally garnered considerable attention for its critique of cable news. "But here's the problem," Carr wrote. "Most Americans don't watch or pay attention to cable television. In even a good news night, about 5 million people take a seat on the cable wars, which is less than 2% of all Americans. People are scared of what they see in their pay envelopes and neighborhoods, not because of what Keith Olbermann said last night or how Bill O'Reilly came back at him." Carr did not stop there. "True, any poll of American attitudes toward the press would suggest a lot of people share Mr. Stewart's distrust of media, [but] if they had a Rally to Restore Respect for the Media, it would draw two people. And one of them would be a hot dog vendor."

Assessment

There is no simple answer to the question, "Do the media do an adequate job of criticizing themselves?"

News media criticize themselves in many ways: corrections, ombudsmen, news councils, media critics, journalism reviews, professionalism, codes of ethics and humor. Each involves some controversy. Are they effective? Do they serve the best interests of the news media and the public? It is possible to answer those questions by analyzing the evidence for or against these measures, beginning with those that do not work well. Research indicates that the ombudsman idea is better in theory than in practice. Meyers showed benefits such as efficiently directing complaints to the right person, and former NPR ombudsman Dvorkin told *American Journalism Review* that the position symbolizes a commitment to high standards. These benefits, however, seem to be overshadowed by problems. As Cline pointed out in the *Journal of Mass Media Ethics*, the position is not effective unless ombudsmen are independent of the news organization, and few are. When ombudsmen are insiders, as Nemeth observed in his book, the temptation is to soft-pedal criticism for fear of alienating coworkers and hurting one's future career options. That leads to a frustrated public.

News councils have advocates such as Bill Babcock, whose concept of "media evangelist" aims to educate audiences and hold the media accountable. But here, too, objections loom large. Ugland and Pritchard showed that a lack of clear standards alienates journalists, who do not know how their work will be judged. Worse, if councils fail to articulate standards, they cannot perform the educational function so valued by Babcock and others. Finally, Rowland Thompson's concerns about potential control over content are unlikely to come true (thanks to the First Amendment), but journalists fear a slippery slope toward some external authority that would compromise their independence. That deters them from participating.

Media critics are considered peers by other journalists, and as Hayes argued, thus enjoy a degree of credibility. D'Angelo and Esser noted that critics can reach a broad audience because they write for the public, not internally. As with news councils, however, critics' failure to explain their standards is problematic. Perhaps most damning is Meyers' argument that credibility does not translate into authority. That leads journalists to ignore critics or even denigrate them. It appears reasonable to conclude that even if critics reach the public, they do not connect with the very journalists whose work they intend to influence.

Journalism reviews fall somewhere between effective and ineffective. They provide a forum for journalists to evaluate their vocation, as Haas and Steiner acknowledged, but their reach is limited. Average citizens probably do not read reviews or even know they exist. Also, as Bunton pointed out in her chapter, reviewers might be too close to the media they report on. Haas and Steiner made the scathing claim that reviews' coverage of the public journalism movement rendered them not "agents of progressive social change, but rather ... agents of social control." However, the critique by Haas and Steiner was narrowly focused on one issue during a particular time period. Ultimately, journalism reviews' role in holding the media accountable cannot be completely dismissed.

The evidence indicates that codes of ethics have more promise. Plaisance and Christians suggested that codes express high ideals, but they are not always translated into action. As with news councils, Bukro wrote, ethics codes have elicited fears of control. But Bukro also explained how the Society of Professional Journalists successfully negotiated a heated debate and created a "green-light" code articulating positive things that journalists should do: seeking truth, minimizing harm, acting independently, and — most important — being accountable.

Two final methods appear to work well. The first is corrections. They encounter resistance from some journalists who want to avoid becoming entangled in conflicts about subjective news judgments, as Nemeth and Sanders wrote. But the arguments in favor of correcting the record are more persuasive. Bowden's experience with his online audience (whom he thanked for correcting his mistakes) helped strengthen the story that eventually became *Black Hawk Down*. Furthermore, as Bugeja has argued, corrections can make people whole — for example, restoring someone's reputation — and thereby demonstrate journalists' commitment to ethics.

That leaves satire. Hart and Hartelius were concerned that Jon Stewart generates cynicism about the news media without suggesting ways to improve it. Countering this fear is a strong and convincing argument that even though comedians are not journalists they are as influential as any traditional critic, as Borden and Tew stated. Stewart and Colbert's performances succeed as a form of self-criticism precisely because they are idealists, not cynics. As Smolkin concluded, comedy illustrates not just what the news media do poorly but how it could be better. The audience's laughter, Painter and Hodges agreed, is "informed by ethical standards."

Given the strengths and weaknesses of the various forms of self-criticism, what can journalists do differently? The answer might lie in the shifting media landscape. This chapter began by noting that new technologies allow virtually anyone to gather and disseminate news. That can be good, but it also contributes to a clutter of unverified information. In such an environment, trust is perhaps journalists' only exclusive commodity. Social networking media could take the process of self-criticism a step further. They have not been extensively studied in this context, but they can achieve some of the goals examined above: engagement, explanation and accountability. Journalists can be more transparent and more authentic. If satire is a critical tool because it reveals a gap between ideal and reality, then social media can be a restorative tool to bridge the gap on an individual level. If the public perceives journalists as trustworthy individuals instead of members of vague and remote "media," that perception could reverse the trend away from traditional news and toward opinionated outlets and online aggregators. Better still, it might help ensure that regardless where people get their news, they can demand — and get — reports that achieve well-articulated and generally accepted standards of accuracy, fairness and responsibility.

Points of View

Books

Commission on Freedom of the Press. *A Free and Responsible Press.* Chicago: University of Chicago Press, 1947. Now a classic, the Hutchins Commission report stirred controversy when it was published but helped establish a key media ethics theory of the 20th century.

Goldstein, Tom. *Killing the Messenger: 100 Years of Media Criticism*, rev. ed. New York: Columbia University Press, 2007. This is the latest edition of Goldstein's accessible history of journalism criticism, in which he lets key figures speak for themselves.

Hayes, Arthur S. *Press Critics Are the Fifth Estate: Media Watchdogs in America.* Westport, Conn.: Praeger, 2008. This engaging study spells out criteria for effective criticism and

takes readers through various approaches from bloggers to comedians.

Nemeth, Neil. *News Ombudsmen in North America: Assessing an Experiment in Social Responsibility*. Westport, Conn.: Praeger, 2003. Nemeth's comprehensive book combines a broad background with studies of individual news outlets that have had ombudsmen.

Wyatt, Wendy N. *Critical Conversations: A Theory of Press Criticism*. Cresskill, N.J.: Hampton Press, 2007. Wyatt acknowledges criticism as a discourse and characterizes journalism as a social practice confronted with challenge and change.

Articles and Book Chapters

Borden, Sandra L., and Chad Tew. "The Role of Journalist and Performance of Journalism: Ethical Lessons from 'Fake' News (Seriously)." *Journal of Mass Media Ethics* 22 (2007): 300-14. Anyone who enjoys *The Daily Show* or *The Colbert Report* can learn why their critiques of journalism are funny — and ultimately idealistic.

Borden, Sandra L., and Peggy Bowers. "Ethical Tensions in News Making: What Journalism Has in Common with Other Professions," in *The Handbook of Mass Media Ethics*, Lee Wilkins and Clifford G. Christians, eds. New York: Routledge, 2009. This chapter compares journalism with other fields such as law, medicine, and engineering to see how each addresses professional tensions.

Bugeja, Michael. "Making Whole: The Ethics of Correction." *Journal of Mass Media Ethics* 22 (2007): 49-65. This article goes beyond the mere mechanics of correcting mistakes and examines what it takes to make corrections more ethical.

Fengler, Susanne. "Holding the News Media Accountable: A Study of Media Reporters and Media Critics in the United States." *Journalism & Mass Communication Quarterly* 80 (2003): 818-32. Journalism critics have considerable power, but they ultimately should serve the public, not just other journalists.

Ferré, John P. "A Short History of Media Ethics in the United States," in *The Handbook of Mass Media Ethics*, Lee Wilkins and Clifford G. Christians, eds. New York: Routledge, 2009. This chapter takes readers through four historical stages as journalism ethics developed in the 1800s and 1900s.

Haas, Tanni, and Linda Steiner. "Fears of Corporate Colonization in Journalism Reviews' Critiques of Public Journalism." *Journalism Studies* 3 (2002): 325-41. The authors probe to see whether journalism reviews are really effective critics or if they are constrained by economic and social forces.

Holt, Kristoffer. "Authentic Journalism? A Critical Discussion about Existential Authenticity in Journalism Ethics." *Journal of Mass Media Ethics* 27 (2012): 2-14. Holt questions whether authenticity actually provides a useful ethical guide for journalists.

Newton, Lisa H., Louis Hodges, and Susan Keith. "Accountability in the Professions: Accountability in Journalism." *Journal of Mass Media Ethics* 19 (2004): 166-90. The authors show how journalism aligns with other professions — or, in some respects, should not be considered a formal profession.

Plaisance, Patrick Lee. "The Concept of Media Accountability Reconsidered." *Journal of Mass Media Ethics* 15 (2000): 257-68. Plaisance dusts off an old concept and redefines it as a fluid, dynamic process and not just a set of static indicators.

Ugland, Erik, and Jennifer Henderson. "Who Is a Journalist and Why Does it Matter? Disentangling the Legal and Ethical Arguments." *Journal of Mass Media Ethics* 22 (2007): 241-61. The authors tease out what distinguishes journalists from other public communicators in today's cluttered media landscape.

3 How Powerful Are the Media?

When *Pediatrics* published a study in 2007 by Victor C. Strasburger that concluded that the connection between media violence and real-life aggression is nearly as strong as the connection between smoking and lung cancer, many people expressed disbelief. After all, medical studies have revealed a direct correlation between smoking and lung cancer. Of course, all who smoke do not contract cancer, but the odds of contracting the disease rise dramatically.

Still, millions of people agree that the effects of media — especially on children and adolescents — are undeniable. They point to a long list of studies and anecdotal accounts to support their contentions. After Hollywood released the *Jackass* series of motion pictures, a number of ambitious teens copied the foolish antics of the movies' star, Johnny Knoxville. One 15-year-old boy from Washington state decided that Knoxville's "human barbeque" suit was a great idea. Knoxville, in a fireproof suit, covered with steaks, set himself on fire. The boy did the same by dousing himself with lighter fluid and setting himself on fire — all with *Jackass*' video camera rolling. The Washington state boy suffered first-degree burns on his face and chest. Two other adolescents were not as lucky. Both died after simulating *Jackass* stunts that involved vehicles, one with boys driving a car down railroad tracks and the other with the teen riding on the hood of a car that slammed on brakes.

Similar events have been happening for years, and some people blame media for those tragedies. In 1993, a 5-year-old boy set his bed on fire with a cigarette lighter. His 2-year-old sister died in the bedroom blaze. Investigators blamed the fire on the youngster's television habits, according to the Children's Protection from Violent Programming Act. He'd been watching the MTV program *Beavis and Butt-head*, where one of the 15-year-old cartoon characters proclaimed, "Fire is cool." In 1997, before a congressional hearing, parents blamed a son's suicide on a recording by explaining that their teen had been listening to the music of Mar-

by David A. Copeland
Elon University

ilyn Manson, according to an Associated Press story published in November. The song the boy repeatedly listened to was titled "Suicide Solution." The committee members agreed, concluding that the music caused the death.

The connection between media and physical harm often can seem blatantly obvious, particularly when people harm themselves or others after either mimicking or being "inspired by" media content they've consumed. A parents' group in 2001, for example, accused the World Wrestling Federation (now the WWE) of being morally responsible after a 13-year-old boy said he was copying wrestling moves when he beat a 6-year-old girl to death. Various media were blamed for the 1999 mass shooting at Columbine High School in Colorado. In fact, in April 2004, according to news reports, the Columbine victims' families filed a class-action lawsuit against a number of entertainment companies that produced the media messages they believed shooters Dylan Klebold and Eric Harris watched or used. The suit claimed the pair would not have killed 13 people and themselves had they not been exposed to violent video games. The suit also mentioned that Klebold and Harris visited websites featuring sexually violent content. Many people other than the parents of those killed at Columbine have argued that music, video games and movies were responsible for nurturing the destructive impulses that eventually led the two teenagers to embark on their shooting spree.

Legally, the courts are loath to find the media responsible for physical harm, but that doesn't mean no causal connection exists. In 1995, Leonard Eron, a researcher who performed one of the groundbreaking studies on media violence, spoke to a Senate subcommittee reviewing the Children's Protection from Violent Programming Act. Eron told senators that children who watch excessive amounts of television are more likely to be convicted for serious crimes. He also warned that even those who did not watch television could be affected by its programming. "You and your child might be the victims of violence perpetrated by someone who as a youngster did learn the motivation for and the techniques of violence from television," Eron's written testimony to the committee chaired by John McCain explained.

On this premise, Congress passed a law in 1996 that established a rating system to alert parents to potentially inappropriate content on television. Today, all new TV sets come with a "V-Chip," which allows parents to determine to what extent violence, sex, language and adult situations enter the home through their televisions.

Legislators in Washington continue to subscribe to the idea of media — especially visual media — as powerful agents of influence. In June 2007, representatives of the American Psychological Association told the Senate Commerce Committee that ample evidence demonstrates the harmful effects of television violence on children. Dale Kunkel, who led the 1990s National Television Violence Study, testified that most violence on television is presented in a way that increases the possibility of harmful effects on child viewers. "Most depictions sanitize violence by making it appear much less harmful than it really is," Kunkel was quoted as saying in "The Impact of Media Violence on Children."

The incidents, lawsuits, congressional testimony and subsequent legislation noted above suggest that many believe media have a powerful and lasting impact on society. But do they? Researchers have attempted to discover the answer to this question since early in the 20th century. This chapter reviews research coming down on both sides of the issue. Before examining findings of recent studies, however, a brief account of early media effects studies provides context for recent conclusions on the topic.

Origins of the Issue

At the beginning of the 20th century, little if any scientific research had been conducted in relation to media effects. The growth of motion pictures and a world war, though, changed that. The large number of people attending movies in relative darkness with oversized visual images looming above them fed into newly developed theories that claimed that large, urban, detached societies react to stimuli. Referred to as the "magic bullet" theory (also known as the "hypodermic needle" theory), social scientists concluded that once mass-mediated messages reach individuals ("targets"), the effect was automatic and as powerful as a bullet hitting a target. In the first two decades of the 20th century, however, ideas concerning media were not tested in any systematic way. Most researchers assumed the "magic bullet" theory to be true, and it became the standard for understanding societal reaction to mediated messages.

By the 1920s, research fueled by concerns about the assumed powerful effects the media had on adolescents and children, who comprised about 44% of the audience, burgeoned. As W.W. Charters said in the preface of his 1933 publication *Motion Pictures and the Social Attitudes of Children*: "Motion pictures are not understood by the present generation of adults. They are new; they make an enormous appeal to children; and they present ideas and situations which parents may not like. Consequently, when parents think of the welfare of their children who are exposed to these compelling situations, they wonder about the effect of the pictures upon the ideals and behavior of the children." Charters then posed questions that launched formal research into media effects: "Do motion pictures really influence children in any direction? Are their conduct, ideals and attitudes affected by the movies? In short, just what effect do motion pictures have upon children of different ages?"

To find answers to these questions, Charters and a team of university psychologists, sociologists and educators were brought together in 1928 by the Motion Picture Research Council. Collectively known as the Payne Fund after the organization that provided the grant money for the study, scholars in 1929 began a series of field projects with young people. Their findings, published in a series of 13 studies in 1933, supported the magic bullet theory — movies did have powerful effects on young viewers.

At the same time, another group of researchers realized that people could be persuaded in a variety of ways. During World War I, Edward Bernays and others through the Office of War Information realized that information properly presented to people through media could create a positive impression for joining the war effort. Properly mediated messages, he realized, could be used for nearly any purpose to influence society, and he proved it in 1929. Calling them "Torches of Freedom" and working with tobacco companies, Bernays orchestrated societal acceptance of women smoking during that year's Easter Day parade in New York City. He persuaded a large number of debutants to "light up" as they marched. Of course, Bernays had already notified the press that something was going to happen at a certain point in the procession. As the women lit up, cameras snapped images, which appeared in papers across the nation the next day. Societal acceptance of women smoking quickly followed. For Bermays, public relations was born, and he used psychological elements to manipulate the masses for another half century along with thousands of other PR and advertising practitioners. As Bernays said in his 1928 publication *Propaganda*, "The conscious and intelligent manipulation of the organized habits and opinions of the masses is an important element in democratic society." This was made possible using media to "pull the wires which control the public mind."

Following World War II, media research's focus quickly turned to television, specifically TV violence. A U.S. Senate subcommittee on juvenile delinquency released a report in 1956 warning of the potential danger of TV violence to young viewers. A 1958 landmark British study, *Television and the Child*, agreed. A similar American study, *Television in the Lives of Our Children*, reached the same conclusions.

The domestic upheaval and violence of the 1960s spurred more U.S. media effects studies. Following assassinations of political leaders, race riots in major American cities and growing violence on American streets, President Lyndon B. Johnson created the National Commission on the Causes and Prevention of Violence in 1968. The commission presented its findings in 1969's *Violence and the Media,* concluding that media, television in particular, were presumed to be the principal cause of these national problems.

Another governmental study followed immediately. The Surgeon General's

Scientific Advisory Committee on Television and Social Behavior, planned a new series of experiments to explore television's effects, something that the 1968-1969 study, which relied extensively on previously published material, had not done. The study concluded that "a preliminary and tentative indication of a causal relation between viewing violence on television and aggressive behavior" existed for "some children . . . in some environmental contexts."

After this, the number of studies into television effects soared. A massive amount of published research into television's influences on behavior took place in the 1970s. In 1975 alone, 2,400 different publications related to television and its effects on people were published. The culmination of this research was 1982's *Television and Behavior: Ten Years of Scientific Progress and Implications for the Eighties*, prepared by the National Institute of Mental Health. It concluded "that violence on television does lead to aggressive behavior by children and teenagers." The study noted that this did not occur among all children, "but the correlations between violence and aggression are positive."

Over the years, violence in television, movies and music has increased dramatically along with public concern about the impact of violent media. In 1997, a public opinion survey commissioned by the American Medical Association found that 75% of parents reported they had walked out of movie theaters and turned off their televisions because of the violent content. Moreover, a solid majority wanted a more effective movie rating system as well as a rating system for television shows, computer games and music. As a result, all major media industries have devised rating systems for their material. The National Association of Broadcasters, the National Cable Television Association and the Motion Picture Association of America, for example, established the TV Parental Guidelines Monitoring Board, which established a set of seven ratings to be used in conjunction with the V-Chip so that parents can monitor and block programming.

Media Effects: Powerful or Minimal?

Since the end of World War II, about 300 studies involving nearly 50,000 subjects have concluded that exposure to violent media increases aggression. Researchers in these studies have concluded that the effects are not immediate but instead create aggregated, long-term effects. Children who are exposed to large amounts of violent TV programming, Brad J. Bushman, L. Rowell Huesmann and Jodi L. Whitaker concluded in 2009, are more likely to behave violently later in life. Similar findings occurred when researchers studied recorded music and video games. In fact, the 2008 "Experimental Study of the Differential Effects of Playing Versus Watching Violent Video Games on Children's Aggressive Behavior," published in *Aggressive Behavior*, suggested that the effects of violent video games were even stronger than that of television and music, because video games are an active medium rather than a passive one.

But do media really produce changes, especially radical changes? Since the 1920s, experiments have produced varying results. Within the Payne Fund Studies alone, for example, some of researchers reported finding powerful effects, while others concluded motion pictures produced limited to no effects on viewers.

Powerful Effects

Powerful effects produce changes in the receiver's actions and attitudes that vary noticeably to those before exposure to the media content. Minimal effects are those that produce only temporary, slight or no changes in the actions and attitudes of receivers, according to researchers Shearon Lowry and Melvin DeFleur. In some cases, effects are immediate and noticeable, but they don't last. In other instances, short-term changes in actions and attitudes are undetected, but cumulative exposure to similar media messages produce a discernible change in actions and attitudes over time.

Early Long-Term Effects Research

The Payne Fund Studies reached a number of conclusions that reinforced that era's fears concerning the negative effects of motion pictures. Payne Fund researchers studied thousands of .young people and adults, and the results often were alarming to a public and research community already threatened by films. Some of the findings in the Payne studies are the following. P.W. Holaday and George Stoddard found that movie retention — remembering what occurred on screen — lasted for months. Herbert Blumer and Philip Hauser determined that what was seen on the big screen contributed to criminal activity. Blumer found that audience behaviors in fashion and mannerisms were influenced by movies. L.L. Peterson and Ruth Thurstone found that when audiences were exposed to movies that proposed the same actions, attitudes or themes at intervals of one week, the movies produced a cumulative effect among viewers by changing their respective attitudes and actions to those seen on screen.

A series of World War II studies conducted by researchers from the U.S. Army identified potential long-term mass media effects that were greater than any short-term effect. The researchers tested the effects produced by exposure to one of director Frank Capra's *Why We Fight* documentary films. They found that even when soldiers could no longer recall the exact details of the film, they remembered the general "feel" of the piece long after. This "sleeper effect" pointed to a potentially powerful media influence, which the authors explained by say-

ing an initial acceptance of a topic in a film made it more probable that a long-term change would occur than a short-term one.

Desensitization in the Short- and Long-Term

As part of a national commission to prevent violence at the close of the 1960s, the Media Task Force authorized a study of television violence based on one week of prime-time network programming in both 1967 and 1968. The study defined violence as "the overt expression of force intended to hurt or kill."

Researchers found that the total percentage of violence on each of the three major networks increased from 1967 to 1968. ABC, CBS and NBC collectively had acts of violence in 81.4% of their programs. The task force concluded that the effects produced by media violence were of "a variety that most persons would deem costly and harmful to individuals and society" and that television had the greatest potential of all media for powerful effects, in both the short-term and long-term. A short-term effect, the committee said, was that "audiences exposed to mass media portrayals of violence learn how to perform violent acts." Consequently, audiences that have learned violent behavior from media are likely to exhibit that learning "if they encounter a situation similar to the portrayed situation, expect to be rewarded for violent behavior, or do not observe disproving reactions to the portrayal of aggression." The committee also suggested that exposure to media violence over extended periods conditions audiences to violence. As a result, those socialized by mass media probably resolve conflicts with violence and use violence to obtain a desired end. Long-term exposure to media violence desensitizes viewers to real violence and lowers inhibitions against the use of violence. Audiences become more likely to use violence and to tolerate its use by others. In addition, TV violence has the effect of producing inaccurate portrayals of class, ethnic, racial and occupational groups that in turn create feelings of fear and hatred toward these groups. Television more than any other mass medium, the task force said, "is re-shaping the traditional, definitional and socializing activities of political, economic, educational, recreational and religious institutions" and "is the primary source of exposure to severe acts of violence for the majority of Americans."

The Office of the Surgeon General directed a new study in 1969 with a $1 million Congressional appropriation. The findings were published in 1972 in the five-volume *Television and Social Behavior* and the accompanying *Television and Growing Up: The Impact of Televised Violence*. The report affirmed earlier studies, concluding that television had the potential for powerful effects in short-term aggressive behavior among young people as well as the potential to produce a cumulative effect toward the acceptance and use of violence.

The effects of television on aggressive behavior also were studied by Robert

M. Liebert and Robert A. Baron, who used a laboratory situation to find out whether watching a 3.5 minute clip of television violence, compared with a sporting event, made children more susceptible to violence when placed in situations where they could help or hurt another child by pushing selected help or hurt buttons. The researchers concluded in their study published in the 1972 three-volume *Television and Social Behavior* that children who watched the televised violence "showed more willingness to engage in interpersonal aggression than those who had observed the neutral program." In addition, these children held the hurt button down longer than children who viewed the sports clip. "[T]he primary effect of exposure to the aggressive program was that of reducing subjects' restraints against inflicting severe discomfort on the ostensible peer victim," the researchers reported.

The cumulative effects of television upon young people were the focus of the study by Monroe Lefkowitz, Leonard Eron, Leopold Walder and L. Rowell Huesmann, published in *Television and Social Behavior*. The researchers looked at the aggressive behavior of a group of children from ages 8 to 18 during a 10-year period (1959-1969). They examined television programs watched, amount of TV viewing time and aggressive behavior as reported by family and peers. The conclusion was clear: The more violence subjects viewed, the more aggressive they became. This effect was particularly noticeable among boys. Researchers also discovered that aggression among these individuals increased when compared with the results from 10 years later. "[T]elevision habits established by age 8 influenced aggressive and other behaviors at that time and at least through late adolescence," the study reported. "This is more true for boys than for girls, although many of the relations for girls are in the same direction as those for boys, though less strong." The study also found that it was not necessarily the type of program watched but the amount of programming that increased the aggressive behavior. Researchers concluded "that preferring violent fare in the third grade leads to the building of aggressive habits" and that the "relation between television violence and aggressive behavior in the third grade is due to the fact that this behavior has already been established."

The study also found that the more violent fare children watched, the harder it became for them to distinguish between television violence and real-life violence. These children conclude that TV violence "is the way life is and the way one goes about solving problems. Inhibitions against expressing overt aggression would thus be diminished."

Researchers coined several terms to explain the effects they observed. Exposure to a stimulus, particularly TV violence, tended to "prime" related emotions, concepts and ideas within a viewer's memory. Priming, as they called it, meant that if a viewer saw violence in a program, it could increase thoughts about aggressive or violent behavior. Young people in particular, researchers said, mimic what they observe. Scientists have even discovered "mirror neurons" that promote this activity, according to *Perspectives on Imitation: From Mirror Neurons to Memes* published in 2005. Mimicry is the term that describes how children are likely to act out the same behavior immediately after observing aggressive behavior in the media. Young children might act as if they could fly or act out fighting scenes to mimic the super hero in *Iron Man* on the Cartoon Network, for example. Mimicry and priming can reinforce each other. If children mimicked violent or aggressive behavior they viewed, the experience would also tap into their memory of other similar behavior, thus priming them to think more often about the collective violence and aggression to which they have been exposed over time.

Long-Term Effects: Cultivation & Social Learning Theories

Cultivation Theory was proposed in 1976 by scholar George Gerbner in "Living with Television: The Violence Profile," *Journal of Communication*, to explain the effects of television viewing on people's perceptions, attitudes and values as television grew to play a key role in American society. Because television has become a cultural storyteller, it has a tremendous impact on how audiences view the world, Gerbner argued. Cultivation research indicates that the potential effects of television viewing are varied and possibly extreme. For example, the "mean world syndrome" identified through cultivation research suggests that people who watch a lot of television often believe that the world is a much more dangerous place than it really is. Gerbner has argued that this exaggerated fear can lead to repression as a way to reduce anxieties. Cultivation research has also investigated the impact of media consumption on the likelihood of being the victim of a violent crime. Almost across the board, frequent television viewers overestimated the negative in their analysis of society, meaning they believed — because of heavy TV consumption and because the media emphasis on violent acts was out of proportion with the true amount of violence within communities — that violent acts and crime within a community occurred more often than they really did.

Cultivation theory was criticized in its early days by researchers who contended that it failed to address adequately the influence that other variables might have on audience fears. As a result, Gerbner and associates revised the theory by adding the concepts of mainstreaming and resonance. Mainstreaming occurs when heavy viewing leads to agreement across groups. For example, heavy viewers in both low-income and high-income groups agree that crime is an important issue, and Gerbner explains that this is because both are exposed to a similar television reality. When reality and TV worldviews reinforce each other,

Gerbner says, the effect of the TV depiction is enhanced. Resonance occurs when the cultivation effect is boosted for a certain group of the population. For instance, heavy viewers are more likely than light viewers to agree that violent crime is a problem. And among that sample, heavy-viewing females agree the most strongly, no doubt because women tend to be more physically vulnerable to violent men, so the effect resonates more with them.

Gerbner and his associates identified violence in 66% of the approximately 3,000 American films produced between 1950 and 1961. That number surely is greater in recent decades. Gerbner observed that more than 75% of television dramas in the 1950s and 56% of all programs in the 1950s contained acts of violence. And recent research has shown that prominent violence continues to remain prevalent in broadcast television. Between 1994 and 1998, in fact, violent content increased by 14% on broadcast television and 10% on cable television, according to a three-year study by Paul Klite, Robert Bardwell and Jason Salzman and sponsored by the National Cable Television Association. The researchers also found that a minimum of six violent acts occurred in each hour of the typical violent program.

Others have joined Gerbner in cultivation analysis research. T. N. Robinson, M. L. Wilde and L. C. Navracruz examined whether reducing use of television, videotapes and video games could reduce aggressive behavior and perceptions of a mean and scary world and published their findings in 2001 in the *Archives of Pediatrics Adolescent Medicine*. Elementary school students in San Jose, California, received an 18-lesson curriculum to reduce media use. Researchers found that children who had been exposed to the experimental curriculum had a significant decrease in physical and verbal aggression compared to the school that did not participate in the intervention program. The authors concluded that by reducing television, videotape and video game usage, aggressive behavior in elementary-school children could be reduced thereby limiting young people's tendency to fall victim to Gerbner's concepts of a mean and scary world produced by media.

While Gerbner argued that TV created a belief that the world outside was violent, Stanford psychologist Albert Bandura went a step further and argued that the violence in television and movies actually made viewers themselves more prone to violence. He based this argument on his social learning theory, which posits a strong causal link between the consumption of media and the behavior that follows. As in Gerbner's cultivation theory, this effect is powerful with heavy media consumption over time. Viewers—especially children—see characters they identify with, begin to learn which behaviors are rewarded and which are punished, and behave accordingly. So if a character like Dirty Harry is rewarded for being violent, adolescent boys will learn to emulate his behavior.

Four hours a day of violent television programming, therefore, can build a strong worldview that violence is acceptable and make a child-like, 13-year-old Lionel Tate into a killer after viewing and copying wrestling moves by Hulk Hogan, the 1980s and 1990s World Wrestling Federation superstar. Bandura's theory doesn't state that the causal link is always there, however. The effect requires four ingredients: attention, retention, motor reproduction (including physical capabilities) and motivation.

The social learning theory also has implications beyond just violence. Kristen Harrison and Joanne Cantor, for example, considered the theory in "The Relationship Between Media Consumption and Eating Disorders," published in the *Journal of Communication* in 1997. Their examination of television's role in influencing audience members' ideas about thinness and ideal body shape argued that images of thinness and dieting are common in mass media and that the mass media often provide instances of thin actors being rewarded. They found that viewers with higher exposure to "thinness" used in depicting and promoting messages tended to have a higher drive for thinness and were more likely to be dissatisfied with their bodies.

Minimal Effects

Just as some researchers have been adamant that the media produce powerful effects in both short- and long-term situations, other researchers have drawn completely different conclusions from their studies, finding a limited relationship between the interaction of individuals and media. Sometimes these conflicting results have come out of the same research reports.

Although Holaday and Stoddard's *Motion Pictures and Youth* (1934), Peterson and Thurstone's *The Effect of Motion Pictures on the Social Attitudes of High School Children* (1932), and Blumer's *Movies and Conduct* (1933) pointed to very strong and long-lasting media effects in their reports, other Payne Fund researchers pointed out that motion pictures might not be the primary cause of behavior. In the 1933 "Motion Pictures and Youth," W. W. Charters pointed out that the relationship between the medium and behavior was at best complicated. He questioned how one could rate the influence of movies properly in relation to what is taught and learned at home, school, church, community customs, peer relationships and street life. Shuttleworth and May's 1933 *The Social Conduct and Attitudes of Movie Fans* determined that motion pictures could have an effect on children, but "this influence is specific for a given child and a given movie. The same picture may influence different children in distinctly opposite directions. Thus ... the net effect appears small." They concluded that movies only further established and confirmed behavior patterns and attitudes already in place among young people.

The *Why We Fight* film series and the studies of the series' effects also produced conflicting findings. The powerful potential for the "sleeper effect" described by researchers Hovland, Lumsdaine and Sheffield in *Experiments on Mass Communication: Studies in Social Psychology in World War II* (1949) was countered, they said, by the discovery that the films had little to no effect on viewers in other areas, especially in changing attitudes and motivation. The films did little to change attitudes or increase motivation that would make soldiers want to fight, accept unconditional surrender of the enemy, think positively of British war efforts or dislike the enemy. According to *Experiments on Mass Communication,* "The films had no effect on the items prepared for the purpose of measuring effects on the men's motivation to serve as soldiers, which was considered the ultimate objective of the orientation program."

In finding answers for the questions dealing with television and its effects on values, addictive behavior and violent activity, 1961's "Television in the Lives of Our Children" concluded that "very little delinquency can be traced directly to television." The study's authors, Schramm, Lyle, and Parker, also said that television broadcasters were not completely free of fault if children's values differed from their parents or if children turned to delinquency and violence. But, according to the researchers, "Television is at best a contributory cause" to violent behavior. Television was not something to be feared or given clemency in its relationship with children, the researchers said. Schramm, Lyle, and Parker explained: "For some children, under some conditions, some television is harmful. For other children, under the same conditions, or for the same children under other conditions, it may be beneficial. For most children, under most conditions, most television is probably neither particularly harmful nor particularly beneficial." They concluded, "If a child has security and love, interests, friendships and healthful activities in his non-television hours, there is little chance that anything very bad is going to happen to him as a result of television."

Joseph Klapper and Reinforcement Theory

Perhaps the most influential minimal effects study was *The Effects of Mass Communication*, written in 1960 by Joseph Klapper. After synthesizing findings from other communications research and much of his own work, Klapper found that mass media had little to no impact on audience behavior. In fact, he identified his reinforcement theory as the only possible effect: The media's impact, if anything, was limited to reinforcing beliefs that the audience already held. Klapper's book was quickly adopted by scholars and industry professionals who questioned the scholarly evidence that had previously shown massive media impact. In fact, there are many other researchers who disagree with this body of research. According to Richard Rhodes in "The Media Violence Myth," only about 200 studies actually involve real research into media violence, and they demonstrate tremendously inconsistent results. Some reports find that boys become more aggressive after exposure to violent television clips, while others find that girls do. In other studies, control groups exhibit more aggression than the kids who are exposed to violence. For example, watching *Mister Rogers' Neighborhood* and *Sesame Street* tripled the aggressiveness of preschool kids, according to Barbara Wilson's research in the 1997 National Television Violence Study. Rhodes, though, articulates another fundamental research flaw common to all the experimental studies: They don't account for the powerful effect called "researcher expectation," whereby the subject easily guesses what the researcher wants him to do and behaves that way.

Steven Messner set out to determine whether metropolitan areas with high audience ratings for television shows with heavy violence also exhibit high rates of violent crime. In "Television Violence and Violent Crime," published in *Social Problems* (1986), he discovered that the inverse was true. That is, areas with large audiences for violent programming tend to exhibit low rates of violent crime. He posited that the "Catharsis theory," which says that viewing of violence on film and on television allows for the vicarious release of aggressive impulses instead of overt acts of aggression, offered the rationale for his discoveries.

The carthasis theory also helps explain short-term media effects in relation to the 1999 Columbine shootings. After the Colorado high school massacre, *Harper's Magazine* published an essay attacking video games and blaming them for contributing to school violence. An unnamed New Jersey teenager responded with a letter in their defense. "As a geek," he wrote, "I can tell you that none of us play video games to learn how to shoot people. For us, video games do not cause the violence; they prevent it. We see games as a perfectly safe release from a physically violent reaction to the daily abuse leveled at us." This statement, quoted in James D. Torr's *Is Media Violence a Problem?* (2001), exemplifies the rationale behind the concepts of catharsis, which were proposed as early as the 1890s by Sigmund Freud. The theory has been adapted to contemporary media, especially with video games. They became a part of the Columbine discussion when the students who did the shooting were depicted as avid players. According to catharsis theory, playing video games or watching violence in movies or on television can reduce violent activities because the actual media experience allows players or viewers to mirror their own aggressive tendencies as they play or watch. Video games, especially, provide players with the chance to act out what their avatar on screen is doing. According to *Understanding Video Games: The Essential Introduction* (2008), this active role allows the players to vent their aggression on elements of the game, not on other people.

The reasoning underlying catharsis theory is that suppressed rage creates tension that is released in violence. The idea that a player can release this anger harmlessly on a surrogate such as a video game character — takes the idea a step further. Perhaps watching others commit violent acts in the media can serve the same purpose — releasing the tension — as committing the acts oneself. Charles Asbach in "Media Images and Personality Development: The Inner Image and The Outer World," *Media, Children and the Family* (1994) said that both children and adults find cathartic release through violent media programming. Children who watch violence in shows targeted specifically at them tend to identify with the underdogs, and they enjoy when the underdog gets the best of an aggressor, as when Tweety in Warner Bros. cartoons gets the best of Sylvester the cat. For adults, the study concluded, can have violent tendencies relieved by watching a "Rambo-type" character wreak vengeance on a host of despicable characters.

Assessment

The power of media effects is just as much in question today as it was at the time of the Payne Fund Study. That visual media can and do affect viewers was assumed in 1929 and today. The question that remains is just how and to what extent these media affect viewers. A class of college students studying media and society, for example, may say it believes strongly that visual media has an impact upon viewers. The class may also admit to viewing dozens of murders on screen, including violent attacks in so-called "slasher" movies. Yet none of the students say they would ever consider such violent acts, a concept affirmed by the 1969 Media Task Force report, "Violence and the Media." "Common sense and observation refute the claim that exposure alone makes all people think and act violently. We know millions of adults and children are exposed daily to television entertainment programming, but a majority of them do not espouse violent norms or behave violently," the study concluded.

Media studies also point to differences in individuals as a component in explaining media effects. The *Why We Fight* studies of Hovland, Lumsdaine and Sheffield found that individuals, more than anything seen in the films, were themselves the source of media effects. And the caveat offered by Schramm, Lyle and Parker, which was repeated in the Surgeon General's Report, also finds the individual at the root of media effects. "For some children, under some conditions, some television is harmful.... For most children, under most conditions, most television is probably neither harmful nor particularly beneficial."

Even if all researchers of media effects concluded that it is individual differences that create visual media effects, that admission would not discount the possibility of powerful media effects. From the Payne Fund Study forward, the cumulative effect that media may have on consumers has been proposed. The Media Task Force reported that repeated exposure to media violence makes violence socially acceptable and desensitizes viewers. Similarly, the Surgeon General's Report pointed out the great cumulative effect of media in acceptance of violence. Lefkowitz and associates in "Television Violence and Child Aggression" observed that aggression among the young people who were part of the 10-year study increased, and it was not necessarily the type of visual media observed but the amount of it. The violent actions that were observed might be learned from repeated viewing; the cumulative exposure to certain actions on screen could trigger behavior that had been learned elsewhere. The same results in cumulative exposure to media have been observed in studies of racism and sexism, too.

Although most of the studies into visual media effects have focused on the power to produce negative influences, the powerful effects of visual media have also been shown to produce long-term positive changes in such things as seatbelt laws and smoking, as seen in studies published by the National Bureau of Economic Research in 2007 and the National Cancer Institute in 2008.

Perhaps one of the best ways to understand visual media effects has been explained by Gerbner and associates. Television, Gerbner says in "Growing Up with Television: The Cultivation Perspective," is a pervasive medium. Its influences on viewers are often subtle, complex and intermingled with influences that have nothing to do with media.

The more that viewers interact with the symbols and messages seen on television, the more those perspectives become a part of life. Television may introduce new concepts or reinforce ideas gained elsewhere in society. Gerbner even hypothesizes that media effects studies that find little or no change in receivers through media-viewer interaction may actually reflect the strength of cultivation. Television's version of the world, in this instance, has in effect become the viewer's version of the world, and the two reinforce each other.

Even with all the effects studies since the 1920s, the discussion still returns to the questions of whether visual media affect individuals and society, and how powerful those effects are. Most research has demonstrated visual media have at least some impact on individuals and society. As to the strength of those effects, cumulative exposure, individual differences and societal norms no doubt all play a part. Can society blame its ills on the media? If all violence on television were replaced by programs espousing acts of kindness, would societal violence stop? The answer is clearly no, because the relationship between visual media and viewers is much more complex. If, as Gerbner suggests, television is but a part of a dynamic interactive process, then television cannot move away from violence or any aspect of life any more than passers-by can avoid slowing down at the scene of a wreck along a highway. And, these suggestions do not even take into account what effects increased online media use will create. As the audience for mass media fragments into literally millions of online sites, consumers will have much better opportunities to find content to which they can closely identify. What effects will this have on people, especially children and adolescents? The dialogue on how media affect society, the power of that influence versus the relative innocuous nature of effects, will continue with more studies, more theories and more disagreement.

Points of View

Books

Bandura, Albert, and Richard Walters. *Social Learning and Personality Development.* New York: Holt, Rinehart & Winston, 1963. Seminal study of media effects by using "Bobo" dolls found that children who saw abusive conduct with the dolls imitated the behavior.

Comstock, George A., Eli A. Rubinstein, and John P. Murray, eds. *Television and Social Behavior.* 5 Vols. Washington, D.C.: U.S. Department of Health, Education, and Welfare, 1972. The Surgeon General's Report. The five volumes examine the amount and nature of TV violence, the circumstances in which violent programming is created, and the formal and informal influences that affect the selection and prohibition of television content.

Grimes, Tom, James Arthur Anderson, and Lori A. Bergen. *Media Violence and Aggression: Science and Ideology.* Thousand Oaks, Calif.: Sage, 2007. Extended critique of the media violence/social aggression debate, proposes to explain why the violence/media aggression hypothesis does not explain or predict the reactions of most people to media, as well as how they react to what they see and hear in the media.

Kirsh, Steven J. *Media & Youth: A Developmental Perspective.* Chichester, England: Wiley-Blackwell, 2010. Kirsh provides a comprehensive review and critique of the research and theoretical literature related to media effects on infants, children, and adolescents, with an emphasis on development.

Potter, W. James. *Media Effects.* Los Angeles, Calif.: Sage, 2012. The media constantly influence individuals and society by focusing on larger social structures and institutions.

Schramm, Wilbur, Jack Lyle, and Edwin B. Parker. *Television in the Lives of Our Children.* Stanford, Calif.: Stanford University Press, 1961. The first major American study into effects of television on children, this book points to children as the actors in the relation between television and viewers, assuming that children use television, not vice versa.

Strasburger, Victor C., Barbara J. Wilson, Amy Beth Jordan. *Children, Adolescents, and the Media.* 2nd Ed. Thousand Oaks, Calif.: Sage, 2009. This book discusses the impact of the varied interactions children and adolescents have with the modern media. It examines

research and seminal studies dealing with advertising, violence, video games, sexuality, drugs, body image and eating disorders, music and the Internet.

Articles

Bogart, Leo. "Warning: The Surgeon General Has Determined That TV Violence Is Moderately Dangerous to Your Child's Mental Health." *Public Opinion Quarterly* 36 (1972): 491-521. A researcher the networks "blackballed" from doing research for the Surgeon General's report provides a critical response to the 1972 Surgeon General's Report.

Feshbach, Seymour. "The Stimulating vs. Cathartic Effects of a Vicarious Aggressive Experience." *Journal of Abnormal and Social Psychology* 63 (1961): 381-5. The author proposes the catharsis theory of media effects, which states that frustrations and violent behavior are relieved by vicariously watching media violence.

Guttman, Monika. "A Kinder, Gentler Hollywood." *U.S. News and World Report*, May 9, 1994, 38-46. This *U.S. News* and UCLA survey of national and Hollywood perceptions of visual media is important because Congress has used the findings for much of its subsequent action.

Maccoby, Eleanor E. "Television: Its Impact on School Children." *Public Opinion Quarterly* 15 (1951): 421-44. This early study into television's effects on children looks at items such as homework time and the supper hour. It suggests that TV and fairy tales serve similar purposes but that TV deserves further study to determine its long-range effects.

Tulloch, Marian I. "Evaluating Aggression: School Students' Responses to Television Portrayals of Institutionalized Violence." *Journal of Youth and Adolescence* 24 (1995): 95-116. This study of students ages 9-16 on situational responses to televised violence concludes that age, gender, and social backgrounds affect responses to that violence.

4

News Media and American Democracy

Consider two scholars named Alex separated by 174 years.

As he traveled around the United States in the early 1830s, Alexis de Tocqueville, a French aristocrat with liberal leanings, observed how ideas and aspirations diffused among America's social and economic groups. He believed identifying the methods of diffusion would explain what political and economic aims each group would pursue, what institutions they would establish and operate, and with what success. He paid little attention to government separation of powers and much attention to which social groups might sustain a democratic outlook. In his considerations, Tocqueville became one of the first observers to recognize the press as a powerful force for promoting and sustaining democracy.

"[The press'] influence in America is immense. It causes political life to circulate through all parts of that vast territory," he wrote in 1835's *Democracy in America*. "Its eye is constantly open to detect the secret springs of political designs and to summon the leaders of all parties in turn to the bar of public opinion." Tocqueville argued that the press "rallies the interests of the community round certain principles and draws up the creed of every party; for it affords a means of intercourse between those who hear and address each other without ever coming into immediate contact."

As he reviewed the state of American news media in 2009, our second Alex, Alex S. Jones, an American journalist with democratic concerns, also observed how ideas and aspirations were disseminated among America's different social and economic groups. Jones *did* pay attention to government separation of powers, and he reinforced a long-held belief in the United States that the news media exist as the public's check and balance on its political system by diffusing "accountability news."

"Traditional journalists have long believed that this form of fact-based accountability news is the essential food supply of democracy and that without

by David J. Vergobbi
University of Utah

enough of this healthy nourishment, democracy will weaken, sicken, or even fail," he wrote in *Losing the News: The Future of the News that Feeds Democracy* (2009). "[T]his core of reported news has been the starting place for a raucous national conversation about who we are as a people and a country."

The similarity of Tocqueville's and Jones' comments — separated by nearly two centuries — reveals how deeply the perception of the press as a democratic catalyst is embedded in American political thought. J. Herbert Altschull called it "The Democratic Assumption." "Indeed," he wrote in *Agents of Power* (1984), "we can say with a large measure of certainty that *one of the primary assumptions held by the American citizen is that democracy thrives in part because of the information disseminated by the news media.*" Altschull himself italicized his words to drive home their significance. This assumption considers the news media "indispensable to the survival of democracy." Political scientist Timothy E. Cook showed in *Governing with the News* (1998) that even politicians accept the Democratic Assumption to the point of planning their campaign and governance strategies based on voter media consumption.

But is it a safe assumption? Does American democracy's survival depend on its news media? Do news media in fact fail American democracy? Or do they simultaneously support and undermine, acting as a contradictory agent "smack dab in the middle" of "this struggle over what constitutes democracy," as Robert McChesney argued in *Rich Media, Poor Democracy* (2000)?

Origins of the Issue

We can trace the Democratic Assumption to the country's founders. James Madison, one of the principal authors of both the U.S. Constitution and the Bill of Rights, argued in his 1789 speech *Proposing the Constitutional Amendments* that the "people shall not be deprived or abridged of their right to speak, to write, or to publish their sentiments; and the freedom of the press, as one of the great bulwarks of liberty, shall be inviolable." When the United States ratified the First Amendment in 1791, Madison reasoned in the *National Gazette* that "[w]hatever facilitates a general intercourse of sentiments, [such] as ... a free press, and particularly a circulation of newspapers through the entire body of the people, is ... favorable to liberty." Late in his life, Madison wrote a letter concerning "Public Instruction" (1822) that emphasized citizen access to government information as the basis of self-governance. "A popular Government, without popular information, or the means of acquiring it is but a Prologue to a Farce or a Tragedy; or perhaps both," he wrote. "A people who mean to be their own Governors, must arm themselves with the power which knowledge gives."

Thomas Emerson connected past to present in "Colonial Intentions and Current Realities of the First Amendment" (1977) when he clarified that a key democratic function of the press is that of purveying critical information. "The public, as sovereign, must have all information available to instruct its servants, the government," he wrote. "[T]here can be no holding back of information; otherwise, ultimate decision-making by the people, to whom the function is committed, becomes impossible."

In other words, the democratic self-governing process depends on an informed citizenry, which in turn depends on the free press — Altschull's Democratic Assumption. The news media use their First Amendment guarantee to bare the secrets of government and inform the people. Scholars argue that news media earn their constitutional protection by providing citizens: (1) a marketplace for discussing diverse, often conflicting ideas; (2) a voice for public opinion; (3) surveillance of the political scene and politician performance; and (4) a public watchdog or checking value that uncovers governmental misbehavior, corruption and abuses of power.

Although they accept the Democratic Assumption's necessity for American self-governance, commentators and scholars have long debated its legitimacy, reality and effectiveness. Some argue that the news media fail their democratic duty. Others disagree. Their arguments cover a variety of views ranging from corporate ownership of the media to the nature of the American citizenry.

News Media Fail the Democratic Assumption

In a chapter in 1998's *Media & Democracy*, Leo Bogart argued that the structure of news media in America means they can be manipulated and thus that they "are not inevitably an agent of democracy." Instead, they are *Agents of Power* (1984), said Altschull. "Americans cling to the idea, the *perception*, of the democratic assumption with a ferocious tenacity," Altschull wrote, but do not recognize or accept their societal and political realities.

In an exhaustive evaluation of the world press, Altschull challenged Fred Siebert, Theodore Peterson and Wilbur Schramm's *Four Theories of the Press* (1956) and their conclusion that the press' social responsibility supported the Democratic Assumption. His study culminated in "The Seven Laws of Journalism." He cited three of those laws to illustrate how forces wielding power in the economic, political, social and cultural environment manipulate news media in their favor. These three laws illustrate why news media cannot fulfill a legitimate democratic role. First, news media are not independent. They are agents for those holding political and economic power. Second, news content inevitably reflects the interests of the news media's economic supporters. Third, college journalism programs indoctrinate future journalists into the society's status quo, which maintains the first law. Two other laws, however, seemingly contradict this power of outside forces. Altschull stated: "All press systems endorse the doctrine of social responsibility, proclaim that they serve the needs and interests of the people, and state their willingness to provide access to the people." The key, wrote Altschull, is that reality contradicts philosophy: "Press practices always differ from theory." Leo Bogart addressed this contradiction when he argued that news media are vital to a democracy because they can make information available, criticize government, investigate wrongdoing, advocate good causes, and create constituencies and common experiences. But, Bogart continued, journalistic *practice* is a matter of who controls the media. "Mass media can serve democracy," he wrote, but "only when those who manage them feel a passionate responsibility to create and maintain it."

Unfortunately, those who control the news media are passionate for money, not democracy, wrote Ben Bagdikian. His first edition of *The Media Monopoly* in 1983 decried the fact that a mere 50 corporations controlled nearly 87% of all American media. He then suggested "that sooner or later a handful of corporations would control most of what the average American sees and hears." It came sooner. In four years, Bagdikian's second edition noted that ownership dropped from 50 to 29 corporations. By the seventh edition in 2004, the number was five. These five intertwined international conglomerates control most of the newspapers, magazines, book publishing companies, motion picture studios, and radio and television stations in the United States. And now they are pursuing the Internet. "This gives each of the five corporations and their leaders more communications power than was exercised by any despot or dictatorship in history," wrote Bagdikian. In 2013, the five largest conglomerates by size were Time Warner, the Walt Disney Co., Rupert Murdoch's News Corp. (Australia), Viacom and Bertelsmann (Germany).

The problem, Bagdikian wrote in the 1987 edition of his book, is the "antidemocratic potential of this emerging corporate control.... What the public learns is heavily weighted by what serves the economic and political interests of the corporations that own the media." By 2004, Bagdikian argued that such control had indeed emerged. The "Big Five" major players altered U.S. politics by promoting laws increasing corporate domination and abolishing government regulations. Media corporations act like corporations, Bagdikian acknowledged, but "with the crucial exception that they are directly related to voting patterns because their product happens to be a social-political one." In the process, with legislation such as the 1996 Telecommunications Act, media political power subsumed the individual citizen's political power. According to Bagdikian, "[C]itizens are presumed to have the sole right to determine the shape of their democracy. But concentrated media power in the news and commentary, together with corporate political contributions in general, have diminished the influence of voters over which issues and candidates will be offered on Election Day."

Bagdikian also reasoned that all large corporations traditionally prefer conservative policies, including the Big Five media. Their corporate and political news sources and content reflect it, as do their political talk show hosts. Bagdikian acknowledged the legitimacy of conservative sources and content but questioned the lack of news balance. He clarified that a democracy needs the perspective of all socio-economic classes. Conservatism, critics argue, limits the news media's democratic effectiveness in other ways, as well. Broadcast journalist Eric Sevareid said in 1976, "The bigger the information media, the less courage and freedom of expression they will allow."

Also expressing concern that a few giant corporations dominated American media, Michael Gurevitch and Jay Blumler argued in a 1990 chapter in *Democracy and the Mass Media* that the very structure of corporate-controlled news media presents four obstacles that undermine democratic ideals the news media are supposed to serve. Obstacle one refers to tensions between editorial autonomy versus citizen access to media; between immediate public tastes and interests versus providing need-to-know socio-political information; and between majoritarian mainstream opinions versus dissident and marginal views. Obstacle two clarifies that the method of political communication through corporate news media divided American citizens between "movers and shakers at the top and bystanders below," which severely limits democratic participation.

In obstacle three Gurevitch and Blumler acknowledged that corporate media, as large business organizations, must first survive in the marketplace and are "linked inextricably" to government institutions through regulations and the interdependence of reporters and sources. News media are part of a larger social system and must respond to it, which has constrained reporting on economic and socio-political issues relevant to the public. Obstacle four contrasts the democratic presupposition of an engaged citizenry versus the freedom to be politically apathetic. The result is that political news must compete for attention with entertainment or lifestyle information. Because political messages lose audience attention to celebrity scoops and "news you can use," economically focused corporate media ultimately fail to pursue their role in a democracy.

Entertainment content in fact dominates the media, said Leo Bogart (1998) in his "Media and Democracy" chapter. Media conglomerates have far broader interests than just delivering the news. "This cannot be categorized as nonpolitical," Bogart said. "It is *anti*-political, because it deflects public time and attention away from real-world matters that invariably carry political connotations." The problem compounds when the news itself becomes entertainment based, through corporate commercialization, as McChesney stated in *The Problem of the*

Media (2004). News has become preoccupied with celebrities, crime and violence. These topics are inexpensive, easier to cover than hard news and attract mass audiences for advertisers. The public enjoys the illusion of controversy and, through repeated exposure, develops a taste for it. McChesney lamented that news media could as easily develop the public's taste for exposing corporate and governmental corruption. But, he concluded, corporate-owned media do not engage in such a role.

The impact of commercialization of the news goes far beyond concerns over entertainment. McChesney echoed Bagdikian's concern that "corporate domination of both the media system and the policy-making process that establishes and sustains it causes serious problems for a functioning democracy and a healthy culture." To promote greater public participation, McChesney sought to debunk eight "myths" that encourage and protect corporate control of the news media. One myth posits that commercial media "unquestionably provide the highest quality journalism possible — the caliber of journalism a democracy necessitates for informed self-government." McChesney argued that the opposite occurs: The need for profits inevitably forces budget cuts, which reduce news staff and resources. As a result, editors and reporters relax journalistic standards, gut investigative reporting and rely on public relations and official sources — all of which play into the hands of the corporate media owners. When corporations provide the news media with self-interested versions of science, for example, or journalists cast political debate in terms of strategies and spin, rather than on facts, McChesney argued, democratic deliberation suffers.

He also argued that commercialization and corporate cutbacks directly affect the flow of information to voters. Journalistic integrity, for instance, suffers when advertisers influence how the news is covered. Commercialism also pushes journalists to select content that attracts demographic audiences pleasing to media owners and major advertisers. While the middle and upper socio-economic classes are served, the lower class and the poor are ignored. Another problem arises when journalists favor their corporate owners' commercial ventures or investments when reporting on public issues or use promotional material masquerading as news. These concerns exemplify distractions from the political realities that should be reported to the voting citizenry, argued McChesney.

James Hamilton's 2005 essay "The Market and the Media" explored how economic forces transform not only news delivery but the news itself, to democracy's detriment. He examined how three economic factors affect news content: technological changes, product definition/differentiation and media ownership. He concluded that these factors encouraged opportunities to report both hard and soft news. But in a case study of evening network news programs, he documented a dramatic change in content resulting from these factors. In 1969, for example, the news was heavy with stories on domestic politics and foreign policy. By 2000, with the exception of war reportage, light features about health and entertainment overwhelmed foreign policy hard news. From 1969 through 1973, 82% of major congressional votes were covered by at least one network within one day of the decision. But from 1994 to 1998, network coverage dropped to 62% of the votes. "An additional dilemma for hard-news consumers," Hamilton wrote, "is the economic pressures that may push some outlets away from offering the type of news they prefer." Advertisers, for example, value younger viewers, who may prefer softer news. Broadcasters thus insert soft news into hard-news programs, emphasizing entertainment and human-interest stories over political issues to attract a more youthful audience. Hamilton concluded that "news is a commercial product" that "has shifted to an increasing emphasis on what people want to know and away from information that they need as voters."

Economics and ownership are not the only reasons critics consider the news media as failing their role in the Democratic Assumption. Doris Graber posited in 2003's *Annual Reviews in Political Science* that media "lack the power, resources, structure, and inclination to perform tasks that have become impossible to handle in a huge, heterogeneous country that must cope with extraordinarily complex political conditions." For one thing, too much news exists to cover and report on a daily basis. Graber agreed that the structure of corporate organizations prohibits systematic government surveillance. Shallow presentations and the lack of diverse viewpoints compound the problem. Graber concluded that the news media "do not assess the soundness of policies and the performance of politicians adequately to make a vigorous participatory democracy possible."

Internet-based media fare no better, concluded Aeron Davis in a 2010 chapter of *New Media, Old News.* He argued that new media are linked to "weakening communicative ties, social capital and public engagement." When market pressures, he wrote, forced politicians and journalists to adopt Internet media hoping to improve communication, understanding and deliberation among citizens, the opposite occurred. Politics and political reporting became more abstract, symbolic and distant from individuals. Davis said that Internet-dependent journalists "present a professional veneer" that disguised the fact they could not produce watchdog journalism. They just tried to keep up with events and resorted to shortcuts to do so, mining their new media technologies and personally interacting less and less with sources and the public. Symbolism rose over substance. "News beats are narrowed, source exchanges limited, news agendas and story information copied from other journalists, [and] political conflict and scandal stories substituted for detailed evaluations of policy and competency." The book's editor, Natalie Fenton, wrote in the introduction that the Internet can "in many ways be seen as contributing to the stifling of journalism for the public good and in the public interest."

Cass Sunstein identified a contributing problem with Internet-based media — namely that they provide too much information with too much self-selection. He wrote in *Republic.com 2.0* (2007) that when "information is freely available, tyrannies are unlikely to be able to sustain themselves; it is for this reason that the Internet is a great engine of democratic self-government." Information overload, however, can defeat self-governance in three ways. One, *unlimited self-filtering*: So much choice produces few common experiences and little shared information. Two, *fragmentation*: Individuals now have unlimited power to customize and filter their news intake, thus fragmenting society into increasingly polarized groups that do not interact. Three, *compromised freedom*: Unlimited self-filtering of information can severely reduce exposure to diverse topics and opinions, which the democratic process requires. Sunstein does not believe people should be forced to read political material. He does, however, believe news media in all their formats must create "a system of communication that promotes exposure to a wide range of issues and views."

News Media Fulfill the Democratic Assumption

Although critics are on philosophical and quantifiable grounds that the media are not fulfilling their duties related to the Democratic Assumption, others contend just the opposite. They see the news media as having the potential to fulfill their democratic mandate, but they do differ in their confidence about how well the media are doing their job.

In 1945, the Supreme Court described the mandate in *Associated Press v. United States*. It declared that the First Amendment "rests on the assumption that the widest possible dissemination of information from diverse and antagonistic sources is essential to the welfare of the public." Four years later, the Court wrote in *Terminiello v. Chicago* that "a function of free speech under our system of government is to invite dispute. It may indeed best serve its high purpose when it induces a condition of unrest, creates dissatisfaction with conditions as they are, or even stirs people to anger." During the same period, in 1947, the Commission on Freedom of the Press, also known as the Hutchins Commission, released *A Free and Responsible Press; A General Report on Mass Communication: Newspapers, Radio, Motion Picture, Magazines, and Books*. The commission concluded that the media play a significant role in the development and stability of society. They have a social responsibility, therefore, to provide citizens with the information they need to self-govern. Some scholars considered the report a bold reassertion of modern media's role in a democratic society. The commission's report was directly "rooted in the democratic assumption," Herbert Altschull (1984) wrote, "and in carrying out this role, the press must be accountable to the public, to the society that it serves."

The Hutchins Commission proclaimed freedom of the press as essential to political liberty and cast the press as the information conduit, arguing that if citizens "cannot freely convey their thoughts to one another, no freedom is secure." The report enumerated five basic services that citizens had a right to expect of the press: (1) an accurate, comprehensive account of the day's news; (2) a forum for exchange of comment; (3) a means of projecting group opinions and attitudes to one another; (4) a method of presenting and clarifying the goals and values of the society; and (5) a way of reaching every member of the society. In other words, Altschull commented, the press should present "not merely objective reality, but objective reality clarified and explained."

No single medium could meet all five ideals, the commission concluded. The key was for media to provide citizens the public discussion necessary for self-governance, which in turn defined the commission's call for press social responsibility: "Freedom of the press can remain a right of those who publish *only* if it incorporates into itself the right of the citizen and the public interest." Within a decade, the commission's refrain of "social responsibility" joined "the public's right to know" as journalistic dogma.

Siebert, Peterson and Schramm's 1956 *Four Theories of the Press* contained the seeds of social responsibility theory. They argued that the media's power and near-monopoly status demanded an even greater duty to society to present information from all sides fairly, allowing the public to make informed decisions. The authors warned that "if the media do not take on themselves such responsibility it may be necessary for some other agency of the public to enforce it." The American Society of Newspaper Editors heeded their call by adopting its Canons of Journalism, which addressed the same obligations to practice responsibility to the general welfare.

Arguing that the news media's traditional social responsibility role often oversimplifies the democratic process, James Curran's chapter in 2005's *The Press* considered the press within the overall political system and explained that news media aid the democratic process in several vital ways. He cautioned against the "grandiose conception" of the press as speaking *for* the people and offered an alternative representational role for the news media. "While the media may speak on occasion for society," he wrote, "their more customary role is to enable the principal organizations and groups in society to be heard — and, where appropriate, be heeded."

Curran then considered news media as forums for political deliberation. Arguing that objective reporting reinforces the dominance of elites, he called for the media system to include partisan and adversarial media that provide alternative and opposing perspectives. He used Internet weblogs to exemplify how adversarial media challenge the tendency of mainstream media journalists to reach group consensus. With a division of labor, Curran claimed, news media might also resolve conflicts in a democracy. "One sector should facilitate activism and conflict," he wrote. "[A]nother should promote dialogue and reciprocity." In other words, news media are not a single entity. They can practice different forms of journalism to make different contributions to the democratic system.

Jack McLeod argued in "For the Affirmative," a 1993 article in *Political Communication,* that news media contribute more to democracy than critics say. Considering the significant growth of media options since 1993, McLeod's conclusions carry even greater context. When tallied, McLeod argued, the press presents far more information and ideas than people are willing to seek out. So, while citizens might fail their democratic duty, the press has met its own.

McLeod also argued that studies have underestimated the level of political learning from the news media. He attributed poor results to weak measures of media exposure in non-experimental empirical research and ineffective variables in experimental work. "Criteria most often used to measure political learning may have little resemblance to what people actually learn from the media," he wrote. "[P]eople do learn enough to make choices, and the news media help them do so." McLeod went further, arguing that the news media both enhance information gained during political campaigns *and* the likelihood of citizen participation. "Jefferson and his contemporaries," he concluded, "might be surprised to learn that, despite the appalling political and commercial pressures placed on them, the news media still operate at least in part guided by public service ideals."

David Demers (1996) agreed that commercial pressures on news media are real and increasing, but the media can and still do deliver on the Democratic Assumption. With *The Menace of the Corporate Newspaper: Fact or Fiction?* Demers analyzed more than 200 U.S. newspapers to measure the degree to which corporatization correlated with journalism quality. He defined "quality" with democratic values: community involvement, job satisfaction, editorial autonomy, quantity of editorials, and letters to the editor. He concluded that "critics have vastly overstated the consequences and adverse effects of the corporate form of organization," adding that the "corporate newspaper has a much greater capacity than the entrepreneurial newspaper to promote social change." Demers essentially concluded that corporate-controlled newspaper journalism is democratically superior to that of independent newspapers.

In "Political Discourse Remains Vigorous Despite Media Ownership," F. Dennis Hale (2003) recounted six of his own studies over an 18-year period that consistently found that chain newspapers were much more similar to independent newspapers than expected. He showed that concern over increasing corporate control of news media has existed almost as long as mass media. He concluded, however, "the marketplace of ideas remains alive and viable despite the growing and unprecedented concentration of modern mass media."

Hale noted that mainstream "establishment" news media publish "a surprising number of facts and opinions" critical of the corporate power structure and the status quo. He also pointed out that alternative and counterculture media offer an even greater variety of societal and political perspectives, citing the evolution of digital technology, desktop publishing and Internet communications. But to "make this diversity meaningful," Hale cautioned, "educational institutions need to institute programs to help citizens become more active in their pursuit of information."

Doris Graber supports Hale's views on the diversity of political information that news media provide and on citizen apathy. When she tested the Democratic Assumption in a 2003 essay, she found it wanting, because it is an impossible-to-meet ideal. But she also argued that, by debunking the myths and considering realities, we find the democratic process does persist despite news media and citizens who fail their idealized roles. Her examination of the overall quality of American news showed two results. One, traditional political campaign stories did indeed decline. Two, and more importantly to Graber, "the supply of political information, including hard political news, has never been more abundant when one considers the totality of offerings, including those available on the Internet." Graber clarified that different political news venues and formats supplement and overlap one another in ways that always provide information for an interested citizen. The public might be frustrated with politics, politicians and political news as the news media present them, she argued, but the media have not alienated citizens from the political process, as some critics allege. Media *do* provide the information, Graber concluded, but citizens do not necessarily use it.

Pursuit of information might in fact be the key determinant for the press' role in the democratic process, according to Thomas Patterson and Philip Seib in their 2005 essay "Informing the Public." "The mark of an informed citizen ought to be an inquiring habit of mind," they wrote, "a tendency to 'think about' leaders, issues, and developments." In this conception, Patterson and Seib argued that family and educational influences precede news media influence, but that news media do play an important, if smaller, role in the democratic process — providing coverage of new developments and events, which is "what it does best." Novelty is what people seek, Patterson and Seib argued. Literally, people want to know what is *new* about today compared to yesterday. In the process, they gather information to help them consider public affairs. The challenge for the news media thus becomes disseminating material that "provokes thought and discussion relevant to public matters," news that "will encourage citizens to think about what they are seeing and hearing." Patterson and Seib cited research studies that suggest news does sometimes have these effects.

Ten years earlier, Michael Schudson argued in *The Power of News* (1995) that idealistic journalists often *think* "their goal should be to educate the people to be shrewd observers of politics and enthusiastic participants in the political process." But then journalists confront the political realities of public skepticism and disinterest, elitist control, moribund political parties and the disproportionate influence of big business. Yet, Schudson concluded that the classical notion of democracy remains "an excellent guide" for news media to follow. The press, for example, represents the public by holding governors accountable, not to the disinterested citizenry, but to the democratic process itself. Or, to counter the influence of corporations on governance, the news media can ascertain and report on how business and government interact. "One task, clearly," Schudson wrote, "is to report more fully and on a regular basis about decision making in the private sphere that directly affects public policy." Through these avenues, he argued, the news media do serve as political educators, because it is impossible for them not to transmit political perspectives. But it is therefore incumbent upon them to recognize this fact and "do so intelligently and critically" and not "unconsciously and routinely."

With the rise of the Internet, futurists saw an opportunity to prove Schudson's optimism true. Nicholas Negroponte, in *Being Digital* (1995), and Wayne Rash, in *Politics on the Net: Wiring the Political Process* (1997), argued that the mass communicative network of the Internet contains the potential for a renewal of direct democracy. Meanwhile, public sphere theorists such as Robert Putnam with *Bowling Alone* (2000) and John Dryzak in *Deliberative Democracy and Beyond* (2002) clarified the Internet's potential for enhancing a direct deliberative democracy.

In 2010, Natalie Fenton edited a series of British-based new media studies that asked whether Web-based news and informational media were reinvigorating the Democratic Assumption or drowning it. Scholars writing in *New Media, Old News,* argued that U.S. online media have done both. "The Internet has modified things," Fenton wrote, "sometimes in positive and productive ways." Nick Couldry's chapter, for instance, pointed to "New Online News Sources and Writer-Gatherers," such as soldiers in war, that provide citizens with insider voices on pressing political and societal issues.

In a chapter titled "A New News Order? Online News Content Examined," Joanna Redden and Tamara Witschge examined whether the Internet would produce more diverse news and increased public participation in the democratic process. Although they found a significant amount of online news, the content from mainstream news outlets was repetitive and offered "little opportunity for the public to participate beyond interpreting and responding to stories." Redden and Witschge, however, clarified that mainstream media online archives, especially in multimedia applications, provide citizens access to information with considerable depth. They also pointed to the wealth of alternative news sites on the Internet, such as Facebook, that provide unique political decision-making content. Such sites organize political interests and show how people use online communication to enhance political participation.

Meanwhile, Bagdikian, in *The New Media Monopoly* (2004), saw the Internet as a point of protest against the political power of media ownership conglomerates. He called it "a moving force that has transformed the world of communications and the mass media." He praised the Internet for challenging existing laws, creating legal struggles with media oligopoly, mobilizing mass protests, accelerating social change around the world and introducing a new political playing field.

These philosophical arguments and empirical studies do suggest that news media are fulfilling their duties toward the Democratic Assumption.

Assessment

Which arguments about the media and democracy should we accept?

McChesney captured the Democratic Assumption in *Rich Media, Poor Democracy* (2000) when he argued that a society's genuine commitment to self-governance depended upon citizen access to information that impacts that society's social, economic and political decisions. He claimed that the news media, as conduits of that information, thus performed "a crucial function" in a democracy as the "battleground for political debate and culture."

But McChesney concluded that the press both supports and undermines democracy. So did Graber, who argued that the Marketplace of Ideas, Voices for Public Opinion, Surveillance Function and Watchdog Function were idealized democratic myths the press could never fulfill. She concluded, however, that "despite a media system that gives too little support much of the time," American democracy does function. News media offer interested citizens at least enough information to make political decisions.

The results of research into the Democratic Assumption can be boiled down to four key terms: *contradictory*, *ideal*, *interested*, and *enough*.

Contradictory: Scholars disagree on whether the press meets its democratic role. But disagreement might actually define disparate research purposes. Each study operated at a micro level that produced building blocks for two opposing macro conclusions: news media either fulfill or fail the Democratic Assumption. Together, however, the research presents a picture that American news media simultaneously support *and* undermine self-governance. We should revel in the contradiction, for it offers a comparative analysis that provides a more complete and nuanced picture of the complicated role private news media play in a democracy.

Ideal: Scholarly disagreement often can be reduced to belief versus reality, an argument between what the news media can do versus what they actually do. In their more philosophical approaches, *believers* define news as an inherent First Amendment responsibility. Speech and press are constitutionally protected, they argue, because free speech and press are the cornerstones of a self-governing democracy. News media thus have a people's mandate, a priority duty to deliver political information. Believer studies showed the press can and has delivered. To such believers, money is a by-product of news, not its end purpose.

With their more quantitative studies, *realists* define news as a commercial product. Face reality, they argue. A news medium must financially survive even to be in a position to inform the public. Profit is thus the necessary means to reach an informed end. But realists also clarify that money too often becomes an end in itself, and political information simply does not sell as well as entertainment-based information. So news media often fail their democratic duties. Yet even realists believe in the democratic ideal. They hope to reawaken business, government and citizens to that ideal by documenting press failures. Recall Bogart's conclusion that mass media "can serve democracy only when those who manage them feel a passionate responsibility to create and maintain it." And Graber contends that "the spirit in which political elites conduct the affairs of government" matters most, for history proves that "democracy is safe in political cultures pervaded by democratic principles." In other words, to make democracy work, everyone must believe the ideal.

Interested: The Democratic Assumption rests upon another assumption — that politically well-informed citizens actively participate in government. Such ideal citizens, though, are difficult to find. Worse, "the decline in participation in civil society signals an impending erosion in democracy and is associated with the decline in political engagement," warned Peter Dahlgren in his article "In Search of the Talkative Public: Media, Deliberative Democracy and Civic Culture" (2002). Yet, hope remains. In *Processing Politics: Learning from Television in the Internet Age* (2001), Graber found that people from all socio-economic levels are politically more sophisticated than civic IQ tests indicate.

In a similar vein, in *The Power of News* (1995), Schudson argued that journalists need not worry about an irrational, uninterested, inactive citizenry but can assume that a small, rational, interested audience will in fact pay attention to political decision-making information. "Then the news media can be viewed not as communicators to the public," he wrote, "but as guardians of the public, stand-ins for public scrutiny, gatekeepers who monitor the political process on behalf of the public." So, to gauge more accurately press effectiveness within the Democratic Assumption, both journalists and researchers should assume an *interested subset* of citizens, not a *fully active* citizenry.

Enough: A Newspaper Guild sticker proclaims: "Democracy depends on journalism." America's founders, justices, journalists, scholars, citizens and even politicians and business people believe in the principle. It also suggests that journalism has disappointed democracy. The question becomes: Does the press provide *enough* information for American democracy to survive? Yes, argued Graber. A citizen's "harvest of significant political information," she concluded in "Media and Democracy" (2003), "tends to be rich ... for making sound political decisions, even when their detailed factual knowledge is sparse."

American democracy might be flawed, chaotic, structurally unsound and undermined by individuals and institutions, including a press that too often provides too little. But it still works — partly because the news media, for all their failures, have provided enough democratic decision-making information to enough interested citizens for American democracy to lean, if not depend, on journalism. Today's press might not impress Alexis de Tocqueville as it did in 1835. But he would still recognize its vital role for democracy in America.

Points of View

Books

Altschull, J. Herbert. *Agents of Power: The Role of the News Media in Human Affairs*. New York: Longman, 1984. An independent press cannot exist. The news media are inevitably agents of those forces that wield power in the economic, political, social, and cultural environment.

Bagdikian, Ben. *The New Media Monopoly*. Boston: Beacon Press, 2004. Monopolization of mass media hurts democracy, and unbiased communication merits and needs an attack on concentrated ownership.

Bennett, W. Lance. *News: The Politics of Illusion*, 6th ed. New York: Pearson Longman, 2005. As the core of the national political system, the news does not fully serve the needs of democracy.

Christians, Clifford G., Theodore Glasser, Denis McQuail, Kaarle Nordenstreng, and Robert A. White. *Normative Theories of the Media: Journalism in Democratic Societies*. Urbana: University of Illinois Press, 2009. Using the Four Theories of the Press as their starting point, the authors explore the philosophical underpinnings and political realities that inform a normative approach to questions about the relationship between journalism and democracy, investigating not just what journalism is but what it ought to be.

Curran, James. *Media and Democracy*. London and New York: Routledge, 2011. A U.S. and European comparative study hypothesizes that more market-oriented media systems foster less serious kinds of journalism that limits knowledge of public affairs. The study both lauds and criticizes American journalism in relation to the democratic process but claims it is only semi-independent of government.

Demers, David. *The Menace of the Corporate Newspaper: Fact or Fiction?* Ames: Iowa State University Press, 1996. An analysis of 200 U.S. newspapers provides evidence that the journalism practiced by newspapers controlled by corporate entities was superior to other newspapers.

Hamilton, James T. *All the News That's Fit to Sell: How the Market Transforms Information into News*. Princeton, N.J.: Princeton University Press, 2004. Ownership issues and economic forces transform not only news delivery but the news itself, to democracy's detriment.

Leigh, Robert D., ed. *A Free and Responsible Press; A General Report on Mass Communication: Newspapers, Radio, Motion Picture, Magazines, and Books*. Chicago: University of Chicago Press, 1947. Beginning with the premise that freedom of the press is essential to political liberty, the Hutchins Commission concluded that any regulation of media must come from within, not from the government. The report is the seminal initial proponent of the social responsibility of the press theory.

Loader, Brian D., and Dan Mercea, eds. *Social Media and Democracy: Innovations in Participatory Politics*. London and New York: Routledge, 2012. The authors investigate the complex interaction between social media and contemporary democratic politics and provide a grounded analysis of the emerging importance of social media in civic engagement.

McChesney, Robert W. *The Problem of the Media: U.S. Communication Politics in the 21st Century*. New York: Monthly Review Press, 2004. The corporate domination of both the media system and the policy-making process that establishes and sustains it causes serious problems for a functioning democracy and a healthy culture.

Schudson, Michael. *The Power of News*. Cambridge, Mass.: Harvard University Press, 1995. The classical notion of democracy remains "an excellent guide" for news media to follow because they do serve as political educators.

Siebert, Fred S., Theodore Peterson and Wilbur Schramm, *Four Theories of the Press*. Urbana: University of Illinois Press, 1956. Analyzed and interpreted in the light of modern thought, the four theories summarize the conflict among communication approaches since Plato. The book established social responsibility of the press as an American stan-

dard.

Sunstein, Cass R. *Republic.com 2.0*. Princeton: University Press, 2007. Concerning free speech and democracy, the task is to avoid "information cocoons" and to ensure that the unrestricted choices made possible by technology do not undermine democracy.

Williams, Bruce A., and Michael X. Delli Carpini. *After Broadcast News: Media Regimes, Democracy & the New Information Environment*. Cambridge and New York: Cambridge University Press, 2011. This historical analysis considers both the benefits and problems of the declining power of journalists to control the media narrative and an increase in the importance of other forms of communication, some new and some old, to influence and/ or dictate media coverage of politics.

Articles and Book Chapters

Curran, James. "What Democracy Requires of the Media." Pp. 120-40 in *The Press*, Geneva Overholser and Kathleen Hall Jamieson, eds. Oxford, U.K.: University Press, 2005. The news media's traditional social responsibility role often oversimplifies the democratic process. But considered within the overall political system, the news media can aid the democratic process in several vital ways.

Graber, Doris. "The Media and Democracy: Beyond Myths and Stereotypes." *Annual Review of Political Science* 6 (2003): 139-60. Democracy can persist despite citizens and media that fall short of their expected idealized roles, suggesting that political culture may be more important than citizen wisdom and media excellence.

Gurevitch, Michael, and Jay G. Blumler, "Political Communications and Democratic Values." Pp. 269-89 in *Democracy and the Mass Media*, Judith Lichtenberg, ed. New York: Cambridge University Press 1990. The very structure of corporate-controlled news media presents four obstacles that undermine democratic ideals the news media are supposed to serve.

Hale, F. Dennis. "Political Discourse Remains Vigorous Despite Media Ownership." Pp. 140-57 in *Media, Profit and Politics: Competing Priorities in an Open Society*, Joseph Harper and Thom Yantek, eds. Kent, Oh.: Kent State University Press, 2003. The marketplace of ideas remains alive and viable despite the growing and unprecedented concentration of modern mass media.

Kaufold, Kelly, Sebastian Valenzuela, and Homero Gil de Zuniga. "Citizen Journalism and Democracy: How User-Generated News Use Relates to Political Knowledge and Participation." *Journalism & Mass Communication Quarterly* 87:3/4 (2010): 515-29. User-generated journalism is negatively related with knowledge of national political figures but strongly and positively associated with higher levels of online and offline participation. Trust in user-generated news amplifies the link between citizen journalism and online participation.

Parmelee, John, John Davies, and Carolyn A. McMahan. "The Rise of Non-Traditional Use for Online Political Information." *Communication Quarterly* 59:5 (2011): 625-40. Non-traditional sites control respondents' online attention as much as traditional media sites in terms of political information, and several factors contribute to accessing traditional and non-traditional media online.

Pinkleton, Bruce E., Erica Weintraub Austin, Yushu Zhou, Jessica Fitts Willoughby, and Megan Reiser. "Perceptions of News Media, External Efficacy, and Public Affairs Apathy in Political Decision Making and Disaffection." *Journalism & Mass Communication Quarterly* 89:1 (2012): 23-39. The survey's findings undercut the frequently made argument that dissatisfaction with media coverage is responsible for voters' cynicism and political apathy.

Trenchard, John, and Thomas Gordon. "Of Freedom of Speech: That the Same is Inseparable from Publick Liberty" (1720). In *Cato's Letters; or Essays on Liberty, Civil and Religious, And other important Subjects. The Third Edition, carefully corrected, Vol.* I. New York: Russell & Russell, 1951: 96-103. Highly influential argument shows that freedom of speech and press "is the great Bulwark of Liberty; they prosper and die together."

5 Public Journalism

In a 1995 essay in the *Journal of Democracy* and later in a book titled *Bowling Alone*, social scientist Robert D. Putnam described a decline of civic engagement in America. He noted that polls found post-Baby Boom generations exhibiting less interest in public affairs than their parents. Participation in public meetings was declining, and "more Americans than ever before were 'turned off' and 'tuned out' from politics." His observations sounded the alarm for professional journalists who believed that civic engagement and newspaper readership are linked.

Editors in Georgia and Kansas and a journalism professor in New York began looking for ways to get the public re-engaged. In Georgia, Jack Swift put his reporters to work interviewing citizens and writing about their perceptions of community needs, then became the leader of a task force that set out to provoke grass-roots action. In Kansas, another editor, Davis "Buzz" Merritt Jr., looked at the declining state of reporting on political campaigns and called for a fresh initiative that asked citizens to define issues and pressed candidates to discuss them.

Jay Rosen of New York University, in a 1992 article titled "The Old News v. The New News," said journalism bore responsibility for "a troubled democracy." He urged the press to "point itself toward a new public philosophy, toward an improved method of explaining its place in politics and its role in public life." He called that new approach "public journalism."

At the core of public (or civic) journalism was a view that the media ought to be reporting on issues ordinary people in communities said they cared about, rather than those raised by editors and political figures. As Rosen and co-author Davis Merritt Jr., argued in their book *Public Journalism: Theory and Practice*, news agendas would be set from the bottom up. The wisdom of editors about what was important to readers counted less than the choices of the readers themselves.

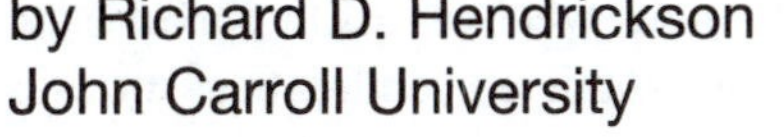
by Richard D. Hendrickson
John Carroll University

Origins of the Issue

Public journalism — which asks journalists to help improve civic discourse — had its genesis before Putnam's writings in a project conducted in 1987 and 1988 by a Knight-Ridder newspaper in Columbus, Ga. Under the direction of its editor, Swift, the *Columbus Ledger-Examiner* published the eight-part series "Columbus: Beyond 2000," which explored citizens' concerns about the city and its future. The journalists interviewed residents in their homes and spoke to experts about the issues the citizens described. The series explored the problems of transportation, low wages, a lack of nightlife in the city, failing schools and the dominance of elites in politics.

After some initial attention, however, the series failed to provoke community leaders into tackling these problems. The newspaper reacted to this silence by sponsoring a public forum that drew 300 people for six hours of discussion about the future of their city. Shortly after that, Swift invited seventy-five interested citizens to a barbecue at his home that resulted in the creation of a new civic organization, "United Beyond 2000." The editor became its chairman, recounted Rosen and Merritt in *Public Journalism*.

Writing about these events, Rosen and Merritt argued that the result was a "different kind of politics, in which public discussion and civic involvement could play a larger part. This became the newspaper's project — political but not partisan."

In 1996's "Getting the Connections Right," Rosen contended that journalists not only should report objectively on public affairs but also "engage people as citizens, to improve public discussion, to help communities solve problems and to aid in the country's search for a workable public life."

The movement found its way into the coverage of traditional political campaigns. Merritt, the editor of the *Wichita Eagle-Beacon* was dissatisfied with coverage of the 1988 campaign for president. Merritt wrote a post-election column decrying campaign professionals' efforts to manipulate press coverage by focusing attention on "pungent but pointless" charges and counter-charges. As he later contemplated the start of the 1990 campaign for governor of Kansas, Merritt dreaded more of the same shallow reporting of polls and tactics. So he and his staff insisted that the candidates address the issues. Journalists could reintroduce Americans to public life by contributing more than information to the civic discourse, said Merritt. They would no longer "maintain a pristine distance, a contrived indifference to outcomes," because a public that no longer pays attention to public affairs "has no need of journalists and journalism." So the newspaper in 1990 undertook the "Voter Project," an eight-week series in partnership with the local ABC affiliate, KAKE-TV. The project reported candidate responses on key issues voters had identified in a survey. Merritt, quoted in Rosen's "Getting the Connections Right," said a survey showed voters liked it. "Daily campaign coverage, horse-race polls, and columns extolling the virtues of voting ranked far down their usefulness list."

Rosen also recounted how in 1992 Merritt and his newspaper asked citizens about their concerns on crime, education and government gridlock, seeking "to move beyond venting about problems and involve people in thinking about solutions." As a result, thousands of people in south central Kansas "spent time and energy in the second half of 1992 in an exercise in public life." Volunteerism in the Wichita school district increased by 37% as the school year opened, and a survey showed reader satisfaction with the newspaper rose an unprecedented ten points, which Merritt said was twice the increase among Knight-Ridder newspapers whose ratings rose at all.

Rosen described how other newspapers undertook similar efforts to engage readers and effect change. The *Charlotte Observer*, also a Knight-Ridder newspaper, decided to focus on environmental issues in North Carolina's U.S. Senate race. One candidate balked at answering the paper's questions during the primary, saying his plan was to save the issue for the general election. He changed his mind after the editor threatened to run white space under his photo. Later, the *Observer* surveyed citizen concerns and then described problems and solutions to local crime. The paper's education writer decided interviewing the superintendent, a school board member and an expert were not enough; she needed to spend time in the classrooms and talk to readers, something she'd been doing as a reporter in Florida before she'd heard of public journalism. The *Akron* (Ohio) *Beacon-Journal*, another Knight-Ridder paper, used public journalism techniques to explore and debunk racial stereotypes about crime and education and business. The series, "A Question of Color," won the 1994 Pulitzer Prize for public service journalism. In Norfolk, Va., the *Virginian-Pilot* assembled a "Public Life Team" with a mandate "to lead the community to discover itself and act on what it has learned."

The Issue

Rosen's examples show how public journalism moved from theory to practice in several cities. Surveys, leaders' responses, calls to action, and volunteerism were key elements in the public journalism mix.

The scholars and journalists who support public journalism say reporters should take a step away from the political figures they write about and get closer to the audiences they write for. News stories should include the views of typical people as well as the usual array of experts, and news organizations should provide opportunities for citizens to identify problems and deliberate on the solutions.

The critics, on the other hand, argue that the press ought to confine itself to reporting news and editorializing on issues and leave the efforts to engender civic action to others. It is enough for journalists to call attention to public issues. They should not take places at the table for the discussion and policymaking that follows. Citizens who are given facts on all sides of a question and exposed to carefully delineated opinions, critics reason, are sufficiently intelligent and motivated to take the lead in engaging others in dialogue.

Voices of Support

Political columnist David Broder was an early supporter of public journalism, saying in a 1991 lecture at the University of California - Riverside that it was time for journalists to break a pattern of politics that was "turning off" the American people. "We have to try to distance ourselves from the people we write about — the politicians and their political consultants — and move ourselves closer to the people that we write for — the voters and the potential voters."

Describing the thinking behind a 1990 *Washington Post* project to examine the impact of campaign advertising, Broder noted that in the past the way a campaign unfolded was up to the candidates. "The axiom is that the campaign and its contents are the property of the candidate. It's up to the candidate to decide what is said and done, because, after all, it is the candidate whose name is on the ballot." The press needed a new operating principle for reporting on the campaign. "[V]oters have a right to have their concerns addressed and their questions answered by the people who have exercised power and who are seeking to exercise power."

Cole Campbell, an editor who served at the *Norfolk Virginian-Pilot* and later the *St. Louis Post-Dispatch*, was among the early practitioners of public journalism. In a 2000 article in *Journalism Studies*, Campbell defined it as having three principles. Through a variety of practices and experiments, he said, public journalism tries to first "treat citizens as experts in their own lives and aspirations — and therefore legitimate sources of news, information and context." Second, public journalists "treat citizens as political actors who can create public knowledge by deliberating together" in print, online or face to face. Finally, public journalists "create new forms of story-telling and reporting to enrich information."

Nancy Grub, who in 1996 offered a reporter's perspective on civic renewal for *National Civic Review*, contrasted public journalism with the practice of parroting solutions offered by experts. "Rather than relying on experts or blue-ribbon commissions to figure out complex issues, the everyday people who are most affected by the problems are mapping their own solutions." Those who practice public journalism "have answered the call of a democracy.... They understand that providing the mortar for building community is not only their privilege but their civic duty. They know that, if there is a bias here, it is no more than the bias of a medical reporter who wants a cure for cancer or of an education reporter who champions a literacy campaign."

Another reporter, Walker Lundy, in a 2003 *Editor & Publisher* story, described useful practices that evolved. "Along the way, civic journalism stopped being just for special megaprojects and started being part of the culture of the newsroom. With daily stories, reporters were more likely to go find real people to quote instead of just the usual sources. They also took stories a bit further than we did before and added breakouts showing readers how they could become involved in the news. Sometimes, we actually talked to readers about our stories...."

Public policy expert Ann E. Beaudry, in a 1996 article in *Editor & Publisher*, saw public journalism's value in encouraging civic engagement. Media-fostered community discussions bring topics into focus for a large percentage of the citizens. "Because [civic journalism] raises questions and features 'real' citizen input, not just the usual array of experts, it encourages average citizens to become engaged with the questions, to see themselves as some part of the answers. The dialogue is not limited to formal organizations but is more likely to move from the family breakfast table to conversations with coworkers to street-corner and backyard-fence conversations with neighbors."

In *Assessing Public Journalism*, edited by Edmund B. Lambeth, Philip E. Meyer and Esther Thorson, Salem College journalism professor Carol Rees Dykers said her review of twelve years of Merritt's newspaper columns showed that over that time "he stopped viewing himself as a detached, aloof observer and began to identify himself as *one* with the readers in a democratic public." The lesson was that although traditional journalists always had applied their values in deciding what to cover and what to keep out of their reporting, public journalists also tried to encourage citizens to talk about and act on issues and choices.

In his book, "Breaking the news: How the media undermine American democracy," journalist and author James Fallows described a public journalism project at the *Norfolk Virginian-Pilot* that included collecting questions from readers that the paper then presented to candidates for their answers. "This approach obviously had potential pitfalls, but so does the customary 'tactics-oriented' approach to campaign coverage, and indications were that the readers felt better served by the new coverage." Journalists didn't give up their duty to decide what to cover, he said. "In the most successful efforts, editors and reporters have listened carefully to public concerns — but have balanced what they learned that way with their own best judgment about the issues of greatest long-term significance to their readers."

Fallows argued that the key reason editors have criticized public journalism is that it lacks objectivity, but the reality is that objectivity is a myth. "One of public journalism's basic claims is that journalists should stop kidding themselves about their ability to remain detached from and objective about public life. Journalists are not like scientists, observing the behavior of fruit flies but not influencing what the flies might do. They inescapably change the reality of whatever they are observing by whether and how they choose to write about it."

Paul S. Voakes, a scholar who surveyed 1,037 newspaper journalists, found in the 1999 article "Civic duties: Newspaper journalists' views on public journalism," that most supported the practices associated with public journalism.

Those good practices included encouraging reporters to seek out and quote typical people, putting an increased emphasis on describing solutions, and offering citizens opportunities to deliberate on those problems and proposed solutions.

Editors in Dissent

Critics of public journalism focus on questions of who ought to be setting the agenda for journalists, the potential for conflicts of interest when journalists become civic leaders, and an inability of some editors to separate journalism from newspaper promotion.

In the November 12, 1994, issue of *Editor and Publisher,* writer Tony Case quoted Leonard Downey Jr., executive editor of the *Washington Post,* describing public journalism as "gimmicky and packaged" and saying his ideal of journalism, "whether you call it public or otherwise, is to provide citizens with as much as possible of the information they need to conduct their lives, private and public, and to hold accountable the increasing number of powerful people and institutions that hold sway in our lives." Downie said journalists should not be put in the position of "forcing candidates to participate in a dialogue with voters, staging campaign events, deciding what the good of the citizenship is and force-feeding it to citizens and candidates and encouraging citizens to vote." His remedy was renewed emphasis on investigative reporting. He also recommended that news organizations report on solutions as well as problems.

Another big-city journalist, Richard Aregood, editorial page editor of the *Philadelphia Inquirer,* told Case that newspapers shouldn't be letting outsiders set their agendas. "We are abandoning a piece of our own jobs if what we are doing is asking people what we should do. Are we to draw up panels of our readers and ask them what they want and put them in the newspaper? We might as well go into the mirror business."

In an October 3, 1994, article "A New Press Role: Solving Problems," *New York Times* columnist William Glaberson quoted *Inquirer* editor Maxwell King as saying that some of what is labeled public journalism, such as aggressive coverage of community issues, simply is a revival of good journalism. But King pointed to the importance of avoiding conflicts of interest. "The traditional rules about the distance and impartiality of reporters from their subjects are a key source of our strength." He saw no reason to break those rules.

The conflict of interest question came up again in a 1995 article in *Columbia Journalism Review*. *CJR* senior editor Mike Hoyt described another *Philadelphia Inquirer* editorial page editor, Jane R. Eisner, worrying in a letter to her readers about the press taking an active role in public affairs. "Our central mission is to report the news, to set priorities, to analyze but not to shape or direct events or outcomes," said Eisner. "Subsume or diminish the central mission, and we become like any other player in society, like any other politician, interest group, do-gooder, thief. I am not willing to relinquish this unique role."

And William Woo, editor of the *St. Louis Dispatch*, expressed concern in a 1995 lecture at the University of California - Riverside about how a newspaper could "objectively report on a burning community issue when the editor sits on the commission that is promoting a particular point of view on the matter."

In a column in *The New York Times Magazine* on May 21, 1995, Max Frankel, former executive editor of the *New York Times*, imagined newspapers sponsoring conferences and bringing heads of public organizations to conference stages to badger them into taking action to fix civic problems. "The emphasis on 'solutions' and 'connections' will inevitably distort the news agenda, devalue problems for which no easy remedy is apparent and end up compromising the paper's independence," he said. "The elemental tasks of describing events and discerning their causes are already beyond the skills and budgets of many American newsrooms. Running forums, finding speakers and raising money are diversions for most television and newspaper staffs even if such activity had no compromising side effects."

In a January 17, 1995, column in the *Washington Post*, former *Post* ombudsman Richard Harwood reviewed the misgivings of others and concluded that he had them, too. "The press already has credibility problems, based on the public perception that it is an arrogant, self-serving institution that more often aggravates than cures the social illnesses that afflict us. To anoint ourselves now as leaders of a new American reformation may be a little more than the market will bear."

Don H. Corrigan, a Webster University professor of journalism and working editor of two St. Louis area weekly newspapers, offered a comprehensive critique of public journalism in his 1999 book *The Public Journalism Movement in America*. He began by questioning one of the movement's basic assumptions: that the loss of interest in political affairs had led to a loss of interest in local journalism. "The major tenets ... that civic engagement is in decline, that political life is in decline, that public discourse is in decline — are all premises that may very well be false," Corrigan wrote. "At the very least, they are questionable."

Americans today are just not interested in the same things that attracted earlier generations, Corrigan wrote. People moved from the big cities to suburbs and turned their attention to issues that were closer to home, as presented in weekly newspapers.

Calls for reform of political journalism are valid but not new, he said. "The critics of horse-race coverage of elections were crying out against it long before public journalists began having epiphanies over the shortcomings of presidential election coverage."

Steve Davis, a former editor of *USA Today*, said in the journal *Journalism Studies* in 2000 that some editors were having trouble separating journalism from promotion. "Good civic journalism projects have been executed by good editors for years; for them, this is a name change. For other good-intentioned editors, there has been a rush to implement something they really do not understand, something they really cannot explain. They have rolled out all kinds of 'community outreach' — special projects, panel discussions, forums and dialogues that have confused staff and readers alike in pursuit of good PR (and better numbers for circulation and advertising)."

Regardless of whether better numbers were the goals of public journalism efforts observed by Davis, it seems clear they were not successful. Reports in media trade publications showed the decline of newspaper circulation persisted through the mid-'90s and the first decade of the new century. For example, the *Norfolk Virginian-Pilot*, one of the early papers doing public journalism projects, saw its numbers slide from 219,482 daily and 237,989 Sunday in 1992 to 196,131 daily and 232,139 Sunday in 2002. Of course, an argument could be made that the decline might have been greater without such efforts.

Assessment

When Robert Putnam observed that Americans were "bowling alone" in the early 1990s, he was seeing a decline in participation in social clubs, recreational activities and other places where people had come together face to face. Some scholars and journalists concluded that people also had similarly lost interest in politics and public affairs. The public journalism movement began with an editor's desire to do something about that declining interest by engaging more "real people" in setting the agendas for political reporting. The idea was expanded to cover other community concerns, such as crime and schools, and it brought journalists closer to their audiences. The movement's critics said asking citizens for their views was just good journalism, and warned that if editors started convening public gatherings to address issues, that would lead to conflicts of interest and take away journalists' strength — their independence.

Today, journalism organizations have discovered new ways to reach audiences through social media and are enthusiastically using those new media forms to deliver news and harvest information and opinion. Reporters "tweet" their accounts of political events-in-progress and prepare articles for the Web within minutes of the news breaks. Individual citizens engage in "micro-blogging" — filling Web pages with local news and opinion. News websites are thriving in communities across the land. Reporters use "crowd-sourcing," the practice of soliciting information from mass audiences, to feed stories.

Presidential campaigns in 2004 and 2008 used e-mail and websites to provide campaign updates and draw large numbers of small contributions from grass roots donors. The surge of "Tea Party" activism in the 2010 congressional elections took advantage of the new networks of electronically connected citizens as well as the voices of television talk show hosts. People who post personal information and "status updates" to a small mass audience of "friends" on Facebook also use the channel to communicate political information. The social media have helped renew civic discourse. Through e-mail, text messaging, Twitter and Facebook, people are connected 24/7 to those they know and, based on political and other interests, even complete strangers.

The Internet permits public journalists to silence claims they have lost their detachment. Those who want to encourage more people to participate in public affairs may do so simply by establishing links on their blogs and websites or inviting comments and responses via social media. They do not need to serve on committees or speak at public forums.

Critics of public journalism wrongly characterize it as a sales gimmick. It is, in fact, a communications tool that can help out-of-touch big-city journalists achieve the level of community connection enjoyed by their small-town and weekly counterparts. In the city or the country, such grassroots research is worthwhile as long as editors and producers continue to fulfill their historic duty to define news as not only what is interesting to audiences but also what has impact on people's lives.

The critics are right, however, in describing public journalism as just "good journalism" with a new name. Campaign correspondents have always been urged to demand that candidates answer questions about issues, though there is nothing wrong with also reporting about tactics and poll results. Reporters have always been instructed to listen to the people in community halls and observe the work of professionals in classrooms, courtrooms and city halls. Investigative reporters have always examined systems and uncovered abuses. Explanatory journalists have always enlightened audiences and helped people understand issues and choose solutions. But public journalism can do more, by inspiring audiences to be informed about issues, repair abuses and develop solutions. And it doesn't matter whether that discussion takes place on an auditorium stage or an electronic screen.

Suggesting that journalists shouldn't attempt to provide advice and leadership in civic affairs ignores the fact that they have always done so on the editorial pages of newspapers. No one should argue that the editorial writers' calls for action on the opinion pages impeach the credibility of the reporters' accounts of events, documents and the opinions of others on the news pages. In his journalism textbook from the late 1950s, Carl Warren described an expectation that the press would "be strictly objective, keeping its news and opinion columns separate and never slanting the news to promote the pet projects or private whims of anybody, including the publisher." Warren said, however, that there was an advocacy role for some of the journalists. "The public demands from a newspaper — and is entitled to — something more than mere parrot-like transmission of bare facts without explanations." There are many who advocate that "a newspaper, as a wide-awake community leader, should use its news as well as its editorial columns to stimulate thought, provoke action, expose wrong-doing and promote progress." Today those advocates would be called public journalists.

Public journalism drew a lot of attention as it was developed and implemented in the 1990s. The debate among scholars and journalists has faded in the past decade, but the techniques it fostered — asking people to identify community needs and political issues and asking community leaders and politicians to respond — continue to be practiced by good journalists, no matter what label is applied or where the discussions take place.

Points of View

Books

Corrigan, Don H. *The Public Journalism Movement in America: Evangelists in the Newsroom.* Westport, Conn.: Praeger, 1999. A journalism teacher and community newspaper editor offers a comprehensive review of public journalism. He labels as false the assumptions that interest in public affairs is fading and that the survival of journalism depends on healthy civic life.

Fallows, James. *Breaking the News: how the media undermine American democracy.* New

York, N.Y.: Pantheon Books, 1996. A leading critic indicts the media for behavior he says has brought lost credibility, including conflicts of interest and a preoccupation with political strategy over public issues.

Friedland, Lewis A. *Public Journalism Past and Future*. Dayton, Ohio: Kettering Foundation Press, 2003. The author examines four newspapers — the *Wichita Eagle, Charlotte Observer, Virginian-Pilot,* and *Colorado Springs Gazette* — as case studies of public journalism's successes, failures, and future.

Haas, Tanni. *The Pursuit of Public Journalism: Theory, Practice and Criticism*. New York: Routledge, 2007. Along with a review of the history and criticisms of public journalism, the author proposes practical solutions for improving it and speculates on its future.

Lambeth, Edmund B., Philip E. Meyer, and Esther Thorson, eds. *Assessing Public Journalism*. Columbia: University of Missouri Press, 1998. Three scholars collect a dozen papers that explore the origins, practices, and measures of public journalism.

Merritt, Davis Jr. *Public Journalism and Public Life: Why Telling the News is Not Enough*. Hillsdale, N.J.: Lawrence Erlbaum Associates, 1995. Merritt provides an editor's perspective on public journalism, why it is needed, and how it came into being in North Carolina, Kansas and other places.

Rosen, Jay. *Getting the Connections Right: Public Journalism and the Troubles in the Press.* New York: The Twentieth Century Fund Press, 1996. An educator outlines the troubles of the American press and the origins of public journalism. The survival of the press depends on the success of efforts to encourage public participation in governance.

Rosen, Jay. *What Are Journalists For?* New Haven, Conn.: Yale University, 1999. The leading proponent of public journalism describes its history and the views of its critics and considers its future with the emergence of the World Wide Web.

Rosen, Jay, and Davis Merritt, Jr. *Public Journalism: Theory and Practice*. Dayton, Ohio: Kettering Foundation, 1994. An educator calls for a shift away from the interests of political figures to the concerns of citizens. An editor advocates a journalism practice that moves away from reporting on problems to promoting discourse that leads to solutions.

Rosen, Jay, and Paul Taylor. *The New News v. The Old News: The Press and Politics in the 1990s.* New York: Twentieth Century Fund, 1992. Essays by Rosen, a college professor, and Taylor, a journalist, introduce the philosophy of public journalism, quote those who explain the need for it, and describe the earliest example, in Columbus, Georgia.

Rosenberry, Jack, and Burton St. John III, eds. *Public Journalism 2.0: The Promise and Reality of a Citizen Engaged Press.* New York: Routledge, 2010. With the means that nearly everyone has, because of websites and social media, to contribute to public discussion, the concept of public journalism is even more important today. This collection of essays offers a variety of views and proposals.

Articles

Campbell, Cole C. "Citizens Matter: and that is why public journalism matters," in "Debate: Public Journalism." *Journalism Studies* 1:4 (2000): 679-94. A leading proponent of public journalism describes its goals and argues that it is good because it tries to fit journalistic practice into democratic theory and practice.

Krub, Nancy. "Public journalism and civic revival: A reporter's view." *National Civic Review* 85:3 (Winter/Spring 1996): 32-34. Public journalism is part of a larger movement spawned by participants asking how the country's public business should be conducted. The civic revival movement was a search for a new social compact.

Stepp, Carl Sessions. "Public Journalism: Balancing the Scales." *American Journalism Review* 18 (May 1996): 38-40. Public journalism is a thoughtful effort to jump-start a tired industry. The author details the founders' critique of the media and expresses concern about unintended consequences of the movement.

Voakes, Paul S. "Civic Duties: Newspaper Journalists' Views on Public Journalism." *Journalism & Mass Communication Quarterly* 76:4 (Winter 1999): 756-74. A national study of 1,037 newspaper journalists found strong support for four practices associated with civic journalism, without reference to the terms "public" or "civic journalism."

Concentration of Media Ownership

In 2009 Comcast announced a $30 billion deal that would give it a 51% stake in General Electric's NBC Universal. This acquisition would create, as Cecilia Kang of the *Washington Post* stated, "a new kind of media colossus that would not only produce some of America's most popular entertainment but also control viewers' access to it." Comcast is the nation's largest cable operator and broadband Internet service provider with, according to its website, 23.2 million cable subscribers and 16.4 million Internet customers. NBC Universal's holdings include broadcast network NBC, television stations, cable networks, television production and distribution companies, a major film studio and amusement parks. The Comcast-NBC Universal merge would create a vertically integrated conglomerate that would benefit stockholders but might bar the way for competitors to enter the market. Kang reported that Comcast chief executive Brian Roberts "touted the synergies of the merger," calling the deal "pro-consumer" because the company would be in a better position to provide consumers with what they want. Critics, on the other hand, expressed concern that the merger could increase cable TV bills and allow Comcast to make some content "off limits" to non-Comcast consumers, favor its own content, and discriminate against competitors. In 2011, the Federal Communications Commission (FCC) and the U.S. Department of Justice approved the merger, with conditions that, as NPR reported, attempted to protect both consumers and competition in the online video marketplace. Despite the conditions, FCC Commissioner Michael Copps, the lone dissenter in the vote to approve the deal, stated, "It's too big. It's too powerful. It's too lacking in benefits for American consumers.... And it continues us down a road of consolidation we've been on for a couple decades now."

Competition, diversity, localism and the public interest stand at the center of the media ownership debate. For Comcast-NBC Universal, the merger allows the combined company to compete with other large conglomerates such as News Corp., Time Warner, Viacom and Disney. But it also might hinder competition, as

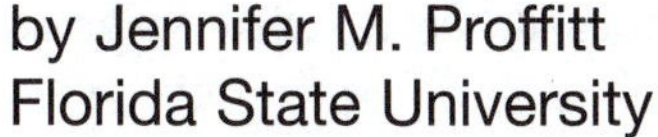
by Jennifer M. Proffitt
Florida State University

fewer and fewer companies dominate the media marketplace at the expense of smaller companies that cannot compete.

Media conglomerates argue that they are in a position to provide better quality and quantity of content. These corporations argue that mergers increase economic benefits that will in turn allow them to serve the public interest by giving the people what they want. Critics counter by positing that fewer owners lead to less content and source diversity. They argue that the public interest is not served by a concentrated media marketplace, one that celebrates profits above all else.

Origins of the Issue

Debates about concentration of ownership, the free market and regulation in the United States have been waged since at least post-Industrial Revolution with the rise of monopolies in the railroad, steel, oil, banking and other industries. The Sherman Antitrust Act of 1890 was a response to public alarm regarding the abuses of monopoly ownership including higher prices and lower quality products and services. This regulation was one of the first of several key federal legislative acts enacted to combat monopolistic, or anticompetitive, practices.

In general, free-market proponents argue for limited government intervention in markets, for regulation stymies economic growth. Critics argue that the free market is not free and that government must step in to correct market failures. It is within this larger context regarding free markets versus government regulation that media ownership debates are contested. The difference is that media corporations sell more than a manufactured product. As Ben Bagdikian, a critic of monopoly, writes, they "manufacture a social and political world."

Concerns about media ownership concentration largely stem from the idea that, in a democratic society, diversity of viewpoints is essential for citizens to make informed political decisions and to combat the possibility of concentrated power. For example, in the late 1930s, the FCC, led by James Lawrence Fly, commissioned a study regarding concentration of ownership in radio broadcasting. As media historian Erik Barnouw noted, Fly believed that the FCC needed to take an active role in preventing concentration of ownership, a trend that was "especially dangerous in an information medium." Under Fly's direction, the *Report on Chain Broadcasting* was released in 1941, which proposed a separation of Radio Corporation of America's (RCA) two NBC networks, Red and Blue. The report found that the two networks used monopolistic strategies that were not serving the public interest because they restrained competition and diversity of content. The networks and the National Association of Broadcasters pressured Congress to block the proposals found in the report. The Supreme Court upheld the report's suggestions, agreeing with the philosophy that diversity of ownership leads to diversity of viewpoints. NBC was thus required to divest one of its networks. The report findings also advanced the creation and adoption of the first commercial television multiple-ownership rule in 1941, which stated that no one person or group could own more than one television station unless it could be shown that such ownership would foster competition. This rule, known as the National Television Station Ownership (NTSO) rule, was changed in the 1950s to allow ownership of no more than seven stations. In another example, in the 1940s, a blue-ribbon panel commissioned by publisher Henry Luce and led by University of Chicago President Robert Hutchins noted that concentration of ownership of newspapers was largely a result of the pursuit of the advantages of economies of scale and high labor costs. However, "exaggerated drives for power and profit ... tended to restrict competition and to promote monopoly throughout the private enterprise system," the Hutchins Commission, as it came to be known, concluded in its report, *A Free and Responsible Press*. Concentration of ownership of the press was viewed as problematic because news media control the flow of information and are protected by the First Amendment, giving them awesome amounts of power. According to this line of thought, the pursuit of profit may benefit commercial interests but not necessarily the public interest.

By the early 1980s, the free-market approach to media ownership became the dominant paradigm. Previously, the idea that media, and broadcasters in particular, were public trustees that should meet the needs of the public served as the basis for regulations regarding media ownership. These regulations included the NTSO rule and other rules limiting the cross ownership of newspapers and broadcast stations in the same municipality. Mark Fowler, FCC chairman during the Reagan administration, and co-author Daniel Brenner, in "A Marketplace Approach to Broadcast Regulation" (1982), argued that a free-market approach for broadcasting, which was already the case for newspapers, would be more effective and efficient than government regulation. They contended that the market, without government intervention, would create more competition because broadcasters would be free to pursue the benefits of economies of scale to compete not only with each other but with other media outlets, such as cable and newspapers. Because there were so many media outlets from which to choose, diversity would be accomplished as well. During and since Fowler's leadership, several ownership restrictions were modified or lifted, allowing for acquisitions and mega-mergers, including Disney and Capital Cities' $19 billion merger in 1995 and Viacom's nearly $36 billion merger with CBS in 1999, AOL's acquisition of Time Warner to create a new company, AOL Time Warner, worth $350 billion in 2000, and the Comcast-NBC Universal deal.

Concentration of Ownership Is Not a Problem

Proponents of media ownership concentration argue that with many different media outlets, media conglomerates are more efficient and cost effective. Large corporations can provide more diverse and professional content.

Many Media Outlets. In his 2005 report, "The Media Monopoly Myth: How News Competition is Expanding Our Sources of Information and Entertainment," media consultant and academic Benjamin Compaine argued that, contrary to critics' concerns about concentration of ownership, "the empirical reality does not support any notion that in the United States ... consumers ... have fewer choices of sources or fewer choices in diversity for any type of content that has been available in the past." For example, in the 1970s, the three television broadcast networks — ABC, CBS and NBC — dominated prime-time programming. With the introduction of new broadcast networks — Fox in 1986 and the WB and UPN in 1995 (UPN and WB merged in 2006 to form the CW) — and the proliferation of cable networks, the three broadcast networks no longer dominate prime time. The networks saw their prime time ratings drop from 60% in the 1970s to about 20% in 2003. In a 1995 article, "The Impact of Ownership on Content," Compaine argued, "Television today has become as diverse as the magazine rack." In radio, consumers in any part of the country have many choices, from numerous local AM and FM terrestrial radio stations to more than a hundred satellite radio channels and thousands of Internet radio stations as well as online music-based systems like Pandora. Media competition, in other words, is thriving. Regulation that restricts growth in terrestrial radio, such as ownership regulations, hampers the ability of companies like Clear Channel to be competitive.

More than any other medium, the Internet offers a nearly unlimited number of choices for consumers and provides serious competition for traditional media sources, including broadcast television, radio and print newspapers and magazines. Compaine and others have noted that the rise of new technologies draws new competitors for traditional media, such as in the case of Google and Apple. Further, with convergence, or the blurring of traditional and nontraditional media, consumer choice is increased. For example, new or less popular sports leagues' games or tournaments are less likely to appear on such U.S. broadcast or cable networks as ABC or ESPN because of cost, lack of advertiser support, small audiences, or other reasons. Instead, viewers can find these games on Internet sites such as ESPN3 and CBScollegesports.com and no longer have to settle for what the television networks provide.

Audiences also have more access to diverse niche media content. *Wired* editor-in-chief Chris Anderson argued in his 2004 article, "The Long Tail," that the Internet has introduced "an entirely new economic model for the media and entertainment industries, one that is just beginning to show its power." Unlike traditional booksellers or video rental stores that have limited selection because of space constraints and reliance on best sellers, such companies as Amazon.com and Netflix allow consumers a plethora of choice for less cost to the distributor. In his 2006 book, *The Long Tail: Why the Future of Business is Selling Less of More*, Anderson expanded upon his article, noting that online distribution has opened up the media marketplace and allows for simpler and faster consumer access to niche titles that otherwise would not be available in traditional retail stores.

Compaine, industry executives and others have argued that concentration of ownership is a non-issue because the industry simply is not concentrated, even after ownership limits were lifted or modified. In his comparison of the concentration of the media industry in 1986 and 1997 in the book *Who Owns the Media?* Compaine used the Herfindahl-Hirschman Index (HHI), which the U.S. Justice Department uses to determine the competitiveness of an industry when evaluating mergers and acquisitions. He found, "The HHI increased from an extremely low 206 in 1986 to a still very low 268 in 1997. Thus, where the measure did show some increased concentration, with HHI levels of under 1,000 indicating low concentration, the media industry remains one of the most competitive major industries in U.S. commerce." In addition, considering the dramatic increase in the number of media outlets and sources of information accessible online, Compaine concluded in his 2005 article that the U.S. media system "is robust, competitive, affordable, and provides access to a vast range of entertainment, culture, news and viewpoints."

Efficiency. Viacom and CBS announced their intentions to merge in 1999, a union that created a conglomerate that would reach consumers of all ages. In the "Joint Statement of Sumner M. Redstone Chairman and Chief Executive Officer Viacom Inc. and Mel Karmazin President and Chief Executive Officer of CBS Corp.," the executives explained: "The assets and markets of the two companies are highly complementary, have very little overlap, and, once merged, will achieve significant economies of scale, resulting in new programming, new jobs, lower costs and an increase in exports of Viacom's brands, for the benefit of Americans and all consumers around the world." One of the primary arguments for mergers and acquisitions is that consumers will benefit from the efficiency of the corporate conglomerate structure, which in turn provides consumers with the content that they want.

As scholar David Pearce Demers stated in the edited book *Mass Media & Society* (1997), "As a social system becomes more complex, competition between media increases, which promotes innovation and economies of scale that, in turn, benefit large-scale organizations over small ones." Within the newspaper industry, for example, chain newspapers are able to benefit from economies of scale as they spread costs across their holdings and have the resources to endure economic threats. As Compaine noted in his "The Media Monopoly Myth" article, "Local owners may not have the economic resources to withstand a local boycott of real estate or banking or similar interests should they risk some criticism of the local industry. Large chains, on the other hand, are far less affected economically by a short-term downturn in any one community." As such, larger companies are in a better position to provide readers with more critical reporting than locally owned papers.

Others have argued that concentrated markets or monopolies are more efficient and more likely to provide diversity than competitive markets. In the 1980s, the FCC argued that the idea that diversity of ownership leads to diversity of viewpoints was not necessarily valid when one considers economic issues. That is, although ownership regulations "tend to increase the number of total owners," a reduction of diversity of programming could occur "due to the inability of station owners to benefit from the program production and distribution opportunities which the efficiencies of group ownership facilitate." In their 1994 book, *Regulating Broadcast Programming*, Thomas G. Krattenmaker and Lucas A. Powe Jr. stated that, "at the purely theoretical level, we cannot say with assurance that the diversity of programs offered will constantly increase with the number of firms in the market, although, once firms are rather numerous, we do expect this to happen.... Nevertheless, it may be that, in some ranges, monopolists will offer more choices than a number of separately owned firms." The authors provided the following example: Three stations have three different programs, each with a production cost of $300. Advertisers are willing to pay $1 for each viewer. Program A attracts more viewers than programs B and C. It is likely that all three stations will then offer programming similar to program A to gain market share. That is, competition leads to imitation. On the other hand, a monopolist could maximize profits by providing all three types of programming so as not to compete with itself.

Similarly, Steven T. Berry and Joel Waldfogel explained in their 2001 study "Do Mergers Increase Product Variety?" that "multiproduct firms do not want their products to compete with each other." As such, "mergers can lead firms to spread similar products apart, to withdraw duplicative products or to crowd products together to pre-empt entry, with ambiguous overall effects on variety." Further, cost savings due to integration "can allow firms to offer additional products, which tends to increase variety." The authors found that the consolidation that occurred in the radio industry as a result of changes in local radio ownership rules in the Telecommunications Act of 1996 — which increased limits on the number of stations one entity could own in a market — actually increased program variety. Previous to the Act, there was a limit of one AM and one FM station in a market. After the Act, a sliding scale was created so that an entity could own up to eight stations in a market with forty-five or more commercial radio stations with no more than five stations in the same service [AM or FM], but for a radio market with fourteen or fewer stations, an entity could own up to five stations with no more than three in the same market. Berry and Waldfogel argued that this concentration "reduces station entry and, holding the number of stations constant, increases product variety." Further, they found that in some cases "concentration increases variety absolutely."

Content. The adage that size matters applies to media outlets. The larger the company, the more resources it has, in theory, to increase production quality and quantity. As Demers noted, "The research suggests that corporate media place greater emphasis on product quality and produce a higher quality product than entrepreneurial media, primarily because they have more resources." For example, Compaine suggested in his 2005 "The Media Monopoly Myth" article that television station-newspaper cross-ownership can be beneficial. Such stations "tend to produce higher quality newscasts" as they have more resources and staff to devote to news. Further, he argued that, despite critics' calls for increased local ownership of television stations, such ownership "offers little protection against newscasts being very poor and does not produce superior quality compared to large group or network owned stations." These findings are consistent with Gregory S. Crawford's 2007 media ownership study, which found that "television stations owned by a parent that also owns a newspaper in the area offer more local news programming." He also found that, "By some methods, television stations owned by corporate parents with larger annual revenue also offer more local news, but by other methods they offer less." FCC Industry Economist Daniel Shiman also found that television stations that were cross-owned with newspapers, owned by one of the four broadcast networks or co-owned with other stations in the same market provided more news programming.

Compaine also noted in "The Media Monopoly Myth" that regulations that were implemented to increase diversity in programming — such as in the case of the Financial Interest and Syndication Rules (Fin-Syn) and Prime Time Access Rule (PTAR) — in fact decreased diversity. The intention of these rules, enacted in the early 1970s, was to reduce the dominance of the three networks, limiting their market share and allowing for more programming diversity by providing time for non-network produced shows (e.g., locally produced and independently produced programming). Citing Mara Einstein's work as an example, Compaine explained that the elimination of these regulations allowed for "vertical integration in production and distribution, which created the economic model that brought about the fourth and subsequent broadcast networks that television's harshest critics had long sought." For example, the combination of the purchase of six television stations from Metromedia and the purchase of 20th Century Fox allowed News Corp. to produce and distribute original programming, which ultimately produced a competitive fourth network. Mara Einstein examined the time around the establishment of the Fin-Syn rules (1966-1974) and the elimination of the rules in 1995 (1989-2002) to see how effective the rules were in promoting program genre diversity. She found that the rules did not increase program diversity and that the number of producers did not affect diversity of program genres. Compaine's 2005 "The Media Monopoly Myth" article and Einstein's 2004 "The Financial Interest and Syndication Rules and Changes in Program Diversity" article both concluded that the reliance on advertising for economic support is more likely than ownership to be the reason for redundancy or lack of diversity in program genres.

Another argument regarding concentration and diversity in content relates to the idea that media corporations are not run by self-interested individual owners. Rather, they are run by managers who are concerned with meeting stockholder expectations as well as providing quality products for consumers, which in theory increases profits. Compaine argued that "profit-driven public ownership" can be beneficial, as "chief executives of these companies have a fiduciary responsibility to their stockholders that they take seriously. Restricting their coverage, their range of films or magazine titles or news shows is not what the big companies are about. They seek to reach the mass market when they can and niche markets when they spot them." Profit-seeking media corporations will provide diverse news, whether in print or broadcast, to reach as many people as possible to maximize profits and thus satisfy shareholders.

An additional line of inquiry regarding content is that media consolidation is not necessarily problematic when we consider how audiences use, reconfigure and influence media content. Henry Jenkins noted in his 2004 article "The Cultural Logic of Media Convergence" that, while "media companies are learning how to accelerate the flow of media content across delivery channels to expand revenue opportunities, broaden markets and reinforce viewer commitments," it is also the case that "consumers are learning how to use these different media technologies to bring the flow of media more fully under their control and to interact with other users." Rather than merely a "top-down corporate-driven process," convergence is also a "bottom-up consumer-driven" process. He argued that with the increase in digital and mobile technologies, traditional media need to recognize that audiences are "active," "migratory," "connected," "resistant," "noisy and public." Additionally, with the rise of Internet sites such as YouTube and cheaper production and distribution tools, people are no longer simply consumers of media content. They are producers of content as well, competing with commercial products and increasing the number of choices available.

Concentration of Ownership Is a Problem

Critics argue that concentration of ownership is problematic for several reasons: Concentration and consolidation create barriers to entry that stymie competition, lead to lack of diversity in content and harm journalism's role in a representative democracy.

Barriers to Entry. When Bagdikian's book, *The Media Monopoly*, was first published in 1983, fifty firms dominated the media industry. In his 2004 updated text, *The New Media Monopoly*, he said that this number dwindled to just five conglomerates. Concentration of ownership can be found in most major media industries, including television and cable networks, cable service, music, film, book publishing, magazines and newspapers. In many cases, the same companies dominate in multiple markets. Concentration of ownership can be found at the local level as well, as most towns in the United States have only one newspaper, one cable provider and a handful of broadcasters, as noted by Bagdikian and others.

Concentration of media outlets creates large barriers to entry for potential competitors. A conglomerate like Disney owns numerous subsidiaries, including television and film production and distribution, broadcast and cable networks, Internet holdings, television stations, radio networks, amusement parks, book publishers, magazines and a music studio. Disney is able to use synergy, which, as scholar Eileen Meehan defines it in her book, *Why TV is Not Our Fault*, is "a series of tactics employed by transindustrial media conglomerates to multiply revenue streams and decrease costs by creating and feeding internal markets." For example, Disney has capitalized on successful programs such as *Hannah Montana* across its business sectors including television, film, music, books and licensing deals, all in-house. Disney is able to use its subsidiaries to produce and promote its product. A smaller company that only produces television shows, for example, does not have the same resources, opportunities or reach, making it difficult to break into the market.

Another benefit for the conglomerate but not for diversity or competition is the stability and access to capital that comes with owning outlets in different industries. If one sector is not doing well, the other sectors can make up the financial losses. For example, if the film industry is less profitable one year, a conglomerate's outlets in other industries, such as Internet and television, can defray the loss. A company that only makes films does not have that insurance, making it much more challenging to compete. Further, benefits from economies of scale lead to concentration. It is much cheaper and more profitable to run several television stations or newspapers than to run just one. Large advertisers also benefit because conglomerates can offer deals to advertise in their multiple outlets, which can in turn funnel advertising revenues away from smaller companies.

Critics reason that the monopoly-like strategies that the dominant media conglomerates use hinder, rather than encourage, competition. As scholar William Kunz posited in his 2007 book, *Culture Conglomerates*, "An important characteristic of an oligopoly, a market in which a few large suppliers dominate, is the interdependence and even collusion between firms," which creates barriers to entry as large firms work together to keep out the competition and share the market. Meehan traced the many joint ventures and deals made between the dominant media conglomerates — Disney, General Electric, News Corp., Time Warner and Viacom — in her book, *Why TV is Not Our Fault.* Since the publication of the book, Viacom has split into two companies, Viacom and CBS, but both remain controlled by Sumner Redstone's National Amusements. Meehan argued that rather than encouraging competition, which presumably results in innovation and content that caters to the public, oligopolistic structures allow for rivalry, "a condition in which each company in an oligopoly strives to be number one without destabilizing the oligopoly from which they all benefit." So while News Corp.'s Fox battles with Disney's ABC and General Electric's NBC for ratings, the three conglomerates are collaborators in other areas, such as the online video service Hulu.

As David Croteau and William Hoynes argue in their 2006 book, *The Business of Media*, the strategies that conglomerates use to minimize risk and cost and to maximize profits "violate basic market principles. Specifically, conglomerates use synergistic strategies and vertical integration to cross-develop and cross-promote cultural products. They use their size to launch large advertising campaigns and branding initiatives to squeeze out competitors." From a market-based approach, critics suggest that the concentrated media industry acts as a cartel rather than as a competitive marketplace. The pursuit of profit in an industry that controls the flow of information also affects the types of news and entertainment that audiences receive. For example, for the first Harry Potter film, Time Warner promoted it through games and sneak previews on AOL, on the cover of its magazine, *Entertainment Weekly*, and in a review in its news magazine, *Time*. In another example, the *Wall Street Journal* reported in March 2011 that Gannett Inc., the newspaper chain that also owns television stations and online media outlets, "launched its first-ever corporate branding campaign to highlight the sum of its parts to advertisers." The *Journal* noted that Gannett "is trying to establish itself as a one-stop shop for national brand advertisers looking to buy media across a variety of platforms instead of just one of its newspapers, websites or TV stations." An independent newspaper owner does not possess such leverage.

Lack of Diversity and Localism. Another concern critics raise is that media concentration affects diversity of content and localism, two values inherent in the concept of the public interest. Kunz argued in his book, *Culture Conglomerates,* that while there may be 500 cable channels available, a fundamental distinction needs to be made between "an abundance of outlets" and "the presence of a full range of voices in the marketplace of ideas." Increasing the number of channels available does not necessarily mean that diverse viewpoints and voices will find an outlet.

Critics suggest that conglomerates in an oligopolistic market structure are profit-seeking and adverse to risk, promoting a homogenized and imitative product. As Croteau and Hoynes argue, "Surely audiences are faced with many media choices, but if the options are somehow all similar in some way, then choice is an illusion." Once a particular media product is successful, whether in television, cable, film, magazines, or music, imitation is likely to follow as such products already have a pre-constituted audience and a successful track record. For example, with the success of CBS's *Survivor* in 2000, reality television programs and their sequels now abound (e.g., fall 2012 marked *Survivor*'s 23rd competition). An online reality television magazine claims to keep tabs on more than 200 reality television programs. Political punditry is to cable news what reality television is to broadcast and cable entertainment — lower in cost and ubiquitous. In terms of film, the summer of 2010 also demonstrated the economic appeal of imitation. According to Standard & Poor's, of the ten films to cross the blockbuster threshold of $100 million, seven were sequels and/or remakes and/or adapted from another source, such as an animated television show in the case of *The Last Airbender.* (Others include *Toy Story 3, Iron Man 2, The Twilight Saga: Eclipse, Shrek Forever After, The Karate Kid* and *Robin Hood.*) In terms of newspapers, a 2008 *Newsweek* article stated that after News Corporation's purchase of Dow Jones and the *Wall Street Journal,* News Corporation made changes to the look of the paper and, more importantly, expanded the focus of the paper to more than business. "By expanding the Journal's bull's-eye," *Newsweek* said, "[Rupert] Murdoch is fulfilling a pledge to compete head-to-head with The New York Times — for readers and for advertisers." Those in the newsroom "feared ... the loss of the newspaper's distinctiveness, given Murdoch's goal to go beyond business coverage," and their fears appear to be confirmed, evidenced by the "slow disappearance of perhaps the newspaper's most revered contribution to journalism — the page-one 'leder,' the long explanatory pieces on either the left or right side of the pre-Murdoch Journal," and the increase of soft news. The result of imitation, as Croteau and Hoynes explain, is that "By following tried and true standardized formulas, Hollywood movies, television entertainment, and other types of media have become formulaic and resistant to new ideas. Despite the potential for quick profits, this kind of media is not likely to serve the public interest."

In regard to serving communities, critics argue that the increase in ownership concentration has led to a decrease in localism, particularly in newspapers and radio broadcasting. Croteau and Hoynes noted that by the late 1990s, only 300 or so of more than 1,500 U.S. daily newspapers were independently owned. Most of them were very small, with circulations less than 10,000. Several radio companies own hundreds of radio stations. They include Clear Channel, which operates more than 800 stations; CBS Radio, which controls 130 stations; and Cumulus, which owns 350 stations. These large groups clearly benefit from economies of scale through centralization and standardization of production as well. With centralization comes less localism, however, as, in the case of radio, pre-recorded programming distributed to all parts of the nation needs to be generalized to remain relevant to diverse regions and tastes. The non-local control also makes it difficult for local musicians to break into the mainstream as playlists are dictated from headquarters. Concentration of ownership has resulted in fewer and fewer radio stations with local news organizations as news becomes centralized as well.

Another problem with centralization involves safety issues. Bagdikian, citing the *New York Times*, relates the infamous case of Clear Channel's ownership of six radio stations in Minot, N.D. In January 2002, a freight train carrying anhydrous ammonia derailed. The emergency alert system failed. So police contacted the radio stations to report the danger. "According to news accounts, no one answered the phone at the stations for more than an hour and a half. Three hundred people were hospitalized, some partially blinded by the ammonia. Pets and livestock were killed." This case became the rallying cry for politicians and critics concerned with concentration of ownership and the potential for even more acquisitions and mergers as the FCC examined whether to lift or modify ownership regulations in 2003.

Harm to Journalism. In his 2004 book *The Problem of the Media*, Robert McChesney argued that the normative goals of the media in a democratic society — "to act as a rigorous watchdog of the powerful and those who wish to be powerful; to ferret out truth from lies; and to present a wide range of informed positions on key issues" — are not being met because the focus of the concentrated corporate mainstream media is profit maximization. Since entertainment conglomerates News Corp., Disney, Time Warner, Viacom/CBS and multi-industry conglomerate General Electric along with Comcast control all major broadcast and cable news outlets, news becomes just one subsidiary of the corporate machine. Further, to increase profit margins each year to placate shareholders, cuts in news resources, foreign news bureaus and staff often occur.

Bagdikian noted that "editorial vigor diminishes under chain ownership," and hard news, including expensive investigative reporting, has given way to soft news, including the trivial and sensational. Croteau and Hoynes argued that "the business logic of lowering expenses and increasing profits results in news that is limited in its range of ideas, favoring those entities that have the resources to aid journalists in their work." Cutbacks leave reporters relying on official sources, press releases and news conferences for information.

Concentration of ownership has led to fewer voices, which critics say harms the democratic process, for multiple viewpoints are necessary for citizens to make informed political decisions. Meehan argued that rivalry has replaced competition. The result is duplicative content across "thousands of media outlets." The same or similar content can be found in news outlets across the United States. For example, newspaper chains share stories across their holdings, and network news outlets provide feeds for network owned-and-operated stations and affiliates. Further, McChesney noted that "the rise in media conglomerates has made it far easier for a firm to spread its editorial budgets across several different media," resulting in even fewer voices as the same journalist can report for multiple media outlets, including newspapers, broadcast and online.

Critics also argue that concentration of ownership leads to concentrated political power. Large media conglomerates in an oligopolistic structure have ready access to political figures. Bagdikian writes: "Many corporations lobby for favorable government treatment, but only media corporations control access to the American mind." For example, critics raised concerns regarding Murdoch's News Corp.'s $1 million donation to the Republican Governors Association in 2010, including how such a large donation might affect news coverage of elections. Fox News, the *New York Post* and the *Wall Street Journal* are News Corp. properties. As Howard Kurtz reported in the *Washington Post*, "It is hardly unusual for media companies to support candidates and political parties." However, none has reached such magnitude as Murdoch's. Kurtz noted that News Corp. executives defended the decision, stating that the donation was made to the Republican Governors Association because of its pro-business agenda and that the news division was not involved. Nonetheless, the corporation has the clout to influence policies due to its size and audience reach.

The News Corp. example also demonstrates critics' concerns that conglomerate business dealings can affect news coverage as news choices often reflect corporate interests. Bagdikian and McChesney argue that news coverage of media concentration, for example, is hard to find. Additionally, in a conglomerate structure, news becomes a small piece of the corporate pie. As such, it is less likely that the news division will criticize its corporate parent or other commercial interests, including advertisers. Journalists or news organizations that are critical of corporate interests are often met by what Edward S. Herman and Noam

Chomsky in their 1988 book *Manufacturing Consent* called "flak," or "negative responses to a media statement or program." For example, the *Los Angeles Times* reported in 2005 that GM pulled its advertising from the paper after the *Times* published a critical review of GM's Pontiac G6 written by Pulitzer Prize winner and car critic Dan Neil. *USA Today* reported in February 2010 that Southeast Toyota pulled its advertising from local ABC stations "to punish ABC-TV for aggressively reporting on its safety problems," even though Toyota had not "publicly complained that any of the ABC reports were factually incorrect." McChesney wrote in *The Problem of the Media*, "The corporate news media have a vested interest in the corporate system," and, thus, coverage of business is largely celebratory. Institutional pressures also affect journalists. A survey the Pew Research Center for the People & the Press and the *Columbia Journalism Review* conducted in 2000 found that market pressures were a primary factor regarding self-censorship, as a majority of the 300 journalists and news executives surveyed reported that they often or sometimes avoid boring or complex stories, and more than a third acknowledged "news that would hurt the financial interests of a news organization often or sometimes goes unreported."

Assessment

Questions regarding the roles and results of media concentration cannot be answered by simply counting the number of media outlets offered at any given time. Although consumers have many options from which to choose, including billions of websites, hundreds of digital television channels and thousands of newspapers and magazines, choice is not necessarily diversity. If we define diversity in terms of differing viewpoints — rather than thinking in terms of the number of media outlets available — then the important questions become who is allowed to speak, what messages are disseminated and how accessible are media outlets. For example, the geographical and market reach of a college radio station is much smaller than that of CBS or ABC. Therefore, it is problematic to compare small, local outlets to the five or six massive horizontally and vertically integrated conglomerates that dominate production, distribution and exhibition, as researchers and the FCC have done to determine concentration of a market. In terms of the Internet, the top search results are not necessarily the websites people go to the most. Rather, they tend to be the sites that pay for higher visibility or use other forms of search engine optimization to be listed near the top. The digital revolution has opened up space for alternatives to the mainstream commercial media. People can be producers of media content, not just consumers of it. Access, however, also remains a concern in terms of broadband penetration and network neutrality.

Proponents of media conglomeration often argue that these corporations give people what they *want* and that critics who suggest that conglomerates are not giving people what they *need* are paternalistic. Nevertheless, it is difficult to say what people want when all they have is a limited choice of products created to sell in the marketplace, to attract advertisers and eyeballs, and to maximize profits and minimize risks. For example, Meehan argued convincingly in her 2005 book that television is not our fault. Rather, the monopolistic ratings process, controlled by Nielsen, is a compromise between meeting the needs of advertisers who want more bang for their buck and television executives who want more advertising dollars. The Nielsen ratings don't count what people really want. Instead, they assess what people choose to watch based on the options available.

Further, bigger is not always better. It does not always create the jobs, reduce costs and increase the quality of content as promised with each new merger and acquisition. For example, when AOL announced that it was going to acquire Time Warner in 2000, the merger was hailed as "historic." The *New York Times* wrote: "Their proposed marriage will be the largest corporate merger in history. The implications of this merger are big too, for the way stocks are valued, for the way information services reach consumers, and perhaps for the way entertainment, politics and journalism evolve in a 21st-century corporate environment." Ten years later, in January 2010, a *New York Times* headline read, "How the AOL-Time Warner Merger Went So Wrong." The article quoted Time Warner CEO Gerald Levin as saying, "The Internet had begun to 'create unprecedented and instantaneous access to every form of media and to unleash immense possibilities for economic growth, human understanding and creative expression.'" The *Times* added, "The trail of despair in subsequent years included countless job losses, the decimation of retirement accounts, investigations by the Securities and Exchange Commission and the Justice Department and countless executive upheavals."

The barriers to entry created by such mergers, however, remain. It is much more difficult for small or new competitors to break into the mainstream to compete with large, vertically integrated conglomerates. For example, even without NBC Universal, according to Brian Stelter of the *New York Times*, Comcast "has long played hardball with competitors and content providers." Local television broadcasters were especially concerned and negotiated conditions to protect their interests. Similar to the original AOL Time Warner merger, promises of "economic benefits and programming opportunities for local communities" were reasons some public officials championed the deal.

Critics have suggested that diversity of ownership should lead to diversity of viewpoints and increased local control, proposing new regulations and stronger enforcement of antitrust law to break up the "media monopoly." If the goals of corporations within capitalism are to minimize risk and maximize profits, however, some of the same issues remain no matter how many outlets exist. C. Edwin Baker, in his 2006 book *Media Concentration and Democracy,* argued that diversity in ownership structure would allow for the disbursement of power and diversity of content. Varied ownership and financial structures would have different goals and motivations in terms of content (e.g., public versus private ownership) and thus would be better able to meet the diverse needs of a democratically functioning society.

Points of View

Books

Anderson, Chris. *The Long Tail: Why the Future of Business is Selling Less of More.* New York: Hyperion, 2006. The Internet has allowed for a new economic model of abundance in which the aggregate sale of niche products rivals sales of the hits.

Bagdikian, Ben H. *The New Media Monopoly*, 7th ed. Boston: Beacon Press, 2004. Increased concentration and consolidation in the media industry harm democracy as a handful of companies dominate news and entertainment, shaping ideology and using their political power to fit their needs rather than the needs of the public.

Compaine, Benjamin M., and Douglas Gomery. *Who Owns the Media? Competition and Concentration in the Mass Media Industry*, 3rd ed. Mahwah, N.J.: Lawrence Erlbaum Associates, 2000. We need to revise our conceptualizations of competition and concentration in the media marketplace in light of the introduction and proliferation of new media technologies.

Croteau, David, and William Hoynes. *The Business of Media: Corporate Media and the Public Interest*, 2nd ed. Thousand Oaks, Calif.: Pine Forge Press, 2006. The pursuit of profit by corporate media, the business strategies used to increase market share and the consolidation of media affect the types of media content produced and influence politics and social relations.

Demers, David. *History and Future of Mass Media: An Integrated Perspective*. Cresskill, N.J.: Hampton Press, 2007. Corporate media have the ability and aptitude to support and encourage social change. In general, mass media become more critical of power relations the more they are corporatized.

Jenkins, Henry. *Convergency Culture: Where Old and New Media Collide.* New York: New York University Press, 2006. New media have opened up space for struggles between corporate controlled media and consumers as consumers use, create and interact with media products in new and exciting ways.

Krattenmaker, Thomas G., and Lucas A. Powe Jr. *Regulating Broadcast Programming*. Cambridge, Mass.: MIT Press, 1994. An increase in the number of media outlets does not necessarily increase programming diversity.

Kunz, William M. *Culture Conglomerates: Consolidation in the Motion Picture and Television Industries*. Lanham, Md.: Rowman & Littlefield, 2007. The conglomerate structure of the film and television industries affects the production and distribution of media content and the public interest goals of competition, diversity and localism.

McChesney, Robert W. *The Problem of the Media: U.S. Communication Politics in the 21st Century*. New York: Monthly Review Press, 2004. The corporate ownership structure, its reliance on advertising and the perpetuation of ideologies that protect the status quo have negative impacts on journalism and the policy-making process.

Noam, Eli M. *Media Ownership and Concentration in America*. New York: Oxford University Press, 2009. Media ownership is much more nuanced and dynamic than either side of the debate suggests.

Articles

Baker, C. Edwin. "Media Concentration: Giving Up on Democracy." *Florida Law Review* 54 (2002): 839-919. Media concentration has adverse economic, legal and social ramifications for democracy. Diversity of ownership structure is necessary.

Compaine, Ben. "The Impact of Ownership on Content: Does It Matter?" *Cardozo Arts & Entertainment* 13 (1995): 755-80. In the television industry, competition rather than regulation leads to content diversity.

Compaine, Benjamin. "The Media Monopoly Myth: How New Competition is Expanding Our Sources of Information and Entertainment." *New Millennium Research Council* (2005): 1-47. Media concentration is a myth. The U.S. media system is robust and competitive.

Einstein, Mara. "The Financial Interest and Syndication Rules and Changes in Program Diversity." *Journal of Media Economics* 17:1 (2004): 1-18. Consolidation of media ownership between 1966 and 2004 did not reduce programming diversity. The broadcasting system's reliance on advertising for revenue "leads producers to create programming that will generate large audiences."

Jenkins, Henry. "The Cultural Logic of Media Convergence." *The International Journal of cultural Studies* 7:1 (2004) 33-43. "[C]onsumers are learning how to use ... media technologies to bring the flow of media more fully under their control and to interact with other users," thus reducing the importance of diversity in media ownership.

"Joint Statement of Sumner M. Redstone Chairman and Chief Executive Officer Viacom Inc. and Mel Karmazin President and Chief Executive Officer of CBS Corp." *Federal Communications Law Journal* 52 (2000): 499-511. The Viacom/CBS merger will allow the combined company to benefit from economies of scale which will in turn benefit the public. FCC regulations that are in place are problematic for broadcasters' competitiveness in the media marketplace.

McChesney, Robert W. "Theses on Media Deregulation." *Media, Culture & Society* 25 (2003): 125-33. Deregulation is regulation that benefits private interests rather than public interests and has led to concentration of ownership.

Schwartzman, Andrew Jay. "Viacom-CBS Merger: Media Competition and Consolidation in the New Millennium." *Federal Communications Law Journal* 52 (2000): 513-18. Mergers like that of Viacom and CBS lead to increased consolidation and barriers to entry and decreased programming standards.

Scott, Ben. "The Politics and Policy of Media Ownership." *American University Law Review* 53 (2011): 645-77. The media ownership regulation debates surrounding the FCC's 2003 Biennial Review demonstrate that policy-making is a political process.

7

Government Funding of Journalism

Journalism is an enterprise that requires money — a great deal of money — to pay for gathering, presenting and delivering the news, whether printed, broadcast or digitized. The business model by which journalists, or their employers, obtain the money to pay for the journalism raises a thorny ethical question: What influence, if any, do the sources of that revenue exert — directly or indirectly — on the journalism? Recent technological changes driven by the Internet have left journalistic enterprises reeling financially, calling into question the viability of journalism. Several observers and even some journalists are on the verge of calling for government to fund journalism. Government funding of an enterprise thought by many to exist primarily as an independent check on government naturally raises a host of ethical questions.

The choice of funding approaches is not an either-or proposition. The financial imperatives of journalism do not mean that news-gathering must be conducted solely for a profit. Nor does the need to pay the bills mean that journalism must be supported by the sale of subscriptions or advertising or by a combination of the two. The commercial business model is the one that was most prevalent as well as financially successful in the United States during at least the last century. Decade after decade, broadcast radio and television stations as well as a wide variety of newspapers and magazines carried countless profitable advertisements of all types, from classified help-wanted ads to display ads for supermarkets, clothing, automobiles, political candidates and the latest electronic gadgets. The advertisers filled pages and airtime as well as corporate coffers while also paying for the newsrooms and news divisions along the way.

While some people listen to public radio or watch public television and subscribe to the occasional publication (printed or online) that shuns advertising, most U.S. consumers have come to accept the presence of advertising alongside news as standard practice for journalism. For most, ads have become a part of the landscape, even if audience members can skip the ads by turning the page,

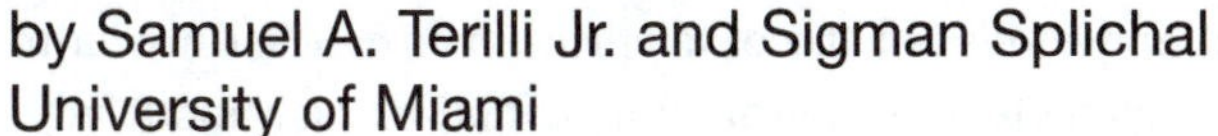
by Samuel A. Terilli Jr. and Sigman Splichal
University of Miami

muting the volume or mastering the fast-forward button on a digital video recording device. Americans typically are familiar with this commercial funding model and the ethical questions that arise when commercial interests influence the journalism, but the commercial model is not the only model.

The financial crisis facing many commercially supported journalistic enterprises has led some journalists, academics, public officials and other interested observers to seek other means of supporting journalism. One response to this crisis calls for using government tax dollars to fund news operations. Involving government and taxes so directly in an activity often characterized as the watchdog of institutions and individuals in power raises fears of a politically neutered press or, worse, one that becomes a propaganda arm of government. This chapter looks at the arguments for and against government support of journalism and the ethical implications of government-subsidized journalism generally.

Origins of the Issue

For most of the 20th century, the national and local news media in the United States were vibrant, though far from perfect. With a few exceptions for failing afternoon newspapers, the news media had large and often growing staffs and acknowledged expertise while delivering strong profits to owners — individuals, families or corporate shareholders and investment firms. Many of these commercial media companies are now fighting for their financial survival.

Newspaper readership began declining in the 1930s during the Great Depression. Economic woes plagued the industry; and the rise of radio and, later, television began to fragment the audience. Still, newspaper profits soared into the 1990s, but those profits were built in large part upon the growth of the U.S. economy and the collapse of afternoon papers, which competed for advertising revenue. The survivors in part grew by cannibalizing their own industry as larger papers took over or merged with smaller ones. Broadcast television and radio stations hardly behaved much differently. Faced with competition from cable and then satellite-based competition for the time of the viewers, broadcasters merged, consolidated and jumped into competing markets, buoying profits even when per-station audiences declined.

Enter a maturing Internet — not merely the hobby of the technologically skilled, but a means of mass communication that even non-engineers could use on a daily basis. The rise of the World Wide Web, browsers and Internet search engines in the 1990s enabled people to find news, information, advertising and entertainment quickly, freely and in great detail. Reasonably skilled users of all ages often found they no longer needed the older print or broadcast media to deliver advertisements for gadgets, jobs, automobiles, food or just about any-

thing else. Advertisers could build brands and move products and services not just through high-concept print campaigns or slick broadcast commercials. Now, they had at their disposal a combination of online banner ads, pop-ups, search-term linked advertisements, viral campaigns and even their own websites and allied bloggers.

The digital revolution did not mean that the old media no longer had any advertising. Newspapers and broadcasters launched their own websites and sold advertising for them, often packaging deals for both online and print displays. In fact, many old media still offer the largest audience or reach in their markets. These markets became, however, more fragmented and competitive. The share of audience and advertising dollars for older media fell, in many cases precipitously.

The economic crisis that began in 2008 only worsened the state of these media businesses. With rampant foreclosures affecting everything from financial to real estate advertising and a general slowing of economic activity causing other advertising declines, the result was dramatic. The legacy news media (newspapers, magazines, radio and television) have faced in recent year what amounts to an economic tsunami. Some large media companies, particularly those most heavily invested in newspapers, found they had taken on too much debt that was difficult to service with declining cash flows. A wave of bankruptcies, restructurings and even closures followed as the companies found they were no longer the darlings of Wall Street and investors. For example, in 2009 the *Rocky Mountain News* closed when the E.W. Scripps Company failed to find a buyer for the financially troubled daily; and the once great Tribune Company, which owns the *Los Angeles Times* and *Chicago Tribune*, among other papers, filed for bankruptcy in 2008. Given this state of affairs, one may understandably question whether the old business model based on the sale of commercial advertising can continue to support journalism and serve as a check on government. Citizen journalism, blogs and social media represent powerful communication tools, but the loss of the institutional or professional press hinders the check the Fourth Estate can have on government or big business. The U.S. government stepped in to help the banking and automotive industries weather their crises. So why not journalism?

The Case for Government Support

Short of moving toward a system of state-run media, those proposing governmental support of journalism call for tax policy changes to favor media outlets, increased funding through existing public broadcasting mechanisms, a new round of antitrust exemptions to allow the old media to negotiate jointly with

Internet news aggregators, the creation of something akin to the National Endowment for the Arts for journalism, other legislative innovations and even for more direct government bailouts of news media companies. As the old saying goes, the devil is in the details.

Leonard Downie, a former *Washington Post* editor and now a professor at Arizona State University, and Michael Schudson, a sociologist and professor at Columbia University, in a 2009 *Columbia Journalism Review* article titled "The Reconstruction of American Journalism," suggested several approaches to support independent news reporting on a local as well as national level. Like the others on both sides of the debate, they acknowledge the revolutionary change facing journalism as they search for what might take the place of the old commercial media that did most of the news reporting. "The questions that this transformation raises," they write, "are simple enough: What is going to take the place of what is being lost, and can the new array of news media report on our nation and our communities as well as — or better than — journalism has until now?"

Then Downie and Schudson pose the million-dollar question: So what can and should be done to shape the future of journalism? They offer several ideas, including favorable tax treatment of independent news organizations substantially devoted to reporting on public affairs, increased philanthropic and university support for news organizations and reporting, greater accessibility of public records and information and, perhaps most controversially, the creation of a national fund for local news collected from license or other fees levied on broadcasters or Internet service providers and administered through open competitions and Local News Fund Councils. Their ideas prompted the *Columbia Journalism Review* in an accompanying editorial titled "A Helping Hand" to label the proposals as "radical."

Professor Robert W. McChesney and journalist John Nichols suggested an interventionist role for government in a 2010 magazine article titled "How to Save Journalism — The Patriotic Case for Government Action" in *The Nation*. Although they oppose government bailouts of commercial media, they strongly support direct subsidies, at least on a temporary basis, for nonprofit, noncommercial news media as well as increases in funding for public broadcasting. The authors also advocated in their 2010 book *The Death and Life of American Journalism* the creation of multiple, competing public stations, an annual tax credit for the first $200 spent by Americans on daily newspapers, elimination of postal charges for periodicals that earn less than 20% of their revenues from advertising, possible tax credits for online subscriptions in the future and requirements that media recipients of certain subsidies make nearly all of their reporting available online without charge. For McChesney and Nichols, as well as others, the necessity and advisability of subsidies is a foregone conclusion. The only question is how best to subsidize the press to serve the public interest.

Their argument for greater government support, like those advocated by many others, starts with the words of Thomas Jefferson and James Madison about the importance of a free press and an informed citizenry. For example, McChesney and Nichols quote Madison's statement, "To the press alone, checquered as it is with abuses, the world is indebted for all the triumphs which have been gained by reason and humanity over error and oppression." A free press and independent journalism have significant roles to play in any self-governing society. It is not the freedom to speak, but the content of journalism that is the concern. No one seriously argues that advocacy journalism and political commentary are dying. Each appears robust on the Internet, cable television and talk radio. Rather, proponents of government support typically point toward investigative journalism and local accountability reporting or the journalism of factual reporting as the type of journalism that most needs public or government intervention and support, as Geoffrey Cowan and David Westphal argued in their 2010 "Public Policy and Funding the News" report published by the University of Southern California. Reporting of facts or news as opposed to commentary is more expensive and more time consuming. Consequently, it is more endangered as news media companies suffer financial reversals.

As summarized in a 2009 essay by C. Edwin Baker in *Balkinization,* this argument is essentially premised on the idea that journalism is a public good that serves society generally and is not merely the producer-sellers (e.g., reporters and media companies) and user-buyers (i.e., viewers, listeners and readers) involved most directly in journalism. As a public good, much like universal education, national defense or highway construction, journalism deserves an allocation of resources by the public and the state.

The proponents, from McChesney and Nichols to Cowan and Westphal, argue that commercial business models that leave journalism to be supported by the sale of advertising and subscriptions cannot be revived to function adequately in the new digital world. Even if advertising sales were to rebound, they contend, profit-seeking media businesses do not adequately serve the many diverse, and at times commercially unsustainable, interests in society. William F. Baker, in the 2009 article "How to Save the News" in *The Nation,* added that philanthropy cannot fill the void. Just as society does not rely solely on private schools to educate either children or adults, society should not rely solely on private for-profit news media to inform the public.

Proponents of a greater role for government also typically make devastating comparisons of the level of government support of public broadcasting in the United States with the levels in other Western-style democracies with similarly free presses and free speech. The amount of federal financial support through the Corporation for Public Broadcasting (CPB) for public broadcasting in all of its forms was about $445 million in the fiscal year 2012 federal budget. Most of the money goes to public television, which does little local or national news reporting. European democracies far outspend the United States in per capita terms and in some cases even in absolute numbers. The United Kingdom invests far greater sums in the BBC and BBC World Services through a television license fee and taxes paid by British citizens. Interestingly, Americans also have benefitted from that investment as the BBC has become more popular in this country not only with viewers, but also with our own public broadcasters who use it as a source of international news. In comparison to smaller democracies such as Sweden and Norway, argued Lee Bollinger, president of Columbia University, in his 2010 *Wall Street Journal* column, the United States lags in these comparisons on a per capita basis. As pointed out by Nichols and McChesney in their January 2010 article in *The Nation*, if the United States invested comparable public resources in public broadcasting, the federal subsidy would increase by several billion dollars and perhaps reach as high as $30 billion. While no one seriously suggests such a dramatic increase in funding is likely or politically feasible in the near term, the comparisons do put these proposals in perspective, internationally speaking. The underlying point of the comparisons is that a modest increase in federal support is both in order and financially plausible for a nation as wealthy as the United States.

The risk that public broadcasting budgets will become a political target does not dissuade advocates of greater funding such as Bollinger, Nichols, McChesney, Downey, and Schudson. First, they call for use of the CPB to shield program producers from political interference, and they cite the decentralized nature of public broadcasting as another shield from orchestrated political manipulation. Second, they laud the success of other, often overlooked forms of federal support for independent institutions or processes that are at times controversial — examples of government support that has not led to official domination or political control. These success stories include, according to the proponents, public universities, public libraries, and even national grants to support the arts and research.

Bollinger also wrote in his 2010 *Wall Street Journal* column that one of the best examples of government funding *not* leading to government control appears in our courts every day: government-paid defense lawyers or public defenders. The key for Bollinger in this regard is a professional ethic that demands that the lawyers hold government accountable regardless of the political pressure to do otherwise — the same ethic one expects of independent, watchdog journalists. Thus, while everyone acknowledges the possibility that some in government might attempt to abuse or manipulate government support for journalism, proponents cite many examples of government support working within a system of safeguards and institutional or professional checks and balances. In addition, the risk of government influence through subsidies often is considered no greater than the risk of the influence of the commercial entities now buying the advertising that supports private, for-profit journalism.

Historically, proponents of government support argue that if government were to subsidize journalism, it would be doing nothing more than replacing subsidies reduced or eliminated in recent years. Nichols and McChesney, in their 2010 *Nation* article, observed that, if the United States today spent on journalism an amount that roughly equaled what the government provided in postal and printing subsidies to the press in the 1840s, the end result, as a percentage of Gross Domestic Product, would be $30 billion annually. Interestingly, that projection tracked what they also estimated would be comparable on a per capita basis to the expenditures of some smaller European nations that have successful, politically independent and well regarded systems of publicly supported broadcasting and reporting.

Proponents of increased government support interpret American history as an ally of government support. This common argument, posited by Westphal and Cowan in a 2009 article in *The Online Journalism Review*, essentially seeks to diffuse the fear of government support of the press by showing that the American government has supported the press in a variety of ways. For example, from the early colonial period through the founding and maturation of the republic, American governments supported the development of a press through a combination of government printing contracts, postal subsidies and advertising. Some early American printer-publishers also served as local postmasters. They circulated news sheets, the proto-newspapers of the day, without charge. Even as Federalists and Anti-Federalists disagreed on many policy issues in the early republic, they agreed in the Post Office Act of 1792 that newspapers should be delivered by the growing postal service at heavily subsidized or discounted rates and agreed that newspapers could exchange copies with one another at no cost.

American governments — state and federal — also supported the development of this nascent press more directly. The printer-publishers of the 18th and 19th centuries earned important revenue through government contracts to print laws and public notices — a practice still in force today. Governments bought advertising or required that private parties buy advertising to publically announce their actions. States throughout the growing country adopted laws requiring litigants or applicants in everything from foreclosure cases to divorces and adoptions to publish public notices in newspapers of general circulation in the relevant communities. Governments published tax rolls, hearing notices and bond issues, to name a few.

The federal government made other investments and policy choices that profoundly benefited the development of the press. For example, the fact that the post office was not only enshrined in the U.S. Constitution but also set up as an essentially nationalized industry at the start of the new republic ensured public investment in the postal network placed at the disposal of the fledgling newspapers. The government, after some prodding, also invested in the experimental electrical telegraph line that Samuel Morse strung from Baltimore to Washington, D.C., in the 1840s. This seed money demonstrated the viability of the new technology that years later would become vital to newspapers and their wire services. State and national investments in and laws favoring roads, canals, railroads and even the Internet would help build transportation as well as communication networks that also would benefit journalism.

Tax policy also supported growth of the press. The British Parliament's missteps with the Stamp Act of 1765, which in part was a tax on newspapers, not only helped fan the embers of a revolutionary spirit, it forever branded attempts to tax specially the press in this country. Advertising for the most part remained untaxed except as part of any generally applicable corporate taxes throughout American history. More importantly, advertising expenditures by businesses are tax deductible. As Paul Starr stated in his 2004 book *The Creation of the Media,* "Cheap print was public policy in America."

Beyond tax policy, government also legislatively tinkered with and supported the press over the course of American history. Take for example the Newspaper Preservation Act of 1970, which created an antitrust exemption allowing the merger of the business operations, though not newsrooms, of a successful newspaper with those of a failing newspaper in the same city. The law amounted to a government attempt to preserve independent editorial voices in communities as afternoon papers began to fail and the industry consolidated. Although many on both sides of the issue question the wisdom of this law, the proponents cite it as another example of government involvement designed to support commercial media.

Proponents of increased government action also cite broadcast regulation as evidence of government's historically close involvement with journalism. Federal policies included the government assignment of radio frequencies under the Federal Radio Act of 1927 with its "public interest, convenience, or necessity" standard, the Federal Communications Act of 1934 and ultimately the now abandoned Fairness Doctrine. All included a commitment to local affairs reporting and the use of the public airwaves in the public interest.

Therefore, proponents argue, while journalism in this country has been essentially left in private hands since the nation's founding, government clearly has been involved in the development of the media and journalism. By citing each of

the above examples of government support over the last 200-plus years, proponents of public support reason that such action will not be a radical departure from tradition that will compromise journalism. Instead, they cite examples from Europe and even from the limited American experience with public broadcasting to suggest that government funding will enhance the quality and breadth of content by freeing the news media from the demands of commerce and the market.

The Case Against Government Support

In many respects, the ethical and policy arguments against government support for journalism begin with the same premise of those who back such subsidies: Journalism is important and must be protected, and the history of American journalism is a valuable guide for what ought to be done in the future. From that shared premise, the two sides of the debate diverge significantly. First, although the opponents rarely question the basic value of journalism, they typically do not consider journalism a classic public good. That is, while journalism is good for the public, opponents such as Michael Arrington, writing for the *TechCrunch* blog in a 2008 entry titled "If 'Real Journalism' Fails As a Business, Should Government Step In?" are not prepared to agree that journalism can only be accomplished through governmental support divorced from commerce. Second, opponents do not draw the same lessons from American history, which they see as underscoring the value of private innovation, investment and markets. Much of the case against government support essentially demands that the market and society, enabled by new technologies, be left free to experiment to deliver quality journalism.

The difference for opponents, as shown by Kevin Klose in his 2010 *American Journalism Review* column, "A Federal Bailout for Papers?" boils down to the concern that once government wades into the world of journalism with some form of subsidy, government inevitably obtains some degree of influence — real as well as perceived — over the content. For the opponents, *private* enterprise, property and ownership of the presses, broadcast facilities or other means of reporting will best protect independent journalism. The opponents tend to be less troubled by the ethical dilemmas posed by commercial support — for example, potential influence exercised by for-profit advertisers or by the demands of private investors — than by those posed by government support. Alternatively, they rely on the diversity of the sources of commercial support and private investment to ameliorate and counter-balance the risks of such influence and, therefore, the ethical dilemmas. In other words, they rely on competition in the marketplace among private actors and a multiplicity of commercial supporters and investors to reduce the risk of government influence and provide for a robust press.

In terms of serving the audience, opponents such as Howard Gleckman, writing for the *TaxVox* blog in a 2009 entry titled "Government Subsidies for Newspapers: Say It Ain't So," argue that government support as opposed to market support, including both advertising and subscriptions, can skew reporting away from what people demand and want toward what the government-paid reporter or enterprise wants. Insulating journalists from market forces would allow them to report on only what they care about themselves (personal-interest journalism) or that which only a government bureaucracy, politician or funding source cares about (propaganda). The journalist will not have an adequate incentive to respond to the market or everyday citizens. Jeff Jarvis of the City University of New York argued in his blog, *BuzzMachine*, in a 2009 entry titled "Giving up on the news business," that the government approach gives up on new, privately funded business models too soon. The government approach runs the risk that new models will never develop, Jarvis wrote, "if we declare surrender and defeat in the hope that the market can support the news a community needs."

More specifically, opponents of government support cite as evidence of inevitable conflicts past problems with government-subsidized expressive activities. As Seth Lipsky said in his 2009 article "All the News That's Fit to Subsidize" in the *Wall Street Journal*, he took "no comfort from the analogy [the proponents] draw with government funding for the arts." For example, one noted controversy arose in 1999 between the Brooklyn Museum of Art and then New York City Mayor Rudolph Giuliani when the mayor attempted to cut off funding for the museum after an art exhibit offended Catholics and others by including a painting of the Virgin Mary in elephant dung. A federal judge ruled against the mayor's efforts on First Amendment grounds before the two sides declared an uneasy settlement of their differences.

For the opponents of government support, the Brooklyn Museum and similar disputes involving the challenged grants of the National Endowment for the Arts and other agencies raise the specter of endless conflict over the process for deciding funding winners and losers. Inevitably, a news story will offend political leaders or their taxpaying constituents. Even if subsidies were structured to be content-neutral, opponents see increased opportunities for vague, and therefore subjective, standards, resulting in favoritism, fraud or, at a minimum, litigation and increased public polarization over the results. The process will be politicized.

Dan Gillmor, author of the influential *Mediactive* blog, argued in the 2009 entry titled "Solutions for Journalism, or Re-Creating a Priesthood" that the subjective nature of any process for evaluating a request for a subsidy or grant endangers the heart of free expression. Furthermore, any time the government has the authority to fund or favor some speakers and not to fund or favor others, we run the risk it will use its position to favor or disfavor some speech, argues Steve Buttry of *The Buttry Diary* blog in a 2010 entry titled "Arguments for government subsidies for journalism: weak and inconsistent." The same arguments arise when discussing state and federal attempts to define who is or who is not a journalist for the purposes of applying shield laws, which protect news gatherers from subpoenas compelling disclosure of confidential sources. Once a law defines the protected class as, say, those who are employed by a recognized media entity, the question of free-lancers, bloggers and alternative journalists immediately arises. Yet, if the law does not draw some distinctions, the courts run the risk of applying such protections willy-nilly and diluting their force. Similar problems arise in the award of government subsidies or grants for artists, poets, journalists and other speakers. Lines must be drawn and judgments made, but by whom, how and with what assurances that government will not abuse its power as it doles out the funds?

Opponents of government support do not limit their arguments to problems inherent in the disbursement or award processes. There is also the cold, hard cost of the subsidies. What are our priorities, and are subsidies to media outlets fair? First, as levels of government are looking to reduce or maintain budgets, avoid tax increases or invest in other public needs, the opponents question whether supporting the news media is a good use of limited resources. Of course, even proponents disagree among themselves over whether any government support should go to private, for-profit media as well as nonprofit media. This concern applies both to direct subsidization and indirect subsidies through tax breaks that result in a diminution of government revenue. While few seriously suggest new or special taxes on journalism, the fundamental argument remains that journalism, as a business, ought to pay the same taxes generally applicable to other for-profit enterprises. Many grand proposals for government support fail to explain how government will pay for those new costs, and those that do nevertheless fail to consider the negative consequences of their new taxes or fees.

One argument against certain proposed subsidies suggests that in the name of trying to treat the disease afflicting contemporary journalism, we may inadvertently hasten the death of the patient. If government subsidies, either in the form of more funding for existing public broadcasters or other grants to media entities, are paid out of new or increased taxes on commercial advertising, use of the Internet or even use of the airwaves, government may further erode the financial viability of the enterprises it is trying to help. At a minimum, further discrimination against one form of communication in favor of another could tip the scales through government power. Battle lines are already being drawn over proposed new taxes affecting the Internet and online commerce.

A related argument is that the rush toward government support may hamper private or market ingenuity that could lead to new, successful business models as technology and demand develop. Martin Langeveld expressed this concern in his 2009 article "First Read: Report Ignores Web's Nimble Nature" in the *Columbia Journalism Review*. Just as the press moved from its ties to local officials during the colonial era to the support of political parties to the commercial basis on which it operates today, this argument rests on the inevitability of change and the risk that government intervention will stifle progress — both technological and financial. Langeveld's argument highlights the risk of propping up old media that may lack public or market support. Opponents point toward the many experiments newspapers and other media companies are attempting — everything from transaction-based commerce from news sites to revenue streams from events to community-focused websites for the collection and dissemination of local reporting. Opponents also fear the power of government will retard the activities and exploration taking place at many universities, think tanks, foundations and press organizations.

The role of the private market is essentially the heart of the argument against government support of journalism. Opponents fear not only the government power over speech, but government interference with the natural evolution of technology and business models. This concern is in part predicated upon a reading of American history that emphasizes private investments, initiative. innovation and markets as the engines of growth and true independence. The fact that proponents cite a long history of government involvement with the development of the communications media is not seen as persuasive. In fact, opponents often read that history quite differently. For example, while the government in the 1840s invested in the experimental telegraph line of Samuel Morse, opponents of increased government support argue that the telegraph took off only after Morse failed to convince Congress to own and control the patents and thus control or license new lines. The market was left wide-open not only to some abuses and duplicative lines, but also for private investment and growth that far outstripped European countries for decades to come.

No one disputes that American governments have historically provided postal subsidies and bought advertising and printing services from individuals and businesses that became the backbone of American journalism. But opponents of public funding of journalism interpret these events through a different prism than do proponents. First, the purposes behind the postal discounts were varied and did not merely serve to build a strong press. Rather, those discounts also helped the postal system develop as a viable entity and helped knit the new nation together by providing a more reliable means of distributing information.

Second, opponents point out the difference between subsidies and payments by government for services rendered (i.e., advertising or printing). The latter represent nothing more than government buying what it needs from the best purveyor just as government goes into the private marketplace to buy construction materials, armaments and other goods and services. Further, legal notices published in newspapers when newspapers were the best means of communicating with the public made good sense as a matter of public policy. Today when the Internet is arguably a more efficient and cost effective means of communication, they contend, the balance of interests must shift.

The history of government involvement with journalism is not, therefore, one that leads toward acceptance of direct subsidies, opponents say. Lesser or indirect, content-neutral forms of support for innovation — ranging from changes in copyright law to tax-code adjustments — to make nonprofit news organizations more flexible draw less opposition for several reasons. The role of government is not as direct, government has less of an opportunity to reward or punish journalists, and government will not stifle market-based innovations. To drive home the risks of direct government support, opponents also cite examples from other countries, pointing particularly to those that show a correlation between government funding and less coverage of government corruption. Joshua Benton's 2009 *Neiman Journalism Lab* study based on Argentina, titled "How government money can corrupt the press: The Story from Argentina," provides an example.

Finally, the 2010 controversy regarding National Public Radio's termination of Juan Williams illustrated many of the reasons behind the opposition to government funding. Williams told Fox News how he had a flash of fear when he saw people dressed in Muslim religious attire on an airplane. NPR's management said Williams had crossed a line, which called into question his credibility on NPR. Heated political controversies about public broadcasting during election years are not new. The Williams tempest was no different. NPR's decision to dismiss him became fodder for cable news and talk radio. Fox News commentators, as well as other journalists, pundits and politicians, responded that NPR was displaying its own politically correct version of intolerance by firing Williams.

Amid the brief storm, opponents, such as Seth Lipsky in his 2010 article "The Real Case for Defunding NPR" in the *Wall Street Journal*, called for Congress to cut funding to public broadcasting, but their reasons were not uniform. Some, as has happened repeatedly in the past, argued that NPR and its television equivalents were inherently biased and liberal. Others argued, however, that whether one agreed or disagreed with the Williams termination and whether one considered the journalism of the public broadcasters excellent or poor, biased or neutral, NPR and the other public broadcasters would never be truly independent until they abandoned all government support — the heart of the ethical argument against government subsidies of any kind. For Jack Shafer writing "Kill NPR to Save It" for *Slate.com* in 2010, NPR has become a classic "political pawn" and will never be independent of government meddling until it is independent, through either commercial privatization or an endowment.

The Williams' dispute and past similar controversies over public broadcasting, whether over the content of children's programming such as *Sesame Street* or at times controversial documentaries such as those on *Frontline*, demonstrate the volatility of government support, opponents say. For those who disagree with the content or perceived bias of the publicly supported journalists, the problem is that tax dollars are being used to support ideas they detest. For those who care more about a robust debate and check on government authority, government-supported journalism is always open to a political attack just as soon as it gets good, that is, really controversial. For them, the only solution is a press standing completely apart from government financing, never beholden to any congressional appropriations bill. The opponents would rather cast their lot with the market and not with the political process or any congressional wrangling.

Assessment

The financial crisis facing contemporary journalism is undeniable. The industry was once supported by profits from commercial advertisers, supplemented by government, nonprofit and political advertising as well as subscription revenues or single issue sales. While that support is still there, it is eroding, and newsrooms throughout the country have experienced drastic cuts in staffing as well as the space, time and other resources necessary for full reporting of the news. Commentary as a form of journalism is still plentiful on cable television, radio and the Internet. However, everyday reporting — from national investigative pieces to local coverage that keeps everyone from the school board to the police honest — has suffered. Citizen journalism, Internet-enabled local exchanges of information and new technologies such as mobile computing and consumer-purchased applications may help in the future, but for now society may see a dearth of quality reporting while consumer demands, business models and new technologies sort themselves out.

The historical evidence marshaled by the proponents of increased government support is impressive. The hand of government policy has been repeatedly used in ways that helped the development and success of American news media from newspapers and magazines to broadcasting and the Internet. Whether in the form of postal subsidies, a favorable regulatory and legal structure or direct purchases of advertising, government action has historically supported the news media that today we value so dearly for their independence from that same government. Further, the proponents have made a strong case that public broadcasting in the United States has been both excellent and independent of government, though underfunded. Clearly, innovative funding mechanisms can be found and administered without turning the news media into government puppets.

The proponents' case is not just about insulating government-funded news media from government manipulation, however. The case in part focuses on the asserted weaknesses of the current commercially based news media. Those media are subject to the financial vicissitudes of the market, but they also are left open to influence by large advertisers and the need to sell advertising and subscriptions. As businesses, they may not have the incentive to cover social or economic issues as deeply as they might if they were funded by other means. This argument shifts the ethical question from merely one of avoiding government influence to one of enhancing the quality of journalism by addressing some of the flaws, ethical and otherwise, in the commercial media model.

The opponents' contrary interpretation of the history also is sound. The proponents at times reach a bit broadly in building the case for historical government support. Yes, the creation of roads, canals and the postal service, to name a few public projects, served the interests of the growing press, but so too did many other fortuitous coincidences in terms of public policy. Further, the opponents correctly distinguish government paying for a service rendered (e.g., advertising or printing) from direct subsidies.

The opponents' oft-stated fear of propaganda and government manipulation is well taken, but perhaps overstated. First, proponents are sensitive to the issue. Even the most far-reaching proposals call for the creation of different processes to avoid such manipulation. Second, no one has suggested that a government-funded media would replace the existing commercial media. In fact, the most salient analyses of the issues extol the virtues of mixed systems with their inherent checks and balances. The opponents have not entirely misstated this issue, however. Recent events involving public broadcasting once again show that anything controversial can become a political lightning rod. The manipulation can take either a direct form or the more indirect, chilled-speech form.

The different sides of the debate perhaps share more common ground than they realize. Both agree a problem exists. Neither claims to have the final answer. Each side raises potential problems with the approach advocated by the other and thus outlines the considerations that governments and citizens must take into account. Anything that might be tried must at a minimum be cost-effective, content-neutral, self-executing and subtle. The likelihood may be slim that contemporary American society could summon the political will or cohesion to fashion anything as grandiose as a bailout of newspapers, a tax credit for subscribing to a newspaper or better funding for public broadcasting. Lesser forms of indirect assistance might garner more popular support and also run fewer risks in terms of government power or political polarization.

The ethical argument against more elaborate forms of government support does not necessarily mean that existing forms of public broadcasting support or the remaining, though often diminished, postal discounts or government printing and advertising contracts ought to be abandoned or further reduced. Great strength may be gained from a mixed media system in which some historically accepted means of supporting journalism, even if indirect, continue and even grow as a counterweight to the problems as well as the inherent conflicts of interest that afflict even an independent, commercially based media system. There is nothing wrong with competition, even if at times that competition comes from those supported in part by government. Competitive, truly independent reporting or journalism is threatened only when *either* commercial and business imperatives or the politics of public policy and government so dominate the media landscape that news reporting and diversity of thought wither and die or limp along while ceasing to inform.

Points of View

Books

Bollinger, Lee C. *Images of a Free Press.* Chicago: University of Chicago Press, 1991. This concise analysis of the competing interests affecting print and broadcast media in the United States provides valuable insights into the advantages of mixed or diverse approaches to media regulation, including a role for government in the broadcast media.

Bollinger, Lee C. *Uninhibited, Robust and Wide-Open: A Free Press for a New Century.* New York: Oxford University Press (USA), 2010. This book surveys the history and legal context of not only the print media, but also television and the Internet in a global context and examines the differences between government regulation and market regulation.

McChesney, Robert W., and John Nichols. *The Death and Life of American Journalism: The Media Revolution that Will Begin the World Again.* New York: Nation Books, 2010. This provocative analysis of the problems facing modern news media offers interesting as well as controversial approaches and solutions, including an argument for greater government support of journalism.

Schudson, Michael. *Why Democracies Need an Unlovable Press.* Malden, Mass.: Polity Press, 2008. This book examines the values served by an independent, often controversial, free press in a democracy.

Starr, Paul. *The Creation of the Media — Political Origins of Modern Communications.* New

York: Basic Books, 2004. This history of the communications industries emphasizes the role of government and public policy choices in the development of American media.

Articles and Other Documents

Anas, Anas Aremeyaw. "State-Funded Journalism – In The Interest Of The State?" February 28, 2011. Writing from the perspective of a Ghanan journalist, the author shares many of the same concerns as American opponents of government funding. He concludes, "Clearly, the idea that government should support the media is one that is difficult to accept. The aversion to state funding or support is rooted in concerns that the state might encroach on press freedom." Available at http://www.ghanaweb.com/GhanaHomePage/features/artikel.php?ID=203960.

Anderson, Kevin. "Government support for journalism is no panacea." *Corante*. May 6, 2009. Proponents of government funding in the United States should learn lessons for the experiences of the BBC. Available at http://strange.corante.com/2009/05/06/government-support-for-journalism-is-no-panacea.

Bollinger, Lee C. "Journalism Needs Government Help." *Wall Street Journal*, July 14, 2010. Bollinger, the president of Columbia University, outlines the case for a government role and a mixed or hybrid system of private enterprise and public support. Available at http://online.wsj.com/article/SB10001424052748704629804575324782605510168.html.

Buttry, Steve. "Five reasons government shouldn't subsidize journalism." *The Buttry Diary* (blog). October 30, 2009. Buttry responds to the arguments of government-funding proponents McChesney, Nichols, Schudson and Downey. Available at http://stevebuttry.wordpress.com/2009/10/30/five-reasons-government-shouldnt-subsidize-journalism/

Corporation for Public Broadcasting Appropriation Request and Justification FY 2011 and FY 2013 (February 2010), available at http://www.cpb.org/aboutcpb/ financials/appropriation/justification_11-13.pdf. This document provides some of the basic facts relevant to the funding debate related to public broadcasting in the United States.

Cowan, Geoffrey and David Westphal. "Public Policy and Funding the News," University of Southern California School for Communication and Journalism, January 2010. Available at www.fundingthenews.org. The research published by USC sets forth the history of the problems facing journalism and outlines a framework for action, including greater government support.

Downie, Leonard, and Michael Schudson. "The Reconstruction of American Journalism," *Columbia Journalism Review*, October 19, 2009. This examination of the crises facing journalism offers several suggestions for government action, ranging from the indirect to the direct. Available at http://www.cjr.org/reconstruction/the_reconstruction_of_american.php.

Jackson, Pamela T. "News as a Contested Commodity: A Clash of Capitalist and Journalistic Imperatives." *Journal of Mass Media Ethics* 24 (2009): 146-63. This article examines the conflict between capitalist and journalistic values and applies commodification theory to the sustainability of a free press.

Lipsky, Seth. "All the News That's Fit to Subsidize," *Wall Street Journal*, October 21, 2009. This commentary critiques the arguments for government support of journalism. Available at http://online.wsj.com/article/SB10001424052748704 59770457448624241703 9358.html.

Martin, Hugh J., and Lawrence Souder. "Interdependence in Media Economics: Ethical Implications of the Economic Characteristics of News." *Journal of Mass Media Ethics* 24 (2009): 127-45. An analysis of the inherent conflicts between independence as an ideal and the need to pay for the costs of producing journalism, this article sets forth ways of ethically balancing those competing realities while serving journalists, audiences and advertisers.

Nichols, John, and Robert W. McChesney. "How to Save Journalism — The Patriotic Case for Government Action." *The Nation*, January 25, 2010, 11-16. This article sets out the essence of the case in favor of government intervention and support for journalism.

Nichols, John, and Robert W. McChesney. "The Death and Life of Great American Newspapers." *The Nation*, March 18, 2009. This article sets forth the problems facing newspapers and possible solutions based largely on government support. Available at http://www .thenation.com/article/death-and-life-great-american-newspapers.

Shafer, Jack. "Kill NPR to Save It." *Slate.com*, October 25, 2010. NPR should abandon government support in order to be truly independent. Available at http://www.slate.com/ tool bar.aspx?action=print&id=2272284.

Stverak, Jason. "Government has no place in journalism." Franklin Center for Government and Public Integrity. Available at http://www.franklincenterhq.org/2303/government-has-no-place-in-journalism/ "[T] the government has no place in the journalism industry and that includes funding any type of media organizations."

Thompson, Derek. "The case for government-funded journalism." *Washington Post*, February 4, 2011. There is no evidence that government funding of journalism is more dangerous than corporate funding.

vanden Heuvel, Katrina. "New models will allow investigative journalism to thrive." *Washington Post*, May 8, 2012. "[T]o combat the corporatization and gutting of media," the United States needs to develop public funding sources.

8

Terrorism and the Media

While some countries have lived with terrorism during their entire existence, Americans were newly awakened to its reality on September 11, 2001, when Islamic terrorists crashed two airplanes into the World Trade Center towers in New York City. The cost in human life was staggering. The economic impact has continued to reverberate in New York and nationwide. America's popular self-perception of immunity from international terrorism was lost forever.

In considering terrorism, the role of the media is an important part of the discussion. The study of terrorism and its relationship to modern mass media is complex. Consider terrorism. Terrorists and their organizations have a pattern of emerging, splintering, and then disappearing, only to reappear again in another part of the world. That fluidity makes it difficult to establish a record of more than seemingly similar but unrelated events and atrocities. Terrorists make the world's most-wanted lists but then vanish as they are killed in skirmishes or disappear into deserts, jungles, and cities. Terrorist organizations change their names, and leaders are shuffled as they are promoted or demoted. The terrorists' activities often seem to be spontaneous and unrelated, some characterized as small and others as shockingly catastrophic. And since there is no traditional military "front," these events are often forgotten or overlooked until the next streetside bomb explodes, the next jetliner is hijacked, or the next public figure is assassinated.

Finding our way through this labyrinth of political and military infrastructure and activity is daunting — until the mass media step in to help make sense of the story. And it is here, in the *media coverage* of terrorism — within the unique craft of explaining the day's events and their meaning to the public — that terrorists' agenda, strategies, and stories get told.

What is problematic about the media role, according to government officials who are trying to prevent further terrorist acts, is that it threatens to achieve

by J. Douglas Tarpley
Biola University

precisely the opposite result. Media coverage gives terrorists a voice to accompany their acts. While the news media insist they are performing their role dutifully, law enforcement and government officials argue that they threaten security and lower the prospects of peace.

Although modern terrorism has been confronted in the Middle East for centuries, and in Europe for at least 100 years, a satisfactory definition of terrorism is surprisingly illusive.

Hundreds of definitions exist. Harvey Kushner explained in a seminal work, *Terrorism In America: A Structured Approach to Understanding Terrorist Threat,* "The term terrorism means different things to different people.... Whereas some blame it on politics, others attribute the difficulty of defining the term to the popular aphorism, 'One man's terrorist is another man's freedom fighter.'" Thus some people might label George Washington, Yasir Arafat, and Osama bin Laden freedom fighters and revolutionaries while others might label them terrorists. As "It should be apparent to all who pursue the literature on terrorism," Kushner added, "that the number of approaches to dealing with the concept of terrorism is limited only by those interested in its study." One encyclopedia on terrorism lists nearly 100 definitions, some rooted in ideology, others in objectives and goals, and still others in tactics and types of terrorist behavior. John Richard Thackrah, an expert on the topic, sums up the apparent difficulty by declaring that the concepts of terror and terrorism are "slippery and much-abused" and that their relation to other forms of political violence and to criminality is often "ambiguous."

For this chapter, terrorism is conceptualized to be the use — or attempted use — of violence by individuals or groups against governments or civilian populations in order to create fear to bring about political or social change. Terrorism manifests itself in acts such as assassinations targeted at public officials or violence against ordinary people at bus stops or in restaurants or in business centers such as the World Trade Center. Generally these activities are designed for political and not military purposes by groups without the military prowess to mount open assaults.

Since one of the driving motivations for terrorist activity is to gain the attention of a large audience in an attempt to influence public opinion and, ultimately, official public policy, the mass media are conceived to be important players in the publicity of the event.

Origins of the Issue

The use of terror has been around at least since Biblical days, but international terrorism is a relatively new phenomenon. Since the 1960s, terrorists have

become better skilled at manipulating the media. With the growth of relatively inexpensive video equipment, they are often able to furnish news organizations with prepared ready-for-television footage. Anita Peresin, in a 2007 article titled "Mass Media and Terrorism" in the Croation journal *Media Research*, observed that "modern technologies have made it possible for small terror groups to use the mass media as a powerful gun." She observed, though, that critics vary in their estimates of just how big and powerful that gun is.

Observers generally agree that there is a "symbiotic relationship" between terrorism and the mass media. Permeating the literature about domestic and international terrorism is the charge that the press — and television journalism, in particular — plays into the hands of terrorists often with live coverage of terrorist activities by providing them with a platform for their "cause." Thackrah, in his 2009 book *The Routledge Companion to Military Conflict Since 1945*, captured the tension of the relationship when he said, "A free people needs a free press; but terrorism needs a propaganda platform. So in all Western countries, the news media faces a dilemma; is it possible to keep citizens informed of daily events, including the often graphic tragedy of terrorism, without becoming, to some degree, propagandists for the perpetrators?" Ultimately terrorists hope that, by striking fear into the hearts of citizens and resultant pressure on public officials to provide for the public safety, terrorists can achieve their goals. Peresin said in her "Mass Media and Terrorism" essay that terrorist organizations are "constantly trying to manipulate and exploit free media for their own purpose. We might say that it is the mass media itself that provide global reach for terrorism."

ABC anchor Ted Koppel possibly said it best in an interview with *Harper's* magazine in the 1980s. "Let me put forward the proposition that the media, particularly television, and terrorists need one another, that they have what is fundamentally a symbiotic relationship," he declared. "Without television, terrorism becomes rather like the philosopher's hypothetical tree falling in the forest: no one hears it fall, and therefore it has no reason for being. And television without terrorism, while not deprived of all interesting things in the world, is nonetheless deprived of one of the most interesting."

The media provide other benefits to terrorists, as L. John Martin and Joseph Draznin say in their 1991 book *The Camera's Eye; News Coverage of Terrorist Events.* They note that publicized terrorism helps secure funds from potential donors who see terrorist groups as successful, helps recruit new members who "really" want to make a difference in the world, reinforces the commitment of existing members, facilitates the freeing of incarcerated terrorist members, and provides a sense of importance to a group and especially to its leaders.

So, the logic goes, the media "feed" on the drama and tension created by terrorist activities because media professionals realize that dramatic terrorist events have the potential to generate audiences for newscasts. Since terrorists need the media, they "play to it" with well-scripted events timed to make the evening news programs. Hence, critics conclude, a symbiotic relationship based on mutual need is created between terrorists and journalists, perpetuating what many people fear may be a never-ending cycle.

The news cycle changed in the last several years with the advent of "new media." Although the term does not exclude the continued use of such traditional media as newspapers, magazines, film, still images, and books, the label is used to identify new and socially expanding technologies such as the interactive power of computer and communications technology, computer-enabled consumer devices, and, perhaps most importantly, the Internet.

These new technologies boast several distinctive qualities. New media, according to the entry on the subject on Wikipedia, "hold out a possibility of on-demand access to content any time, anywhere, on any digital device, as well as interactive user feedback, creative participation and community formation around the media content." As the Egyptian political revolution in 2011 that forced Hosni Mubarak out of office illustrates, new media may have a very real political effect with the creation, publication, distribution, and consumption of content for various purposes.

Terrorism uses media in any one of three ways. The first is the most traditional, occurring when terrorists merely make an attack and expect the traditional media to report on it. They try to influence the coverage with attention to matters such as location, time, and target; but they are "at the mercy" of the traditional news media to cover such an event. With a second approach, terrorists carry their messages directly to the media outlets with a decision about what to say or how to frame the narrative. Ultimate authority, of course, still rests with the media gatekeepers, who may or may not use or edit terrorist material. The third approach occurs today in great part because of the advent of new media. Terrorists may fully control the media outlet. They start their own traditional media outlets of newspapers or satellite television — or, especially important, they begin disseminating their message via the Internet, and they reach all of the social media outlets available relatively easily to disseminate their message.

Daniel Kimmage, an expert on Islamic terrorists' use of new technology, noted in a 2008 essay in the *New York Times*, that al-Qaeda "made its name in blood and pixels with deadly attacks and an avalanche of electronic news media." The Internet, he said, "can be and has been" used by terrorists in a variety of ways, including but not limited to cyber-terrorism, coordination of attack plans, publicity, propaganda, and communication between and among terrorist cells. Michael Moutot, l'Agence France-Presse' lead reporter on terrorism, concluded that "terrorists do not really need us anymore to convey their message. The 'official' media have been replaced by the Internet which, in the end, is much easier to use, much quicker and much more effective."

Lebanese Hezbollah's al-Manar television channel provides one of the best examples of terrorist "home-grown" TV. Broadcasting Hezbollah's point of view about social and cultural events and issues, it provides a propaganda platform to an audience unable to distinguish between its propaganda and fare from bona-fide news organizations. Although such operations are more expensive for terrorists than is the use of the Internet alone, terrorists successfully combine them for maximum impact.

New media present terrorists with an opportunity to *become* the media directly and bypass traditional journalists. Thus, the relationship between terrorists and the media has the potential to become one in which the media become an arm or extension of terrorist activity, a tool for propaganda. The *Transitional Terrorism, Security & The Rule of Law Project Report* declared in 2008 that for the Internet, the situation is clearly different from that of traditional media. Most authors for the *Report* agreed that terrorists use the Internet in order to achieve their own objectives just as they do while using traditional media. However, they said that "people are more likely to accept banning media that is directly related or even part of a terrorist organization."

Law enforcement and government officials — as well as a significant segment of the general population — wonder if the cycle can be broken by more responsible media behavior. What is the mass media's answer?

The Government Perspective

Coverage legitimizes terrorism. The communication researchers Paul Lazarsfeld and Robert Merton observed some years ago that, in a number of contexts and situations, mass media publicity "in and of itself confers status." Thus, some people fear that coverage of terrorists and their activities can bestow positive status on terrorists and their causes, a much-desired commodity for terrorists who must recruit "believers" and raise money.

Law enforcement and government officials fear that journalists contribute unwittingly to the propagandistic goals of terrorists. That is, reporting of terrorists' heinous acts can give terrorists the status of a Robin Hood or even of respectable politicians with a worthy cause, distracting attention from their crimes.

The charge against the media as an ally of terrorist propaganda does not imply that the media co-sponsor terrorism. Rather, the supposition is that the media may, inadvertently, become involved in disseminating propaganda as they report about terrorism. Regardless of intent, the fear is that the media become an arm of terrorist efforts to reach for and shape public perceptions and thereby legitimize terrorists as well as their ideas and causes.

This legitimization is indefensible, a few critics point out, when the media magnify terrorist exploits even if the activities or organization warrant little attention. Critics charge, for example, that terrorist groups numbering perhaps a dozen members have been described as armies and their official communiqués discussed on countless television shows and radio broadcasts as well as in numerous articles and editorials. In a few cases even non-existent groups have been given a great deal of publicity.

Critics offer several reasons for why media coverage presents a problem.

One is that coverage influences public perceptions. To the extent that media images of political terrorism affect the public's perception, the nature of the images is of paramount importance. The impact may range from the mere transfer of information (what scholars call the agenda setting function of media) or to attitude change. The Task Force on Disorders and Terrorism of the U.S. National Advisory Committee on Criminal justice Standards and Goals declared, "Depictions of incidents of extraordinary violence in the mass media are ... a significant influence on public fears and expectations."

Part of the critics' concern is that airing terrorists' claims can make them seem legitimate and socially acceptable. Some scholarly research concludes that there is often, in media coverage, an uncritical interchange of terms such as atrocity and act, event and attack, revolutionaries and terrorists, freedom fighters and guerrilla fighters. As Baljit Singh said in the 1977 book *Terrorism: Interdisciplinary Perspectives*, edited by Yonah Alexander and Seymour Maxwell Finger, word choice has tremendous potential to influence an audience's perceptions. Other scholarly studies suggest that news operations around the world reveal predictable tendencies to use either positive or negative "labeling."

Abraham Miller discussed the importance of the public's perception of terrorists and their activities in his 1982 book *Terrorism, the Media, and Law Enforcement: An Introduction and Overview*. He suggested that terrorists' motives when explained in the media can make the public begin to question its own assumptions of morality and the political system. The concern rests in the belief that the public's perceptions of the world influence public policy alternatives, a view inherent in terrorists' efforts to capture public attention. Public attitudes may, especially in a democracy, even undermine the political infrastructure as citizens consider the "merits" of alternative ideas and their systems. For terrorists, that is precisely a significant part of their goal.

The other major reason critics give for why the media present a problem is that they often — though not always — "get in the way" of law enforcement's efforts to do its jobs. The charge is that journalists may unintentionally obstruct

the attempts of law enforcement personnel to deal with terrorists who have taken hostages and are negotiating for their release, or that journalists may impede efforts to manage a terrorist situation by releasing information that retards official investigative or negotiating efforts. For example, some feared that Osama bin Laden's television addresses after the attack on the twin towers might signal "sleeper" al-Qaeda cells into action. Thus, most American TV journalists decided not to air videotaped addresses by bin Laden and his accomplices unless convinced that the messages contained no "hidden codes" designed to activate terrorist activity among followers around the world.

The Fourth Estate's Perspective

Despite the critics' concern, many journalists think the concern is exaggerated, and they oppose changing journalistic practices as a consequence of terrorism. They offer three main arguments: (1) informing the public is the purpose of news, (2) the news media must report on terrorism because it is newsworthy, and (3) concern about terrorism could erode civil liberties.

Informing the Public

The tradition in the American press is the belief that vigorous debate of competing ideas and perspectives in a "marketplace" of ideas strengthens a nation and ensures its vitality and health. Libertarian theory envisions a press committed to the nourishment of debate, believing that the truth ultimately will win because of its innate strength and power. Thus, traditionally the press has been devoted to protecting an intellectual, political, and social environment of unencumbered freedom. A corollary to this concept assumes the press should be in an adversarial relationship with the government. As the "eyes and ears" of the public, the Fourth Estate works on behalf of the public by reporting on government activities, players, and policies. "By definition," wrote British scholar Robin Clutterbuck in his book *The Media and Political Violence*, "those who wish to live in a free society must accept a free press and must develop the art of living with it." On the issue of terrorism, David Paletz and Alex Schmid, in *Terrorism and the Media*, declared, "The media have made every effort to discover and reveal the news. Dictatorships may do their best to conceal the news and distort the facts, but the essence of democracy is openness. In a democracy, the media have an obligation to keep the public informed."

Journalists generally see reporting about terrorists and their atrocities much as they see reporting on everything else. However, some do believe that a distinction should be made between reporting about terrorism and other events because of the concomitant dangers of terrorism to the well being of individuals and to the stability of societies. For example, Paletz and Schmid posited that if editors and news directors do not thoughtfully reflect on the issue, "They might then take an attitude of 'Terrorist news is like any others news' — it has to be reported, independent of the consequences." Nonetheless, most journalists argue that they must be free to report on events and issues, including terrorism, in a vibrant marketplace. Only then will citizens know about important events and significant issues to talk about and think through. Then social institutions such as law enforcement agents are activated as they become aware of those same events and issues.

It is in this context that tension is often created between the press and law enforcement agents when the police demand information about news sources and request journalists' research and notes. Journalists argue that they do their job of informing the public, and it is the job of law enforcement agents to investigate, arrest, and prosecute criminals once they are aware of problems. Journalists maintain that they are not an "arm" of the police and that the distinction should be protected.

Writing about journalists' "take" on terrorism reporting, Paletz and Schmid provided an insightful conclusion about the role of journalists: "If," they said, "for no other reason, the media have an obligation to fulfill their critical function because they not only keep people informed, they also serve as an obstacle to excesses of all kinds. Without truly free media, there can be no free democracy.... [The media must] decide for themselves what to present as news, and how they want to do it."

Newsworthiness

Journalists believe they have a contract with the public to provide information. Part of their "professional" craft involves defining the newsworthiness of events. Terrorism, they say, is newsworthy most of the time. Moreover, reporters, news directors, and editors as well as corporate media executives — not government — are the ones who have the authority to decide what is news.

The scholarly, professional, and journalism textbook literature consistently identifies several "news values" such as conflict, nearness to audience, uniqueness, and timeliness. Within the context of terrorism reporting, the literature emphasizes that three qualities govern journalists' selection of newsworthy events. These qualities include (1) the media's evaluation of the relative importance and significance of a specific event in contrast to other current events vying for coverage, (2) the specific event's "sensational" appeal — conflict and novelty, for example, and (3) the particular medium's policy toward covering such events. The question regarding coverage of terrorism becomes, of course, what responsibility for the public safety and continuity of a stable society do journalists have, if any? Is their job simply to report information and let the public decide what to do, if anything?

A survey of journalists reported by Paletz and Schmid identified the following "ethical principles that should be applicable with regard to the coverage of terrorism." The guidelines advised journalists (1) not to serve as spokesmen/accomplices of terrorists, (2) to avoid endangering lives of hostages, (3) not to portray terror as attractive, romantic, or heroic, (3) to focus on facts, (4) to avoid encouraging further terrorism, (5) to encourage the basics of good journalism as much as possible — accuracy, clarity, truthfulness, impartiality, editorial independence — and (6) to distinguish — as in all good journalism — between news and commentary. The study concluded that fewer than 20% of the journalists indicated that their professional "units" had a special policy for handling news on terrorism. In some cases the existing guidelines were verbal and informal, while in others they were formal and written. However, a majority of the respondents said that although their media had no written and formal guidelines, they had "a certain policy for handling news on terrorism." The basic principle was "not giving more publicity to the particular group than is necessary."

Terrorists, though, became skilled at taking advantage of journalism practices to increase the propaganda success of terrorism. Thus, journalists themselves had to confront the issue. As Thackrah said in *The Routledge Companion to Military Conflict Since 1945*, "The question of whether information is news or propaganda is very important. Even straightforward news stories about terrorism can involve agonizing decisions. Do they contribute to the free marketplace of ideas [by] helping people to understand the central issues of their day? Or do they give terrorists a megaphone through which to spread their message of fear to their ultimate target — the public at large?" The tension may be expressed another way: Should journalists be concerned with getting the scoop and informing the public or with providing for the public safety?

Civil Liberties

One of the fears of journalists is that perhaps, in efforts to defend against and prevent terrorism, legislators and police will erode citizens' civil liberties by expanding the powers of police and security agents. After the September 11, 2001, terrorism attack on the World Trade Center, Congress passed the PATRIOT Act, which gave authorities greater authority to do such things as eavesdrop on suspected terrorists. In an effort to gather information about al-Qaeda's infrastructure, operations, and plans, law enforcement and military personnel detained a number of people suspected of terrorism or of having ties with terrorists. Many journalists, media outlets, and professional organizations criticized the law as a great danger to Americans in general. Trade journals and professional associations continue to discuss what many media professionals and civil libertarians fear is an erosion of the civil liberties of private citizens and journalists.

Assessment

The news media are central at the intersection of terrorism, government, and the public. Thus, the issue of the media and terrorism raises many important questions. Which terrorist activities should be reported? How prominently are they to be displayed? How should they be framed conceptually? Whose views should dominate the reporting?

These questions are important because they influence the behavior of terrorists, the policies and behavior of government officials, and the perceptions of citizens. Moreover, the role to be played by the press may be relatively factual and benign as they become "mirrors" or mere chroniclers of terrorist actions, or they can become "projectors" and influence terrorists and citizens. The role to be played may be disruptive of official negotiation efforts or cooperative in those efforts. The media may endanger the lives of hostages or thwart the plans of terrorists. So, how are journalists to be responsible, covering terrorism without becoming pawns of terrorists? At the same time, how are they to protect the First Amendment freedoms and editorial independence that are critical to the vitality of America without becoming an "arm" of the government and law enforcement communities or a pawn of terrorists?

What do journalists themselves say needs to be remembered when covering terrorism? First, they generally consider the *traditional* professional earmarks of good journalism to apply to terrorism reporting — accuracy, truthfulness, timeliness, clarity, etc. Second, probably fewer than 25% of news operations possess some type of *distinctive*, formal, written guidelines for coverage of terrorism.

At the top of the list of traditional professional values that journalists hold to be important are these three: credibility, newsworthiness, and editorial independence.

Credibility. Credibility is one of the most valued commodities professional journalists possess, and it is no exception in the context of reporting about terrorism. One of the news media's greatest challenges is maintaining credibility with the public, and that is especially true in the context of terrorism reporting.

Newsworthiness. Journalists almost unanimously believe that terrorist activity is newsworthy. They also believe, though, that coverage should not sensationalize terrorism. Some editors and news directors take the position that terrorism news is like any other news and should be reported without any special consideration to restrain or sensationalize the narrative. Other editors and news directors have prepared guidelines about how to report terrorist activities. Whether exercising some restraint or a more free-wheeling approach to reporting about terrorism, journalists in the West understand that terrorists acts are unacceptable because they spill other people's blood, including the blood of innocents, to get their message out and to influence public policy and police behavior. In his chapter "Terrorism, Journalism, and Democracy" in Yohan Alexander and Richard Latter's book *Terrorism and the Media: Dilemmas for Government, Journalists and the Public,* Alan Protheroe explained that "the art of responsible news judgment on the part of an editor consists of finding a suitable balance among the public's need to know, its mere desire to know, the terrorists' wish to intimidate and/or to propagandize the public or sectors thereof, and, last but not least, the hostages' and other victims' right to survive."

Independent editorial voice. Journalists also are concerned about maintaining editorial independence from the government and law enforcement agents. It is the "contract" between journalist and citizen that journalists report with accuracy, integrity, truthfulness, and independence. Despite such concern, few news operations have complained about government or law enforcement pressure to compromise their independence. Paletz and Schmid observed that "public officials and the police forces want coverage (to the extent they want any coverage) that is minimally intrusive and non-inflammatory, and that lends no credibility to terrorists."

Along with concern about traditional news values, journalists deal with several pressures when reporting about terrorism. The most important ones are (1) sensitivity to the battle for minds and hearts, (2) independence of journalistic reporting practices, (3) understanding of the very real life-and-death "human dimension" of terrorism reporting, and (4) a balance of presentation within the context of terrorism news with other news.

Battle for minds and hearts. Many journalists realize that the central battles of the day-to-day politics in democracies are increasingly fought in and through the media. Terrorists understand this and attempt to create violent "real" situations in order to have a shock effect on the public at large. Journalists understand this, too, and try to distinguish between pseudo-events — or stunts — of terrorists and those of actual news value. Most journalism codes and guidelines do not, however, directly address the terrorist perception that the anticipation of reporting can have a causal effect on terrorist activities.

Real life stories to be taken seriously. Journalists need to be aware that terrorism stories are actually based on someone else's real-life experiences, and the matter of when and what to report might have life-and-death implications for somebody. The news scoop is important, but life is, too. Some critics of the news media's terrorism reporting suggest that journalists do not have to "scoop" other journalists to get out the story. The story can be told later when the event reaches a "natural" end. "The real issue, in many cases," say Peletz and Schmid, "is not one of self-censorship versus freedom of the press, but a question of timing, of telling the full story now or a little later.... A good story is not worth a life.... While freedom of the press is a precious good, citizens' lives should not be sacrificed to the scoop." Unfortunately, journalists have been known to be sensitive only to the scoop and careers.

Display and emphasis of coverage. Balancing the news stories of the day is often neglected when dramatic visual footage is available. The professional drive to get a "scoop" and the economic pressure to secure and hold an audience sometimes outweigh concerns about balancing. As some media guidelines suggest, journalists should try to avoid the temptation to sensationalize reports about terrorist activity and seek to keep the "grading" — display on a page and prominence in a newscast — in proper balance.

So, what do journalists need to do?

First, it is clear that a symbiotic relationship between terrorism and traditional mass media exists. Therefore, coverage of terrorism in news stories can be an incentive for terrorist action. One of the implications for journalists is that they need to consider thoughtfully and carefully when and how to report on terrorism. They need to make a clear assessment between "pseudo" and "real" events. They also need to discriminate between propaganda and actual news events and information.

Second, since a strategy of terrorists is to use violence to try to gain access to the media as a platform to speak to large audiences, it is incumbent upon media professionals to show the human suffering caused by terrorism. While informing the public about terrorists' heinous crimes, journalists also should help citizens understand that terrorists' ultimate goal is to de-stabilize society and replace existing political and social infrastructures with their own.

Third, using the traditional professional value system when identifying news, journalists find themselves "drawn" to terrorist acts — as heinous as they are — and reporting on them. One of the implications for journalists is the need to balance stability of a society and the value of human life with the professional goal of "scooping" the competition. That is to say that the value of a news story may diminish when the cost of its dissemination is the life — or lives — of human beings. A second implication is the need to identify and develop sensitivity to distinctive pressures experienced when reporting about terrorism such as an increased sensitivity to the battle for minds and hearts of citizens, independence of journalistic reporting practices to retain a credible voice apart from both terrorists as well as law enforcement personnel, understanding of the very real life-and-death "human dimension" of terrorism reporting, and balance of presentation within the context of terrorism news with other news. This increased sensi-

tivity does not make journalists social engineers. It makes them responsible reporters.

Fourth, a vibrant and independent press is necessary for a democracy to function. The media must be free to report about terrorism as it must be free to report about anything else so that citizens are informed and are enabled to make responsible decisions. Terrorists' exploitation of media will only work in the short-term until citizens "see through" the propaganda and realize the human suffering — and therefore, the moral vacuum as well as political iconoclasm of terrorism. Terrorists will be unsuccessful ultimately in a campaign to destroy civilized democratic societies because people will not allow it. In the long run, in our democratic system, citizens seek to discover the truth, to embrace moral and civilized values and behavior, to dispel the evils of uncivilized behavior, and to reinforce and strengthen our political system.

Points of View

Books

Altheide, David L. *Terror Post 9/11 and the Media*. New York: Peter Lang, 2009. "[T]he mass media, including news and popular culture, have cast terrorism, propaganda and social control post 9/11.... [F]ear works with terrorism to alter discourse, social meanings, and our sense of being in the world."

Barnett, Brooke, and Amy Reynolds. *Terrorism and the Press: An Uneasy Relationship*. New York: Peter Lang, 2009. This critical analysis of media coverage of terrorism examines the nexus of terrorism, media, political processes, and government. Both terrorists and government officials are becoming very sophisticated in dealing with the media.

Centre of Excellence. Defense Against Terrorism. *The Media: The Terrorists' Battlefield*. NATO Advanced Research Workshop on the Media, Vol. 17. Amsterdam, Netherlands; Washington, D.C.: IOS Press, 2007. "[I]n contemporary conflict ... strategic success cannot be achieved unless the government and its agencies can both maintain the consent of its population and discredit the goals of the terrorists they face. The media have a vital role to play ... : they must challenge the methods used by governments ... , and they must find a balance between reporting incidents of terrorism and serving the terrorists' interests."

Dass, Niranjan. *Media and Terrorism*. New Delhi: MD Publications, 2008. Fifteen essays by different authors analyze "the larger issues surrounding media's portrayal of terrorism ... particularly the tension between government and the press."

Ethiel, Nancy, ed. *Terrorism: Informing the Public*. Chicago: McCormick Tribune Foundation, 2002. Written in the aftermath of 9/11, this book represents a conference report of the effort to understand the relationship of media and terrorism. All "responsible" parties will have to work together to successfully cope with terrorism. There needs to be a balance between freedom of the press and the public's need for a secure and stable society.

Greenberg, Bradley S. *Communication and Terrorism: Public and Media Responses to 9/11.* Cresskill, N.J.: Hampton Press, 2002. This book "brings together research findings that encompass the full range of social communication issues relevant to Sept. 11." Chapters cover such topics as "the communication behaviors — mass and interpersonal — of varying segments of the public ... [and] content dimensions of the news coverage."

Hess, Stephen, and Marvin L Kalb, eds. *The Media and the War on Terrorism.* Washington, D.C.: Brookings Institution Press, 2003. This collection of essays by eyewitnesses and journalists "takes the reader up-close and personal and shows how difficult it is to know the degree to which such observations are typical or representative of what is going on the overall conflict in which they are embedded."

Hoskins, Andrew, Akil Awan, and Ben O'Loughlin. *Radicalisation and Media: Connectivity and Terrorism in the New Media Ecology.* New York: Routledge, 2011. "[E]merging threats to security and stability ... [are presented by] individuals and groups holding or espousing radical views about religion, ideology, often represented in the media as oppositional to Western values. This book asks what, if anything is new about these radicalising discourses, how and why they relate to political acts of violence and terror, and what the role of the mass media is in promoting or hindering them."

Izard, Ralph S., and Jay Perkins. *Lessons from Ground Zero: Media Response to Terror.* New Brunswick, N.J.: Transaction Publishers, 2011. "Many lessons were evident to journalists as they sought to cope with the challenges of covering 9/11. The long-term question, however, is whether the answers they found served as catalysts for better journalism in the future, or whether they have been forgotten, put into the closet of old memories with no noticeable long-term impact."

Martin, Andrew, and Patrice Petro, eds. *Rethinking Global Security: Media, Popular Culture, and the War on Terror.* Piscataway, N.j.: Rutgers University Press, 2009. "[O]ur notions of fear, insecurity, and danger are fostered by intermediary sources such as television, radio, film, satellite imaging, and the Internet.... [T]he proliferation of digital technologies ... has transformed our knowledge of near and distant events so that it has become impossible to separate the politics of war, suffering, terrorism, and security from the practices and processes of the media."

Miller, David, and Tom Mills. *The Politics of Terrorism Expertise: Knowledge, Power and the Media.* New York: Routledge, 2012. "[T]he knowledge produced and the expertise provided by the experts are a product of the social and political forces which have sponsored the emergence of the field, and ... in particular these experts are responsive to the strategic and ideological requirements of Western states, and the closely associated corporate interests represented by the private think-tanks and security companies which constitute ... the 'terrorism industry.'"

Nacos, Brigitte Lebens. *Mass-Mediated Terrorism: The Central Role of the Media in Terrorism and Counterterrorism*, 2nd ed. Lanham, Md.: Rowman & Littlefield, 2007. "Terrorists exploit global media networks and information highways to carry news of their violence along with propaganda of the deed."

Nacos, Brigitte Lebens, Yaeli Bloch-Elkon, and Robert Y. Shapiro. *Selling Fear: Counterterrorism, the Media, and Public Opinion*. Chicago: University of Chicago Press, 2011. After 9/11, "the Bush administration hyped fear, while obscuring civil liberties abuses and concrete issues of preparedness. The media, meanwhile, largely abdicated its watchdog role, choosing to amplify the administration's message while downplaying issues that might have called the administration's statements and strategies into question."

Norris, Pippa, Montague Kern, and Marion R. Just, eds. *Framing Terrorism: The News Media, the Government, and the Public*. New York: Routledge, 2003. "Headlines matter as much as the act, in political terms. Widely publicized terrorist incidents leave an imprint upon public opinion, muzzle the 'watchdog' role of journalists and promote a general one-of-us consensus supporting security forces."

Paletz, David, and Alex Schmid. *Terrorism and the Media: How Researchers, Terrorists, Government, Press, Public, Victims View and Use the Press*. London: Sage, 1992. Each chapter examines the media-terrorism relationship from a distinctive perspective — terrorist, government, media, victim, etc.

Schaffert, Richard W. *Media Coverage and Political Terrorists*. New York: Praeger, 1992. Citizens need to understand how terrorists exploit media and how to minimize that exploitation. The book covers such topics as the history of state sponsored terrorism, the causes of terrorism, terrorists' media tactics, and responsible media coverage of terrorism.

Schlesinger, Philip. *Media, State and Nation; Political Violence and Collective Identities*. London: Sage Publications, 1991. This book explores the concepts of violence, terrorism and the mass media, and terrorists' and officials' techniques to capture the media's attention.

Selb, Philip, and Dana M. Janbek. *Global Terrorism and New Media: The Post-Al Qaeda Generation*. New York: Routledge, 2010. "[T]errorism 1.0 is migrating to 2.0 where the interactive nature of new media is used to build virtual organization and community."

Singh, Anand Shanker, and Dhirendra Dwivedi. *Role of Media in War and Terrorism*. New Delhi, India: Sunrise Publications, 2011. "Technology has made the media an active and influential participant in armed conflict informing and influencing nation's public opinion. War begins in the minds of men and therefore the minds of men need to be influenced through the mass-media."

Van Der Veer, Peter. *Media, War, and Terrorism*. New York: Routledge 2006. After 9/11, "while the US, and to an extent European, media seems largely unified in their coverage and silence in public debate of the events surrounding the attacks on the World Trade Centre, there exists open, critical debate in other parts of the world."

Venkatraman, S., ed. *Media in a Terrorized World: Reflections in the Wake of 9/11*. Singapore: Eastern Universities Press, 2004. Six papers by various Asian authors examine the media's impact during times of terrorism. It "reviews whether they have fostered balance over bias, communication over confrontation, and insight over ignorance in addressing these critical issues."

9

The Media in Wartime

The United States was engaged in nine wars from 1898 (the Spanish-American War) to the second war in Iraq that began in March 2003. This list does not include the Spanish Civil War from 1936 to 1939, in which the United States was not a direct participant, and a war in 1999 during which American air power eventually halted Serbian aggression against residents of Kosovo. In all nine wars, the nation received its primary information from the news media: at first newspapers and magazines, later radio, television, cable television and finally the Internet. The public has used all these media to get up-to-date information on the ongoing war in Afghanistan and how the Iraq War was fought. Journalists, and perhaps Internet bloggers, were the most vital link in keeping the public informed about what was happening. Since the early 1900s, even Hollywood films have come into play.

But in each war, relations between the military and journalists were strained because of the fundamentally different ways in which soldiers and journalists perceive their duties to the public. Journalists believe that openness and transparency are necessary to provide people with the information they need to make critical decisions in a democratic society. This belief entails telling the public the truth about a war with little regard for whether the truth helps or hurts the war effort.

Military officials, conversely, believe their most important goal is to win the war. Sometimes they must keep secrets, manage the flow of information and block the media from printing or broadcasting any information that might harm the war effort. In his 1991 work *Newsmen & National Defense: Is Conflict Inevitable?* retired military officer Lloyd J. Matthews put it this way: "War attracts two varieties of men — the soldier who prosecutes it and the newsman who reports it. The soldier finds that operational security is an absolute condition for the successful prosecution of the war; the newsman finds that operational security interferes with what he regards as his absolute right to report that war." British

by Francis Ward
Syracuse University

writer Susan L. Carruthers said in her 2000 book, *The Media at War: Communication and Conflict in the Twentieth Century,* "Both journalists and soldiers take a certain professional pride in seeing themselves as locked in a mutually antagonistic relationship, each bound by irreconcilable working practices and codes of honour."

Phillip Knightley is a British journalist who wrote a critical history of wartime reporting, *The First Casualty: The War Correspondent as Hero and Myth-Maker from the Crimea to Iraq*. He addressed the media-military relationship in his preface. "The military wants to win the war as quickly as possible and preferably," he wrote, "because the face of battle is horrific, away from the public eye. The media wants [sic] to observe the military in action, bear witness and record the first draft of history. If doing that as objectively and as truthfully as possible means writing and broadcasting stories damaging to their nation's war effort, what are correspondents to do? Does the correspondent within the journalist prevail? Or the patriot? And what if reporting patriotically involves telling lies? Is that journalism or propaganda?"

One of the most important decisions the public has to make is whether to support any decision for the nation to go to war and continue that support as the war progresses. During the decision-making process, journalists feel obligated not to take sides.

The tense military-media relationship has raised many questions about how news media have reported past wars and continue to report them: Does wartime reporting require censorship? If so, how strict should it be? When is it necessary not to tell the public the whole truth about war? Should the press maintain its traditional role as independent watchdog of government, or should news media become "team players" to mobilize public support for the war? How do journalists satisfy the public's right and need to know information while simultaneously protecting military secrets from the enemy? And what, precisely, *is* a military secret? Journalists and military officials invariably take different sides on these and other issues.

Origins of the Issue

Any discussion about relations between the media and military inevitably leads to what has become a seemingly endless debate about how the press reported the Vietnam War from about 1963 until the fall of Saigon in 1975. Journalists argue that their reporting was truthful and very much in the public's interest. Military officers and enlisted personnel argue that the reporting (including coverage of the anti-war protests on the home front) helped to mobilize public opposition to the war, which undermined the military's efforts to win the war. Bernard

Trainor, a retired military officer and respected journalist, wrote a chapter in the book 1991 *Newsmen & National Defense*. His chapter, "The Media and the Military: A Troubled Embrace," said, "Although most officers no longer say the media stabbed them in the back in Vietnam, the military still smarts over the nation's humiliation in Indochina and still blames TV and print media for loss of public support for the war. Today the hostility manifests itself in complaints that the press will not keep a secret and that it endangers lives by revealing details of sensitive operations. The myth of the media as unpatriotic, left-wing, anti-military establishment is thus perpetuated."

William V. Kennedy, a longtime military officer and journalist, wrote in 1993 in his book, *The Military and the Media: Why the Press Cannot Be Trusted to Cover a War*, "... All of the public opinion evidence subsequently gathered by Burns W. Roper and other analysts indicates that television had no impact whatsoever on the public at large, although it did have enormous impact on Washington decision makers ... who *assumed* that the public was as dismayed as they were by the sensationalistic television reporting."

Since the end of the Vietnam War, the military-media relationship has been framed by three major issues: the ability of journalists to cover a war from actual battle sites, the use of a "pool system" for wartime news coverage and the experiment in embedded journalism that began in 2003 in the Iraq War and still exists today.

Access to Battle Sites

At the heart of the debate over media coverage of the Vietnam War was the military's decision not to impose official censorship of news media coverage. This decision was a major departure from the strict government censorship in World War I and less strict censorship in World War II and the Korean conflict from 1950 to 1953. Military and government officials decided to set forth only voluntary guidelines for journalists to follow in Vietnam, not a mandatory censorship regime.

In 1991, a journalism think tank, the Gannett Foundation Media Center (now named The Freedom Forum) at Columbia University in New York City, concluded a study of how censorship has worked in conflicts since the Spanish-American War. The study, "The Media at War: The Press and the Persian Gulf Conflict," said that government and military planners decided not to impose mandatory censorship during Vietnam because they were convinced it would not work. These same officials also feared that censorship would anger journalists at the very time the government needed the support of the press to help cultivate public support for the war. "Even if that consideration had not existed, however, military officials doubted that a strict censorship policy could have been enforced effectively. The military in Vietnam did not control the movement of civilians into and out of the war zones; non-military aircraft arrived and departed daily at Saigon's airport. In addition, journalists could easily rent small private planes and fly into the interior," said the study.

The absence of control over journalists' access to battle sites in Vietnam had unintended consequences for the military. Television reports from the front began to show horrible scenes of death and destruction. A memorable photograph showed a South Vietnamese officer executing a member of the Vietcong (Communist fighters from South Vietnam). It inflamed domestic public opinion because it repeatedly aired on television worldwide. Imagine how wide the circulation would have been had there been YouTube and Facebook in the 1960s.

Especially after the Tet Offensive of 1968, American public opinion began to shift dramatically against the war. The massive anti-war protests of the late 1960s and early '70s contributed to the shift. What probably sealed the fate of the war in the public's mind was the killing of four students during an anti-war protest at Kent State University in Ohio in 1970.

The bitter Vietnam experience heavily influenced military decisions on whether to allow media access to battle sites for years to come. Journalists were kept away from combat areas during the U.S. military overthrow in 1983 of a pro-Communist government in the Caribbean island nation of Grenada. The press similarly was excluded from most battle zones when the United States invaded Panama in 1989 and overthrew the government of Gen. Manuel Noriega, who at one time had been an American ally. The administration of George H.W. Bush argued that he had become a danger to American interests in Central America because he aided international drug smugglers by allowing them to transport drugs into the United States from Panama. After his capture, Noriega was brought to the United States, tried and convicted of drug smuggling, money laundering and related crimes.

Determined not to repeat what military planners firmly believed was the mistaken Vietnam experience, the U.S. government and military established a policy of press pools for coverage of the buildup to the Persian Gulf War and the fighting itself in 1991. In the pool system, selected reporters and photographers gathered essential information and pictures and distributed them to other journalists, who were not allowed the same access to battle sites. Press pools had been used in the brief Grenada war and in Panama. In the months after Iraq's invasion of Kuwait and overthrow of its government in August 1990, the first Bush administration led in the formation of a 28-nation Allied coalition to oppose the invasion and demand an Iraqi withdrawal from Kuwait. During the massive buildup of American and coalition forces in Saudi Arabia in October,

November and December 1990, most reporters and photographers were denied access to areas where troops and materiel were stationed. When the war began on January 16, 1991, only pool reporters and photographers were allowed access to battle sites. "When gathering news in the war zone, pool reporters were obliged to accept a military escort if U.S. military commanders deemed one necessary," said Gannett's The Media at War study. "The requirement meant, in effect, that reporters would have to conduct many of their field interviews with soldiers under the watchful eyes of public affairs officers."

Many journalists objected to the pool system in Iraq. But in the end, news organizations accepted its limitations. Victory in the Persian Gulf War was hugely popular with the American public, which overwhelmingly sided with the military's restrictions on news media. The Media at War study noted that "Public opinion polls showed that though the majority of Americans thought that the media were doing a good job of covering the gulf war, most also approved of the press restrictions imposed on the press by the military.... Senior Pentagon officials pronounced themselves satisfied with the reportage produced under the press ground rules and accompanying guidelines — and so, too, did the majority of the public, as measured by the most reputable public opinion surveys." Newspaper columnist Cal Thomas praised the military's actions and suggested that restrictions on media coverage were essential to America's winning the war. In his syndicated column of February 28, 1991, he observed, "The press has been tightly controlled in four recent military conflicts: the British invasion to take back the Falklands Islands [from Argentina in 1982], the liberation of Grenada from Marxist communists, the toppling of the dictator Manuel Noriega from Panama and, now, the liberation of Kuwait from the clutches of Iraq's Saddam Hussein. Is it a coincidence that each of these was successful?"

His point was unmistakable: America wins wars when the press is restricted from war zones.

Mark Van Ells, a professor at the University of Wisconsin-Plattville, studied antiwar protests in Madison, Wisconsin, in 1990 and 1991. The opening paragraph in his report, "No Blood for Oil: Protesting the Persian Gulf War in Madison, Wisconsin," read, "The Persian Gulf War of 1990-1991 enjoyed great public support in the United States. The destruction of the Iraqi army in just weeks provided Americans with a powerful anodyne for the painful memories of defeat in Vietnam. Americans sported countless yellow ribbons on their lapels and on their homes to demonstrate their affection for the US troops in the Gulf. At the war's conclusion, the returning heroes received lavish homecoming parades." Ells concluded that protesters were largely ineffective because they relied too much on the messages and tactics used in the 1960s to protest the Vietnam War.

Embedded Journalism

The current system of "embedding" journalists with troops in the field, used in the second war in Iraq that began March 21, 2003, and in Afghanistan, is the latest effort to fashion a relationship that will work for both media and military. Embedding places journalists with units in the field doing the fighting. It gives journalists the kind of firsthand look at warfare that the public seldom sees. The system has won praise for the access it provides, but critics have also charged that embedding severely restricts what journalists can report based on what they see. Another criticism has been that journalists embedded alongside troops in the field become too heavily identified with the troops, on whom journalists must rely for their protection. Objectivity is thus compromised, say critics.

Some experts have strong opinions for and against the embedding system. Knightley argued in *The First Casualty*, "No matter how determined embedded correspondents may have been to maintain their distance and objectivity, once the [Iraq] war had started, almost without exception, they soon lost all distinction between soldier and correspondent and began to use the pronoun 'we' in their reports...."

Knightley also repeated the most prevalent criticism of embedding: that it blurs if not completely destroys the reporter's ability to remain detached and objective. "In order for embedding to be a successful wartime strategy," he wrote, "correspondents would need to bond with their unit — 'get up close and personal,' provide warm human-interest stories about soldiers, go for maximum imagery but with little insight into the wider picture."

Geert Linnebank, editor-in-chief of the British news service Reuters, argued the same point when he said in an op-ed column for *USA Today* on March 31, 2003, "I have an uneasy feeling about embedded reporters in the Iraq theater presenting only one side of the story. An embedded correspondent is part of the war effort. Even when a reporter resolves to be detached, the fellowship of the battlefield can influence his or her dispatches. If you share a foxhole with a U.S. or British Marine, he is your buddy. The incoming artillery belongs to the foe. Comrades become heroes. You demonize the enemy. Embed more than 500 journalists within an army — as the Pentagon has done in Iraq — and this effect may well be magnified."

Others have called the embedded program a success. "Allowing journalists to move with combat units," concluded a report by the RAND Corp. in 2004, "appears to be the best solution to date at balancing the needs of three core constituencies — the press, the military and the public." The study, however, cautioned that problems may lie ahead. "Embedding journalists with troops will be a model for the future," it said. "But the embedding program could create tensions between the press and the military in future combat operations if US military forces should suffer serious setbacks or heavy casualties." The study was conducted by RAND's National Defense Research Institute, described as "a federally funded research and development center supported by the office of the secretary of defense." Likewise, Fran Unsworth, head of newsgathering for the British Broadcasting Corp., said the following in *The Guardian* of London on September 15, 2009: "Embedding reporters can provide a unique insight into the situation from the perspective of the troops who are often operating in demanding and difficult circumstances."

In a similar vein, the Project for Excellence in Journalism, a Washington, D.C., think tank that studies journalism issues, distributed a report, "Embedded Reporters: What Are Americans Getting?" in 2003. Its findings were mixed but, on the whole, favorable to the embedding system. The PEJ report said in part, "In an age when the press is often criticized for being too interpretive, the overwhelming majority of the embedded stories studied, 94%, were primarily factual in nature.... On balance ... Americans seem far better served by having the embedding system than they were from more limited press pools during the Gulf War of 1991 or only halting access to events in Afghanistan."

Censorship and Propaganda

In every war beginning with the Civil War, the U.S. government has censored press accounts of the fighting. Some censorship regimes have been harsher than others, but some form of censorship has been present in every war the United States has fought since 1861. The justification in each war was to prevent publication or broadcast of information that might be helpful to the enemy. The North and the South both censored the press during the Civil War. And there was censorship in the Spanish-American War of 1898. By far the most severe censorship restrictions, however, were established when America entered World War I in April 1917. At the behest of President Woodrow Wilson, the government created America's first official censorship and propaganda agency, the Committee on Public Information, headed by a former newspaper editor, George Creel. Wilson believed censorship was necessary to build a solid consensus of public support for U.S. entry into the war. He had long been convinced of the need for American entry on the side of the Allied forces, but he knew he needed public support.

The CPI's role was to enforce regulations that the U.S. Departments of State, War and the Navy had drafted before Congress had even approved a declaration of war. "Those regulations, which the press voluntarily accepted, forbade publication of such militarily sensitive information as troop movements within the United States, ship sailings and the identification of units dispatched overseas," said The Media At War, the Gannett study.

But more severe restrictions were yet to come. Congress later passed two sweeping pieces of legislation that added considerably more strength to the government's power to censor the press. These were the Espionage Act of 1917 and the Sedition Act of 1918. The Espionage Act made it illegal for anyone, while the nation was at war, to "wilfully make or convey false reports or false statements with intent to interfere with the operation or success of the military ... or to promote the success of its enemies." It punished those found guilty with fines of up to $10,000 and jail sentences of up to twenty years. The act also allowed the U.S. postmaster to withhold mailing privileges to any publication the postmaster believed had violated the law.

The Sedition Act imposed fines and imprisonment for publishing anything disloyal or abusive about the United States government, flag, or armed forces, explain historians Wm. David Sloan and David A. Copeland in their book *The News Media: A Documentary History*. The Act "prohibited the use of 'disloyal, profane, scurrilous, or abusive language' about the government, flag, or armed forces during wartime. It also empowered the postmaster general to exclude from the mails newspapers and periodicals containing treasonable or seditious material. The Post Office Department threatened to deny mailing privileges to more than seventy-five publications and actually did to a handful. Radical, Socialist, and German-language papers were hardest hit."

The Justice Department used both laws to pressure African-American newspapers to halt (or at least minimize) publication of stories about the lynching of African-Americans and other forms of racial discrimination at home and against African-Americans serving in the military at home and abroad. The Justice Department argued that such stories inflamed and upset black soldiers in such a way that they would be less likely to fight. A special target was the *Chicago Defender*. Before the war, it ran hundreds of articles that encouraged southern blacks to leave the South, in order to escape virulent racism and terror and to resettle in the North and Midwest, where there were better jobs and relatively less racism. The *Defender's* campaign caused outrage among Southern white business and farm owners, who were losing thousands of cheap laborers. Southern white politicians, who accused *the Defender* of running scurrilous and inflammatory articles, complained to the Justice Department. Patrick Washburn, in his book *The African American Newspaper: Voice of Freedom*, says, "The *Defender*, as well as two other black newspapers, the *Baltimore Afro-American* and the *St. Louis Argus*, were warned by the government in 1918 that they should be careful in what they ran."

Mainstream newspapers and magazines did not come to the defense of these black papers or the radical socialist or German-language papers. "Once America entered the war, a wave of super-patriotism spread across the country. Two months after the United States' entry, the *Literary Digest* invited readers to clip and send to that journal any editorial that seemed 'seditious and treasonable,'" says historian Debra Reddin van Tuyll. Her chapter, "The Media in National Crises: 1917-1945," appears in Wm. David Sloan's edited book *The Media in America: A History.*

None of the black weekly newspapers actually was prosecuted for violating the Espionage or Sedition Acts. But J. Edgar Hoover persisted into the 1940s, during World War II, trying to persuade the Justice Department to prosecute some black papers for printing stories about racial oppression in the United States. Hoover, at the time a young lawyer, was named head of the Justice Department's Bureau of Investigation in 1924 and was director in 1935 when it was renamed the Federal Bureau of Investigation (FBI). Throughout his career until his death in 1972, Hoover remained an implacable opponent of the civil rights movement, often linking it to subversive or Communist influences. The same charge was hurled against black newspapers in 1942 by the conservative columnist Westbrook Pegler, who had won a Pulitzer Prize the year before. "Pegler said that the *Chicago Defender* and *Pittsburgh Courier*, vigorous papers read regularly by Negro servicemen, 'are exploiting the war emergency as an opportunity to push the aspirations of the colored people.' He likened [the papers'] obvious, inflammatory bias to the slant of 'such one-sided publications as the Communist Party's *Daily Worker* and [Father Charles] Coughlin's *Social Justice*." This was the observation of Armistead S. Pride and Clint Wilson II in their book *A History of the Black Press*. However, despite the fulminations of Hoover, Pegler and others, the Justice Department took the position that publishing stories about racial oppression and the atrocities of lynching did not violate the law.

Government censorship of the press during World War II, while less severe than during the previous war, was much in evidence. Television news had not come of age. News coverage was provided by daily and weekly newspapers, magazines such as *Life* and *Time*, and the newest medium of mass communication, radio. "When war came on December 7, 1941," the Gannett Foundation/Freedom Forum study recounted, "the FBI assumed temporary control over both news censorship and telecommunications traffic into and out of the United States. Eight days later, [President Franklin D.] Roosevelt named Byron Price director of censorship, relieving FBI chief J. Edgar Hoover of that responsibility. Congress authorized Price's actions and the creation of the Office of Censorship by passing the War Powers Act on December 18, 1941."

The government then established a set of censorship guidelines called the Code of Wartime Practices, which took effect in January 1942 and remained in effect until the war ended in August 1945. Added to the censorship guidelines was an Office of War Information, created in 1942 as the country's official wartime propaganda agency and headed by former journalist and news commentator Elmer Davis. "The OWI's job was to oversee foreign propaganda (except for Latin America); supervise government war information programs on the radio, motion picture and other mass media; and serve as a liaison between the press and the government," says Debra Reddin van Tuyll.

The office censored dispatches from the main theaters of war in Europe, North Africa and the Pacific. The most severe censorship was in the Pacific under the region's top military commanders, Army Gen. Douglas MacArthur and Adm. Ernest King, the chief of naval operations. "MacArthur required each correspondent's copy to go through a multiple censorship review before being released and pressured journalists to produce stories that burnished the image of troops and their supreme commander. The story was different in North Africa and Western Europe. There officials of the U.S. military cooperated with their British counterparts in drawing up a censorship scheme that was less restrictive," according to the Gannett/Freedom Forum study.

Great Britain and the Soviet Union were America's main allies during World War II. The British government had set up its own censorship mechanism before 1941. The British had been at war with Japan since the late 1930s after Japanese troops invaded and overran British colonial possessions in Asia. Britain's war with Germany began shortly after Germany invaded Poland on September 1, 1939. British writers Miles Hudson and John Stanier in their book *War and the Media: A Random Searchlight* say that the British system of voluntary censorship worked well. "Editors only sent material to the Censorship Bureau if they required advice as to the desirability of suppressing the information in the piece concerned. However, if any printed material prejudiced the defence [sic: British spelling] of the realm or might be directly or indirectly useful to an enemy, editors were liable to be prosecuted under the defence regulations. The censor's approval was a complete defence against such prosecution."

Hudson and Stanier, who remember the horrors of World War II as young boys, argued that censorship in Britain worked reasonably well because the journalists and censors were of one mind: Both believed their No. 1 priority was for Britain and its allies to win the war, and this belief guided their selection of what was or was not to be printed or broadcast.

Censorship was also considered necessary during the Korean War and in every other war the United States fought thereafter except for Vietnam. How it was applied and the extent of its coverage may have differed in Grenada in 1983, in Panama in 1989 and Iraq in 1991, but some form of censorship was always present.

Wartime Challenges to Media Independence

One of the bedrock principles of American journalism is the "watchdog theory" — the idea that journalists must closely watch and keep the public informed about the actions of governments to prevent the abuse of government power. The theory is that an informed public in a democratic society is the surest bulwark against government abuse. A closely related principle is that the press and governments in democratic societies must be independent of one another — that the news media must always be free of government influence, control and coercion. The public's acceptance and understanding of these principles is most severely tested during wartime. When the nation goes to war, the immediate public response is to rally behind the government in the spirit of national resolve to win the war. Citizens often think this national sense of unity and resolve should also include the news as well as entertainment media. The question becomes: Does wartime change the rules for the press? In times of national crisis and emergency, should the media continue their independent watchdog role, or should they become "team players" to help win the war?

The independence of the media got its most severe test during World War II, which began before the American entry on December 8, 1941, a day after Japan bombed the American naval base at Pearl Harbor. "The paradigmatic wartime experience most commonly evoked since 1945, in Britain and elsewhere, has been the Second World War, upon which many states continue to base their expectations of media compliance," said Susan Carruthers in her book *The Media at War.* Hudson and Stanier also pointed out, "The objective of all was to win the war — and to be fair to the media, that objective superseded thought of commercial success during what was seen as a war of national survival.... The media, both in Britain and the United States, were virtually unanimous in their unwavering support in principle for the governments of both countries in their determination to bring about the defeat of their enemies by force of arms."

World War II — probably more so than any other war the United States has fought — was the clearest example of good versus evil, of the need for democracy to triumph over totalitarianism. This was the only time in recorded history that militarily powerful dictatorships — Nazi Germany, fascist Italy and imperial Japan — joined forces in a war that was fought literally all over the world. (In contrast, hostilities in World War I from August 1914 to November 1918 were confined to Europe, Russia, parts of the Middle East and the seas.) World War II became the war when true believers and civil libertarians were willing to put aside their reservations about government power and join in an unprecedented national effort to defeat this tri-partite enemy of democracy.

During World War II, the U.S. government didn't, except on rare occasions, resort to the blunt instruments of the Espionage and Sedition Acts that heavily restricted the media in World War I. The government relied more on the voluntary compliance of journalists. The evidence suggests that news and entertainment media's voluntary compliance was almost complete. Evidence also suggests that in World War I, but particularly World War II, journalists overwhelmingly believed that their highest priority was to cooperate with the government and military to defeat an autocratic enemy that posed history's greatest threat to democratic values.

World War II was also fought after the founding of the Hollywood film industry, and Hollywood produced a number of movies and documentaries that supported the war effort. Before the attack on Pearl Harbor, the majority sentiment in America was that the nation should stay out of foreign wars. Phillip Knightley put it this way in his book, *The First Casualty*: "When the war broke out in Europe, it was doubtful whether the United States would fight at all. There was strong resistance to sending American soldiers overseas again, and, even if this feeling changed, the United States Army was in no state to go, ranking nineteenth among the world's armed forces, after Portugal but barely ahead of Bulgaria." The attack on Pearl Harbor, however, immediately changed American opinion. Then, after the war started, Hollywood produced many films with themes of courage, bravery, patriotism and self-sacrifice — all of which fit with the government's and military's view.

One of the best films was *Mrs. Miniver*, produced and distributed by Metro-Goldwyn-Mayer (perhaps the most powerful of all the Hollywood studios) in 1942. The film starred Greer Garson as Kay Miniver, a British housewife who displayed epic heroism and bravery during Germany's "blitz" bombing of London in 1940. Stacey Endres and Robert Cushman described the importance of *Mrs. Miniver* in their book, *Hollywood At Your Feet: The Story of the World-Famous Chinese Theatre.* "President Franklin D. Roosevelt," they wrote, "had the film run in his private screening room before its premiere and was so impressed that he asked for the quickest possible release and urged that everyone see it. The picture premiered at New York City's Radio City Music Hall on June 4, 1942 ... and was seen by an unprecedented 1.5 million people during its ten-week run there."

One of Hollywood's most celebrated film directors of the 1930s and 1940s, Frank Capra, made a series of films under the general title *Why We Fight* that helped to convince Americans it was necessary to fight and win World War II. The famous British film director Alfred Hitchcock made two propaganda films for the British Ministry of Information in 1944. Another famous Hollywood film director of the 1940s, George Stevens, served with the U.S. Army in Europe during World War II, during which time he directed a crew of cameramen who documented the war on film. Sam B. Girgus, in his book, *Hollywood Renaissance: The*

Cinema of Democracy in the Era of Ford, Capra and Kazan, said of Stevens: "From D-Day to the liberation of Paris and the fighting in between, to the gruesome and momentous combat at the Battle of the Bulge, to the liberation of Dachau concentration camp just a week before the German surrender, Stevens and his crew were there."

The best-known Hollywood stars of the 1940s joined in promoting the sale of war bonds, which millions of Americans bought to help pay the costs of the war. Many film starlets such as Hedy Lamarr, Rita Hayworth and Betty Grable regularly entertained soldiers and sailors, at times on the war front, but most often at USO facilities at home.

Assessment

1. The Military-Media Relationship

Phillip Knightley is incorrect when he says that the demands of media and the military are irreconcilable. It's a difficult relationship, to be sure, but the Iraq War of 2003 and the war in Afghanistan have shown that Americans can be reasonably well informed about day-to-day events in a war without compromising military secrets or battlefield security. Most important are the policy questions and debates leading to the decision to go to war. The media should cover these decisions thoroughly, giving all sides a chance to be heard and understood. If an issue of secrecy or national security arises during the debates, the burden of proof for the necessity of secrecy should be on the military or government officials who insist on it.

Regarding battlefield security, military officers and their civilian counterparts in government have a valid point that troops in the field should not be endangered for the sake of public disclosure. But secrecy can and should be maintained only as long as public disclosure is likely to threaten human life or the overall success of the war effort. What may be kept secret during the war probably should be fully disclosed after the war has ended. One can make a case-by-case argument for continued secrecy, but the burden of proof must be on those military or civilian officials to justify continued secrecy, compared with the costs of keeping the public uninformed. Advocates of secrecy sometimes forget that one of the bedrock principles of American democracy is the public's right and need to know about their government.

2. The Vietnam Syndrome

Those advocates who continue to insist that the media (especially television) "lost the Vietnam War" are wrong. What the unrestricted reporting from Vietnam bared for all to see was the horrors of war — the suffering, the dying, the grotesque weapons of mass destruction (like Napalm) at work, thousands of displaced persons and huge damage to Vietnam's infrastructure and overall society. Any decision to go to war must of necessity be based on war's true costs — death, destruction, mass relocation of refugees and suffering. Such a fateful decision should be made with the clearest understanding of what the ultimate costs and sacrifices will be.

News media worldwide, especially television, told some of the true story of what war is about, but the grotesque scenes were precisely what the military advocates and their allies wanted to keep away from public view. This argument says Americans cannot know the real costs of war because, if they did, they would never approve going to war. Pro-war advocates sometimes argue that the benefits of going to war outweigh the short and long-term negatives. There is persuasive evidence that it was necessary to defeat the Axis powers (Germany, Italy and Japan) during World War II. It is less certain that America needed to go to war in Vietnam.

3. Embedded Journalism

Both sides in the debate about embedded reporters have reasonably good arguments. Some media historians insist, correctly, that the experiences of World War II correspondents like Ernie Pyle and Walter Cronkite were similar to the experiences of embedded journalists in Iraq and Afghanistan. The biggest difference, of course, was that Pyle, Cronkite and other World War II correspondents did not report in real time.

Embedded journalism provides a special kind of look at warfare. But it can potentially compromise a reporter's objectivity. And the embedded reporting must always be accompanied by analysis and interpretation by others. It's important to note that any journalist who is embedded with a fighting unit first must agree not to publish or broadcast any information about the war that the government and military want to keep secret. This policy means remaining silent when the war goes badly or when U.S. forces suffer an embarrassing defeat.

One of the issues of American media reporting on both Iraq wars, in 1991 and March 2003, was their failure to tell the full story of Iraqi deaths, injuries and suffering. We should not expect the embedded journalist to complete this part of the picture, but responsible reporting must always fill in the spaces left blank by the reporter's limited view of the war.

Points of View

Books

Carruthers, Susan L. *The Media At War: Communication and Conflict in the Twentieth Century*. New York: St. Martin's Press, 2000. The media play a decisive role in forming public opinion leading up to war, and they sustain public support for the war once underway.

Flores, Jessie J. *Military-Media Relationships: Analyzing U.S. Navy Officers' Attitudes Towards the News Media*. Monterey, Calif.: Naval Postgraduate School, 2012. "[M]aintaining a good rapport with the media is vital to bridge [the] 'civil-military gap.' Military cooperation with the media by allowing appropriate access enables journalists to communicate with the military base of support in the public, and thus may prove vital to effective military operations."

Hammond, Philip. *Framing Post-Cold War Conflicts: The Media and International Intervention*. Manchester and New York: Manchester University Press, 2007. Since the end of the Cold War, the news media face increasing challenges in explaining the reasons for conflicts around the world. The old Cold War framework — Communists vs. anti-Communists — is no longer valid.

Hoskins, Andrew, and Ben O'Loughlin. *War and Media*. Malden, Mass.: Polity Press, 2010. With the advent of electronic, immediate distribution of news and information, institutions such as governments have had difficulty adapting to the new environment. Thus, the inter-relationship among citizens, governments, the military and the media is often chaotic.

Hudson, Miles, and John Stanier. *War and the Media: A Random Searchlight*. New York: New York University Press, 1998. British censorship of news media during World War II succeeded mainly because reporters and editors believed it was necessary to win the war.

Kennedy, William V. *The Military and the Media: Why the Press Cannot Be Trusted to Cover a War*. Westport, Conn., and London: Praeger, 1993. The media can't be trusted because there aren't enough journalists trained to accurately write about the military.

Knightley, Phillip. *The First Casualty: The War Correspondent as Hero and Myth-Maker from the Crimea to Iraq*. London: André Deutsch, 1975; rev. ed., Baltimore and London: Johns Hopkins University Press, 2004. This critical history of the role of war correspondents, from the Crimean War of 1854 to the Iraq War of 1991, examines the role of journalists "in the promotion of war and urge[s] them to reconsider the burden they bear — every time they write a story, they have an unmeasurable but definite responsibility for what happens next."

Matthews, Lloyd J., ed. *Newsmen & National Defense: Is Conflict Inevitable?* Washington, New York, and London: Brassey's, 1991; published under the auspices of the U.S. Army

War College Foundation, Inc. This collection of essays by authors with military backgrounds gives the military's point of view on media coverage of various wars. "These essays ... portray the structurally embedded tension between the soldier and the press as it has expressed itself at several important junctures over our nation's history."

Sloan, Wm. David, and David A. Copeland. *The News Media: A Documentary History*. Northport, Ala.: Vision Press, 2012. Chapters 10, "The Press and World War I, 1914-1919," and 13, "The News Media and World War II, 1935-1945," are particularly useful in understanding the thinking of journalists and the military. The accounts are based primarily on writings during the wars, and both chapters include full texts of many important documents. "Because of their greater access to the front lines, the dangers [for journalists] increased significantly over those that World War I correspondents had faced. Yet they managed to cover the war, for the most part, accurately and with integrity."

Stewart, Ian, and Susan L. Carruthers, eds. *War, Culture and the Media: Representations of the Military in 20th Century Britain*. Wiltshire, England: Flicks Books, 1996. This collection of essays examines how British media have covered wars from World War I to Iraq.

Articles and Book Chapters

Arnett, Peter. "Vietnam and War Reporting." *Media Studies Journal* 11:2 (1997): 32-38. Arnett persuasively answers the critics of media coverage of the Vietnam War.

Pritchard, Robert S. "The Pentagon Is Fighting — and Winning — the Public Relations War." *USA Today Magazine*, July 2003, pages 12-15. Reprinted in *Mass Media 2005-2006*, Joan Gorham, ed. Dubuque, Iowa: McGraw Hill/Dushkin, 2005. Embedded reporting offers both strengths and potential dangers.

Roeder, George H. "Missing on the Home Front: Wartime Censorship and Postwar Ignorance." *National Forum: The Phi Beta Kappa Journal* (Fall 1995): 25-29. Reprinted in *Mass Media 1999-2000*, Joan Gorham, ed. Dubuque, Iowa: McGraw Hill/Dushkin, 1999. There were specific reasons behind the censorship of certain kinds of photographs during World War II.

van Tuyll, Debra Reddin. "The Media in National Crises: 1917-1945," chapter 17 in Wm. David Sloan's edited book *The Media in America: A History*, 8th ed. Northport, Ala.: Vision Press, 2011. This survey history of the news media during World Wars I and II provides a solid, thoughtful account. "Total wars, like World War II ... bring problems with access, information flow, and government restrictions. Considered in that light, press errors during momentous national and international crises may not be easily excusable, but they become more understandable."

10 Political Bias

"With the constant drum beat of radio show hosts, TV pundits, and book salesmen insisting there is a big liberal bias, it is quite an irony the exact opposite is true. That the media exhibits and conducts itself consistent with a right wing bias is readily apparent with even a cursory analysis of the facts and behavior shown by the mainstream media." — www.rushlimbaughonline.com (a website for criticizing Rush Limbaugh and conservative views)

"Just don't ask a liberal if there is a liberal bias in the national news media. In answer to that question you'll continue to hear what conservatives have been hearing for decades. No matter how many times the obvious is proven, and no matter how many ways that evidence is documented, the response from the liberal elites is always the same. Noise." — Brent Bozell, Media Research Center

The two quotations above, the first from a liberal and the second from a conservative, offer a clue about how strongly the sides feel about media bias. They also reveal how difficult it is to come to any agreement about the nature of bias. The liberal critics are just as certain as the conservatives that the media are biased. The issue of partisan bias has been strong enough to see at least fifty books published on the subject.

Conservatives and liberals, Republicans and Democrats, all claim the media color political candidates and agendas along partisan lines. Each side accuses journalists of framing issues to present an inaccurate view of opposing ideologies and present the best possible view of the side they favor. The issue of bias has been complicated by the recent growth of ideological media outlets. Competition for the market also may contribute to the debate about bias as radio, television, and publications strive to increase audience size by appealing to listeners, viewers, and readers who share their particular ideological views.

In the debate about bias, part of the difficulty is defining what constitutes

by Wm. David Sloan and Michael Andrews
University of Alabama

bias — at least in a way that both conservatives and liberals can agree on. Even a particular selection of facts or choice of words can lead to charges of bias. Thus, for example, the media's aggressive pursuit of "facts" can appear to be biased. Newsgathering and other practices, which may in themselves not reflect any partisan bias, sometimes make it difficult to distinguish between true bias and merely innocent behavior. The issue often boils down to what the audience is predisposed to believe. In fact, it is virtually impossible to eliminate audience predispositions from the debate about political bias.

Three views dominate the debate. The first and longest-lived is that the media have a liberal bias. For fifty years or so, proponents of this view have argued that, even though there may be occasional conservative voices among journalists, the dominant bias is clearly liberal. As a response to that position, liberals have in the last several years fashioned an argument that a conservative bias dominates the news media. They point to such things as conservative talk radio, the Fox News cable channel, and corporate ownership of the media. The third view is that, even though one can find instances of both liberal and conservative bias, the news media as a whole are generally objective and unbiased.

Origins of the Issue

Since the beginning of America's news media, people have claimed they were politically biased. It is easy to find examples from the media to justify the claim. The first continuing newspaper, the *Boston News-Letter* (1704), for example, served as a voice for the governor of Massachusetts, and the *New-England Courant* (1721) provided an organ for Anglicans. During the American Revolution, most newspapers published as patriot voices. For decades after the United States had become a nation, newspapers aligned with political parties and became partisan advocates. Even after newspapers broke away from party affiliation during the middle of the nineteenth century, partisanship remained strong, and politicians could count on the support of newspapers that labeled themselves as either "Democratic" or "Republican." By the 1930s and into the 1950s, critics claimed that most newspapers were conservative in their editorial policy, reflecting the views of their owners. They pointed to the fact that the large majority of newspapers editorially endorsed Republican candidates in all eight presidential elections from 1932 to 1960.

In the 1960s, though, criticism about political bias switched sides, and the modern debate appeared. Conservatives and Republicans began to claim that the news media had a liberal bias and that they treated Democrats better than Republicans. Their concern, however, did not arise from presidential endorsements, for from 1968 to 1988 a majority of newspapers endorsed the Republican candidate in each election. Conservatives and Republicans began to criticize news coverage as well as editorial opinion. Republicans, professors Debra and Hubert van Tuyll explained in the book *Media Bias: Finding It, Fixing It* (2007), "moved from vague dissatisfaction to specific and sustained criticism.... Republican criticism of the media became more organized through the establishment of special-interest groups such as Accuracy in Media." In 1971 Edith Efron published her book *The News Twisters*, which claimed that the media were under the control of an "Eastern liberal establishment." At about the same time, Richard Nixon's vice president, Spiro Agnew, in a memorable quotation denounced journalists as "nattering nabobs of negativity." Just as conservatives were growing concerned about the media's partisan bias, journalists at the national level were becoming more adversarial toward the government. Such criticism of the established order was easy to perceive as criticism of conservatism.

Now, for half a century, conservatives have argued that the news media have been biased against them. They point to such things as the ideological views and voting patterns of journalists, the nature of media coverage of political candidates and issues, and the differing language that journalists use in referring to conservatives and liberals.

Responding to such arguments, liberals have developed their own. They claim that the media are conservative. To buttress their argument, they point to such things as corporate ownership of the media, the preponderance of conservatives on talk radio, and the existence of conservative television commentators and newspaper editorial writers.

Some journalists, on the other hand, take satisfaction from the fact that both sides criticize them. They argue that the reason *both* sides are upset is simply because the media are unbiased and thus conform to the ideology of neither side. Conservatives, they say, criticize the media because they are not conservative, and liberals criticize them because they are not liberal. Along with journalists, many journalism professors seem to hold that view. The number of people, though, who argue that the news media are unbiased has been declining for many years.

The Media Are Liberal

"Over 40-plus years, the only thing that's changed in the media's politics is that many national journalists have now cleverly decided to call themselves moderates. But their actual views haven't changed.... Their political beliefs are close to those of self-identified liberals and nowhere near those of conservatives. And the proportion of liberals to conservatives in the press, either 3-to-1 or 4-to-1, has stayed the same. That liberals are dominant is now beyond dispute. Does this affect coverage? Is

there really liberal bias? The answers are, of course, yes and yes. It couldn't be any other way." — Fred Barnes, "Evidence of a Liberal Media," *The Weekly Standard*, May 28, 2004

As the quote from the website of the *Weekly Standard* indicates, conservatives insist that for years the mainstream media have favored the liberal left. Liberals, they insist, have controlled the mainstream media for far too long, and the elite liberal media have promoted liberal ideology and denigrated conservative views. Until recently, they say, the liberal media held a monopoly, putting conservative voices at a clear disadvantage.

The main arguments that conservatives make are that (1) most journalists are liberal, as demonstrated by such evidence as their voting records in presidential elections; (2) journalists use different language in referring to conservatives and liberals — such as calling conservatives "conservatives" while not attaching a "liberal" label to liberals; and (3) media content, on the whole — both news stories and comments — paints conservatives negatively while treating liberals favorably.

Many writers have argued that the media have a liberal bias, and the Internet has added voices to the debate. Among the best known critics are Bernard Goldberg and Brent Bozell. Their arguments cover the main ones that most conservative critics present.

Goldberg's book *Bias*, published in 2002 with the subtitle *A CBS Insider Exposes How the Media Distort the News*, was not the first to present the argument that the media are predominantly liberal, but it was the first to become a national bestseller. Goldberg, a former reporter with CBS News, wrote from his perspective of twenty-eight years as a member of the mainstream media. Correlating the mainstream liberal media and the fictional organized crime family of *The Sopranos* TV show, he satirically termed the liberal media the "news mafia." However, he said, he meant "no disrespect to the mafia."

Despite repeated denials to the contrary, Goldberg said, the liberal bias of the elite media has been evident for several decades. While at CBS, he began to recognize a pattern of liberal bias in story choice and structure. Bias was an accepted fact, he said, but the "liberals in the newsroom" frowned upon discussing it. After critiquing liberal media bias in a 1996 article in the *Wall Street Journal*, Goldberg said, his fellow journalists at CBS viewed him as a traitor and a "right-wing ideologue." Goldberg says he is not a conservative and points to his views and records on a number of issues as evidence. His fellow journalists, though, thought anyone who described journalists as liberal must be a reactionary conservative.

Liberal bias can be seen in several ways, Goldberg wrote, even if it is not always overt. It can be inferred when a news report describes one person as conservative while not describing another as liberal. The fact that journalists label conservatives but not liberals reflects journalists' liberal leanings, Goldberg said. They don't think of liberals as having an ideology, for in their view only conservatives are ideological. "[T]he media label conservatives far more often than they do liberals," he explained, "because the media elites think conservatives need those warning labels; they think conservatives are *out of the mainstream* — and therefore must be identified — while at the same time thinking that liberals *are the mainstream*."

Unlike some conservative critics, Goldberg does not believe that "elite" liberal journalists have an agenda. Their problem is that they think they are "middle of the road," but Goldberg reasons that in that belief they are delusional. They are simply "out of touch" with the public and with reality. In fact, the greatest problem on the bias issue is that national reporters believe they have no liberal bias. The ultimate reason for the success of conservative news programs on cable channels such as Fox, Goldberg said, is that a liberal ideology is so ingrained in the thinking of the majority of journalists that average Americans no longer trust the mainstream media to keep them informed.

Journalists' voting patterns, Goldberg wrote, also indicate their liberalism. For example, two 1996 studies by the Freedom Forum and the Roper Center found that Washington journalists, in comparison to typical voters, are far more likely to vote liberal and Democratic. Liberal journalists, though, brush off such evidence. Dan Rather, for example, on Tom Snyder's program *Tomorrow* in 1995 declared, "It's one of the great political myths, about bias. Most reporters don't know whether they're Republican or Democrat, and vote every which way." The fact that Rather, like many journalists, can maintain such a stance in the face of clear evidence, Goldberg reasons, simply indicates how out of touch they are with reality.

In a second book, *Arrogance: Rescuing America from the Media Elite*, published in 2003, Goldberg expanded on the denial aspect of the liberal media and argued that liberal writers twist the truth in order to claim that instead of a liberal bias there is a conservative bias. He elaborated his belief from *Bias* that there is no "liberal conspiracy" but that liberal bias stems from the personal views of left leaning journalists. Being so convinced that they are without bias, they find it is easier to blame conservatives as conspiracy theorists than to recognize their own bias.

For evidence, Goldberg wrote, one can look at research such as that conducted by Ted Smith III, a professor at Virginia Commonwealth University. His survey of journalistic attitudes found that the majority of journalists identify themselves as liberal on major social issues. Despite similar evidence from a variety of such research projects, liberal elites continue to reject the idea of liberal media bias. Journalists, most of whom are clearly more liberal than the general population, are elitist enough that they consider themselves, and only themselves, to be professional enough to avoid bias.

Liberal journalists, Goldberg wrote in *Arrogance*, view bias in a good-guy vs. bad-guy scenario. The bad guys are conservatives, and they're the only ones who are biased. "Lots of reporters think conservatives are either scary or morons or both," he said. The liberal media have little or no respect for conservative views. As an example, Goldberg told of a newspaper reporter's reaction to a press release by a student conservative group before a speech Bill Clinton made in 2003 at the University of Texas. In a derogatory email to the group, the reporter referred to the members as "heartless, greedy, anti-intellectual little fascists." Reporters, Goldberg declared, frequently express such views, although often only to one another.

The liberal media, Goldberg wrote, tend toward political correctness, with the result that incomplete or inaccurate reporting on minority-related stories and issues is commonplace. Part of that problem results from what he terms "white liberal guilt." Such a mindset obstructs progress in race relations by restricting "open public discussion on vital issues." Journalists' fear of being labeled as racist results in an inequality of reporting. Fear of offending minority groups, or even giving the appearance of being unsympathetic, Goldberg concluded, can "hamper full and honest coverage."

Similarly, the impact of diversity groups in the media results in liberal bias. Professional associations whose purpose is diversity can have an agenda that influences media performance. For example, the National Association of Black Journalists, according to Goldberg, watches for news items that may be "offensive to black sensibilities." He suggests that issues such as affirmative action do not receive full and open coverage because the appearance of opposing it seems to such groups to be the same as racism.

Like Goldberg, Brent Bozell says liberal journalists believe their views are not biased but are the norm. He is the founder of the Media Research Center, a group he formed in 1987 to "document the existence of liberal media bias." His 2004 book *Weapons Of Mass Distortion: The Coming Meltdown of the Liberal Media* presents some of the main arguments about liberal bias. Despite years of documented evidence of bias in the liberal media, Bozell wrote, members of the liberal media have repeatedly refused to acknowledge it. They hold to that outlook despite the fact that they vote overwhelmingly for Democrats and hold views on social, moral, and political issues that are far more liberal than those of the general public. Furthermore, they think they have an understanding and social conscience that are superior to those of conservatives. Only recently has there been even the slightest admission of occasional bias.

The elite liberal journalists, Bozell reasons, are arrogant, believing themselves to be "enlightened" and conservatives to be "the great unwashed." As an illustration, he quoted an editor as saying, "You just don't get it: We are the social conscience of this country and we have an obligation to use the media." Such a sense of superiority, Bozell said, inevitably leads to distortion of media content, for it trickles into various aspects of news coverage and commentary.

An obvious example is the double standard that exists in the coverage of political parties and figures, Bozell said. Republicans often find themselves on the defensive from liberal media attacks simply for expressing conservative ideas. These attacks sometimes have been vicious and yet prompted no media outcry because journalists consider objectionable actions to be the outcome of Republicans' conservative agenda.

Furthermore, Bozell declared, the liberal media hold conservative political figures to a higher standard than liberals. Bias is evident repeatedly in media coverage of conservative vs. liberal views. Liberal figures or issues receive the benefit of the doubt while conservative ones generally receive harsher treatment. Pointing to a variety of studies of news content, Bozell wrote that it is "a quantifiable fact that the news media routinely find fault with the actions and personal behavior of conservatives even when the accusations are mere allegations."

Among the most prominent examples of a double standard, Bozell said, are differences in the coverage of recent U.S. presidents. The media treated Democrat Bill Clinton much more leniently than it did Republican George W. Bush. During Clinton's presidency, many journalists did their best to present beneficial coverage and to downplay scandals. In the case of Bush, though, there was much more negative rhetoric, some of it so sharp that it bordered on "hatred," even in the wake of the 9/11/2001 attacks and the beginning of the war in Iraq. When left leaning activists and journalists criticized Bush, other "mainstream" media let the attacks go unquestioned.

As another example of liberal bias and a double standard, Bozell points to the treatment the media gave former conservative reporter David Brock. While Brock was a conservative, his investigations of President Clinton and Democrat-related scandals got little attention. It was only when his views turned toward the Left, and toward praise for Bill and Hillary Clinton, that his reporting and books became acceptable and made him popular with journalists.

Several writers have — as Goldberg did with CBS — singled out individual media outlets for criticism. An example is Bob Kohn. In his 2003 book, *Journalistic Fraud: How The* New York Times *Distorts the News and Why It Can No Longer Be Trusted*, he claimed that America's most prominent newspaper displays a consistent liberal bias. In attempting to demonstrate that bias, he quoted *Times* employees who were disillusioned with the paper's approach and referred to media observers' comments that the *Times'* has become a predictably partisan paper.

He also analyzed several standard practices that journalists can employ to give a slant to the news. The *New York Times,* he concluded, consistently uses the techniques to slant the news to its perspective. One of the practices is interpretive reporting, which has replaced much of the traditional "inverted pyramid" approach to writing news stories. Another is what headlines say and how they are placed on a page, making it possible to give a reader scanning a page an erroneous impression of the facts that the story reports. Similarly, labels that reporters choose when referring to people and ideas can give a slant. For example, stories in the *Times'* much more frequently identify some people as "conservative" than they designate others as "liberal," and they refer to conservative ideas as "extreme" much more frequently than they do liberal ones. How a reporter selects quotations and opinions to use in a story can affect the perspective, and a liberal perspective can be seen easily in the *Times'* selection of such material. Even facts, Kohn wrote, can be used in a way that contributes to bias. They can be distorted, chosen selectively, omitted, or even falsified to create certain impressions, and the *Times* often employs facts in such ways. If that use were random, one might find the *Times'* coverage balanced, Kohn concluded, but instead it almost always seems to favor a liberal perspective.

The most systematic study that has been done to assess media bias reached similar conclusions. It was titled "A Measure of Media Bias" and appeared in the scholarly publication *Quarterly Journal of Economics* in 2004. The researchers were Dr. Tim Groseclose, a professor of political science at UCLA, and Dr. Jeffrey Milyo, a professor of economics at the University of Missouri.

Since a criticism of arguments about media bias is that "bias is in the eye of the beholder," Groseclose and Milyo first devised a method of measuring bias by calculating "ideological scores for several major media outlets." To compute the scores, they "count[ed] the times that a particular media outlet cites various think tanks and policy groups, and then compare[d] this with the times that members of Congress cite the same groups." In essence, they identified the average view of members of Congress as representing a middle point in ideology, that is, halfway between liberalism and conservatism. Then they compared views in major media outlets with congressional views. They included twenty major American newspapers with a national readership — such as the *New York Times* and *USA Today* — and national television news programs. They examined only the news content and not such opinion material as editorials.

The results showed, they concluded, "a strong liberal bias: all of the news outlets we examine, except *Fox News' Special Report* and the *Washington Times,*

received scores to the left of the average member of Congress. Consistent with claims made by conservative critics, *CBS Evening News* and the *New York Times* received scores far to the left of center. The most centrist media outlets were PBS's *NewsHour*, CNN's *Newsnight*, and ABC's *Good Morning America*. Among print outlets, *USA Today* was closest to the center."

The Media Are Conservative

"Those of us who pay close attention to the news media have known for years that the So-Called Liberal Media was a myth perpetrated by the GOP.... [T]he GOP has complained about an alleged liberal media bias for years as a tool for browbeating the media towards favorable and sheepish coverage, while wanting voters to ignore that it is conservative Corporate America that actually owns the large majority of that same media and dictates its content." — Steve Soto, "Democrats Show Signs of Realizing Conservative Bias In Media," www.theleftcoaster.com, January 12, 2004

Compared with the arguments against liberal media bias, the liberal case is a latecomer. In the early years of conservative criticism of "liberal" media, liberals gave no response, perhaps unconcerned that the criticism would ever grab hold. As, however, the criticism grew more widespread, liberals began to fashion a response. One of their main arguments is that the conservatives' criticism is merely a tool, taking advantage of journalism's precepts of objectivity and balance, to try to beat the media into giving positive treatment of the conservative side. Liberals argue that conservatives are aggressively pursuing an agenda of denouncing a so-called liberal media (SCLM) simply to silence opposition to conservative issues.

Eric Alterman has been particularly vocal in arguing that "SCLM" is merely a myth that conservatives created, a right-wing propaganda tactic. "The myth of the 'liberal media,'" he wrote in his 2003 book *What Liberal Bias? The Truth About Bias and the News*, "empowers conservatives to control debate in the United States to the point where liberals cannot even hope for a fair shake anymore." The "myth" for decades has been an effective tool to counter media disagreement with conservative ideas or issues. "Smart conservatives," though, do not necessarily believe in the myth. They simply make use of it, Alterman said, to publicize their issues or impede the publication of liberal views. Since if you "repeat something often enough ... people will believe you," conservatives have, by constant repetition, browbeaten journalists into spreading the "baseless accusations of liberal bias."

Despite conservative claims of liberal bias, Alterman said, conservatives actually dominate the media. The key to conservative media power is conservatives' extensive access to and use of publications, talk radio, and the Internet to spread the myth of liberal media. This extensive influence makes it possible for these "deeply biased and frequently untrustworthy outlets" to circulate their distorted and poorly informed opinions. In fact, the sheer volume of conservative media is overwhelming.

The use of pundits, for example, is an effective means of dispersing conservative views, Alterman wrote, while denigrating liberal ones. These pundits are the "shock troops" of the conservative media and are far more widespread than the "so-called liberal media." As a result, "[a]cross virtually the entire television punditocracy, unabashed conservatives dominate, leaving lone liberals to offer themselves to be beaten up by marauding right-wingers...." Alterman characterized conservative punditry in one of two ways: either ignorant belligerence or sitcom-like silliness. Without saying which category Fox commentator Bill O'Reilly falls into, Alterman described him as the "undisputed king of cable today." O'Reilly has no hesitation about arguing with better informed persons, Alterman opined, and continually insults liberal guests on *The O'Reilly Factor* in a vain attempt to discredit them.

Fox News, however, is not the only forum for conservative pundits, Alterman lamented. They dominate talk radio. The growth in conservative voices has made the medium a haven for right-wing hosts. Rush Limbaugh, for example, has rapidly become one of the strongest voices for conservative issues and often "pushes the bounds of good taste." Despite all his faults, Alterman concluded, Limbaugh has had considerable influence on political issues.

Despite what conservative apologists such as Goldberg and Bozell say about the treatment of Republican and Democratic presidents, Alterman argued, the media are easier on Republicans. During the 2000 presidential race, for example, the SCLM treated Republican candidate George W. Bush as well as or better than Democrat Al Gore.

Along with Alterman, David Brock has been a prominent voice advocating the liberal view of media bias. A self-avowed former conservative, he has denounced conservative political tactics, including use of the media. In his 2002 book, *Blinded by the Right: The Conscience of an Ex-Conservative*, he admitted he had been a right-wing journalist for the *Washington Times*, the Heritage Foundation, and the *American Spectator*. He painted a dark picture of the conservative media. They carry out a no-holds-barred campaign against liberals, he said, while at the same time diverting attention by complaining about so-called liberal media.

While he was a conservative writer, Brock covered a wide array of subjects, including the Whitewater scandal and the impeachment of President Bill Clinton.

He described within conservative circles an environment of "visceral hatred and unfathomable hypocrisy." Conservative political leaders worked hand-in-hand with conservative media to coordinate attacks on liberals. "I had learned," he wrote, "… that right-wing journalism had to be injected into the bloodstream of liberal media for maximum effect."

Brock said he himself took part in efforts intended to discredit Bill and Hillary Clinton. The objective was to gather information that could be used to damage their reputations and then to spin it to the benefit of the Right. One of the episodes was the so-called "Troopergate" affair, in which critics claimed Bill Clinton as Arkansas governor used state troopers to assist him with sexual liaisons with several women. Brock was the first journalist to report the story. However, he said he grew increasingly suspicious of the motives of witnesses and lost confidence in their accounts. Having converted from a conservative to a liberal, he now describes his resulting article as "a cruel smear disguised as a thorough 'investigation.' … I pushed ahead because my role at the *Spectator* — as a right-wing hit man, a hired gun in every sense of the word — was more than a job; it was who I was. I had a hit to pull off."

After his change of ideology, Brock eventually wrote a letter of apology to Clinton for his role in the Troopergate article. When the matter of Troopergate came to court, witnesses recanted statements they had made to Brock. Conservative media used Brock's published apology and the recanted statements, Brock said, to make him the "object of a right-wing smear."

Brock's 2004 follow-up book, *The Republican Noise Machine: Right-Wing Media and How it Corrupts Democracy*, adopted the view that Alterman emphasizes: Liberal media bias is a myth. In fact, Brock wrote, "[t]he mainstream media is actually influenced by wealthy benefactors who use it as a front group for the Republican Party." He described substantial gains that conservatives have made in cable television and talk radio. The conservatives' political philosophy, he said, is "It's the media, stupid." Conservative talk radio and cable news channels such as Fox News are convenient and effective propaganda tools for the Republican Party. Conservatives now have the media advantage, Brock declared, which they use to good effect, leaving a visible pattern of victims, including the Clintons, Al Gore, and virtually every major Democratic political figure.

Conservatives use the term "liberal bias," Brock said, as a cover for the real media bias, that is, conservative bias. He described Bozell as both a conservative and an activist. Bozell, Brock said, understood that conservatives could use the "liberal media" label to expand and enhance the conservative media, and as many as 90 per cent of liberal media bias stories, at least in the press, originated from Bozell's Media Research Center.

The Internet, Brock said, has become a powerful outlet for the right wing, which commands greater resources than liberals do. Conservatives have used the Internet more successfully because liberals, unlike conservatives, are not "devoted to pushing misinformation into the rest of the media." An example of conservative Internet success is the far-reaching *Drudge Report*. Although it initially was merely a gossip site, according to Brock, the Right soon began to use it to further a political agenda. From 240 million hits annually in 1996, by 2004 it was getting 6.5 million hits daily, Thus, the *Drudge Report* became a juggernaut of the right-wing media.

Like Alterman, Brock criticized Rush Limbaugh for his prominent role in conservative talk radio. In his early days in radio, according to Brock, Limbaugh was fired at least four times, twice for "alienating listeners and advertisers," before finding his place in Sacramento, California, in 1984. As a self-described anti-liberalist, Limbaugh drew in an audience of lower-middle-class white men by focusing their attention on what he described as liberal threats to their cultural status. Limbaugh's attacks included religious groups, feminists, the NAACP, and other minorities. Despite denouncing "lifestyle liberalism," Limbaugh was an "unlikely conservative warrior," for he had two ex-wives but no children and did not attend church. As a precursor to later conservative media channels, though, Limbaugh's program tapped into a growing "right-wing hostility toward the media" that included "right-wing propaganda" and "relentless attacks on liberals and liberalism." His popularity spawned a multitude of similar right-wing programs.

The lack of liberal opposition to such fear-mongering, according to Brock, was a factor in the success of the "right-wing campaign" to dominate the media. Fortunately, Brock concluded, groups like the Center for American Progress and Democracy Radio were attempting to level the playing field.

Like Brock and Alterman, Joe Conason says the idea that the media are liberal is fraudulent. "Conservatives," he wrote in his 2003 book *BIG LIES: The Right-Wing Propaganda Machine and How It Distorts the Truth*, "complain so habitually and so monotonously about their exclusion that usually nobody notices the relative scarcity of liberal voices." He considers it paradoxical that so many conservatives appear in so many conservative forums to complain that the conservative view is never heard. He compares professional conservatives harping about liberal media to "grifters working on an old but reliable con." The charge that the media are liberal, he said, is an "inside joke" among "self-respecting rightists." Conservatives have simply used the liberal media myth to cover their own mistakes.

Conason compares media and politics to children's sports, using a "work the ref" metaphor. Children try to use the tactic to intimidate a referee into second-guessing a call. Unfortunately, conservatives have used it successfully to convince the public that the "liberal media" have excluded their views. Conservative media — unlike the mainstream, so-called "liberal" media — rarely give liberals a voice, Conason insisted, because conservatives know there is really no liberal bias in the mainstream media, and "they just prefer a fixed fight." While the mainstream media may provide both sides of an issue, the conservative media are consistently one-sided.

As evidence, Conason quoted one conservative writer as saying, "Fox News is obviously biased to the right. It's simply loopy to pretend otherwise." Fox, Conason said, is not interested in being credible. It prefers being influential. He quoted Brit Hume, who at the time of Conason's book was a main Fox anchor, as saying after Republicans won big in the 2002 elections: "We have become so influential now that people watch us and they take their electoral cues from us. No one should doubt the influence of Fox news in these matters."

Despite their claims of liberal media bias, Conason said, conservatives actually have the advantage of a vast network of conservative media. Those outlets present a skewed view of political reality. They are quick to defend conservatives in response to what they consider liberal attacks, and they give great attention to scandals involving liberals and Democrats while virtually ignoring those involving conservatives and Republicans.

Conservatives use an arsenal of propaganda tactics not only to attack liberal ideology, Conason said, but to attack liberals personally. The conservative media are coordinated and serve as the voice of these attacks, carrying them, sometimes, to extremes. Typical charges include calling liberals and Democrats unpatriotic, morally deficient, and fiscally irresponsible, among other things. For example, conservatives have pressed the "politically correct" issue so that they can label liberals as anti-freedom and criticize colleges and professors who promote it. Even though the media embraced the issue, Conason said, there was never a concerted effort by "liberal academics" to stifle free speech. Rather, the Right created the issue of political correctness as a tool to incite fear of the so-called liberal "thought police." The Right's propaganda was simply a tool to try to fool the public into thinking that "liberals" were trying to promote ideology, restrict freedom, and embarrass and discredit the Right.

The Media Are Unbiased

In the general population, there appear to be few who argue that the media are not biased. Despite the widespread claims of bias, though, many working journalists stick to the traditional view that the media are unbiased. In fact, they take comfort in the conflicting claims of liberals and conservatives. They reason that if both liberals and conservatives think the media are biased, then the media must not be taking sides. The only reason liberals are mad at the media, journalists say, is because the media are not liberal. The same is true for conservative arguments: the only reason that conservatives claim the media have a liberal bias is because the media are not conservative. Thus, journalists reason that the mainstream news media adhere, for the most part, to the standards of fairness, balance, and objectivity. They agree that some outlets are intentionally ideological, but those outlets should not, they say, be considered mainstream and do not reflect the general practices of journalism.

Journalists' views get support from some political liberals and academic writers. For the most part, they conclude that research studies provide little empirical evidence of partisan bias.

David Niven is one such researcher — although one who writes from a Democratic perspective. He is best known for his book 2002 *Tilt? The Search for Media Bias.* At the time he wrote it, he was a political science professor at Florida Atlantic University. He left that position to become a speechwriter for Ted Strickland, the Democratic governor of Ohio. "Of all the authors who have attempted to frame a Democratic response to the Republican critique of the press," write Debra and Hubert van Tuyll in their overview of partisan media bias in the book *Media Bias: Finding It, Fixing It*, "... Niven has been one of the few to go after hard, quantitative evidence."

In *Tilt?* Niven first dealt with the issue of how to define partisan bias. He proposed this definition: Treating a member of one party differently from a member of another party in the same situation. "Bias," he said, "cannot be substantiated without a comparison." He then devised a study to measure bias. Rather than examining something such as how the media treat two candidates of different parties in the same election, he studied how the media have treated different U.S. presidents in similar situations. He did the same type of study for political officials at other levels, from city mayors to members of the U.S. Congress. For the question of media treatment of presidents, he selected periods during the administrations of George H. W. Bush and Bill Clinton when the unemployment rate was the same. He asked this question: "Does a Democrat president with a high unemployment rate get better or worse coverage than a Republican president with a high unemployment rate?" He found little difference in the coverage of Bush and Clinton. On a larger scale, he compared and contrasted newspaper coverage of more than 450 political figures who had similar accomplishments while in office. There was "simply no evidence of partisan bias," he concluded.

The main reason that so many members of the general public believe the media have a liberal bias, Niven said, is because the media report such claims. In that view, he resembles a number of other critics writing from a liberal perspective. The extensive coverage of media bias, real or imagined, keeps the topic in the minds of the audience and adds to the conviction that bias does exist. The reason the public believes there is more liberal than conservative bias is that, even in the absence of provable bias, conservatives are more adept at presenting a view of liberal bias than are liberals of presenting the opposite case. Conservatives' charges get more attention, Niven concluded, because they tend to be "mean, sarcastic and unflattering."

Even though Niven wrote from a Democratic perspective and appears to have the goal of refuting Republicans' charges, his study is notable for the fact that he did not claim that the media have a conservative bias — as critics such as Alterman and Brock have claimed — but that there is no media bias. "Those who have a firm ideological commitment," Niven concluded, "tend to view the media as hostile to their perspectives and to embrace those data that appear to confirm their belief."

Some academic writers reason that what appears to be media bias is not ideological at all but is simply the natural result of professional journalistic practices. For example, in their 2003 book *The Press Effect*, Kathleen Hall Jamieson and Paul Waldman reasoned that the public mistakes the results of standard journalism methods for bias. "[M]any biases, most of them professional, not political," they wrote, "shape the news. Reporters have a bias toward the use of official sources, a bias toward information that can be obtained quickly, a bias toward conflict, a bias toward focusing on discreet events rather than persistent conditions, and a bias toward the simple over the complex." Journalists, Jamieson and Waldman concluded, don't discriminate based on party affiliation in their use of such practices.

Assessment

Jamieson and Waldman's book illustrates the difficulty in reaching a definitive assessment about the issue of media bias. It may appear on the surface to present a detached study. One of the problems, though, in evaluating their conclusion that bias does not really exist is that one cannot be certain how their own biases might affect their conclusions. Jamieson is a journalism professor at the University of Pennsylvania and might be detached in her political views. We would hope that would be true in academic studies. Waldman, on the other hand, is a writer for MediaMatters.org, which is openly liberal and describes its website as a "progressive research and information center dedicated to comprehensively monitoring, analyzing, and correcting conservative misinformation in the U.S. media." He is also the author of two books that are staunchly partisan: *Being Right is Not Enough: What Progressives Must Learn From Conservatives* (2006) and, in collaboration with David Brock, *Free Ride: John McCain and the Media* (published by

MediaMatters.org during the 2008 presidential campaign). The second book claimed the media were biased toward McCain, the Republican opponent of Barack Obama. The same question about whether authors are biased can be raised about nearly everyone who writes about the issue of partisan bias. The potential bias is easy to spot in those writing from the conservative and liberal camps. Unfortunately, even writers who claim to be presenting an uncolored view may actually have a partisan agenda.

The majority of "evidence" cited in accusations of either liberal or conservative media bias is anecdotal rather than empirical and appears to boil down to matters of opinion. Thus, one will not find a large number of studies that seem to be detached from partisanship. So, in attempting to assess the evidence, both the liberal and conservative arguments suffer from some of the same weaknesses.

The proponents of the liberal side have several problems. Among them are the following:

• They base most of their arguments on anecdotal rather than empirical material.

• In the argument that corporate ownership results in conservative content, they present little verifiable evidence to document the connection.

• They tend to critique personalities and media outlets — such as Rush Limbaugh and Fox News — that obviously take a partisan position, and they pay little attention to the traditional "mainstream" media, which are, after all, the main focus of conservative critics.

Similarly, the conservative critics have problems in their arguments.

• Like their liberal counterparts, they rely on anecdotal material for much of their case.

• They write much of their critique (as do their liberal opponents) from a strong partisan perspective so that much of the material they perceive as biased probably is, in the whole context of news reports, merely innocent.

In comparing the liberal and conservative cases, though, the conservatives seem to come out ahead. One of the strongest points in their favor is simply that many more people believe the media have a liberal bias than believe the bias is conservative. Several studies, including respected ones by the Pew Research Center, have reached that finding. James Hamilton (in *All the News That's Fit to Sell: How the Market Transforms Information into News*, 2004) posits that audience members perceive more bias as media content gets farther from their own views. Similarly, Daniel Sutter (in "An Indirect Test of the Liberal Media Thesis Using Newsmagazine Circulation," 2004) has shown that audience members who can be identified as leaning Democratic tend to like the "mainstream" media better than Republicans do. The evidence that a large majority of journalists vote for Democratic candidates and have social views that are more liberal than those of the general public also seems to support the conservative argument. Finally, there is some significance to the fact that, in the face of conservative criticisms, it was many years before liberals began arguing that the media were conservative. That suggests that they did not see any reason to argue earlier that the media were conservative because they did not think the media were biased against liberalism.

Even though the majority of arguments that partisans make seem to be biased themselves and are largely anecdotal, occasional researchers have attempted to gather empirical data and analyze it, apparently, without an ideological motive. The Pew studies are a good example. The academic study that has been most frequently cited is Groseclose and Milyo's 2004 article "A Measure of Media Bias." It is the best study to incorporate a way to define bias, and it offers a systematic examination of possible bias. Its concludes that liberal bias dominates the media. Groseclose followed up on the article with a book-length study in 2011 titled *Left Turn: How Liberal Media Bias Distorts the American Mind.* In it, in contrast as he and Milyo did with their article, he reveals clearly that he views politics from a conservative perspective. Still, he approaches the issue of media bias in a rigorous manner. First, he identifies the "political quotient" of the "average American" — that is, a numerical rating of views on political and public issues. Then he compares it with the content of a wide range of media outlets. He concludes that most outlets are more liberal than is the average citizen.

Even though the Groseclose-Milyo study received considerable applause, it also has critics who claim it has problems. One, for example, is that the average views of members of Congress or of think tanks may not equate to centrist ideology. Another criticism is that the study does not measure liberal vs. conservative bias at all but instead assesses media content in terms of how it varies from dominant views in government authority structures. After the publication of Groseclose's book, liberal critics argued that it simply proved that the Groseclose-Milyo study was biased.

Despite the weaknesses of much of the writing about media bias, we can make some brief conclusions. The most obvious one is that some media content has a conservative bias, some has a liberal bias, and some has no apparent bias at all. Every story may not be biased, and the degree of bias may not be the same on every issue. Furthermore, we should not assume that all media outlets and journalists are biased one way or the other or that, even among those that are, everything the outlet or journalist does is biased. Most writing about media bias has focused on national media. It would be a mistake to assume that every local media outlet reflects national views or is the same as every other one. So it is a mistake to say "the media," if we mean the media as an entire group, are biased one way or the other. Beyond these obvious conclusions, the fact that so many readers and viewers perceive bias still raises a red flag — a good indication that media bias really exists. Members of the media — just like real people — have their own values, their own biases. The principle of objectivity is not revered as much as it was a few decades ago, but most journalists still acknowledge the principle that journalism, at least news reporting, should be balanced and fair. Yet, even though journalists may be trained in such practices as objectivity, they have a human tendency to favor those views and principles that they consider to be "right." Thus, bias sometimes creeps into both news and opinion without the writer recognizing it.

Points of View

Books

Alterman, Eric III. *What Liberal Media? The Truth About Bias and the News.* New York: Basic Books, 2003. So-called "liberal bias" is a myth that Republicans made up to gain political power.

Anderson, Brian C. *South Park Conservatives: The Revolt Against Liberal Media Bias.* Washington, D.C.: Regnery Press, 2005. Liberal bias has dominated for many years, but now new media outlets are challenging it.

Bozell III, Brent, *Weapons Of Mass Distortion: The Coming Meltdown of the Liberal Media.* New York: Crown Forum, 2004. Numerous studies have shown that the mainstream media are liberal. Their refusal to recognize public disapproval will result in the demise of the liberal media.

Brock, David. *The Republican Noise Machine: Right Wing Media and How it Corrupts Democracy.* New York: Crown Publishers, 2004. Right-wing media have tried to close off debate about important political issues and have the power to destroy the American democracy.

Conason, Joe. *BIG LIES: The Right-Wing Propaganda Machine and How It Distorts the Truth.* New York: St. Martin's Press, 2003. The idea that the media are liberal is fraudulent. "Conservatives complain so habitually and so monotonously about their exclusion that usually nobody notices the relative scarcity of liberal voices."

Franken, Al. *Lies (and the Lying Liars Who Tell Them: A Fair and Balanced Look at the Right).* New York: Dutton, 2003. The claim that the media are liberal is a smoke-screen that Republicans use to try to make the public distrust the media. Conservative media figures are dishonest.

Gillard, Arthur, and Stuart Kellen, eds. *Media Bias.* Farmington Hills, Mich.: Greenhaven Press, 2004. This collection includes essays about media bias written from different

points of view.

Goldberg, Bernard. *A Slobbering Love Affair: The True (And Pathetic) Story of the Torrid Romance Between Barack Obama and the Mainstream Media.* Washington, D.C.: Regnery Press, 2009. The mainstream national media, liberal as they are, overwhelmingly supported Democrat Barack Obama in the 2008 presidential election.

Goldberg, Bernard. *Bias: A CBS Insider Exposes How the Media Distort the News.* Regnery Publishing: Washington, D.C., 2002. Most journalists at the national level are liberal and think that anyone who is not liberal is odd. That attitude results in systematic bias in most major news media outlets.

Groseclose, Tim. *Left Turn: How Liberal Media Bias Distorts the American Mind.* New York: St. Martin's Press, 2011. Compared with the "average" political views of American citizens, most media outlets are liberal.

Kohn, Bob. *Journalistic Fraud: How the* New York Times *Distorts the News and Why It Can No Longer Be Trusted.* Nashville, Tenn.: WND Books, 2003. The *New York Times* uses a number of journalistic practices to give a consistent liberal twist to its news. It has become a predictably partisan paper.

Niven, David. *Tilt? The Search for Media Bias.* Westport, Conn.: Greenwood Press, 2002. The media are biased, but the bias is not of a partisan nature or liberal. It simply reflects journalists' tendency to be negative.

Sheppard, Si. *The Partisan Press: A History of Media Bias in the United States.* Jefferson, N.C.: McFarland, 2008. Although historically partisan and conservative, the media turned toward liberalism in the 1960s.

Sloan, Wm. David, and Jenn Burleson Mackay, eds. *Media Bias: Finding It, Fixing It.* Jefferson, N.C.: McFarland, 2007. Essays on a variety of issues present the opposing arguments about media bias.

Articles

Eisinger, Robert, Loring Veenstra, and John Koehn. "What Media Bias? Conservative and Liberal Labeling in Major U.S. Newspapers." *Harvard International Journal of Press/Politics* 12:17 (2007): 17-36. While newspaper labeling of both conservatives and liberals varies, that fact does not necessarily indicate a media bias.

Groseclose, Tim, and Jeff Milyo. "A Measure of Media Bias," *Quarterly Journal of Economics* 70:4 (2004): 1191-237. Groseclose and Milyo's original report can be found at http://www.sscnet.ucla.edu/polisci/faculty/groseclose/Media.Bias.8.htm. Content analysis comparing media views with politicians' views shows "a very significant liberal bias." Most news outlets "received a score to the left of the average member of Congress."

Lee, Tien-Tsung. "The Liberal Media Myth Revisited: An Examination of Factors Influencing Perceptions of Media Bias." *Journal of Broadcasting & Electronic Media* 49:1 (2005: 43–64. "Findings based on two large national surveys suggest that audiences' ideologies and partisanships affect how they view the media" and that "conservatives and Republicans are more likely to distrust the news media."

Websites

Accuracy in Media (AIM). http://www.aim.org/ AIM describes itself as a "watchdog of the news media that critiques botched and bungled news stories and sets the record straight on important issues that have received slanted coverage." It represents the conservative point of view.

Fairness and Accuracy in Reporting (FAIR). http://www.fair.org/ FAIR describes itself as "the national media watch group [that] has been offering well-documented criticism of media bias and censorship." It represents the liberal point of view.

Media Matters for America. http://mediamatters.org/ Media Matters describes itself as a "progressive research and information center dedicated to comprehensively monitoring, analyzing, and correcting conservative misinformation in the U.S. media."

Media Research Center (MRC). www.mediaresearch.org/ The MRC describes itself as "a conservative media watchdog group dedicated to bringing political balance to the news and entertainment media."

11 Objectivity — Ideal or Unreal?

"The uncorrupted ideal of objectivity, in the sense of reporters driving to dig out verified facts and present them fully and fairly, is indispensable in journalism." — Doug McGill, "The fading mystique of an objective press," *The McGill Report*, 2004

"In fact, there is no such thing as objective reporting.... We should stop pretending that objectivity is possible, and stop asking our news providers to practice it." — Theodore Dawes, "Why the news makes you angry," *The American Thinker*, 2010

The two quotations above present professional journalists, and, indeed, society as a whole, with quite a conundrum. Those who favor objectivity consider it a hallmark of professional journalism, employed by individuals who have received specialized training and are willing to abide by well entrenched standards. Those who dismiss it believe that such detachment is impossible to achieve because each individual's worldview is subjective.

Part of the challenge stems from not having an agreed-upon definition of the term "objectivity." It is best known by its characteristics — fairness, balance, factual accuracy, neutrality, impartiality and detachment. The tradition of news objectivity called for reporters to "provide straight, unbiased information," according to Steven Ward in his 2004 book, *The Invention of Journalism Ethics*, to inform citizens of the day's events. Although many researchers and some journalists argue that those traditional roots have changed, we still see many news media practices incorporating these characteristics. Proponents such as Bill Kovach and Tom Rosenstiel in *The Elements of Journalism* and others continue to laud the role of the news media to report verifiable information, provide multiple viewpoints fairly and keep personal biases out of news reports.

Adding to the challenge is that objectivity no longer gets mentioned in the leading news media ethics codes. For example, the Society of Professional Jour-

by Lois A. Boynton
University of North Carolina at Chapel Hill

nalists removed the terms "objective" and "objectivity" when it revised its Code of Ethics in 1996. The new code does, however, address many of the characteristics of objectivity mentioned previously, including seeking truth, being thorough and accurate, detaching from conflicts of interest and avoiding expressions of personal bias. Similarly, the Code of Ethics of the American Society of Newspaper Editors, last updated in 1975, does not refer to objectivity but calls on editors to "assure that the news content is accurate, free from bias and in context, and that all sides are presented fairly" and to employ "independent scrutiny." In the digital media arena, the Radio Television Digital News Association (formerly Radio Television News Directors Association) Code of Ethics and Professional Conduct from 2000 uses phrases including "pursue truth aggressively and present the news accurately" and "resist distortions that obscure the importance of events," but does not refer to these practices as objectivity. Even a 20-page Company Policy on Ethics in Journalism produced in 2005 by the *New York Times* eschews the word, opting instead for terms such as impartiality, neutrality, fairness, "unvarnished truth," and "professional detachment, free of any whiff of bias."

Although proponents see objectivity as an essential means of providing the public with accurate information needed to make informed decisions, some critics argue that it simply is not realistically attainable. For example, Richard Reeb, Jr., in his 1999 book *Taking Journalism Seriously: Objectivity as a Partisan Cause,* considers objectivity a valid ideal, but "manifestly impossible," and David T. Mindich stated in his 1998 book, *Just the Facts: How 'Objectivity' Came to Define American Journalism*, that true objectivity cannot be attained because human beings are flawed. Hence, some opponents have proposed alternatives, ranging from pragmatic objectivity that embraces human limitations, to feminist standpoint theory, which calls for journalists to understand better their inherent biases and write from the position of marginalized groups rather than power elites.

Origins of the Issue

The roots of the idea of "objectivity" may be found in both philosophy and science as a tool to ascertain the truth. Some ancient Greeks including Aristotle employed reason, logic and mathematics to draw conclusions, rather than relying on myths or religious beliefs. They also acknowledged, however, the role of human fallibility and understood that it was imperfect humans who employed these skills to arrive at what truth they could determine. Such a context is also crucial in journalistic objectivity, in which the human observer — reporter or photographer — is inherently flawed. As the columnist Walter Lippmann wrote in *Liberty and the News* in 1920, "The sensible procedure in matters affecting liberty of opinion would be to ensure as impartial an investigation of the facts *as hu-*

manly possible" (emphasis added). Objectivity within scientific inquiry bloomed during the Renaissance period, with an emphasis on testing and replication rather than observation or speculation. As with the ancient Greek approach, scientific inquiry did not ensure absolute truth but allowed access to the most achievable truth.

In the Age of Enlightenment in the 18th century, philosophers such as John Locke, Auguste Comte and Denis Diderot continued to rely on reason, observable fact and disengagement to achieve truth, which snowballed to refer to complete detachment. Although science and philosophy embraced objectivity, journalism did not take up the banner until the 1800s. From the beginning of American newspapers during colonial times, printers and the reading public thought papers should be impartial. With the Revolution against England, though, and in the decades that followed, the press became staunchly partisan. In Steven Knowlton and Karen Freeman's 2005 book *Fair & Balanced: A History of Journalistic Objectivity*, chapter authors Carol Sue Humphrey and Hazel Dicken-Garcia explained that owners used their newspapers to espouse their favored platforms, and readers knew the positions of the newspapers they were reading.

What became known as journalistic objectivity took root in the 1830s with technological advancements such as the speed of printing presses and the telegraph, along with the emergence of a literate, urban population. Additionally, newspapers moved away from a subsidized model to an advertising-based model, wherein neutrality would not offend advertisers or readers. The change from partisanship to objectivity was societally motivated, argued Dicken-Garcia in her chapter in *Fair & Balanced*, as readers called for more information to help them navigate the complexities of their world. This information model focused on the public's right to know and ushered in the watchdog role. Journalists attempted to move away from opinionated reporting to presenting factual information with "independence, detachment and balance." Story structure also changed. Newspapers had occasionally used a form of the inverted pyramid structure, which lent itself to factual writing, as early as the colonial era, but it became more popular during the Civil War. Mindich wrote in *Just the Facts* that the modern structure was first used to report President Lincoln's assassination. Rather than telling the story chronologically, the initial story indicated the horrifying end result: Lincoln had been mortally wounded while attending a theatrical performance. Other historians have said that the inverted pyramid came into common use in the Progressive era, as an outgrowth of the rise of science and education. The ideal of detachment has not always been practiced, however. Today's news media still present much biased material, despite ethical standards to the contrary.

By the early 1900s, impartiality and dedication to fact-seeking became known by the term "objectivity." These practices were codified in the 1920s by professional associations such as Sigma Delta Chi, the forerunner of the Society of Professional Journalists. The public shifted from expecting opinions and distortions to news that was free of reporter bias. As Steven Ward explained in *The Invention of Journalism Ethics*, it was the reporter's job to present facts that readers could use to draw their own conclusions. This approach placed reporters on the outskirts of what German philosopher Jurgen Habermas referred to, in his 1984 book, *The Theory of Communicative Action*, as the public sphere, where debate and persuasion take place.

Traditional news objectivity enjoyed its heyday from the 1920s to 1950s. By the 1950s, objectivity encountered serious criticism for being too unrealistic and preventing journalists from providing news analysis or interpretation. Further, critics grew concerned that objectivity reduced reporters to mere stenographers who did not challenge powerful sources. For example, reporters initially did little to challenge U.S. Sen. Joe McCarthy's anti-Communism campaign of the 1950s. They used proper sourcing and attribution techniques, considered foundations of objectivity, but did not stand up to false allegations and efforts to curtail free expression. Today, investigative reporting, public journalism and social media have led us to revisit objectivity's role. Can objectivity continue to provide the framework for effective reporting?

Proponents of Objectivity

One of the early proponents of news objectivity was Walter Lippmann, a noted columnist who wrote a series of essays in the 1920s decrying the "crisis of journalism." He wrote that facts needed to be the basis of reporting. "True opinions can prevail only if the facts to which they refer are known," he argued. "If they are not known, false ideas are just as effective as true ones, if not a little more effective." He promoted "disinterested reporting" as a method for journalists to keep their personal and political views out of their stories. "Emphatically, he [the reporter] ought not be serving a cause, no matter how good." It is also important to note, explained Julien Gorbach in a 2009 paper, "When the Journalist Becomes the Story: Lippmann, Stone, Liebling, Jewish Identity, and the Arab-Israeli Conflict," that Lippmann did not advocate the "pure" version of objectivity. Rather, he recognized that humans have limitations. He believed that impartiality, observation and discipline were hallmarks of sound journalism, but he also noted that community standards would call for journalists to take personal responsibility and avoid clouding the truth.

This "honest effort" may come from *how* information is gathered in the first place. Philip Meyer, a retired professor and journalist, said in a 1995 speech to the Investigative Reporters and Editors Conference that objectivity should not focus so much on the resulting news stories, but more on the methods by which reporters gather the information. Objectivity, he said, "means standing so far from the community that you see all events and all viewpoints as equally distant and important — or unimportant.... The result is a laying out of facts in a sterile, noncommittal manner, and then standing back to 'let the reader decide' which view is true." Journalists, Meyer argued, should focus on *how* the information is gathered and interpreted. That is, verifying whether that information is accurate with an informed and structured process helps ensure that what reporters present — even on sensitive or volatile topics — is as objective as humanly possible. "Scientific method was developed to protect human investigators from the unconscious tricks of self-deception that afflict us all. Its procedures of peer review, replicability, and falsifiable hypotheses protect journalists as well...," Meyer said. Michael Ryan, in "Journalistic Ethics, Objectivity, Existential Journalism, Standpoint Epistemology, and Public Journalism," a 2001 article, also noted that journalistic objectivity has many of the same characteristics as scientific objectivity: accuracy, precision, skepticism, "receptivity to new evidence and alternative explanations," impartiality and honesty about personal biases. Whether or not news reports are objective, he added, depends on how well practitioners live up to professional standards of obtaining and sharing newsworthy information.

Similar to Meyer's arguments for objectivity of method, Leo Bowman argued in a 2006 article titled "Reformulating 'Objectivity': Charting the Possibilities for Proactive Journalism in the Modern Era" that merely relying on the final product as the main artifact of objectivity is not enough. Rather, he said, it is important to explore how journalists "*do* objectivity" in collecting information for their stories. His research showed that broadcast reporters did not passively report what official sources said, but often developed procedures to challenge authoritative views and ensure story balance.

Other supporters of the idea of objectivity see it as a worthy ideal rather than as an achievable result. David Mindich wrote, in his book *Just the Facts,* that objectivity is more of a goal than a practice because "journalists do and must construct stories, because of their membership in the world of humanity.... Information cannot be conveyed without an organized narrative, and stories cannot be told without conveying information." It is difficult — perhaps impossible — for a reporter to detach from the world. The challenge for the reporter, then, is to maintain standards of the professional journalist, argued Suite101.com writer Adam Williams in his 2008 blog, *Objectivity in News Reporting.* "That such a caring person maintains any notable degree of objectivity as a newspaper reporter attests to that individual's professionalism, and the ability to maintain honest credibility as a messenger in the community," he wrote. Mindich also contended that nonpartisanship, "insofar as it is defined as keeping personal political preferences ... out of news stories" — rather than pure objectivity — is attainable, primarily because he believes most news reporters do not hold strong partisan positions but tend to be middle-of-the-road politically. "Journalists take pride in the fact that they are both praised and criticized by people of all political persuasion...," he wrote. It is important to note here that Mindich and other objectivity supporters are referring to news reporters, not columnists and pundits who have decided views that they present openly.

Proponents point to a number of attributes that may contribute to this objectivity goal:

- Reporting verified facts
- Representing an issue's multiple viewpoints fairly and in a balanced manner without taking sides
- Keeping personal biases, interests and distortions out of stories (Note that this standard does *not* say that reporters do not have opinions. Rather, they are called on to keep those opinions out of their stories.)
- Avoiding real or perceived conflicts of interest to ensure the journalist is not beholden to anyone

Dan Gillmor, a proponent of participant journalism and founder of Grassroots Media Inc., despite calling his 2005 blog column "The End of Objectivity," said that four practices may serve the same purpose as the somewhat obsolete definitions of objectivity. First, he identified thoroughness, which he contends must include gathering views beyond the comfort of official sources. The second practice is accuracy, which involves discovering facts and admitting what is not known. Third, he calls for reporters to practice fairness by gathering many viewpoints. Unlike the concerns raised about traditional objectivity as a passive exercise, Gillmor stated, "It does not mean parroting lies or distortions to achieve that lazy equivalence that leads some journalists to get opposing quotes when the facts overwhelmingly support one side." His fourth practice is transparency, which involves reporting where information comes from.

Furthermore, both Michael Ryan, in his 2001 *Journal of Mass Media Ethics* article, and Carrie Figdor, in a 2010 *Journal of Mass Media Ethics* article, argued that objectivity does not mean values-free reporting. Many news topics are reported because the subjects conflict with widely held values — sex trafficking, genocide, abortion, capital punishment and physician-assisted suicide, for example. But journalists still can report objectively even when reporting such topics. Ryan contended that reporters must learn to acknowledge their own biases as they begin the newsgathering process, consult reliable sources and focus on gathering the most relevant information possible. Again, supporting Philip Meyer's objectivity of method, both Ryan and Figdor contend that reporters can be reasonably accurate if they verify the information they gather rather than take statements at face value. Although journalists will not be perfect, they can employ standards of practice so that their reporting process allows them to come as close to an accurate description as is humanly possible. Objectivity can be achieved in degrees, Figdor argued, if the focus is on reporting accuracy. Hence, objective practices can lend credibility to the news media.

Other authors support a new approach that Steven Ward named "pragmatic objectivity" in 2004. It focuses on the goals of objectivity while recognizing human fallacy in the process. This pragmatism, wrote Brian Turner and Judith Kearns in 2010 in the *Canadian Journal of Communication*, acknowledges that humans yearn to learn what is true and employ the best methods available to them to get as close to that truth as possible. "Traditional objectivity," Ward wrote, "is flawed by the mistaken belief that objectivity requires claims to be based on absolute standards or facts, as ascertained by neutral, perspective-less agents." Rather, "journalism objectivity needs to be fallible and practical." This approach acknowledges that detachment is not wholly possible, but journalists can and should acknowledge any shortcomings, suppositions or biases as part of the news gathering and reporting process.

Ward continued this contention in his 2009 chapter in *The Handbook of Mass Media Ethics* by arguing that objectivity cannot be boiled down to merely repeating reports of what individuals state or telling audiences what the facts are. Rather than passively recording events, he said, reporters should test the veracity of claims and interpretations and question beliefs when doubts arise. Truth emerges from inquiry. What is true now may not have been true in the past, a foundation that dates to poet John Milton's 1644 argument for a marketplace of ideas in his treatise *Areopagitica.* Consider, for example, what you learned in grade school about the number of planets in our solar system. In 2006 Pluto was dropped from that list because planetary scientists decided it does not meet their definition of a "planet." Seeking truth, then, is a valid exercise in and of itself, according to the pragmatic approach. Ward further identified how pragmatic objectivity might be employed in practice. First, journalists must seek the truth, using the skills of inquiry that are both inherent to humans and taught professionally. Journalistic investigation, like scientific investigation, must observe, inquire, construct,and reconstruct interpretations as new data emerge, and then report on them accurately and fairly. Journalists also must acknowledge their own presuppositions that may, despite best efforts, affect a story. Reporters can avoid the obvious pitfalls of judging situations and sources by employing accepted standards of practice as outlined in company and association codes of conduct. In other words, disciplined interpretation of events by employing reason and logic may help ensure that reporters present a viable account of what is true. These standards emphasize fact gathering, compare new knowledge to what is already known, and focus on fairness, openness and impartiality. The final result should balance the inherent passion to seek interesting and substantive topics with an objective process that justifies interpretations. "Journalism based only on passion is reckless," Ward argued, and "a journalism based only on objectivity is accurate but lacks depth."

Critics of Objectivity

While Walter Lippmann promoted the disengaged, fact-focused reporter, his contemporary Henry R. Luce, co-founder of *Time* magazine, believed such a focal point reduced reporters to the role of stenographers, wrote James Baughman in his 1987 biography of Luce. Consider, for example, Luce's barb against neutrality in journalism: "Show me a man who thinks he's objective and I'll show you a man who's deceiving himself." Because he created *Time* and then *Life* magazines to be interpretive rather than purely objective, he also argued that "objective accounts could be written with such attention to accuracy and attribution as to confuse the lay reader." Luce believed that providing an analytic approach to reporting the news actually helped divorce the media outlet from partisan causes. This view also has been raised in recent years, with researchers Margaret Duffy, Esther Thorson and Fred Vultee, in their 2008 paper "Advocating Advocacy," calling for journalists to make a concerted effort to let their views be known and "interpret news in terms of that position."

Critics also have raised their voices against elements of traditional objectivity, noting, as Pamela Shoemaker and Stephen Reese contend, in their 1991 book, *Mediating the Message: Theories of Influences on Mass Media Content*, that reality cannot be observed objectively. Rather, reality is a construct of what people in a society think it is. Kevin Stoker, in his 1995 *Journal of Mass Media Ethics* article, disparaged what has been called the "spectator role" of journalists, who attempt to maintain neutrality and distance, almost to an extreme of segregating themselves from their humanity. For example, *The Atlanta Progressive News*' news editor, Matthew Cardinale, went on record in a 2010 column, "Notes on News and Objectivity," stating that his publication is not designed to be objective. "The premise of objectivity is literally to remove the observer from what it is that is being observed and simply to report what 'is,'" he wrote. "However, that is an impossibility. It cannot be done. In fact, there is nothing that 'is,' separate from the observer or multiple observers who construct and interpret what reality is." Duffy, Thorson and Vultee, in "Advocating Advocacy," recommended that reporters not hide their persuasive intentions but acknowledge their use of narratives that crusade, praise, condemn or chastise. Rather than merely spout facts and rely on readers to find their own meaning, media should concede that "[r]allying the public around a wrong that must be righted is clearly a persuasive function."

Objectivity critics have focused on the flaws of the concept, either from the perspective that objectivity leaves reporters without significant power or that it places too much power in the hands of mainstream communicators. Those who express concern about the lack of power believe, as publisher Henry Luce did, that objective journalists are permitted only to state what happened in a sanitized fashion without contextual analysis or criticism. These results played out in the 1950s when Sen. Joseph McCarthy instigated a campaign to rid the country of Communist sympathizers. For some time, the media seemed to assume a stenographer's position, in essence parroting McCarthy's views, albeit through proper sourcing and attribution, without regard to whether the statements were valid or not.

Others, however, point to the power held by journalists who keep their newsgathering process from public view or scrutiny, revealing only the result. Michael Karlsson wrote in *Visibility of Journalistic Processes and the Undermining of Objectivity* in 2008, "Journalists have the cultural authority of both deciding news and defining journalistic standards in the newspaper." Sociologist Gaye Tuchman, in her 1972 article "Objectivity as Strategic Ritual: An Examination of Newsmen's Notions of Objectivity" in *American Journal of Sociology*, suggested that this lack of transparency allows reporters to hide behind a banner of objectivity, in large measure to protect themselves from criticism or litigation.

One root of journalistic power comes from the reporters' ability to determine which sources they will interview. Because reporters seek readily accessible expert views — traditionally those in leadership positions including governmental officials and business executives — authors including Herbert J. Gans, in his 1979 book *Deciding What's News*, have argued that news media only reinforce the status quo of the elite, rather than serve as watchdogs of those in power. Diversity of viewpoints does not necessarily appear in news stories. Tuchman also worried that reporters might cloak their own opinions with selective use of sources and their quotations. Journalists also decide for readers what information from those interviews is significant enough to put into a story. For example, the traditional inverted-pyramid structure, which places the most important information first, has its shortcomings as a tool of objectivity. The concern frequently raised is *who* determines what is most important. If those individuals — that is, reporters and editors —do not represent the diversity of voices in their community, objectivity and balance may be further compromised.

Power is also evident through news framing, argued researcher Meenakshi Gigi Durham in a 1998 article in *Communication Theory*. Framing is the process by which journalists determine what is included and excluded from their stories. Based on well-established news routines, frames can affect how readers and viewers perceive issues and their players. Hence, framing "can convey values and moral judgments while hewing strictly to known and verifiable facts," explained Duffy, Thorson and Vultee in "Advocating Advocacy."

The balancing act of news reporting has also garnered its share of criticism. Creating a balanced story stems from the journalistic practice of presenting counterclaims when an initial claim cannot be verified. The presumed result, then, is a "balanced" story that gives an issue's two sides. The reader then discerns what is true. As more facts emerge, they are reported, thereby bolstering the claim of objectivity. But does a story only have two sides? Feminist theorists and others have argued that viewpoints are more nuanced, and a truer balance will emerge when many perspectives can be seen and heard, particularly from those who are outside the power elite. Further, balance can be contrived by introducing weak alternative views as being equally valid as more credible views. Duffy, Thorson and Vultee, in "Advocating Advocacy," used coverage of global warming as an example of this "inappropriate evenhandedness." That is, although few scientists reject the view that global warming is a concern, their viewpoints get equal billing with those of the substantially larger contingent of scientists who argue that global warming exists.

Critics have proposed several replacements for the objectivity model. For example, participatory journalism — providing news consumers access to information planning, gathering and reporting — garnered support in the late 20th century through the public journalism movement. Although the approach has fallen out of favor recently, the goal of advocates such as Jay Rosen, author of *Community Connectedness Passwords for Public Journalism* in 1993, was to provide in-depth reporting with less polarization of issues that concerned communities. Philip Meyer explained, in his 1995 speech to the Investigative Reporters and Editors Conference, that public journalism would foster deliberation by "helping and encouraging members of a community to make that earnest attempt at reciprocal understanding." Reporters practicing public journalism seek nontraditional voices to provide useful insights. For example, in a 1994 series called "Taking Back Our Neighborhoods," the *Charlotte* (N.C.) *Observer* made a concerted effort to start its in-depth investigation with individuals who lived and worked in some of the city's poorest communities, and it called upon nonprofit leaders more frequently than city and police officials.

Interactive models of journalism may also challenge traditional ideas of objectivity. The potential for direct communication with news consumers may further diversify how information is gathered and from whom, as well as what is published or aired in the final news product. Michael Karlsson, in his 2008 conference paper "Visibility of Journalistic Processes and the Undermining of Objectivity," argued that transparency "involves the producer of information being open to the consumers of news ... to monitor, check, criticize, and even intervene in the journalistic process." This approach can be accomplished by including links to source materials, admitting and correcting errors with the original story and seeking public input. Whether transparency becomes the new standard of news remains to be seen, but because of the openness of the digital media platform, journalists may need to adjust expectations of how news consumers get, process and react to available information.

Another concept gaining visibility is the application of feminist standpoint theory. This approach posits that scientists (or reporters) should start their investigations from the position of marginalized groups rather than power elites. In media terms, the voices of others dissimilar to reporters and their official sources may provide useful insights, thereby "increase[ing] our ability to understand a great deal about the distorted way the dominant groups conceptualize politics, resistance, community, and other key history and science notions," Sandra Harding argued in her 2004 book, *The Feminist Standpoint Theory Reader*.

Durham, in her 1998 *Communication Theory* article, argued that standpoint theory's emerging "strong objectivity" can lead journalists to better understand their own biases and inherent problems associated with social marginalization. "Truth," she argued, may have multiple and conflicting layers that may be interpreted differently depending on an individual's social status. Hence, the journalist should consider his or her role and presuppositions about an issue at various stages of news production — source selection, interview questions, news production, etc. Durham does not advocate abandoning all aspects of objectivity, such as the popular ideology of the journalist's role to "afflict the comfortable and comfort the afflicted." Rather, she asks reporters to pursue less obvious sources to ensure the story provides adequate context.

Assessment

Many proponents of objectivity as a news standard do not believe that it is possible — or even helpful — for reporters to attempt *complete* detachment from what they cover and to present only raw facts without context or analysis. Rather, most concede that objectivity represents an ideal for which reporters should strive through such practices as verifying facts, presenting multiple viewpoints fairly, keeping personal interests out of stories and avoiding conflicts of interest.

Likewise, critics of objectivity don't suggest that the norm should be abandoned entirely. Instead, they believe that reporters should venture beyond the comfort of traditional sources and routines to get a "truer" picture of reality.

Both supporters and critics believe journalists need to focus on how information is gathered. As Philip Meyer recommended in his 1995 speech to investigative reporters, objectivity of method requires journalists to employ rigorous standards when seeking information, which may reduce the chances that personal biases will influence the final news product. Reporters and editors should test and verify claims judiciously, challenge authoritative views, be skeptical and open to alternative explanations, and seek new evidence. Critics also have pointed to information-gathering flaws and have offered solutions including transparency of process and product and reporters acknowledging their personal biases.

Additionally, the "strong objectivity" approach of standpoint theory provides a broader method of inquiry than traditional objectivity by first seeking views of marginalized groups. This approach is not totally foreign to news media. Public journalism long has advocated that reporters seek non-official and non-traditional sources to comment on issues of the day.

Steven Ward's pragmatic objectivity and Sandra Harding's strong objectivity bring similar practices to the table. They believe in the importance of seeking truth while also acknowledging that flawed humans have preconceptions that may affect their reporting and news production. They also believe that reporters should be transparent about their limitations but not allow those limitations to stymie the quest for as much truthful reporting as possible.

Hence, it may be argued that both pragmatic objectivity and strong objectivity fall within a continuum of the extremes of the sanitized detachment of pure objectivity and the make-no-judgments approach of relativism. Both extremes have been challenged — pure objectivity for being impossible and relativism for being impractical. Rather than pitting pragmatism against standpoint theory, it would behoove researchers and practitioners to discuss their common foundations, with the ultimate goal of helping ensure that mass media continue their significant role in democratic societies.

Finally, it also will be useful for journalists to understand the impact of media on society by donning the hat of the news consumer. Learning — or remembering — how media can affect individuals, groups and society as a whole serves as a reminder of the importance of making sure news is reported in pragmatic, strong and viable ways. One approach is through concepts of media literacy, which W. James Potter's 2004 *Theory of Media Literacy* defined as the study of how we attend to and interpret media messages. Media literacy education, explained Elisha Babad, Eyal Peer and Renee Hobbs in their 2009 paper "The Effect of Media Literacy Education on Susceptibility to Media Bias," teaches individuals to explore "how bias exists in both the production and reception of messages, to identify the difference between well-supported arguments and spurious claims, and to assess the credibility and veracity of information about current events."

Returning to the quotes at the beginning of this chapter — yes, objectivity involves fairness and verification of information, but the concept has evolved since the mid-19th century. And, yes, pretending that *traditional* objectivity retains its viability is problematic, as researchers have shown. The potential exists for a "new" objectivity that reflects the pragmatic reality of human fallacy with the importance of affecting change through inclusive, rigorous and thorough reporting.

Points of View

Books

Baughman, James L. *Henry R. Luce and the Rise of the American News Media*. Boston: Twayne Publishers, 1987. Luce did not believe that pure objectivity was possible, and he criticized those who believed otherwise. Rather, he supported an analytic approach to journalism that is the hallmark of many news magazines to this day.

Diamond, Edwin. *Behind the Times: Inside The New New York Times*. New York: Villard Books, 1994. Diamond describes a "wild streak" that appears in the *Times*, with editor Max Frankel urging greater interpretation in the news pages as a way of attracting and keeping a younger readership.

Evensen, Bruce J., ed. *The Responsible Reporter*, 2nd ed. Northport, Ala: Vision Press, 1997. Michael Buchholz's Chapter 2, "History of Reporting," provides a particularly useful overview of the development of objective and interpretive reporting.

Fallows, James. *Breaking the News: How the Media Undermine American Democracy*. New York: Pantheon, 1996. The erosion of objectivity has damaged American democracy.

Gans, Herbert J. *Deciding What's News: A Study of CBS Evening News, NBC Nightly News, Newsweek and Time.* New York: Vintage Books, 1979. Gans observed and interviewed journalists to ascertain how they pursued and determined news content in the 1970s. His work explores the ideals of journalism and objectivity, including news values and professional standards.

Goldstein, Tom. *Journalism and Truth: Strange Bedfellows*. Evanston, Ill.: Northwestern University Press, 2007. Journalism, while emphasizing accuracy and objectivity, has never had strong, universal principles or standards for achieving them.

Harding, Sandra. *The Feminist Standpoint Theory Reader: Intellectual and Political Contro-*

versies. New York: Routledge, 2004. This book addresses the feminist perspective of standpoint theory, which argues for reporters to understand fully the perspectives of marginalized groups rather than solely the views of power elites. This type of context may provide a truer picture of what is happening in society.

Jones, Alex S. *Losing the News: The Future of the News that Feeds Democracy*. New York: Oxford University Press, 2009. "[A] great deal of what makes journalism good is entwined with what I would term authentic journalistic objectivity, as opposed to the various flavors of phony or faux objectivity. I believe it is essential that genuine objectivity should remain the American journalistic standard, but we may be living through what could be considered objectivity's last stand."

Kaplan, Richard L. *Politics and the American Press: The Rise of Objectivity, 1865-1920*. Cambridge: Cambridge University Press, 2002. Based on a study of newspapers in Detroit, Mich., journalistic objectivity appears to have originated because of the changes in the American political system, not because of changes in newspaper economics.

Knowlton, Steven R., and Karen L. Freeman, eds. *Fair & Balanced: A History of Journalistic Objectivity*. Northport, Alabama: Vision Press: 2005. This edited volume traces objectivity's roots from colonial times through the present. In America's formative years, objectivity reflected what readers believed to be true, and colonial printers often favored neutrality as a strategy to maintain business with diverse customers. Objectivity took a back seat during the American Revolution, and the modern age of journalism with its focus on objectivity strengthened in the 1800s.

Ladd, Jonathan M. *Why Americans Hate the Media and How It Matters*. Princeton, N.J.: Princeton University Press, 2012. Although not solely devoted to media objectivity, this book addresses some of the concerns associated with journalistic principles, including media bias, fairness, trust and potential polarization.

Lippmann, Walter. *Liberty and the News*. Princeton: Princeton University Press, 2008. Essays written by the noted columnist in the 1920s emphasized the need for early 20th century journalism to move from partisanship to fact-based, neutral reporting.

MacDougall, Curtis D., and Robert D. Reid. *Interpretative Reporting*, 9th ed. New York: Macmillan, 1987. This journalism textbook shows the shift in abandoning objectivity as a professional paradigm.

Maras, Steven. *Objectivity in Journalism*. Boston, Mass.: Polity Press, 2012. Maras provides a survey of views and arguments about objectivity.

Mindich, David. T. Z. *Just the Facts: How 'Objectivity' Came to Define American Journalism*. New York: New York University Press, 1998. This book charts the development of the ideal of objectivity as the foundation of American journalistic practice and uses well-known cases to show the strengths and weaknesses of the concept.

Schulte, Henry H., and Marcel P. Dufresne. *Getting the Story: An Advanced Reporting Guide to Beats, Records and Sources.* New York: Macmillan, 1994. This textbook for journalism students is typical of dozens of manuals now on the market deploring objectivity as a nostalgic and self-limiting practice of yesteryear's journalistic establishment.

Shoemaker, Pamela J., and Stephen D. Reese. *Mediating the Message: Theories of Influences on Mass Media Content,* 2nd ed. White Plains, N.Y.: Longman, 1996. The authors view news as a construct of reality. Hence, it cannot be viewed objectively. This book details the myriad influences on media content, including individual media workers' views, organizational factors, sources and ideology.

St. John III, Burton, and Kirsten A. Johnson, eds. *News with a View: Essays on the Eclipse of Objectivity in Modern Journalism.* Jefferson, N.C.: Mcfarland, 2012. "[J]ournalists' impulse to hold onto objectivity, and to ignore the increasing subjectivities to which citizens are attuned ... contributes to the news media's disconnect from today's news consumer.... [T]raditional journalism needs to incorporate 'post-objective' stances."

Tumber, Howard, and Marina Prentoulis. *Journalism and the End of Objectivity.* New York: Bloomsbury USA, 2012. "[T]he new communications environment, marked by technological, social and political innovations," raises issues about objectivity. The authors examine such topics as "citizen and participatory journalism, literary journalism, public journalism, peace journalism, online journalism, and journalism of attachment."

Ward, Stephen J. A. *The Invention of Journalism Ethics: The Path to Objectivity and Beyond.* Montreal: McGill-Queen's University Press: 2004. The author introduces a new approach to objectivity, "pragmatic objectivity," to overcome the shortcomings of traditional objectivity. Journalists should acknowledge their shortcomings and biases while pursuing the truth. They should not be passive in accepting what sources say, but should investigate viewpoints to get closer to the truth.

Articles

Black, Jay. "An informal agenda for media ethicists." *Journal of Mass Media Ethics* 23:1 (2008): 28-35. This article presents nine issues emerging from the Media Ethics Summit II that the media should consider to ensure the craft is practiced professionally, particularly in the age of digital and social media communication. One of these issues is the pursuit of truth. Black supports Ward's concept of pragmatic objectivity and encourages journalists to focus on accountability and transparency.

Bowman, Leo. "Reformulating 'Objectivity': Charting the Possibilities for Proactive Journalism in the Modern Era." *Journalism Studies* 7:4 (2006): 628-43. Reporters should challenge authoritative views to ensure story balance and serve the public interest, rather than passively reporting what sources say and merely reinforcing the status quo.

Figdor, Carrie. "Objectivity in the News: Finding a Way Forward." *Journal of Mass Media*

Ethics (January-March 2010): 19-33. After defining the concept of objectivity in news, the author addresses inherent flaws of objectivity. She notes that, although bias is a human trait, it does not mean that biased news must be the end result. Journalists must distinguish between emotional detachment and objectivity.

Ricchiardi, Sherry. "Over the Line?" *American Journalism Review* (September 1996): 25-31. An Indiana University professor analyzes advocacy journalism in the reporting of the war in Bosnia.

Ryan, Michael. "Journalistic Ethics, Objectivity, Existential Journalism, Standpoint Epistemology, and Public Journalism." *Journal of Mass Media Ethics* 16:1 (2001): 3-22. Each individual's worldview is subjective and may affect how a story is reported. Whether objectivity materializes depends on how well reporters live up to professional standards of obtaining and reporting newsworthy information.

Tuchman, Gaye. "Objectivity as Strategic Ritual: An Examination of Newsmen's Notions of Objectivity." *American Journal of Sociology* 77:4 (1972): 660-79. Reporters use objectivity to protect themselves from criticism. They also sometimes quote certain sources to help reinforce their own beliefs.

Wien, Charlotte. "Defining Objectivity within Journalism." *Nordicom Review* 26:2 (2005): 3-15. "[I]t is one thing to operate with objectivity as a beacon, and something else to operationalize objectivity in the everyday task of journalism.... Journalism has made several attempts to break free of the positivistic objectivity paradigm, none of them very successful."

19 Political Correctness

A political correctness debate has permeated the halls of academia and has been argued in the pages of major newspapers since the 1990s.

Many actions have given rise to charges of political correctness — or political incorrectness. Here are some examples:

• In a city council discussion concerning taxi drivers in Lynn, Mass., one councilman argued that drivers should speak English, opening the door to media and organizational accusations of racism. In an interview responding to the situation, the councilman said, "It's all about political correctness. The only way to be politically correct is to say nothing at all or it's going to offend someone."

• In 2012, New York's Department of Education drew controversy because of its request to ban 50 particular words from standardized tests. The words included "birthday," "divorce," "dinosaurs," "swimming pools," and more. Among other reasons, the city said the terms "could evoke unpleasant emotions in the students." Because of the negative backlash, the city reversed the decision and abandoned the list.

• The changing of numerous names (of lakes, streams, bluffs and valleys) has proven challenging for various states. Oregon in 2001 ordered the elimination of the term "squaw," which had been used historically for labeling geographic locations but now deemed offensive by some American Indians (the term now considered politically correct instead of Native Americans). In an agitated reaction to a state decision in the mid-1990s, Minnesota's Lake County formally resolved to change the name of Squaw Lake and Squaw Bay to "Politically Correct" Lake and "Politically Correct" Bay. Eventually, all "squaw" terms were changed throughout the state. In Maine, frustration brought one county to change "squaw" names to "moose" across the board.

• Two graduates brought Stanford University notoriety through their well-publicized book, *The Diversity Myth*, a scathing review of the "multicultural" curriculum they were forced to take.

by Douglas Tarpley and Tamara Welter
Biola University

• James Finn Garner's popular *Politically Correct Bedtime Stories* spoofed serious liberal and conservative efforts to protest and censor classic literature, films and other works of art.

• In 2007 after much public and internal debate, MSNBC and CBS canceled Don Imus' syndicated morning talk show after his derogatory remarks about members of the Rutgers University women's basketball team. Critics called the cancellation an example of political correctness holding sway over the media.

The term *political correctness* has rallied support and dissent from both sides of the aisle. Events in the wake of the 9/11 terrorist attacks kindled new debate as attention to the Muslim community increased. A 2009 national Rasmussen Reports survey reported that 63% of voters said that "political correctness prevented" necessary response by the U.S. military to warning signs in the case of Maj. Nidal Malik Hasan (a Muslim U.S. military psychologist who turned radical) which could have possibly prevented his massacre of thirteen people and wounding of many others at the military base at Fort Hood, Texas. Political cartoons of Muhammad from artists in Europe as well as the United States fueled attacks from some Muslims around the world. Participation as well as outrage ensued over cartoonist Molly Norris' creation of an "Everybody Draw Muhammad Day," her effort to speak against censorship (specifically that of Comedy Central's censoring of a *South Park* episode with satirical representations of Muhammad after the creators received death threats). With FBI encouragement after threats to her life, Norris went into hiding.

Political correctness and political incorrectness are particularly provocative concepts as they relate to the mass media, especially news organizations. Critics say that the news media popularized the terms but failed to define them adequately for audiences. Some also accuse the media of being politically correct or incorrect as well through their role as agenda-setters. Still other observers say the media reflect ways of thinking and forms of behavior that have permeated the American culture in recent years or may have existed long before these popular terms emerged. Certainly signs of political correctness and political incorrectness can be found throughout newspaper, magazine, television, film and other media, as advertisers, public relations specialists, journalists, creative writers and other communication professionals have attempted to adapt to an increasingly pluralistic society.

Origins of the Issue

Merriam-Webster's online dictionary defines political correctness as "conforming to a belief that language and practices which could offend political sensibilities (as in matters of sex or race) should be eliminated."

The meaning for the First Amendment has continued to be a source of debate in intellectual circles, specifically on college campuses in the U.S. Wrapped up in the hate speech issues university campuses were dealing with during the 1980s came controversies surrounding political correctness in the early 1990s. But it was the publication of related stories and books that took this debate from the college campus to the public sector, connecting it to other social and political issues. Admitting that the origins and meaning of political correctness are "muddled," D. Charles Whitney and Ellen Wartella trace the early development of the term in their article, "Media Coverage of the 'Political Correctness' Debate." They argue that the news media were greatly responsible for transforming what was a relatively innocuous 1980s debate limited primarily to university settings, between left-leaning proponents of multiculturalism, minority rights and women's rights and those defending conservative ideas and the basic value of free speech — into a widespread popular debate by the early 1990s.

The media framed the debate in three ways. First, they gave publicity and credence to a series of books produced by conservative authors who attacked conditions on college campuses and contemporary higher education as a whole. These include Allan Bloom's *The Closing of the American Mind*, Charles J. Sykes' *Prof. Scam: Professors and the Demise of Higher Education* and *The Hollow Men: Politics and Corruption in Higher Education*, Bruce Wilshire's *Professionalism, Purity and Alienation*, Page Smith's *Killing the Spirit: Higher Education in America*, David E. Purpel's *The Moral and Spiritual Crisis in Education*, Roger Kimball's *Tenured Radicals: How Politics Has Corrupted Our Higher Education* and, most of all, the highly popular *Illiberal Education* by Dinesh D'Souza. The media also dramatically increased the number of political correctness stories they carried, particularly in 1991 as the revised perspective of the issue became entrenched in the American culture. And finally, they treated specific revelations or apparent instances of politically correct thought or behavior as "crimes."

Although many critics considered efforts to impose political correctness on speech to be repressive, Tom Foster Digby in *The Humanist* article "PC and the Fear of Feminism" echoed the claims of some that the political influence of university radicals, on or off campus, was highly overestimated. In "Freedom of Expression, the University, and the Media" in *Journal of Communication*, Everette Dennis noted that political correctness was a term critics and journalists coined to reflect longstanding ideas about multiculturalism and minority rights that became threatening when they were manifested in the form of "new courses, theories of history and other considerations" by faculty members and their students who were basically recruited to add diversity to university communities. T. Kenneth Cribb agreed in "Dumb and Dumber," a *National Review* article, that it was politically correct thinking that inspired actions on college campuses, such as changing curricula, modifying reading lists, developing new speech codes and attempting to re-define acceptable behavior outside the classroom that drew the increasing public concern and media attention in the early 1990s.

Although there are still conflicting viewpoints about minority rights, academic freedom, free speech, the future of higher education and other college campus concerns, the term "political correctness" and resistance to what it is perceived to represent have spilled over from academia into every dimension of society since the early 1990s. What was a nebulous term to begin with is linked today to a variety of activities and given a number of meanings that have become widely embedded in everyday American cultural consciousness.

Now, political correctness is commonly perceived as a battle, says Greg Lukianoff in his 2010 article "P.C. Never Died," that was "fought and won in the 1990s." Roger Kimball observed the same in his 2003 article in *National Interest*, "Political Correctness, or the Perils of Benevolence." "[W]e are often assured," he said, "that political correctness — whether or not it posed a threat in the past — is no longer a menace. It has, the argument goes, either been defeated or simply faded away." Both of these writers, though, argue that political correctness (and its residual struggles) is still present in universities, the media and society as a whole. Political correctness and political incorrectness are commonly perceived today as minority-rights issues. Minority or repressed groups have used politically correct terms such as "diversity" and "multiculturalism" as a rallying cry. Although many people support such traditional civil rights concepts as equal opportunity and affirmative action, negative reaction to political correctness has been considerable when it has been linked to extreme efforts to demand reparations for past oppression or subjugation or revision of facts in favor of egalitarian values and goals.

Political correctness in this sense relates to "radical egalitarianism," a perspective that in its extreme demands that every cultural subgroup, no matter how small, or even every individual, no matter how bizarre, has the right to be heard and demand equality in all areas of life. Political correctness has been associated, confused and equated with a host of popular terms such as "multiculturalism," "diversity" and "pluralism." These three words are overlapping terms that represent ideals and goals. Within the mass media industries, "diversity" has been used to reflect the need to encourage or even demand through Federal Communications Commission rulings and other means that minority groups and political viewpoints be heard through the limited communication channels that exist. More recent struggles surround the intent of media organizations to accommodate such considerations in recruiting, training and maintaining a work force that represents all minority groups and women and of depicting them fairly and carefully in media content.

Many define political correctness and political incorrectness in a much larger sense. In his article "Being Politically Correct in a Politically Incorrect World," Lawrence Grossberg suggests that the terms reflect a "culture war," basically a product of ongoing tensions between the worldviews, life-styles and agendas of liberals and conservatives. In *Politically Incorrect*, Ralph Reed views the issue as essentially a conflict between those who "no longer believe that religion can make a legitimate and rational contribution to civic discourse" and those who believe it is foolish to separate religion and politics. In this climate, politically correct and politically incorrect have become both derogatory rhetorical labels for opponents and convenient means of virtuous self-identity. The terms have also been used by both liberals and conservatives to direct people toward "correct" and away from "incorrect" positions on particular, important public issues of the time such as abortion, euthanasia, capital punishment, animal rights, creationism/evolution and media bias.

Others view political correctness and political incorrectness in even broader terms. No longer are the ideas perceived as a matter of minority views or actions being forced upon others. Instead, political correctness has become attached to any group, institution, or movement that seeks to re-define the terms of a debate to favor their viewpoint. Being politically incorrect often means standing up against any effort to silence the views of others or failure to respect their rights. It is standing up with pride against governmental entities, dominant political parties, powerful corporations, pervasive media organizations and prominent political movements such as environmentalism or world government. It is resistance to authority of any kind.

The evolution of these terms and ideas has given them even more sweeping meaning. Political correctness often represents prevailing norms and fashions or efforts to impose them. Political incorrectness, by contrast, refers to any individual or collective effort to resist them. It is essentially non-conformity and taking pride in it. Furthermore, it is this manifestation of the concepts that now seems to be used most frequently. Historical figures or groups, for example, have been referred to as politically incorrect for being out of step with the norms of their time. Contemporary musical works have been judged politically correct or politically incorrect because they did or did not conform to the latest tastes, styles or techniques. Politicians have made generic use of "politically incorrect" to identify themselves and their constituents.

Perhaps most of all, political correctness and incorrectness have been perceived as a language issue that has affected every professional field and prompted discussion, debate and humor throughout the American culture. Political correctness has come to mean a rigorous effort to eliminate intimidating, outdated words and jargon from media content, books, religious works and other materials and from workplace, educational and other environments. The goal has been to replace them with sensitive, extremely tolerant, non-sexist, non-racist, non-ethnic, non-religious terms that will offend no one.

On the surface, political incorrectness has involved reaction, much of it in the form of ridicule, to what have been perceived to be excessive, picayune efforts to redeem the cultural vocabulary and eliminate distinctions within sexes, races and other cultural groups. Politically correct terms are continually being parodied, and many people are laughing at new terms created primarily for the sake of humor. Being politically correct itself has even been labeled "category challenged" and "logocentric." Beneath this particular form of resistance appears to reside an unwillingness to accept what one element of society is attempting to impose on another.

Old Issue with a New Label?

Some people have suggested that political correctness and political incorrectness are merely new terms representing old ideas and power struggles in American society. They are terms that are helping to crystallize thinking and behavior at a moment in history, but they and some of what they have come to represent will eventually fade away and be replaced by new terms and ideas. Chuck Green of the *Denver Post* contends that "political correctness is just a new label for what's been around forever." Many journalists shrug off concerns about political correctness in the newsroom, equating the political correctness criticisms with the old "liberal media bias" label. But those cases in the media continue to show the evident consciousness of the mere term "politically correct."

One of the underlying assumptions of journalists who regard political correctness as a "no-issue" is that news media professionals are not personally affected by the social and political pressures of political correctness. Others suggest, however, that this assumption begs the question of news objectivity. If our postmodern society and intellectual climate have accepted the idea that objectivity is simply one person's or one group's socially constructed subjective perceptions of certain phenomena, then the journalist who works within that postmodern culture cannot argue that he or she is unaffected by the preeminent egalitarian value system underlying the construct of multiculturalism so closely associated with political correctness.

In his 2003 article "Political Correctness Or, the perils of benevolence," Roger Kimball wrote that that by "refusing to speak the truth," those promoting PC feel they "can change the truth." He told of the BBCs requirement for employees to use the term "partner" as opposed to "husband" or "wife" in order to keep from favoring one sexual orientation to another. He explained that major newspapers refuse to run advertising that mentions "views" because the word is unfair to the blind, along with other terms along the same lines. He also told about the removal of a student newspaper editor because he had "insufficient coverage" of minority happenings on campus. Gary North, freelance writer and co-editor of a Knight-Ridder newspaper, agrees that political correctness operates in the newsroom but states that it is nothing new, only much more "in the open." He argues that journalists should be aware of their own political bias when producing news. The late Robert Novak suggested that the influence of political correctness on journalists is difficult to perceive and control because journalists are elitist in nature. Innocent elitism or simple arrogance are two additional reasons why journalists may dismiss the influence of political correctness on the news.

Yet the value of the openness that has come as a result of the popularizing of the discussion in society has brought about change in the newsroom and even in the reporting process. Sensitivity to terms that might be offensive can reduce complacency towards otherwise abusive and condescending language. This allows the conversation to move to another level. A 1999 study by the "International Women's Media Foundation" (IWMF) in Washington, D.C. addressed issues of diversity in the workplace, relating those issues specifically to black women in the media. The report says, "There is a large disparity in how women of color and managers see the newsroom environment. The vast majority of managers — 82% — say that management respects cultural differences in the newsroom, but only 32% of the women journalist respondents agree. Likewise, 77% of the managers believe that co-workers respect cultural differences, but just 40% of the women consider that to be the case."

Resistance over time wanes as the awareness in language becomes more commonplace. In Philadelphia, a white news anchor was dismissed because he used the derogatory "N-word" in internal discussions during a budget meeting. In 2011 he sued the station, portraying himself as a victim of "political correctness run amok." The defendants said they are employers who responded to an employee who uttered repeatedly "the most noxious racial epithet in the contemporary American lexicon," resulting in difficulties in the workplace.

PC Struggles in the Newsroom

Although some critics say political correctness is an inflated or rhetorical issue, most newsrooms already have incorporated politically correct decisions concerning personnel as well as content.

Regarding the dismissal of NPR analyst Juan Williams in 2010, journalists filled the blogosphere with disagreements over his right to speak his opinion.

Williams had made comments in an interview on Fox News that he felt uncomfortable when he saw Muslim people dressed in cultural attire at the airport. "Even though I disagree with much of what Mr. Williams says," said H. Dean McSpadden in his October 28 entry in the Delaware Online blog post, "political correctness poses threat to the entire nation. I'll defend his right to say it with my last breath." On the other hand, Joshua Rosen, opinions editor of *The Miscellany News*, says that after he read Williams' comments that were made on Fox News, "the decision made by NPR seems quite reasonable." And Greg Sargent in his blog "The Plum Line" on TheWashingtonPost.com, said, "Put me down as someone who wasn't comfortable with Williams' firing over this. When the news broke I saw no reason why he shouldn't have had a chance to clarify. But now he has, and he's failed to acknowledge what was problematic about his initial remarks." Mark Tapscott. editorial page editor at washingtonexaminer.com, said in a commentary titled "Political Correctness runs amok at NPR," on October 21, 2010, "Williams' firing may be the most blatant illustration yet of the utter hypocrisy among too many journalists who claim to stand for freedom of expression and the press, yet lack the cojones to stand up for it when it is under attack."

William McGowan, senior fellow at the Manhattan Institute, who has written for the *New York Times*, *Wall Street Journal* and other national publications, said in his 2002 book *Coloring the News: How Political Correctness Has Corrupted American Journalism*, that newsrooms in the early 1990s began crusades to diversify their staffs and the news coverage those staffs produced.

Mirroring society as a whole, the backdrop for debate among journalists is the apparent "culture war" between liberals and conservatives. Individual journalists and news organizations representing both sides have viewed each other as political correctness culprits for what they perceive to be an erosion of traditional journalistic standards. Claiming that only two conservatives exist among about 500 otherwise liberal, elitist reporters and editors who are based in Washington, D.C., conservative journalist Robert Novak, in a *USA Today* article titled "Political Correctness," charged that American journalism now prints "all the news that's 'politically correct' to print." On the other hand, Dorothy Giobbe in an *Editor & Publisher* article "Political Correctness," quotes one editor as saying, "Political correctness is a label foisted on dissident voices by those who want to maintain the mainstream views in media and education."

Journalists have also debated, to some extent, the nature, merits and difficulties of political correctness within the context of minority rights issues, although the term and ideas behind it are often lost under the banner of diversity and, to a lesser degree, multiculturalism. It is clear that many in the news industry have become advocates for educating, hiring, training, promoting and effectively utilizing African Americans, Hispanics, Asian Americans, American Indians, gays, other minority groups and women. They have also challenged peers and students of journalism to produce news content that is devoid of offensive language and stereotypes. Moreover, news events and issues involving any of these groups should be reported more thoroughly and fairly, they say.

The idea of diversity in journalism has been prompted by current realities in the news business: declining readership and the threatened demise of daily newspapers; fragmentation of audiences spurred by the expansion of cable television, movie rentals, online television shows, movies and news, along with other media alternatives; shrinking viewership of major television networks; and other changes. Tailoring new or existing media to particular minority markets is viewed as an opportunity for growth. In their *Journalism Monograph* "Objectivity Revisited: A Special Model of Political Ideology and Mass Communication," Ekaterina Ognianova and James W. Endersby argue that the convention of news objectivity itself is shaped more by mass media economics than political, cultural, technological and philosophical influences. Appearing neutral and inoffensive is the best way to attract big audiences.

Like those in other professions and parts of society, many journalists perceive diversity as an ideal that goes well beyond news media economics and whose fulfillment is long overdue. Biased coverage and distorted, stereotypical depictions of women and particular racial and ethnic groups have been documented by many scholarly studies through the years. The Society of Professional Journalists several years ago revised the organization's Code of Ethics to include the statements: "Avoid stereotypes in covering issues of race, gender, age, religion, ethnicity, geography, sexual orientation and social status" and "Strive to give voice to all segments of society in public discourse."

As in other contexts, however, diversity has generated debate when it has been perceived as a matter of certain cultures forcing their ideas, values and agendas into the newsroom and news content. Politically correct diversity in this sense has been opposed on a number of grounds. First, it is insensitive to traditional news standards and those who have pursued them. It is advocacy disguised as "objectivity." Moreover, it is an attempt to promote the goals and ideals of special interest groups at the expense of striving for accuracy, facts and a variety of sources and viewpoints. In addition, it demands extreme changes in hiring policies that threaten quality, stability and well established, successful newsroom norms, policies and practices. Its use is also opposed by some because they believe it imposes confusing, stringent, or even ridiculous uses of language in the reporting and editing process. In addition, it is charged, to demand that the only morally and socially acceptable perspective is tolerance for all races, genders, ideologies, cultures and alternative lifestyles tramples on the personal beliefs, values and freedoms of those who disagree. Finally, it is opposed by some who believe that treating all groups and viewpoints as equally newsworthy is wrong in both principle and practicality.

Many practitioners suggest that news organizations need to take advantage of diversity by utilizing the unique perspectives and understandings that minority journalists bring to the newsroom. Others, such as Gary North, in an *Editor & Publisher* article, "Being politically correct in the newsroom," have posed compelling questions: At what point should a member of the newsroom become an advocate for his or her minority? At what point should an editor in authority defer to that minority member? And at what point do several minority newsroom members become a pressure group like any other, advocating the group's preferred language or outlook be published or broadcast?

The most vociferous critics of current journalism practices contend that failure to answer these and other political correctness questions has caused many of today's news organizations to mimic politicians who are afraid to offend special interest groups and continually succumb to the pressures imposed by such groups both inside and outside the newsroom. Editorializing is no longer confined to the editorial page or the commentary segment of a newscast. Added to the debate are questions about how far minority group representation should extend in the newsroom and news content.

Journalists concerned about political correctness also view the issue in terms of freedom of speech. For example, in the *Editor & Publisher* article "'Homojournalist' loses his job," Allan Wolper reviews the freedom of expression debate surrounding the firing of a Canadian college journalism professor who is a self-described "gay prostitute" and defender of pedophilia. Some news media professionals wonder what the limits of free speech are in a culture that increasingly condones views and behaviors that were once socially unacceptable — and still are in the case of pedophilia — in the name of political correctness.

The political correctness dialogue among journalists who contend it is a growing problem has also been crystallized in the matter of language. Numerous articles written by journalists for other journalists deal with difficulties and offer advice about choosing inoffensive, non-stereotypical labels and terms when reporting on women, ethnic minorities and other groups. The AP Stylebook and other news organization stylebooks have undergone revisions to accommodate such concerns, but there is as yet no unanimity about a politically correct style.

Journalists struggling with political correctness issues have generally depended on anecdotal rather than statistical evidence to support their contentions. Those pushing for "diversity," for example, regularly update and report conflicting evidence about minority hiring and refer to occasional studies dealing with treatment of women and others in news content.

There are a number of current, widely debated news media trends and

issues that would appear to make those within the field susceptible to both the most innocuous and devious forms of political correctness. They include the following:

- The increasing development and influence of organized special interest groups within the field of journalism, such as the National Lesbian & Gay Journalists Association, Asian American Journalists Association, National Association of Hispanic Journalists, Native American Journalists Association and National Association of Black Journalists.
- Well-documented evidence that news organizations are overly dependent on a narrow range of news sources, as well as "official" news sources, news releases and other materials provided by image-conscious organizations and special interest groups.
- The growing use of diversity consultants, training, workshops, committees within news organizations, leading to a greater understanding, but also greater demand that the causes of particular groups be forwarded.

Political Correctness as Advocacy Journalism

Other journalists, critics and scholars who perceive strong pressures of political correctness at work within the journalism field regard this trend as a reflection of a move toward a press system built on advocacy. In "Political Correctness Has No Place in the Newsroom" from *USA Today*, Robert Novak declared, "A free press is one of the foundations of a free society. Yet, Americans increasingly distrust and resent the media. A major reason is that many journalists have crossed the line from reporting to advocacy." In his *National Review* article, "PC Comes to the Newsroom," Daniel Seligman points to examples of a number of large-market, reputable newspapers that seem to "reflect increased fears in editor's offices that something might be published that would offend various movements represented in the newsroom." In "The Other Side of the Rainbow," a *Columbia Journalism Review* piece, William McGowan bemoans the departure of the *New York Times* from its "vaunted tradition of frank, fearless, and forthright exposition of the news." While it "may not be the Pravda of p.c.," he says, "it is certainly something less than a model of detached neutrality." Joseph Epstein, in a *Commentary* article, "The Degradation of The New York Times," agrees, noting that "the only news that stays news" in the publication are the obituaries.

Proponents of advocacy are not upset with these observations, conditions and trends. They argue that a media system comprising many alternative voices best fits an increasingly pluralistic society that spawns a seemingly endless variety of special interest groups and causes. Opportunities for the needs and viewpoints of diverse groups to be expressed have increased because of the fragmentation of mass media in recent years, they contend. A press system built on the idea of advocacy is compatible with this trend. In addition, supporters of an advocacy press note that the whole notion of objective journalism has always been misleading, since the predisposition of reporters, editors and other news media personnel and many other "gatekeeping" and "agenda setting" influences shape and bias news content.

This response to the tension exerted by these external and internal pressures on news journalists is to see them as an expression of the postmodern fragmentation prevalent in modern American culture. Specifically, journalists in this camp embrace these tensions as a reflection of the fragmentation of American culture, as a positive step away from traditional objective American journalism and a positive step toward an advocacy paradigm. In "PC And The Press" in *Change*, Huntly Collins concludes that this advocacy has "forced news organizations to confront their own racism and sexism," even though the journalistic attention the political correctness movement has been given is somewhat exaggerated. And in "Political Correctness In The Newsroom" from *Editor & Publisher*, David Harpe, editor of the *Louisville Courier-Journal*, says that "U.S. newsrooms operate under the sway of a politically correct orthodoxy."

Some journalists declare that the freedom to advocate particular points of view should be the norm. In "Being politically correct in the newsroom," Gary North says, "I prefer an assertive ... editor and a publication or program with a point of view." He says this is preferable to a "wishy-washy, pandering product that tries to please everyone and ends up pleasing no one.... As to minority community members within a newsroom, I subscribe to a mild, collegial way of influencing: suggest, nudge, offer a well-stated opinion.... [j]ournalistic integrity means, above all, being true to yourself, be it a question of coverage or calling someone 'pro-choice' or 'pro-life' vs. 'pro-abortion' and 'anti-abortion,' or 'AIDS victim' vs. 'AIDS patient' vs. 'person with AIDS' or 'gay' and 'homosexual' or 'black' vs. 'African-American.'" Similarly, in "PC Comes To the Newsroom," Daniel Seligman represents the thinking of some journalists when he declares, "The mighty American media have begun moving down the politically correct road long trodden by the colleges, and are doing so for many of the same reasons." He concludes that content analyses of big stories show that political correctness is "solidly based in scores of newsrooms." He quotes a *New York Times* editor who said that "the single most important issue this newspaper faces is diversity." He adds that "[t]he more diverse staff will do a better job of reporting."

A number of journalists see a link between economic pressures and content as a justification for advocacy journalism. Because of declining readership and the threatened demise of daily newspapers, fragmentation of audiences, shrinking viewership of major television networks and other changes, many journalists see the need to tailor new or existing media to selective minority markets as a means of survival and even growth. In our "hypersensitive society," John Leo argues in his 1994 article "Our Hypersensitive Society" in *U.S. News & World Report* that in response to this economic need for success in the marketplace, journalists even resort to a sensationalism, capitalizing on the public's "victim culture" mentality. He notes, for example, that stories about politically correct issues of gender and race are often displayed with sensational headlines that the story details may not even support. "This negative twist on news is really quite positive" for the circulation of newspapers by generating fear in the audience, he explains. He adds that it also enhances the continuation of influence by advocates and "is fairly common in reports on women's progress." Columnist William Raspberry, Leo notes, dealt with this "mentality quite shrewdly ... referring to 'feminist leaders' who find it impossible to acknowledge serious progress toward gender fairness — not because there has been progress, but because their power derives from their ability to keep portraying women as victims." Likewise, in "The Degradation of The New York Times," Joseph Epstein quotes a managing editor of the *New York Times* as saying, "we have to grab young readers by the lapels because they are less interested in reading."

Journalists and scholars following the PC debate often frame the discussion within the larger context of society's contemporary postmodernism. As many scholars explain, the United States is segmenting into antagonistic groups. A "tribalism" is splitting the culture. Indeed, the term "culture wars" is part of the popular culture's vocabulary, reflecting conflict among groups regarding such moral issues as abortion, euthanasia, cultural diversity and education. In fact, the traditional values of Western civilization are being questioned, deconstructed. A number of polls indicate that the majority of Americans no longer believe that such a thing as absolute truth exists. They reject modernism because of its belief in an absolute, discoverable truth. Postmodernists do not believe in this objective truth, preferring instead to embrace a relativism and a new aesthetic framework devoid of absolutes. Postmodernist thinking results in the splintering of our culture into various subcultures based on ethnicity, sexuality and social relationships, ultimately calling for a new social order.

This worldview has profound implications for the journalist, whose social function is four-fold: (1) to inform the public of events and issues; (2) to interpret and analyze the meaning of those events in a way to bring some sense of their meaning to the public; (3) to entertain the audience; and (4) to socialize or pass along values of the culture to new members of the community or to subsequent generations. As many scholars have explained, the mass media do not exist in a vacuum, but function as part of a social system. Journalism is no exception.

As Michael Burgoon and William Bailey declare in "PC at Last! PC at Last!

Thank God Almighty, We are PC at Last!," political correctness "rejects the traditional, commonsense notion of an objective reality, and therefore rejects also the notion of external value-free criteria by which the truth or falsity of discourse can be judged. Instead, reality is socially constructed through language, and the dominant culture's ideology is imbued in that reality." And later he summarily declares, "We have bought from whole cloth the notion that we can rename a problem out of existence." For example, in "A session on political correctness," David Astor observes that many journalists are concerned that "they are getting increased pressure from angry readers and worried editors over the content" of their work. The reason? Readers are just more sensitive now than in years past. He quotes one panelist who said, "There is more division in the country, and a higher sensitivity level. Groups are splitting farther and farther apart on issues." Another panel member observed that "many Americans strongly identify themselves as Christians, gays, blacks, or as part of some other group and want that group to be perceived favorably in the media." Hence, the pressure on the journalist mirrors what is happening in American society. But according to William McGowan in his 2002 book, *Coloring the News*, news organizations with the greatest commitment to diversity have begun to have liberal values almost as a requirement for employment. And then when reporters or editors who don't fit that liberal worldview do get hired, McGowan says, they "find that their perspectives and experience aren't always valued, particularly those with strong religious or moral beliefs. In fact, many put considerable effort into keeping their opinions and beliefs hidden, much like homosexuals did in decades past."

Documentation exists to indicate that a host of daily newspapers have introduced hiring programs explicitly identified as "quotas" to achieve diversity in the belief that the new personnel will change the nature of news content and its form and thus appeal more to readers and viewers.

Other journalists, however, view this advocacy in the newsroom with concern, even fear — because of the potential impact on words and behavior. They object to what they see as a deliberate effort by special interest groups — within and outside of the newsroom — to distort, manipulate and willfully intimidate journalists. For example, in "Political Correctness Attacks Black Right Wing," Stephen Goode charges that although the polls show that only about a third of blacks claim to be liberals, a third moderate and a third conservative, "blacks in the media come from the same liberal one-third and editors turn to that segment for quotes." He adds that they "intimidate white editors and corporate leaders and they get away with it." And, in "Political Correctness: Speech Control or Thought Control?" Gerald Kreyche says, "Political correctness is not so much about words, as it is about action and conduct, for words lead from ideas into real life." And then he recalls several anecdotes through which newspapers and mag-

azines influenced a number of events, including even a Smithsonian Institution's exhibit that was ultimately "pared." The real tragedy, he declares, is that political correctness "may be paved with good intentions, but so is the road to Hades. It not only hides truth, but denies it. PC insinuates untruth and sacrifices truth for compromise." He is afraid that the "backers of political correctness, also known as the 'word police,' would like to graduate to 'thought police.' Those who didn't conform would undergo re-education, as do many faculty members accused of insensitivity in the classroom."

Others agree. In "Political Correctness: Journalists attempt to define what it means today," Dorothy Giobbe quotes Margaret O'Brien Steinfels, editor of the *Commonwealth*, as saying that "unprofessional" PC is "shaping, deforming the news." And in "A session on political correctness" in *Editor & Publisher*, David Astor quotes a journalist who charges that a liberal agenda manipulates the content of news. "[T]he media target some people but not others," the journalist said. "The media have no problem talking about the 'Bubba vote' in the South but they don't go to New York and talk about the 'Jose vote' or the 'Vinnie vote.'"

Other journalists suggest that this advocacy is served by withholding coverage of stories or failing to tell "the whole story." In his *National Review* article "PC Comes to the Newsroom," Daniel Seligman fears that journalists, in an effort to accommodate concerns of special-interest groups, don't always tell "the story." A growing number of editors of newspapers with large staffs, he believes, are afraid of offending groups on their staffs that have their own agendas.

Assessment

In his book *Coloring the News*, McGowan argued that "news organizations have always played a crucial role in our democratic political culture, raising important questions and supplying factual information in order that policymakers and the public at large can make sound choices about the kind of society we want to live in. This function is doubly important today as we proceed through a crossroads moment of profound ethnic, racial and cultural change. The country has never been more in need of clear, candid discussion and debate—a service that only a frank, free and forthright press can provide." Resolving issues related to political correctness can be a complicated task, depending on the basic views to which the audience and members of the journalistic community adhere. If political correctness is perceived as merely a rhetorical issue or a label attached to news profession problems that have existed for a long time, then it is essentially a non-issue and the term will eventually fade away — even as the recurring issues continue to be debated within and outside of the professional community. However, there seems to be considerable reason to believe that the accelerating, bold, passionate efforts of special interest groups and causes, the product of an increasingly pluralistic society, are exerting new pressures and are changing the thinking and behavior within many newsrooms. News professionals who dismiss political correctness as an issue have underestimated its complexity and impact.

Journalists and news organizations who view PC as a reflection of and desired step toward a media system that permits greater advocacy and thus better meshes with changing cultural conditions may find, like the New Journalists of the 1960s and 1970s, that mainstream journalism may ultimately continue to embrace traditional — if modified — professional conventions of form, content and practice. Only time will tell whether or not traditional journalism will lose out to a new paradigm of "partisan" journalism. Simply, this perspective also fails to deal with the apparent fact that strong tensions between journalists who intentionally or unintentionally act as advocates for particular groups or causes and those who are committed to traditional standards of news objectivity do exist as they have historically. At the least, individual journalists and news organizations need to openly debate and determine what they want to be in this respect. If the decision is to be advocates of particular groups, causes, points of view, or agendas, they should clearly state to audiences that this is the personal or organizational mission and editorial philosophy that will shape and reflect all news content rather than misleading viewers, listeners, or readers into thinking standards of objectivity are being pursued and met.

For journalists and news organizations conscious of, concerned about, or familiar with conflicts regarding political correctness and political incorrectness in the newsroom, serious effort needs to be made to find balance in a number of contexts. For example, a balance could be struck between upholding traditional standards of news objectivity and responding to the legitimate cries of minority cultural groups. In addition, effort could be made to develop readers or audiences in a diversifying culture and an extremely competitive media environment.

A number of steps can be taken. Media practitioners need to gain a better understanding of political correctness and political incorrectness and their many underlying ideas and issues. And they need to cover political correctness stories and the "culture war" with more balanced and indepth analysis, encouraging more substantive dialogue about the nature and implications of the issue. In addition, they need to research systematically in order to discover the extent and many specific ways in which this issue has influenced editorial decision-making, reporting practices, news values, stylebooks, personnel matters, marketing strategies, internal communication, the effects of news content on audiences and other concerns of news organizations. Moreover, they need to pursue diversity in news organizations through representatives of various groups and views. In addition, they could re-focus on the basics of good reporting by seeking facts, a fair representation of views on an event or issue and other time-tested news values. They could also avoid being either politically correct or politically incorrect by conscientiously resisting those conditions that seem to make news organizations and individual journalists susceptible to these influences. Finally, they could teach media literacy to audiences or sponsor efforts to do so in order to show them how to recognize political correctness in news content and why news objectivity is an ideal that is never fully achieved.

Whether they attach political correctness or political incorrectness to their work or not, news organizations and individual journalists practice their profession today in an atmosphere where these terms and their challenges are a prominent part of media cultures and the larger cultures in which they reside. The terms seem to beg for further debate, dialogue, questions, research, resolutions and actions.

Points of View

Books

Bledsoe, Jerry. *Death by Journalism? One Teacher's Fateful Encounter with Political Correctness.* Asheboro, N.C.: Down Home Press, 2002. The author, a veteran journalist, investigated a newspaper's coverage and subsequent national attention to a professor and course on the civil war and slavery. Behind the controversy was "a bigger, more important story about free speech, academic freedom, political correctness, racial politics, and journalistic ethics and responsibility."

D'Souza, Dinesh. *Illiberal Education: The Politics of Race and Sex on Campus.* New York: Free Press, 1991. Many suggest that this book sparked media interest in the political correctness issue and led to its popularization.

Kimball, Roger. *Tenured Radicals: How Politics Has Corrupted Our Higher Education.* New York: Harper & Row, 1990. Kimball's was one of several books critical of American higher education that prompted the initial political correctness debate.

Lea, John. *Political Correctness and Higher Education: British and American Perspectives.* New York: Routledge, 2009. Writing from a British perspective on U.S. political correctness (and the influence it has had in Britain), the author examines what the term invokes. He gives British readers a picture concerning "the fuss" that America has made over the idea.

Levine, Lawrence W. *The Opening of the American Mind.* Boston: Beacon Press, 1996. Political correctness is nothing extraordinary, but rather a reflection of old patterns of conflict among groups and an inevitable result of changing demographics in a new era of multiculturalism.

McGowan, William. *Coloring the News: How Political Correctness Has Corrupted American Journalism*. San Francisco: Encounter Books, 2002. News organizations' striving for diversity influences newsrooms as well as the news gathering and disseminating process.

Reed, Ralph. *Politically Incorrect*. Dallas: Word Publishing, 1994. The political correctness issue is part of a larger culture war between liberals and conservatives, particularly religious conservatives.

Williams, Juan. *Muzzled: the Assault on Honest Debate*. New York: Crown Publishers, 2011. PC has stifled debate in America, from Congress to the media. (Williams was fired by NPR after he made comments about Muslim dress as a guest on Fox News).

Articles

Bowman, James. "Unhappy is the land." *New Criterion* 28:6 (February 2010): 57-61. Political correctness has had "deleterious effects ... on public policy, and some media outlets practice a "politically correct form of journalism.... [C]utting off debate is precisely the aim of the politically correct in seeking wherever possible to moralize political matters."

Chong, Dennis. "Free Speech and Multiculturalism In and Out of the Academy." *Political Psychology* 27:1 (2006): 29-54. Chong explores how free speech norms — as they changed — impacted political tolerance.

Collins, Huntly. "PC and the Press." *Change* (January/February, 1992): 12-16. Political correctness is an overrated issue made popular by news media and journalists who misunderstood or distorted the issue and events in the context of higher education.

Epstein, Joseph. "The Degradation of the 'New York Times.'" *Commentary* (May 1994): 34-9. The *New York Times* has succumbed to the pressures of political correctness.

Fish, Stanley. "Boutique Multiculturalism, or Why Liberals Are Incapable of Thinking about Hate Speech." *Critical Inquiry* 23 (1997): 378-95. The author's discussion of multiculturalism and tolerance helps define the political correctness issue.

Kimball, Roger. "Political Correctness — Or, the perils of benevolence." *National Interest* 74 (2003): 158-65. The managing editor for *The New Criterion* connects what he sees as political correctness struggles throughout history and around the world.

Lukianoff, Greg. "P.C. Never Died." *Reason* 41:9 (2010): 26-31. Considering recent cases of political correctness on college campuses, Lukianoff says speech codes and episodes involving student media demonstrate that PC is very much alive on campuses.

Whitney, Charles, and Ellen Wartella. "Media Coverage of the 'Political Correctness' Debate." *Journal of Communication* 42 (1992): 87-92. Political correctness originated as a media-created issue.

13 Gender Stereotypes in Sports Media

What comes to mind when you think about a male figure skater? How should he look, act or dress? Picture him in your mind. Now, jot down a few adjectives you would use to describe this athlete — and be honest. Do the same thing for a female pro golfer. What does she look like? How does she dress? How does she act? If you examine your adjectives, you may find a list of stereotypes. You're not alone. The truth is, most of us expect athletes in certain sports to look, act and dress a certain way. Athletes frequently are stereotyped by their gender, race, age, athletic ability and the type of sport they play.

A vast amount of research illustrates that these same stereotypes are prevalent in sports media coverage. Male athletes are portrayed differently from female athletes, even when they compete in the same sport. Also, athletes who compete in masculine sports (such as basketball and hockey) are portrayed differently in media coverage from athletes who compete in feminine sports (such as gymnastics and figure skating). Scholars agree that gender stereotypes exist in sports media and society. From media coverage of certain athletes or certain sports, researchers have culled a long list of stereotypes. The results suggest that gender stereotypes in sports media exist.

But scholars disagree on why those stereotypes exist. Some argue that the media's use of gender stereotypes infuses those same stereotypes into the minds and language of fans. Others argue that stereotypical media coverage reflects the thoughts of sports journalists, who are predominantly male. Therefore, the journalists themselves cause the stereotypical media coverage. A third group argues that the desires and expectations of society force media to use stereotyped language; society forces the media to market and portray sports using gender stereotypes to maximize profits.

So, who is responsible for gender stereotypes in sports coverage: media content, journalists or society?

by Amy Head Jones
University of West Alabama

Origins of the Issue

Historically, male athletes and officials have dominated the sports industry, as have "masculine" sports. According to the U.S. Department of Education, only 15% of collegiate athletes in 1972 were female. Statistics were similar in high school athletics as well, which was mirrored in funding provided to women's athletics at both levels. Partly in hopes of improving the gender equality of athletics in governmentally funded schools and universities, the department developed Title IX of the Educational Amendments of 1972. After nearly four decades, figures indicate an increase in participation of female collegiate athletes by more than 450% since Title IX was introduced. Title IX started arguments about gender stereotypes in sports media content. Nevertheless, because most sports journalists and commentators were male, men dominated decisions about how these emerging sports, athletes and coaches were covered.

As women's sports participation increased, so did the interest of women in society to view televised sporting events. In a 1995 article titled "Fanship and the Television Sports Viewing Experience" in *Sociology of Sport Journal*, Walter Gantz and Lawrence Wenner found that women were significantly more interested in participating in sports, watching sports and learning about sports in the post-Title IX era. In fact, no major differences regarding interest in sports existed between the sexes. Furthermore, in an article in *Gender Issues*, "The Athletic Director's Dilemma: $$$ and Women's Sports," Charles Kennedy stated that Title IX resulted in the addition of eighteen women's collegiate sports. He reported, however, that these advances created a financial hardship for most athletics departments, which rely on revenue generated from men's sports. One reason is that society does not support female athletes and sports as much as they do men's.

In the last few decades, rapid changes have been made in the sports industry to bring about gender equality. However, gender stereotypes were already formed and may take a long time to change. Sports media content, the values of sports journalists and stereotypes in society both seem to move at a slow pace in terms of gender equality.

Sports Media Content Influences Stereotypes

Media provide some of the means by which we view society. We rely to some extent upon the media to "show" us what the real world is like. The same is true for sports media. If we have never attended the Winter Olympic Games in person, how do we know what The Games are like? Most likely, we learned about them (and other sporting events) from media coverage. So if media coverage presents a certain view, will society have that same view about a sport, athlete or event? Most scholars say "yes." They argue that exposure to gender stereotypes in sports media coverage influences similar stereotypical views in the minds of media consumers. In other words, sports media content influences a variety of gender stereotypes in society.

Imagine the last time you tuned to ESPN, picked up *Sports Illustrated* or flipped through a media guide from your favorite team. Do you remember if you were following a men's team or a women's team? Were you more likely to see a male athlete or a female athlete? The history of sports tells us that sports are a man's domain, and this stereotype is reflected in media coverage. In the 2004 article "ESPN's SportsCenter and Coverage of Women's Athletics: 'It's a Boy's club'" in *Mass Communication & Society*, Terry Adams and Charles Tuggle analyzed the gender breakdown of sports coverage on ESPN's *SportsCenter*. They found that only 5% of the airtime was devoted to women's athletics, which they contend grossly under-represents the percentage of female sports participants. They further argue that the under-representation of female athletes in the media negatively influences society. They suggest that exposure to gender discrepancies in sports media coverage cause society to label women's sports as less important than men's sports. Therefore, as long as sports media coverage lacks gender equality, society will continue to believe that sports is "a boy's club."

Research comparing the amount of media coverage of male athletes and female athletes is common. This body of literature suggests that the under-representation of female athletes is a trend at all levels of media, including local, national and collegiate. Suzanne Huffman, Charles Tuggle and Dana Rosengard researched gender equality in collegiate media (collegiate newspapers and television broadcasts) in a 2004 article titled "How Campus Media Cover Sports: The Gender-Equity Issue, One Generation Later" in *Mass Communication & Society*. Despite efforts made in collegiate communities as a result of Title IX, they found that male athletes received the bulk of collegiate media coverage. Specifically, 73% of collegiate sports newspaper coverage and 82% of collegiate sports broadcast coverage focused on male athletes. The authors argued that the under-representation of female athletes in collegiate media was especially concerning. Public colleges and universities are required to offer equal opportunities to male and female athletes as result of Title IX. Therefore, news about women's athletics is not hard to come by on a college campus. It is equally concerning, the authors wrote, to identify the producers of collegiate media. The present generation of college students producing campus media are likely to choose media production as a career. Thus, those who distribute gender stereotypes through collegiate media eventually will go on to distribute them to society. By portraying gender stereotypes in sports to college students through student media, the authors argued, gender stereotypes are likely to gain foothold within this younger generation.

In "Media Coverage of the Female Athlete Before, During, and After Title IX: Sports Illustrated Revisited," a 1988 article in *The Journal of Sport Management,* Mary Jo Kane found that female athletes are more likely to receive sports media coverage when they participate in gender-appropriate sports. For example, female athletes who play tennis (which Kane identified as historically typed as feminine) receive more media coverage than female athletes who play softball (which Kane identified as historically typed as masculine). In her content analysis of more than 1,200 issues of *Sports Illustrated,* Kane analyzed a 16-year span of the magazine (eight years pre-Title IX and eight years post-Title IX). She found that female athletes were less likely to be shown in an athletic role than male athletes. Specifically, they were more often portrayed posing as models than standing in an action pose and wearing athletic gear or uniforms, whereas male athletes frequently were shown in an athletic position and wardrobe. Kane also found that female athletes were rarely pictured on *Sports Illustrated* covers. The cover shot was reserved for "token" athletes or the most valuable player of the times. Since the media coverage indicated that male athletes were mostly portrayed as the "token," Kane argued, society would presume that male athletes were more valuable than female athletes.

Some researchers argue that stereotyped sports coverage not only shows favoritism to male athletes and masculine sports but also suggests that female athletes are limited physically and athletically. In a 2002 article, "An Imperceptible Difference: Visual and Textual Constructions of Femininity in Sports Illustrated and Sports Illustrated for Women," in *Mass Communication & Society,* Janet Fink and Linda Kinsicki argued that the image of the female athlete in media coverage was limited. Female athletes featured in the media were often of the same race, age, athletic ability and body type. The media tended to avoid showing female athletes who were overly muscular or masculine. Society therefore is likely, they argued, to believe that male athletes are more muscular and athletic than female athletes. The results from this content analysis research of *Sports Illustrated* and *Sports Illustrated for Women* show that female athletes are often pictured in sexy poses and are shown with children or husbands to emphasize their femininity. Furthermore, female athletes are under-represented, are portrayed only in gender-appropriate sports and are frequently shown in a non-sports setting. Fink and Kinsicki concluded that these unobjectionable portrayals lead to stereotypes in society that a female athlete's femininity should supersede her athletic ability. In other words, following exposure to sports media content, individuals in society are likely to believe that a female athlete's sex appeal, appearance and sexual preference are more important than her sports performance.

Depicting female athletes in this manner may have unintended consequences. A content analysis by Michael Messner, Margaret Duncan and Faye Wachs suggests that media portrayals may cause society to discount the importance of female athletes all the more. Their 1996 article, "The Gender of Audience Building: Televised Coverage of Women's and Men's NCAA Basketball," in *Sociological Inquiry* involved a comparative analysis of the men's and women's Final Four basketball tournaments. They found that the men's event was produced (through camera angles, pre- and post-game shows, editing and amount of commentary) to appear as a historic, dramatic and "must watch" event, while the women's event was produced as "just another game." They argued that the difference in production techniques influences audiences to perceive the men's Final Four as more powerful, pleasurable and exciting than the women's.

In each of these studies, researchers have argued that the stereotypical media coverage of female athletes results in similar stereotypes in society. Other researchers have said, though, that all male athletes are not treated like kings in media coverage. The type of sport an athlete plays affects the portrayal he or she receives. In "Study Examines Stereotypes in Two National Newspapers," a 2008 article in *Newspaper Research Journal*, Edward Kian found that both male and female athletes received stereotypical media coverage. In this content analysis of men's and women's March Madness national newspaper coverage, he found that male athletes received more coverage than the female athletes. Female athletes got only one-fourth of the overall coverage of March Madness.

Upon further analysis, Kian also found stereotypical trends in text about both male and female athletes. Both sexes were described in terms of their personal lifestyles. Female basketball players were portrayed in roles as good mothers, wives, daughters and girlfriends, while male athletes were described as promiscuous "players." He contended that sports news with a personal focus is common for both male and female athletes. He argued, however, that athletes who participate in gender-inappropriate sports (male athletes who participate in feminine sports and female athletes who participate in masculine sports) are more likely to face stereotypical media coverage. He also argued that under-representation in media coverage affects some male athletes. The majority of media coverage is awarded to male athletes who participate in the "big three" masculine sports: football, baseball and basketball. Therefore, female athletes, or male athletes who do not participate in one of these three sports, are likely to be under-represented in media coverage. Exposure to sports media coverage that is stereotyped by athlete sex and type of sport, he argued, influences the same gender stereotypes in society. Therefore, gender stereotypes in sports media coverage likely cause those in society.

In summary, some researchers believe that stereotypical sports media coverage has a mirroring effect on society. They reason that society is likely to think less of male athletes who compete in gender-inappropriate sports and female athletes who compete in any sport. Researchers contend that the amount of media coverage exposure influences the audience's perception of value and importance. Furthermore, society will perceive female athletes who are depicted in feminine roles (as models, mothers and wives) as more feminine and less athletic. Likewise, male athletes who are depicted in masculine roles will be perceived as more athletic and muscular by society. Finally, the production techniques used to cover a game can influence the audience's perception of viewing pleasure. In each of these examples, researchers point the finger of blame at the sports media content for influencing gender stereotypes in society.

Media Content Reflects Journalists' Values

Editors, producers, photographers, writers, sideline reporters, directors and play-by-play commentators decide daily how the sports they cover are presented. Is it possible that gender stereotypes in sports result from sports journalists' biases? If journalists hold personal opinions about the roles of men and women in the sports world, is it possible that the stereotypes in sports media content reflect the opinions of sports journalists?

Some scholars believe they have found evidence of this behavior. They argue that sports media coverage reflects the beliefs and values of the sports journalists themselves. So are journalists making key decisions that influence sports media coverage? Learning more about sports journalists could potentially answer questions about why sports media coverage includes stereotypes.

Some researchers argue that gender stereotypes in sports media coverage result from the shortage of female sports reporters. In a 2003 study, "Using a Content Analysis to Examine the Gendering of Sports Newspaper Personnel and their Coverage," in the *Journal of Sport Management*, Paul Pedersen, Warren Whisenant and Ray Schneider found that, in the sports newspaper field, 91% of sports reporters, 79% of sports photographers, 100% of national newspaper editors and 91% of sports editors were male. They argued that men and women have differing opinions regarding sports, including favorite sport, perception of athletic skill, definition of athleticism and even perceptions about male and female athletes. Furthermore, they resoned that the lack of female sports journalists in the newspaper industry has led directly to the under-representation of women's athletics. Sports media, they contended, consist of images and sports that the journalists themselves want to see. Therefore, the values of these journalists are reflected in sports media coverage.

What do *female* sports journalists think about their future in the sports industry? They say that women are interested in the field but lack the opportunity to build a career. In "Female Sports Journalists: Are We There Yet? 'No!'" a 2005 article in *Newspaper Research Journal*, Marie Hardin and Stacie Shain conducted focus group discussions with female sports journalists to find out. They found that women working in the industry encountered numerous challenges, which led to the shortage of female sports journalists. Women faced gender-related salary inequities, and female sports journalists encountered a "glass-ceiling" effect when seeking promotions. No women were working in management in sports media. Female sports journalists felt extra pressure from media consumers to establish their credibility as sports experts. Hardin and Shain concluded that women are interested in pursuing careers in sports journalism but lack the opportunities to make long careers worthwhile.

Female sportscasters fulfill specific roles on television, especially when reporting about a masculine sport. In traditionally masculine sports, female reporters are limited to reporting news as sideline reporters or anchors and are rarely seen giving their opinions (as analysts or play-by-play announcers). Researchers argue that if society accepts only male sports reporters, then media coverage will be limited in scope. In Hardin and Shain's focus-group study, female sports reporters stated that many male journalists stereotype sports based on the sex of the athlete and type of sport. They thought that, in the minds of male reporters, sex appeal sells, athletes are under-valued and masculine sports are the big-ticket items. Hardin and Shain argued that since these same stereotypes exist in sports media coverage, then the coverage reflects the views of the sports journalists.

Sports journalists are mostly men. But do they cover sports differently than female sports journalists? John Vincent conducted research to find out whether sports media coverage differed based on the gender of the journalist. In his 2004 article in the *Sociology of Sport Journal*, "Game, Sex, and Match: The Construction of Gender in British Newspaper Coverage of the 2000 Wimbledon Championships," he found that a journalist's gender significantly influenced the portrayal of female athletes. Female athletes were under-represented in media coverage. Verbal and visual portrayals of female athletes focused more on sex appeal than athleticism. Vincent pointed to Anna Kournikova as a prime example. She had received countless endorsements and was frequently portrayed in media coverage of women's professional tennis. She was not the dominant athlete in the game (considering winning percentages), but she dominated media coverage because of her good looks and sexuality. Vincent argued that male sports journalists were significantly more likely to portray female athletes using cultural stereotypes and sexual innuendos. Therefore, a large number of male sports reporters tended to use stereotypes when depicting women in sports.

Jennifer Knight and Traci Giuliano contend that male sports journalists apply a "homophobic" attitude to sports media coverage as well. In a 2003 article titled "Blood, Sweat, and Jeers: The Impact of the Media's Heterosexist Portrayals on Perceptions of Male and Female Athletes" in the *Journal of Sport Behavior*, they highlighted the stigma of lesbianism in women's sports and the homophobic attitudes surrounding male athletes who compete in feminine sports. They suggested that because of commentary and media focus, athletes face scrutiny for sexual preference. An emphasis on orientation, Knight and Giuliano argued, creates a fear in society that women participating in sports or men participating in non-masculine sports will become gay. In particular, if a female athlete appears masculine or a male athlete appears feminine, society is likely to think they are gay. In this survey research, the authors found that the media audience more favorably perceived athletes who were portrayed as clearly heterosexual (athletes shown with a significant other of the opposite sex or with biological children). Male heterosexual athletes were also perceived as more masculine and athletic than those with unknown sexual preference. This research suggested that the gender of the athlete and type of sport can influence perceptions about an athlete's sexual preference. Knight and Giuliano said that sports journalists can influence these perceptions through commentary and the focus of stories. The journalists themselves determine the focus of a story, the specific commentary accompanying a video, the quotes selected for the article and other features. Therefore, they influence how media coverage perpetuates stereotypes.

Other researchers suggest that gender disparities can result from approaches to media production. In a chapter titled "Gender Warriors in Sport: Women and the Media" in the *Handbook of Sports and Media* (2006), Margaret Duncan reviewed research that suggests that the technical quality of the production of women's athletics differs from that of men's. Her focus was on coverage in countries in addition to the United States, and she found that female athletes were under-represented in the amount of coverage internationally. Female athletes received fewer slow-motion replays, fewer statistics in commentary, fewer camera angles to cover an athletic event, slower editing of an athletic event, fewer graphics and lower-quality sound. She concluded that women's sports media coverage revealed few improvements in quantity and quality over the four decades after Title IX. She argued that sports journalists themselves continued to emphasize gender stereotypes, which was reflected in media coverage. By constructing differences between male and female athletes, she concluded, journalists suggest to the audience that these differences indeed exist.

Society's Expectations Drive Media Content

If the ratings for sports media television programs were to drop suddenly, the producers and journalists likely would scramble to improve the content. To succeed, producers and editors need to know the needs and desires of their audiences. Thus, on the issue of gender stereotypes, the question becomes, "Does society — the audience for sports media — influence coverage?" And do athletes themselves emphasize gender stereotypes in an effort to receive favorable perceptions from the media audience? Some researchers suggest that gender stereotypes in society are driven by audience expectations. They argue that the sports media audience dictates coverage. After all, the target market for this business venture is the sports media audience. In terms of gender stereotypes in sports, the term "appropriately" applies to the actions, appearance, wardrobe, physical fitness level and behaviors of athletes. To put it simply, male athletes are expected to be masculine, and female athletes are expected to be feminine. But do these societal expectations drive media coverage?

Daniela Baroffio-Bota and Sara Banet-Weiser explored how the expectations of the media audience can influence decisions made in the sports industry. In *The Handbook of Sports and Media* (2006), they examined how the WNBA, as a league, fought to ensure society would embrace female, professional basketball players. In their chapter titled "Women, Team Sports, and the WNBA," they argued that fashion, personality, motherhood and sexuality helped to characterize WNBA players as feminine. The WNBA reached out to potential fans to create a feminine appearance to the league. The media audience was invited to vote on whether the athletes would wear dresses, tunics, skirts or the traditional shirts and shorts during games. The poll sought to determine whether a feminine wardrobe in the WNBA would allow the female athletes to be perceived more favorably. The strategy to promote WNBA athletes as "true women" was a decision that league executives made to increase revenue and media coverage. The authors thus argued that audience expectations drive revenue, which in turn drives league decisions and eventually media coverage.

Societal expectations of athletes, sports fans and the sports media audience have been found to influence athletes of all ages. Peter Crocker concluded that social influences accounted for decisions regarding sports participation and sports media consumption among adolescents. In his 2008 article "Exploring Self-Perceptions and Social Influences as Correlates of Adolescent Leisure-time Physical Activity" in the *Journal of Sport & Exercise Psychology*, he found that the parents and best friends of adolescents accounted for 49% of the sports decisions. Society influenced the decisions of young athletes on whether to participate in sports, which sports to participate in, which sports to show an interest in and which sports to follow in the mass media. Expectations influenced parents' and adolescents' sports decisions. In turn, these decisions influenced sports media consumption. Therefore, it is possible that societal expectations also influence sports media content.

Much sports media research exists to identify such expectations in society. Some scholars argue that the gender gap in sports media coverage reflects the sex of the sports media audience. Arguably, since a sport is a masculine domain, then the media audience is likely dominated by men. In "Men, Women, and Sports," a 1991 article in the *Journal of Broadcasting & Electronic Media*, Walter Gantz and Lawrence Wenner found that the sports media audience consisted of more men than women. In fact, they found that twice as many men were interested in sports than women. Finally, they found that many women who did consume sports media, did so to spend time with family.

The results from such research (conducted during a period spanning two decades) potentially explain why sports media content is under-representative of women's sports in society. The media coverage is not about the sports or the athletes. It is about targeting the appropriate audience. If the sports media audience consists of more men than women, then the media content should target the values and expectations of the predominantly male audience.

Since sports consumers are predominantly male, what do men want to see in coverage of female athletes? Is it sex? When men consume coverage of female athletes, sex sells. In "Sex Appeal Still Overpowers Sports Skill When it comes to the Marketing of Female Athletes," an article in the *New York Times* on August 9, 2000, Bernard Stamler argued that sex appeal is still the best marketing tool for women's sports. When marketing female athletes to a male-dominated sports media audience, he reasoned, athletic skill is not as important as a female athlete's appearance.

Numerous examples of popular female athletes with sex appeal exist. Professional tennis has Anna Kournikova, racing has Danika Patrick, and the LPGA has the "Beautiful Seven," to name a few. These female athletes have become household names for their beauty and bodies rather than their athletic ability. Even female sports journalists face pressure to look sexy. ESPN's Erin Andrews has won several unofficial titles as "America's Sexiest Sportscaster" by male sports viewers. Clearly, men expect and prefer for females in sports to look sexy and feminine. Therefore, some believe the marketing of women's sports revolves around the feminine image of female athletes.

Few women's sports require sexier clothing than women's beach volleyball. The athletes acrobatically dive around in pits of sand, wearing "barely there" bikinis. Researchers argue that sex is used to sell this sport to the media audience. In "Bump, Set, Spike: An Analysis of Commentary and Camera Angles of Women's Beach Volleyball during the 2004 Summer Olympics," a 2007 content analysis research article in *the Journal of Promotion Management*, Kimberly Bissell and Andrea Duke found that the commentary and camera angles used to televise the

2004 games sexualized the sport and its athletes. More than 20% of the camera shots were tight shots focused on the athlete's chests. Additionally, 17% of the shots were tight shots of the athlete's buttocks. In all, more than one-third of the shots focused on sexual body parts of the female athletes. Commentary also consisted of sexual themes.

This display of athlete sexuality was an attempt to promote the physical attractiveness of the athletes, said Bissell and Duke. They contended that "sex and sexuality were used to not only promote the athletes but to sell the sport to viewers around the world." Viewers expect to see feminine female athletes, and viewers are more concerned about the physical appearance of the athletes than their athletic skill. Therefore, the expectations of the audience are reflected in sports media coverage to market the sport and its athletes.

The female athletes themselves recognize expectations in society and feel pressured to fit the "proper" label of femininity. In a 2004 article in *Sex Roles*, "Living the Paradox: Female Athletes Negotiate Femininity and Muscularity," Vikki Krane and a number of colleagues found that sportswomen feel pulled in two directions. Results from this research involving a focus group of female collegiate athletes suggest that athletes feel pressured to prove their athletic ability for the sports culture but also pressured to prove their femininity to society. Lack of athleticism would reduce a female athlete's credibility, while lack of femininity would increase negative stereotypes about a female athlete (such as lesbianism). The athletes recognized that they are different from "normal women." They felt that they had to find the perfect balance between "athletic" and "feminine."

Female athletes regularly opt to pose in feminine positions for advertisements. Whether by personal choice or pressures to meet societal expectations, they frequently wear makeup and feminine clothing, display emotion and show off their spouses and children. They feel pressured to act feminine. These displays emphasize the femininity of a female athlete and appeal to the sports media audience.

Likewise, the sports media audience has similar expectations that coincide with society. Women are supposed to act and look feminine; men are supposed to act and look masculine. These expectations are reflected in sports media coverage to satisfy the audience. After all, the audience is the consumers who invest in the sports media industry. With this argument, the financial success of sports and the sports media depend upon the perceptions of society. Therefore, sports media content is driven by societal expectations.

Assessment

The issues surrounding gender stereotypes in sports media coverage are complicated. The body of literature indicates that stereotypes in sports exist, but why? Some argue that gender stereotypes in coverage affect the opinions of media consumers. Others suggest that sports journalists have the ability to alter media content and therefore potentially influence the stereotypical coverage of athletes. Finally, another group of researchers argues that society already possesses a set list of rules, which serve as expectations placed upon the actions and appearances of athletes. These expectations influence the sports media content.

This debate is similar to the one about the chicken and the egg. Which came first, the journalists who influence sports media content, the stereotypical media coverage that influences the perceptions of sports in society or the societal expectations placed on sports media producers that lead to stereotypical sports coverage? The answer lies in all three arguments, as the sports media, journalists and consumers appear to feed off one another.

Each argument has its strengths and weaknesses. First, the analysis of media content shows a clear picture of gender stereotypes in sports coverage. Researchers argue that exposure to stereotypes in media is linked to stereotypes in society. On the other hand, survey and focus group data suggest that the audience already possesses gender stereotypes. Both of these arguments have data to support them. Research, however, attempting to connect the dots between these arguments is hard to find. The problem with the research is that it only suggests that stereotypes in media content and stereotypes in society are somehow related.

Finally, a close look at journalists provides an understanding of who produces sports media content. Sports journalists are mostly male, and they have the ability to alter media content to reflect their own beliefs. Surveys or interviews of journalists, however, are needed to assess what the journalists actually believe and whether those beliefs influence media content.

Researchers and scholars typically point the blame at one of the three scenarios discussed in this chapter. They blame gender stereotypes on either sports media content, the sports journalists or the consumers of sports media. All, however, use circular reasoning.

One pressing argument needs greater attention. Researchers and media consumers should consider the responsibilities of each of the parties in creating the gender stereotypes that athletes face. While the media and journalists have a financial responsibility to satisfy consumers, they have an even greater responsibility to present an unbiased view to the media audience. This principle is the foundation of journalism. Intentional portrayals of gender stereotypes, from

camera angles focused on sexual body parts, to frequent feminine themes in commentary, to the disregard of certain sports in amount of coverage should not be tolerated. In giving the benefit of the doubt, the media and journalists perhaps have no intention of portraying sports in a stereotypical light. Time will tell if this is the case, as today's journalism students are becoming educated about this topic. This generation of students one day will decide which sports get covered and how athletes are portrayed.

Points of View

Books

Creedon, Pamela. *Women, Media and Sport: Challenging Gender Values.* Thousand Oaks, Calif.: SAGE Publications, 1994. This textbook links gender, sport and media theory to identify multiple gender stereotypes in media coverage.

Lenskyj, Helen. *Out on the Field: Gender, Sport and Sexualities.* Toronto, Canada: Women's Press, 2003. Stereotypical media portrayals of women in sports influence societal opinions.

Articles and Book Chapters

Adams, Terry, and Charles Tuggle. "ESPN's SportsCenter and Coverage of Women's Athletics: 'It's a Boy's club.'" *Mass Communication & Society* 7 (2004): 237-48. Gender inequality in sports media coverage leads to perceptions in society that sports is a "boys" club.

Bissell, Kimberly, and Andrea Duke. "Bump, Set, Spike: An Analysis of Commentary and Camera Angles of Women's Beach Volleyball during the 2004 Summer Olympics." *Journal of Promotion Management* 13 (2007): 35-53. Sex is used to sell televised coverage of beach volleyball, and the media audience guides these expectations.

Duncan, Margaret. "Gender Warriors in Sport: Women and the Media," chapter 14 in Arthur Raney and Jennings Bryant, eds. *Handbook of Sports and Media.* Hillsdale, N.J.: Lawrence Erlbaum Associates, 2006. Gender stereotypes in sports are caused by stereotypical media content.

Fink, Janet, and Linda Kinsicki. "An Imperceptible Difference: Visual and Textual Constructions of Femininity in *Sports Illustrated* and *Sports Illustrated for Women.*" *Mass Communication & Society* 5 (2002): 317-39. Stereotypical portrayals of female athletes cause the media audience to believe that a female athlete's femininity is more important than her athletic ability.

Gantz, Walter, and Lawrence Wenner. "Men, Women, and Sports." *Journal of Broadcasting and Electronic Media* 35 (1991): 233-48. Women consume more sports media than ever before, and the gender gap in sports media consumption is closing.

Kane, Mary Jo. "Media Coverage of the Female Athlete Before, During, and After Title IX: *Sports Illustrated* Revisited." *The Journal of Sport Management* 2 (1988): 87-99. Male athletes are portrayed in sports media coverage as more valuable than female athletes, which in turn leads to negative perceptions about female athletes in society.

Kennedy, Charles. "The Athletic Director's Dilemma: $$$ and Women's Sports." *Gender Issues* 24 (2007): 34-45. While gender equality in sports is important, men's sports generate all the revenue, indicating that society influences decisions in the sports industry.

Knight, Jennifer, and Traci Giuliano. "Blood, Sweat, and Jeers: The Impact of the Media's Heterosexist Portrayals on Perceptions of Male and Female Athletes." *Journal of Sport Behavior* 26 (2003): 272-84. Sports journalists can influence a story through commentary and focus and in turn can influence the audience's gender stereotypes.

Krane, Vikki, Prescilla Choi, Shannon Baird, Christine Aimar, and Kerrie Kauer. "Living the Paradox: Female Athletes Negotiate Femininity and Muscularity." *Sex Roles* 50 (2004): 315-29. Society pressures female athletes to fit societal norms and influences decisions made in the sports industry and in media coverage.

Messner, Michael, Margaret Duncan, and Faye Wachs. "The Gender of Audience Building: Televised Coverage of Women's and Men's NCAA Basketball." *Sociological Inquiry* 66 (1996): 422-39. Gender stereotypes in production techniques lead to similar gender stereotypes in society.

Pedersen, Paul, Warren Whisenant, and Ray Schneider. "Using a Content Analysis to Examine the Gendering of Sports Newspaper Personnel and their Coverage." *Journal of Sport Management* 17 (2003): 376-93. The majority of sports reporters are male, which leads to masculine decisions in media coverage.

Stamler, Bernard. "Sex Appeal Still Overpowers Sports Skill When It Comes to the Marketing of Female Athletes." *New York Times*, August 9, 2000, C-2. Society expects female athletes to fit a feminine image, which results in stereotypical media coverage.

14

Giving Readers What They Want or Need?

Late in the last century, news industry trade journals periodically published prophetic stories about a journalism crisis. The *Columbia Journalism Review* framed the crisis succinctly with this cover-story headline: "Money lust: How pressure for profit is perverting journalism." The magazine pronounced that a "new era has dawned in American journalism." It then quoted a *New York Times* editor describing the era's hallmark as "a massively increased sensitivity to all things financial."

A few prominent editors created a splash by resigning and directing attention to their disgust with corporate pressure on profits. In 2001, for example, Jay Harris, a 16-year veteran of the Knight Ridder chain, stepped down as publisher of the *San Jose Mercury News* because he believed that proponents of quality journalism at Knight Ridder were losing the battle against corporate priorities. The *CJR* article quoted Harris as saying, "Newspapers are a trustee, not just a business.... [T]he best and most important journalism is in the public interest — and is, on average, done less well, less frequently and less consistently than was once the case." The magazine noted that Harris' resignation "came to symbolize journalistic concern over Wall Street's relentless profit pressure" and "the tension between profit margins and journalistic mission."

Harris was not the only distinguished editor who quit over the quality-versus-profits debate. Most notable was the resignation of Bill Kovach, editor of the *Atlanta Journal* and *Atlanta Constitution,* in 1988. The resignation of Kovach, a former Washington bureau chief of *The New York Times,* created a stir in journalism circles for somewhat different reasons than Harris' departure. Critics credited Kovach with improving the Atlanta papers, giving them the look and tone of the *New York Times* and bringing them stature that goes with winning Pulitzer prizes. But the papers' publisher, Jay Smith, was looking at another newspaper — *USA Today,* then only 6 years old — for clues about new direction for his own organization. He had said that techniques borrowed from *USA Today* might pro-

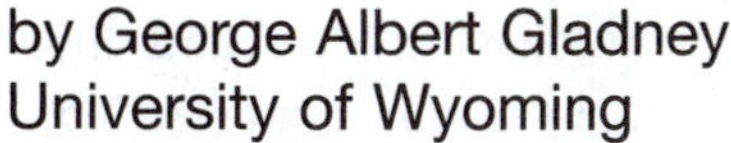
by George Albert Gladney
University of Wyoming

vide the dramatic change needed to attract young readers and buoy sagging circulation. Six months after Kovach was gone, the Atlanta papers hired Ron Martin, executive editor of *USA Today*, to replace him. What was at stake was the legitimacy of a potent but controversial trend that began in the newspaper industry in the 1970s. The trend went by the catch-phrase, "Give readers what they want."

What has happened to the newspaper industry since the turn of the millennium is astonishing. For one, the clarion call of "giving readers what they want" has been turned on its head with the growing phenomenon of "citizen journalism" (often labeled in other ways, including "grassroots journalism," "participatory journalism," "hyperlocal journalism," "networked journalism," "distributed journalism," "user-generated content" and "open source journalism"). In the oddest of twists, "the people formerly known as the audience" (journalism educator Jay Rosen's apt term) are gathering and reporting the news, sometimes in partnership with and sometimes in competition with traditional or legacy newspapers. They are carrying out the philosophy of Matt Drudge, the blogger of "The Drudge Report" fame, who declared, "Anybody can report anything."

Slowly, cautiously and reluctantly — with no certainty of making sustainable profits — the industry has migrated to the Internet by adopting news websites, a presentation-delivery system alien to its experience. Newspapers have long valued eyewitness accounts and photographs, but nothing like what has occurred since the spread of social networking sites including Facebook and Twitter, the vast blogosphere, SMS (text messaging), Google, YouTube, wiki websites that rely on "crowd sourcing," and smartphone and other mobile devices capable of recording and sending sound and video images to the Internet. To varying degrees, traditional media feel pressure to relinquish some gatekeeping and agenda-setting control. Newspapers have adopted these delivery forms with a sense of urgency, because the young have championed the new media technologies, staying away from traditional print newspapers in droves. What we do hear about is devastating declines in circulation and advertising revenues and massive reductions in newsroom staffs. Many long-established news organizations have closed (e.g., *Rocky Mountain News, Honolulu Advertiser, Albuquerque Journal*), sought bankruptcy protection (e.g., Tribune Co., Chicago; Freedom Communications Inc., Irvine, Calif.; Star Tribune Media Co., Minneapolis), or moved to hybrid print/online or Web-only production (e.g., *Seattle Post-Intelligencer, Christian Science Monitor*).

Amid this stormy environment, we don't hear of editors resigning over corporate concerns about profits. The call of "give readers what they want" has subsided. Why make an issue of it when the industry is hemorrhaging? But traditional editors, though perhaps not as outspoken today, still have grave doubts about whom or what will carry the banner for journalism in the public interest. Many

quietly fret about how to support serious journalism focused on what is important for the broad community, even if it is not particularly colorful or amusing.

Origins of the Issue

Throughout the history of American journalism, newspaper editors have disagreed about whether they should give priority to readers' wants or needs. In the past 30 or 40 years, more and more editors have fallen into the camp of giving readers what they want, and the current outlook suggests this trend will continue indefinitely. Many editors say changes are essential if the newspaper industry is to survive. The changes that have swept the industry have altered the form and content of newspapers, including methods by which readers access the news. Traditional editors, however, worry that with the changes, newspapers are failing to keep the public adequately informed about important public issues, thus posing a threat to the health of our representative democracy.

Editors' worries over the want-needs debate came in two stages. First, in the 1970s, editors witnessed a drop in circulation and noticed it was harder to attract younger readers. So, beginning in the 1970s and continuing through the 1980s and 1990s, the majority of daily newspapers revamped their form and content, with many papers emulating *USA Today*, launched in 1982. The new national newspaper became known for championing a brand of "reader-friendly" journalism, basing much of its innovation on market research aimed at discovering what exactly readers want in a newspaper.

The second stage was driven by dazzling 21st-century advances in digital communication technology that gave readers virtually unlimited access to information from the Internet. These technologies marked a shift toward customizable and interactive content, allowing for broad user participation. With the rise of citizen journalism, more and more traditional newspapers and their news websites began confronting and sometimes partnering with content provided by "the people formerly known as the audience." In some cases, this has meant that news organizations are not just giving readers what they want; they are letting readers help shape and determine some content.

The experimentation and changes in newspaper form and content that began in the 1970s was nothing revolutionary or entirely new. Doug Underwood in his 1993 book, *When MBAs Rule the Newsroom*, argued that modern newspaper marketing and packaging may be seen simply as a more sophisticated way of doing what newspaper executives have traditionally done whenever they were worried about their market share. This modern approach is simply a new twist on trying to build circulation by giving readers what they want, attract more advertisers by target-marketing customers and producing a more attractive newspaper, Underwood contended.

Periodically, newspapers have experimented with things for which *USA Today* is known. For example, truncated or digest-form news stories flourished in Chicago newspapers in the 1870s and again in the sensationalist "yellow journalism" papers in New York City in the 1890s. The yellow press was, like *USA Today* and its modern imitators, infatuated with the use of color and illustrations. In a chapter in the 1993 book, *Ruthless Criticism*, edited by William S. Solomon and Robert W. McChesney, journalism historian Gerald Baldasty quotes one editor from that era saying that "the man who manufactures the newspaper must as surely cater to the public taste as he who manufactures tobacco, or neckties, or candies, or groceries, or any other article of consumption."

Newspaper experimentation with changes in the 1970s was guided by market research, something new to American newsrooms. Newspaper researcher Leo Bogart, writing in *Presstime* in 1990, said the idea of "giving readers what they want" was not a *USA Today* innovation but had become a "catch-phrase among editors" in the late 1970s. Following the trend toward *USA Today*-style innovation, the typical American daily began to feature more positive, upbeat news, more "soft news," written in short, easy-to-understand stories that invited readers' personal involvement. Newspaper pages also featured more color, photographs, sports and celebrity news. The redesigned pages allowed readers to find and digest stories more quickly and easily.

But why, suddenly in the late 1970s, all this interest in satisfying readers' wants? The answer was clear — ominous circulation trends. Since the 1940s, newspapers had experienced a gradual, steady rise in circulation, only to see it wane in the 1970s while the population continued to grow. In the 1980s, circulation was mostly flat, peaking at 62.8 million in 1988. In the early 1990s, print circulation dipped below 60 million for the first time since the 1960s. In 2002, total circulation was down to 55.2 million. By 2008, amid a galactic explosion of Internet competitors offering news and information, the figure had dropped to 48.6 million — a scary number for editors.

Give Readers What They Want

Libertarian theory, which harkens to the early days of the American press, sets out two primary press functions: to inform and to entertain. A third function, a necessary correlate to the others, is for the press to ensure its financial independence through circulation and advertising. In the classic *Four Theories of the Press* (1956), co-author Fred Siebert asserted that the media's purpose is to help discover truth and assist in solving political and social problems by presenting all manner of evidence and opinion as the basis for decisions. According to liber-

tarian theory, however, press freedom was viewed as a purely personal right of press owners. The Founding Fathers believed that for truth to emerge there must be a free marketplace of ideas. The best way to ensure a free flow of diverse opinion is to guarantee an unfettered press. If a newspaper does not satisfy citizen wants or needs (market demand) for information, presumably a competitor will.

Four Theories co-author Theodore Peterson wrote in the same book that social responsibility theory, which grew out of recommendations of the Commission on Freedom of the Press (informally known as the Hutchins Commission) in the late 1940s, criticized the American press — then operating largely under libertarian theory — on a number of counts. Among its recommendations for change was a call for the press to provide a "truthful, comprehensive, and intelligent account of the day's events in a context which gives them meaning," Peterson wrote. Many journalists believe knowledge about readers' interests is necessary to fulfill this recommendation.

This background helps us understand the arguments of those who believe the press should give readers what they want. These are the advocates of reader-friendly, or market-driven, journalism associated with *USA Today.* Today, as newspapers have adapted to societal changes wrought by the Internet, virtually all newspapers have embraced to some degree this style of innovation of form and content.

The first argument for giving readers what they want resorts to the libertarian claim that newspapers have a right or obligation to ensure their own financial independence. Advocates of this position argue that for the sake of a newspaper's owners, employees, stockholders, advertisers and readers, a newspaper has a right or obligation to survive and make a profit. As the newspaper scion E.W. Scripps once observed, "The newspaper's first duty is to make a profit, so that it can continue to publish." Reader-friendly advocates argue that the newspaper industry's financial health — indeed its very survival — is threatened by numerous worrisome trends, not least the growing competition on the Internet. The best way to buck these trends, they insist, is to give readers what they want; if newspapers don't give readers what they want in today's era of digital on-demand news delivery, readers will quickly and easily enough find it online.

To examine the reader-friendly argument, it's worth looking more closely at circulation trends in the industry. A 2010 news consumption survey by the Pew Research Center for the People and the Press showed that 26% of Americans said they read a newspaper in print the day before, down from 30% two years earlier and 38% in 2006. But editors perhaps fret even more about the continuing drop-off among younger readers, a prime demographic target for advertisers. The 2010 report said that only 8% of adults younger than 30 read a print newspaper the day before. Web delivery of news, however, offers some hope. In 2009,

17% of Americans said they read a newspaper website the day before, up from 9% in 2006. Although readership of newspaper content is growing online, circulation declines for the print product have translated into a serious drop in ad revenues. According to the Newspaper Association of America, advertising revenues stood at $48.7 billion in 2000, before the Internet seriously entered the picture. In 2005, that figure rose slightly to $49.4 billion, when online revenue was included, but by 2009 combined revenues plunged to $27.6 billion. According to the 2010 Pew survey, less than 10% of newspapers' overall ad revenue is Net-driven, explaining why drops in print circulation are so taxing to newspapers' bottom lines. Without increases in advertising revenues and print circulation, earnings per share cannot grow at an acceptable rate to attract investors. In turn, investors hold the key to raising capital for newspapers' equipment and plant modernization, including investment in websites operated by newspapers. Further, the deteriorating financial health of newspapers damages the morale and well-being of workers in the industry. This effect reached epic proportion as newspapers downsized sharply in the century's first decade. Writing in *Corante* (corante.com) in 2008, Vin Crosbie, a futurist who teaches visual and interactive communications at Syracuse University, predicted that more than half of the 1,400 U.S. daily newspapers will be out of business by the end of 2020.

Proponents of reader-friendly newspapers argue that these financial problems are compounded by two other developments. First, large, family-owned newspapers are almost a thing of the past. Most daily newspapers today are units of large, publicly traded corporations competing with the most profitable and speculative enterprises and investments; the pressure for short-term, bottom-line results couldn't be stronger. Small newspapers and weeklies, which often are the sole providers of local news, are somewhat immune to this pressure.

The second development is the proliferation of competing forms of media that are in an ideal position to give audiences — and advertisers — what they want. The impact of new competition on newspapers began in the early 1920s with radio, but radio did not significantly affect newspaper circulation. It did, however, cut into the advertising-dollar pie, and television cut into that pie further. The rate of growth in newspaper circulation began to decline when Americans started to turn to television as their primary source of news in the early 1960s. Total circulation began to decline after peaking in 1973. Today, direct mail (catalogs and fliers delivered by mail) competes successfully for newspaper advertising dollars, offering firms the advantages of precise market targeting, blanketing of ZIP codes, or 100% market saturation. Newspapers' actual dollar volume of total U.S. advertising expenditures has gone up, but the percentage of all expenditures has dropped as advertising for other media (i.e., magazines, direct mail, radio-television and Internet sites) has grown at a faster rate.

Given these fretful trends, proponents of reader-friendly journalism argue that newspapers must be marketed like any other commodity. To do that, they say, newspapers must do market research to find out what readers want in a newspaper (or news website) and then satisfy those wants.

The second argument for giving readers what they want arises from the complaint that editors are elitist and arrogant if they believe — in their infinite wisdom — that they can decide what's best for readers. This was the attitude of legendary TV news anchor David Brinkley, whose career spanned 1956-97, who famously said, "News is what I say it is." In a similar vein, journalism educator Walter Gieber wrote in 1964 that "news is what newspapermen make it."

This second argument brings to mind the philosophy of Edmund Burke, the 18th-century British politician and statesman who distinguished between the roles of delegate and trustee in a representative democracy. Applied to the U.S. system of government, members of the House of Representatives serve as delegates of the people, voting according to the wishes and views of their constituents. Members of the Senate, designed as an elite body, serve as trustees who are valued for their wisdom and vote their conscience. Applied to journalism, one can say editors who attempt to give readers what they "want," as opposed to what they "need," act as delegates for their audience. Editors who see themselves as trustees, on the other hand, select news on the basis of their professional judgments and conscience.

Subrata Chakravarty and Carolyn Tortellini, writing in *Forbes* in 1989, observed that the trend toward *USA Today*-style form and content — the "delegate model" — represented an effort by newspapers to "win back readers" after years of "telling readers what they should read and shoving the fare down readers' throats." In his 1987 book, *The Making of USA Today*, Peter Prichard noted that the creators of *USA Today* intended it to be edited "not for the nation's editors, but for the nation's readers."

This line of thinking carries forward with an important new twist in the digital era — more than ever, users decide through RSS feeds, e-mail alerts and search engine searching what news or news topics to expose themselves to, leaving professional editors largely out of the loop. The online world does not wait for editors to decide what people "need" to read. And with the rise of independent bloggers and citizen journalists using mobile digital communication devices, more readers are taking on the role of journalists and, in some cases, partnering as amateurs with traditional or legacy newspapers to produce news and opinion.

The Project for Excellence in Journalism's 2010 "State of the News Media" report noted the gradual passing of the old model in which editors assembled a wide range of news based not on its popularity but on its value to the aggregate audience, the community at large. "That model is breaking down," the report said, adding that online consumers "are not seeking out news organizations for their full news agenda ... [they are] hunting the news by topic and by event and grazing," getting news from four to six different platforms (on- and off-line) on a typical day. More and more, the report said, Americans are "on demand" consumers, "seeking platforms where they can get the news they want when they want it from a variety of sources." The 2010 biennial news consumption survey by the Pew Research Center for the People and Press reported that use of search engines is sharply on the rise, with one third of Americans regularly using search engines to get news on topics of interest, up from 19% in 2008. In some ways, this situation represents a victory for those who want a news media that provides readers with what they want, as opposed to what they need.

The final argument favoring reader-friendly journalism asserts that the long-term downward circulation spiral stems in part from the fact that traditional editors lost touch with changing reader interests and lifestyles, as well as changes in the way citizens access and process information. Too many newspapers bored readers by providing too much in-depth reporting that too often lacked any personal relevance to readers. Reader-friendly advocates say that because newspapers traditionally have been averse to change and market research, the old trustee model of editing a newspaper did not adapt to a new era of double wage-earner families who lack the time to pore over comprehensive, in-depth, analytical, interpretive, explanatory or critical reporting. More and more, readers found newspaper coverage too boring and difficult to read. Besides, many people said important news was already covered on the nightly television broadcast and on round-the-clock cable news networks.

This third argument goes beyond mere lifestyle changes to include changes in epistemology, or "ways of knowing." Young people today have learned to process information differently than the previous generation thanks largely to television and the multimedia mix of information delivery by the Internet (e.g., Twitter, Facebook, Google, YouTube, etc.). This new style of information seeking has led to a rethinking of literacy, traditionally defined in print terms, to include visual-audio and interactive-participatory terms.

Prichard made it clear that designers of *USA Today* were mindful of different literacies, and they made a conscious effort to attract a generation of readers weaned on television. *USA Today* became known for what media critic Thomas Rosenstiel said was a "personality as a newspaper designed for the TV generation, with its hopeful tone, its mixing of entertainment and news and its quick-bit, non-linear way of delivering information."

As *USA Today* was accepted by the public and became popular with many newspaper editors who emulated its form and content, newspapers were transformed to attract the visually literate (those raised on TV) and attract less serious readers. The refurbished American daily was no longer drab and heavy with gray text. Instead, it was full of color and visuals, including drawings, charts and graphs (or "infographics"); more and bigger photographs; more news summaries, digests and indices; front-page teasers about stories inside the paper; provocative quotations (similar to a TV "sound bite") displayed to tease a story; one dominant story on page one; large, full-color weather maps; expanded sports coverage; increased use of first-person plural pronouns ("we," "our"); stories about personalities and celebrities; more stories with soft news and upbeat themes; a bright, snappy prose style that used short, declarative sentences; and more human interest stories and "news you can use" (columns relating to personal finance, health, career, beauty). If all of this sounded a little like the 10 p.m. newscast, that's because it was supposed to.

The epistemology of online news reflects the convergence of traditional media (one to many) with digital media (many to many, few to few) that are interactive, personalized, portable and participatory. The Internet and multimedia technologies are radically changing the way we store and access information and, indeed, the way we read and think and process thoughts. (Sherry Turkle's 2011 book, *Alone Together*, provides an absorbing and incisive look at how social media in particular are altering the ways we communicate and learn about the world around us.) The technologies also are changing who is defining what is news as new voices enter the picture. Citizen journalism by amateurs, whether connected with traditional newspapers or not, is increasingly available on the Internet. While some argue that the future of citizen journalism has been overblown, there can be no doubt that ordinary citizens, equipped with mobile digital recording devices, will continue to widely distribute valuable news content, much of it suitable for established news organizations. However, independent bloggers (many with no formal journalism training or background), and dedicated blog sites connected with Web newspapers, are playing a growing communication role, especially in the area of news analysis and opinion and specialty subjects such as food, fashion, entertainment and politics. In a sense, this may signal progress for those who advocate giving readers what they want.

Give Readers What They Need

The argument that editors should give readers the information they "need" — the "trustee model" — is rooted in classical democratic theory and the First Amendment, as well as tension between libertarian and social responsibility theories. At heart is the idea that for a representative democracy to function properly, citizens must be informed about important public matters.

According to classical democratic theory, the government is a creation of the people, and the people elect representatives (servants of the people) to deliberate over public policy and administer the government. For the system to work, the people must take an interest in political matters, have an adequate level of knowledge about political matters and participate in politics at least at the most basic level — by voting. Trustee editors assert that this system works only if an independent press keeps people abreast of important public matters.

Trustee editors embrace the part of libertarian theory that holds that the press should be a vehicle to present evidence and arguments, on the basis of which people can check the actions of government and shape public policy. These editors also embrace the call for a free marketplace of ideas and information, with the press operating unfettered in a free-enterprise system. Editors turn to social responsibility theory, however, in the hope of fulfilling that call.

Modern social responsibility theory holds that, given the tremendous concentration of media ownership and the newspaper monopolies in most areas, the press too often fails to provide a free marketplace of ideas and information. To be socially responsible, the press must ensure that all sides of important public issues are fairly presented and that the public has enough information to make intelligent decisions in the polling booths.

This interest was expressed by Bill Kovach, a prominent media critic whose 1988 resignation from the *Atlanta Journal-Constitution* was noted early in this chapter. According to Richard Shumate, writing in the *Washington Journalism Review* in 1992, Kovach declared not long after the affair: "The only interest I have is public service, public interest and public information journalism. The business of journalism is protected in the Constitution for a reason ... and if you choose to publish a newspaper, you inherit that obligation." The same sort of thinking prompted former *Denver Post* editor William Hornby to declare in a 1976 article in *Quill*: "The newspaper is a quasi-public institution with a constitutional purpose.... The press has never been and never should be in the business to give the people just what they want. The editor who does his editing predominantly from market research isn't worth a damn." The same attitude is found on some Internet news sites. In 2008's *Understanding Media Convergence*, Dean Wright, former editor-in chief of MSNBC, was quoted as saying, "We have to serve the public but we can't give them just the candy they want ... we have to tell them things they don't know and things they already know but in different ways."

Proponents of the trustee model offer rebuttal to the three primary arguments of the delegate model. First, they argue that no one is opposing a newspaper's right to make a profit. The issue is whether they can do that and simultaneously fulfill social responsibilities that transcend counting-house values. Sir Harold Evans, who served for many years as editor of Sunday *Times* of London, once said the challenge of U.S. newspapers "is not to stay in business — it is to stay in journalism."

Further, trustee model supporters believe that editors have made too much of their fear of declining readership, pointing out that for decades newspaper industry profits were the envy of most other industries. As late as 2000, the average newspaper profit margin peaked at 22.7%. In 2001, when newspaper industry profit margins averaged 21.5%, industry analyst John Morton observed in *U.S. News & World Report*, "A recession for the newspaper industry just means you can't take as many truckloads of money to the bank." By the end of that decade, when it seemed the financial picture for newspapers couldn't get much worse, the 2010 annual "State of the News Media" report from the Project for Excellence in Journalism and the Poynter Institute said that even with newspaper earnings plunging in 2009 "most companies were squeaking out an operating profit by year's end."

During the century's first decade, the World Wide Web grew at breakneck pace, providing an endless array of sources for news and information — online social networks, Google and other search engines, the blogosphere, YouTube, text-messaging, Twitter, smart phones and other mobile devices, e-mail and list-servs, chat rooms and a variety of news aggregators. To offset advertising losses to these vehicles, newspapers cut costs by eliminating pages and trimming the size of the printed page, severely reducing staff, reducing the number of days of delivery to subscribers and shrinking their distribution areas. At the same time, newspaper companies tied their hopes to their websites. Even *USA Today*, suffering a collapse in ad revenue and circulation and losing its hold on the national media market, announced in 2010 it would shift its business model away from the print edition and focus on its digital operations. In 2009, newspaper industry analyst Suzanne M. Kirchhoff said in a 2009 Congressional Research Service report that the industry outlook was uncertain as online advertising revenue, which accounts for only 10% of newspapers' overall ad dollars, saw its first decline since 2002. She noted that major newspaper companies' profits in 2008 declined to just over 10% amid severe budget cuts and newsroom layoffs.

As for the delegate advocates' second argument — that the trustee model is elitist and arrogant — trustee proponents counter by saying that delegate editors are arrogant as well, in a different way. Although delegate supporters sneer at editors who presume to know, through professional training and experience, what information readers need to know, trustee supporters argue that the "dumbing down" of newspapers to borrow from the epistemology of television is essentially patronizing. In effect, the argument is that delegate editors demonstrate little confidence in their readers' ability to handle complex, extended exposition and in-depth analytical reports.

Supporters of the delegate model argue that market research should guide the gatekeeping process so that readers get what they want rather than what some elitist editor assigns. But trustee advocates counter that readers are not on the front line, as are journalists, where the raw events of news are occurring. They argue that journalists are able to track developments over time and gain perspective about which events are likely to be most important to the community and about which readers likely are unaware. Market research can't do that.

With the advent of citizen journalism, with ordinary audience members now defining and distributing news, the delegate advocate might ask: What could be more democratic? Yes, the trustee advocate will agree, but many problems arise when surrendering editorial responsibility to citizens. For one, as Dan Gillmor points out in his 2006 book, *We the Media*, citizen journalists aren't always interested in reporting news from the journalistic trenches — e.g., state capitals, the halls of Congress or local zoning boards. As for in-depth, investigative reporting, institutional journalism has a distinct advantage over amateur news-gathering because of journalists' greater experience and newspapers' superior commitment to resources and time.

Newspaper researcher Bogart pointed out that without someone to select, package, measure and label information, news content becomes random and chaotic and produces mental indigestion. Any traditional newspaper has to judge the day's events to decide whether readers should be informed about them and present the news so that readers know what stories the editors consider most important. When news important to the community and polity is buried or ignored by delegate-minded editors, readers begin to get the impression that sports and celebrity gossip are more important. This problem is exacerbated by readers' ability to customize digital news delivery to match their interests. Although their news is personally relevant, it is narrowly focused, tending to confirm one's views or outlook and thus contributing to the public's growing political polarization. Futurologist Paul Saffo, who teaches at Stanford University, observed that we "can create our own personal-media walled garden that surrounds us with comforting, confirming information that utterly shuts out anything that conflicts with our world view." He wrote, "This is social dynamite" and could lead to "the erosion of the intellectual commons holding society together.... We risk huddling into tribes defined by shared prejudices."

Writing in 2010's *Public Journalism 2.0*, Aaron Barlow observed that blogs particularly, "with their unconscious and often amateur attempts to organize information," contribute to disorganization. With millions of active, independent blogs, the information they try to present becomes cacophony. Myriad attempts to aggregate blogs, he said, have done "very little to organize and evaluate entries in an efficient and elegant fashion." News reports furnished by citizens have been valuable to the mainstream press usually during catastrophes or when an eyewitness is there and the press is not. The classic example is the famous Zapruder film footage of the Kennedy assassination. Recently, many citizens, equipped with digital communication devices, have provided the earliest images and accounts of events: the Southeast Asian tsunami, the London and Madrid train bombings, the Mumbai terrorist attack and the Virginia Tech massacre, for example. But Barlow contended in his book that there is a "fundamental difference between reading hundreds of people's stories and understanding the 'real' story." Without the order that traditional news professionals impose, it's much harder "to make sense of what's happening in the world." Trustee advocates argue that many news websites lack a suitable replacement for a traditional "front page" that gives readers an organized understanding of the events of the day that are likely to have maximum relevance and impact for the broad community.

These concerns dovetail with trustee editors' response to the reader-friendly advocates' third argument — that newspapers are too boring, too in-depth and lack relevance to readers' personal lives. Trustee advocates point out that classical democratic theory says nothing about allowing people to ignore certain issues because they are boring, require too much effort to comprehend or seem unconnected to people's lives.

Trustee advocates argue that newspapers that emulate television to accommodate visual literacy and shortened attention spans compound the attention span decline and hasten the death of traditional literacy. This argument was forcefully articulated by the cultural critic Neil Postman in 1985's *Amusing Ourselves to Death,* in which he argued that print is best for people who think conceptually and deductively and engage in contemplative, deliberative and reasoned discourse. For Postman, print fosters introspective, analytical and abstract thought, it is fundamentally propositional in character, and it is inclined toward serious, rational argument and logical, orderly (linear, sequential) arrangement of acts and ideas. Postman maintained that television, on the other hand, with its random-like mosaic presentation of non-discursive symbols (pictures), presents the world as object and images rather than ideas. For Postman, television essentially trivializes serious discourse by presenting all subject matter as entertainment. Postman's concerns apply to the Internet to the extent that multimedia presentations (e.g., YouTube, podcasts, etc.) reflect broadcasting's epistemology.

One has to wonder what Postman's reaction would be to people's Internet reading habits, particularly how they access, gather and process news online. The authors of the 2010 "State of News Media" report note that online consumers "are not seeking news organizations for their full news agenda." Unlike the way they read traditional newspapers, they are "hunting the news by topic and by event and grazing across multiple outlets." Trustee advocates would be alarmed by the report's finding that more and more people, especially younger readers, begin their news consumption through search and end it there, "deciding that all they need is the headline, byline and the first sentence of text. In short, news consumers young and old get a good deal of news without ever actually clicking on the story." Print newspaper trends toward brevity starting in the 1980s (shorter stories, shorter paragraphs and shorter sentences) pales in comparison to this latest style of reading the news.

A final concern here deals with an epistemological twist to the Web, with its ability to embed text with links to other texts at different sites. In a 2008 article ("Is Google Making Us Stupid?") in *Atlantic* magazine, Nicholas Carr argued that Google is conditioning us to reading text embedded with these links, so much so that it is rare that we read an in-depth article from beginning to end. This, too, no doubt would appall Postman, who greatly valued books for their ability to take a subject from beginning to end in a thorough, comprehensive and nuanced way.

Trustee advocates believe that giving readers a heavy dose of shallow, abbreviated news high in entertainment value and visual appeal is likely to develop in readers a weakness for things passive and pleasurable. Even more serious is the charge, articulated by Postman in *Amusing Ourselves to Death*, that newspapers emulating television may accelerate the trend toward declining public literacy, shortened attention spans and widespread voter apathy. In short, reader-friendly newspapers may be more part of the problem rather than the solution.

With respect to news over the Internet, trustee advocates argue that if newspapers or news websites provide readers with only what they want, readers won't know what they're missing. They will unknowingly forego the satisfaction of finding something agreeable or valuable not sought for. In their 2007 book, *News Values*, Paul Brighton and Dennis Foy argue that the pull model of news, in which news receivers draw in only those items that are of direct relevance to them, produces "dull" news that fails to extend "beyond preconceived world views." They argue that a newspaper's mission is to educate readers, and that means educating them about things they are unaware of — not just what they think they want to know. Bogart explained, "Editors have to know what readers will tolerate, but their job is to push up constantly against the limits of that tolerance and thus to expand it."

Assessment

No newspaper attends exclusively either to the wants or the needs of its readers; to some extent all newspapers mix news and entertainment. It is a question of degree. Think of it as a continuum, with wants and needs at opposite ends.

If there is to be resolution in the debate, the media must seek a position somewhere near the middle of the continuum. There is justification for this if we consider the wisdom of Aristotle's principle of the golden mean, whereby moral virtue is situated between the extremes of excess and deficiency. If we take that advice to heart, we should be open to the possibility that both sides of the debate, delegate and trustee, raise valid points and reach a compromise resolution.

A compromise would acknowledge that newspapers should not eschew market research entirely, but at the same time they should not be slaves to its findings. Similarly, newspapers should attempt to balance their mission to inform and entertain, dual media functions identified by the Hutchins Commission. Too much emphasis on the informational needs of readers will repel some readers from newspapers, but too much emphasis on entertainment will accomplish the same. In either case, the result is likely to be a less informed citizenry.

A compromise also would ask editors to acknowledge that newspapers are not purely businesses. All newspapers will acknowledge a higher purpose of the press if they will seriously consider constitutional concerns, the public's right to know and the watchdog role of the press. The latter includes investigative and in-depth or explanatory journalism that educates the public about the inefficiencies and wrongdoings of government and business. Lastly, a compromise would perhaps forgive a few newspapers in robust, competitive markets, blessed with an assortment of newspapers, to ignore pleas to be socially responsible. But it would require newspapers that are local print monopolies — the only newspaper in town — to concede that monopoly status is not what the Founding Fathers had in mind with the guarantee of a free press. Monopoly status should impose a moral obligation to be socially responsible.

If editors insist on catering more to the one than the other, then readers' needs should be served before their wants. Charles McCorkle Hauser, former executive editor of the *Providence Journal-Bulletin*, asked in a 1995 article he penned in *Editor & Publisher,* "If newspapers don't take seriously the informational needs of readers, who will?" He didn't see television or any other medium providing enough serious coverage for people who are genuinely interested in a full accounting of the day's activities. On the other hand, if newspapers ignore their entertainment function, there are plenty of other media to fill the void.

Hauser argued that although some segments of the population are unconcerned about the future of newspapers — and easily could do without them — two significant segments of the population consider newspapers to be essential to their day. The first is "a literate, sophisticated and intellectually curious group that believes the printed word is the most efficient and most satisfying way to attain lots of information on subjects of importance." The second is "an intensely local and involved group that depends on newspapers as the only medium providing detailed coverage of hometown and home state news."

Hauser asserted that the dominant trend is toward a small and loyal readership made up primarily of these two groups. But he pointed out that most editors remain in denial over the irrevocable loss of readers. "They keep searching for magic formulas to restore newspaper reading to levels of the good old days when people had longer attention spans and fewer demands on their time." Hauser's prescription for newspapers: Drop the search for magic formulas and forget television. Instead, commit to serving core readers.

During the past decade, the reshaped media landscape has fueled the wants -versus-needs debate. The new landscape is the product of technological advances associated with powerful search engines like Google and Bing, news aggregators like Google News and Yahoo News, social networks like Facebook and Twitter and a dizzying array of other inventions. As with most material found on the Internet, this content is menu driven. Users select their content from a variety of topics. Readers may choose to access only what they want, or say they want. MyYahoopage.com, for example, allows users to create tailored news reports. It is technically possible for online news sites to go a step further and monitor reading patterns to fine-tune delivery based on patterns of reader preferences.

To some extent, readers of traditional newspapers have always browsed them, choosing what stories they want to read or ignore. It is difficult for readers of traditional print papers, however, to escape exposure to the front page, even if they glance quickly at only the headlines. With the development of online newspapers, especially at the level of local news where news aggregators are not so much of a factor, reader exposure to a front page as we have known it has largely disappeared. Online reading is more personalized and less focused on the broad community. With rapid growth of citizen journalism, the gathering and reporting of news is often limited to the individual interests of the amateur reporter or commentator. Advocates of reader-friendly journalism may not have a problem with that as long as readers' wants are being satisfied. But both delegate- and trustee-model editors are likely to worry about news edited completely to personal interests of readers; this would create solipsistic journalism that ultimately views the community as a fragmented collection of private interests. Missing are news stories that assume broad interdependence among the community's inhabitants and seek to report the shared experience of the collective life. Without a common page to be shared by all readers; and without a common frame of reference, how can a newspaper foster a civic spirit or help shape a vision of public community?

A final concern of trustee editors is how citizen journalism is affecting the balance between providing readers with what they want and need and how it is affecting journalism more generally. In a 2008 article in the *Columbia Journalism Review*, Ann Cooper observed that "freedom of the press now belongs not just to those who own printing presses, but also to those who use cell phones, video cameras, blogging software and other technology to deliver news and views to the world." She said some online writers applaud this development and criticize traditional journalism for being "calcified, too self-important to correct its errors or own up to its biases, too pompous to talk *with* its audience, rather than *at* it." Conversely, she noted, many traditional journalists complain that their new online competitors were "acerbic ego-trippers, publishers of opinion and unconfirmed gossip with no professional standards," and were stealing the hard work of mainstream reporters.

Cooper and many journalists today agree that the pressing question now is: Who is a journalist? For Cooper, anyone can be a journalist, "if and when they choose to be." Rosen, the New York University journalism professor who made popular the phrase "the people formerly known as the audience" and who writes about cutting-edge changes in journalism at his PressThink website, has written about an emerging hybrid model of digital journalism in which online writers, who subscribe to traditional standards, embracing a commitment to accuracy and avoidance of conflicts of interest, can work successfully with traditional journalists. Cooper says Rosen's hybrid model shifts the focus from defining "who is a journalist" to "what is journalism." The answer provides another part of the resolution in the needs vs. wants debate.

To answer the question "What makes something journalism?" Kovach and Rosenstiel, in their 2007 book, *The Elements of Journalism*, turned to the late William Safire, who was for many years a top columnist for *The New York Times.* Safire said part of the answer lies in a commitment and allegiance to hard facts, to truthfulness, to accuracy, to citizens, to the watchdog role of the press. Just as important, journalism must provide a forum for public debate, put readers first and remain staunchly independent.

Kovach and Rosenstiel went on to assert that the Internet, blogosphere and citizen journalism have not made obsolete the need "to decide what people need and want to know to self-govern." But they said the gatekeeper role — "deciding what information the public should know and what it should not — no longer strictly defines journalism's role." They said that in the new era, a journalist's role is to make order out of the news, to make sense of it, to verify it.

Points of View

Books

Gillmor, Dan. *We the Media: Grassroots Journalism, by the People, for the People.* Sebastopol, Calif.: O'Reilly Media, 2006. A national columnist at *San Jose Mercury* and long-time blogger, Gillmor has been following the subject as long as anyone, and his book is as insightful as it is thorough.

Grant, August E., and Jeffrey S. Wilkinson, eds. *Understanding Media Convergence: The State of the Field.* New York: Oxford University Press, 2009. This varied collection of essays illuminates the most important media changes of contemporary times.

Kovach, Bill, and Tom Rosenstiel. *The Elements of Journalism: What Newspeople Should Know and the Public Should Expect.* New York: Three Rivers Press, 2007. Two prominent journalists and media critics defend the traditional trustee model of editor.

Prichard, Peter. *The Making of McPaper.* New York: Andrew, McMeel & Parker, 1987. The author gives an insider account of what went through creators' heads as they invented *USA Today.*

Rosenberry, Jack, and Burton St. John III, eds. *Public Journalism 4.0.* New York: Routledge, 2010. This timely overview of citizen journalism by practitioners and academics focuses on the promise and reality of a citizen-engaged press, including both public journalism and the newer citizen journalism.

Articles

Cooper, Ann. "The Bigger Tent." *Columbia Journalism Review,* September/October 2008, 45-47. On the issue of citizen journalism, the question is no longer Who is a journalist? but rather What is journalism? (and how are citizens doing it?).

Gladney, George Albert. "*USA Today,* Its Imitators, and Its Critics: Do Newsroom Staffs Face an Ethical Dilemma? *Journal of Mass Media Ethics* 8 (1993): 17-36. This survey of staffs at 40 U.S. dailies (comparing heavy adopters and non-adopters of *USA Today*-style innovation) gauges attitudes about the changes in newspapers in the decade following the newspaper's launch.

Harper, Christopher. "The Daily Me." *American Journalism Review,* April 1997, 41-44. The issue of customized online news services that allow readers to receive news content tailored to their interests, raises the question: Do readers risk missing important news that doesn't fit their profiles?

Hornby, William H. "Beware the 'Market' Thinkers." *Quill,* January 1976, 14-17. The author sounded an early warning and plea for newspapers not to let marketing executives encroach on the newsroom.

Stepp, Carl Sessions. "When Readers Design the News," *Washington Journalism Review,* April 1991, 20-24. Changes in newspapers following the rapid spread of *USA Today*-style innovation raised the issue of whether newspapers were dumbing down or wising up.

15 Tabloid Journalism

Tabloid news media have rarely been uncontroversial. Although "tabloid" is technically a description of a newspaper presentation style, it is also used to describe a form or genre of journalism.

Tabloid journalism, or "tabloidism," often is accused of highlighting particularly emotional, sensational, celebrity-oriented or shallow stories and using shoddy, if not downright crooked, journalism practices. Tabloidism stands accused of being substandard journalism, or "churnalism," and of not meeting journalism's essential standards. Tabloid journalists brazenly and carelessly put profit before public service, according to critics, while traditional mainstream news media reverse that order, albeit still with an eye to making a profit. But tabloids and tabloidism are also defended as democratizing news by freeing it from the self-imposed limitations of traditional mainstream news media, and for drawing more people into broader social debates about issues. Advocates also argue that tabloid news media embody a working cultural "multivocality," a way for more voices with more points of view and accents to be seen, heard, recognized and joined by a wider variety of news consumers.

Traditional news media supporters argue that by prioritizing the most exciting and emotional aspects of stories, tabloid-style journalism demotes or even abandons aspects of a story that are essential to public awareness of what is going on in society but that do not conveniently fit the tabloid story model. Or worse, triviality drowns out or becomes more important than more valuable information about politics, culture and society. Celebrity stories are perhaps the poster children for this argument.

Tabloidism uses a formula that emphasizes bold headlines, lots of photographs and graphical elements and fast-paced, succinct writing. But at the same time, critics say, it panders to the public's baser instincts and its thirst for sensationalism. This generic, lazy, one-size-fits-all form ignores nuance, subtlety, comparison, context, transparency, thoroughness, broadness and distinction. With-

by John Latta
University of Alabama

out these characteristics, say critics, there is no value to the journalism. Tabloids also are charged with disguising their inferior product as good journalism, essentially deceiving and shortchanging the public.

Yet defenders say that a "tabloid" story can indeed serve the public good, just as a mainstream news story can. The tabloids are influential elements of our cultural politics. Citizens read the tabloids, and thus their influence reaches into the public sphere — just like mainstream news.

Furthermore, supporters of tabloid journalism also maintain that their mainstream critics are not so much defending the faith as finding a scapegoat on which to blame their shrinking audiences and reach. And mainstream media are not above borrowing tabloid techniques and templates to regain dwindling audiences without giving up their claim to being democracy's town crier.

Origins of the Issue

Tabloid journalism is not new, nor is the controversy surrounding it.

In the 17th and 18th centuries, what were commonly called broadside ballads and newsbooks were popular. They were filled with tales of the weird, gory and scary, and they relied on stories of murder, mayhem and mistresses — much like the staple of modern tabloids. These early publications also exhibited strong moral and religious tendencies.

In 18th century newspapers, sensationalism, moral and religious sermonizing and distinct political biases were commonplace. The moralizing tone and political bent would fade as the 19th century began, but the sensationalism would remain.

In the first half of the 19th century, the rise of the "penny press" — mass-circulation dailies — brought popular news to far more Americans. In 1830 no newspaper in the United States had a daily circulation of more than 4,500. By 1835, the pioneering penny paper, the *New York Sun*, was selling 20,000 copies a day. Meanwhile, photographs began appearing in newspapers and were hugely popular. An easier-to-read style pioneered by the likes of the *Sun* and the *New York Herald* meant more working class people could read newspapers. And by lowering prices, owners made sure they did, boosting circulation beyond the educated and well-off. The "penny press" was named for the newspapers' highly competitive one-cent-an-issue price (making them widely available compared to competitors charging five or six cents). They built their readerships on what we would recognize today as a popular model. Veteran tabloid researcher Sue Bird observed in her groundbreaking 1992 book focused primarily on supermarket weekly tabloids, *For Enquiring Minds,* that, "The short, clear, active style became the model for journalism from then on — tabloid journalism simply developed the style at its most formulaic."

America's cities expanded rapidly. By the end of the 19th century, newspapers were profitable commercial enterprises based on advertising and circulation. Joseph Pulitzer's purchase of the *New York World* in 1883 inaugurated the era of "new journalism." When William Randolph Hearst bought a competing newspaper in 1895, new journalism quickly morphed into "yellow journalism," a fast-paced, sensational, aggressive style of journalism that enticed, informed and entertained mass urban audiences with stories of crime and corruption. Eventually, one-third of America's daily newspapers became "yellow."

As a counterpoint, beginning in the early 1900s, some newspapers, led by the *New York Times* under Adolph Ochs, were increasingly relying on objective, professional reporting techniques and presentations, finding commercial success in apolitical, unsensationalized journalism that not only described events but also explained them and put them into context.

Sensational newspapers used a variety of techniques. Comics, introduced by Hearst in the *New York Journal* in the 1890s, and unabashedly sensational stories would change readership demographics by attracting even more working classes readers. Tabloid-style editors realized that a big story did not have to be socially important, just one that gripped and held readers. Photographs, sometimes grisly and graphic, would be a mainstay of the tabloids until the advent of television. Supermarket tabloids — weeklies that were sold in the checkout lines of stores — began reaching mass audiences in the second half of the twentieth century. They especially relied on exclusive photos and scandals. They began mostly as city-wide popular newspapers, and their owners converted them into national publications.

Tabloid television, and the beginning of more respectable weeklies such as *People*, bit deeply into newspaper circulation. Tabloid television developed the same relationship with mainstream quality television journalism as tabloid newspapers did with quality ones. Some tabloid TV was outrageous and lacked any link to the standards of good journalism. Other shows made attempts to present good journalism, albeit with a sensationalist base. Most of these shows saw their audience drift away after the turn of this century, drawn off by the wide variety of sensationalist material available on the Web.

In the days when newspapers, radio and television, or a mixture of them, dominated news (the days before the Internet and the cable industry), the tabloid/mainstream debate was relatively simple. But the modern age of journalism, an age of constant and rapid change, makes the comparison a little muddier with the increasing number and variety of news-delivery organizations (including individuals) and methods. It is no longer a simple binary situation. Both traditional mainstream journalism and tabloid journalism have, in terms of how we define them, changed from the pre-cable, pre-Internet and pre-social media eras and are continuing to change. Social media are perhaps the most visible stage upon which this change is happening. This process has meant simple definitions of tabloid journalism are often no longer adequate.

There are, though, distinctions within the tabloid field. For example, weekly supermarket tabloids are not the same as big city dailies such as the *New York Daily News* or the *New York Post.* City tabloids are blatantly tabloid in their approach but sometimes dig into important stories, and they have a far greater connection to their readers. Some city papers print in the tabloid page format, but their content resembles that of general-interest, responsible broadsheet newspapers. The tabloids you see at the supermarket checkout counters are designed simply to follow stories that will maximize readership, regardless of their importance within a community. Tabloid television news programs run the gamut from laughably substandard to infringing upon mainstream territory.

Tabloidism Is Never a Good Thing

Tabloids have many critics, some of whom are severe. Aben Kandel, for example, called tabloids a menace that was "converting readers into witless gossips, gutter vamps, and backyard sheiks." They mocked privacy, he said, and were wont to "finger in glee all the soiled linen they can discover." He asserted that tabloids "fill the mouths of readers with intimate details of all the illicit love affairs they can uncover" and "fire their restless minds with lewd photographs." Worse, he said, they target the young and teach them "the vocabulary and lurid ritual of illicit love!" He particularly attacked journalists who worked for the tabs. "The tabloids make eavesdroppers of reporters, sensual meddlers of journalists, and reduce the highest ideals of the newspaper to the process of fastening a camera lens to every boudoir keyhole." Kandel issued that warning in *Forum* in 1927. And there are critics today who would repeat his jeremiad.

In the modern era, critics take tabloidism to task for producing "news" that is little more than a reader-grabbing, one-dimensional thriller story. Sensationalism, rather than the core values of journalism, dictates how the story is presented. Tabloidism trivializes important topics, relies too heavily on gossip and stresses the bizarre, lurid or violent in human interest stories. Critics argue that some events that are important to the public are reported by tabloid journalists in a way that maximizes sales or ratings, and more serious stories are ignored in favor of silly or salacious non-events.

Bill Kovach and Tom Rosenstiel in their 2001 book *The Elements of Journalism,* a primer for journalism students looking to understand the most basic qualities of journalism, argue that tabloids present stories as secrets they are letting you in on. Increasingly, Kovach and Rosenstiel said, "secret" means salacious or scandalous. "These are the classic gimmicks of tabloidism — the news as revealed truth, as sex, or as celebrity scandal." Revealing secrets becomes the essential news value. Tabloids must assemble a narrative of sensational or scandalous revelation from the information their reporters gather. Traditional news values are secondary to the need to build suspense and deliver the secret. Social responsibility, context and privacy go out the window. Any secret is newsworthy, and any story with a secret is worth pursuing. Exposing secrets sells papers. So tabloid editors, Kovach and Rosenstiel argued, choose stories based not on their value to the public but for their value to their owners' income.

Proponents of traditional news media also argue that tabloidism cannot fulfill journalism's most important functions for their audience because the format does not allow for development or explanation of the essential information in the stories. A complete, well-researched and important story is likely to have some boring but necessary sections that include context and detail. Tabloid stories omit those parts. As Bird sees it, 'Tabloid style has come to be understood as a particular kind of formulaic, colorful narrative related to, but usually perceived as distinct from standard, 'objective' styles of journalism. The tabloid is consistently seen by critics as inferior, appealing to base instincts and public demand for sensationalism." Graeme Turner, in his 2008 article "Tabloidization, Journalism and the Possibility of Critique" in the *International Journal of Cultural Studies*, wrote that tabloidization is a generic, one-size fits-all form without subtlety or distinction. According to Stephen Harrington, in his 2008 article "Popular News in the 21st Century: time for a new critical approach?" in the academic journal *Journalism*, tabloids do shallow and shoddy work, but they disguise it with bells, whistles and exaggerated teasers or headlines so that it appears, to the average reader, as "real" journalism. Tabloids, Harrington said, misuse the trappings of traditional mainstream media — print, type, photographs, graphics, headlines and paper — to suggest they are practicing solid, thoughtful journalism. They deceive audiences into thinking that tabloid news essentially is the same as mainstream news. So even though there is a school of thought that argues that if the substance of the tabloid story meets the highest standards of news journalism, then its popularized presentation is actually good journalism, critics say the essential qualities of superior journalism are lost in the popularization process. As a result, the "news" stories will be tabloid trash and have no redeeming features. And popularized news that lacks the essential qualities of journalism will deny the public the chance to be adequately informed of what is happening. A balance must then be achieved if tabloidization is to have a role in keeping news relevant to the widest possible audience in our democracy: the popularization process must go on without the loss of the accepted standards of quality journalism. As Michael Serazio wrote in his chapter in Barbie Zelizer's 2009 book, *The Changing Faces of Journalism*, "The tabloid story might win out, but the cheap story should not." John Street wrote in his 2001 book, *Mass Media, Politics and Democracy*, that claims about the increasing tabloidization of news are typically grounded in the idea that commercial decisions, especially the need to attract advertisers or cut costs, affect journalistic practices. And there is evidence that an increase in tabloid reporting has decreased the volume of traditional reporting, according to Harrington.

Critics accuse tabloidism of using a narrow range of storytelling structures. These structures limit public access to the full depth and breadth of subjects and at the same time push mainstream media into aping these practices. Bird, in her chapter in the Zelizer book, said these practices allow some kinds of stories to proliferate while marginalizing others. Tabloids have been influential in narrowing the range of storytelling techniques used to deliver news, she said, thus curbing audience members' willingness to appreciate nuances and complexity in stories and reducing the number of storytelling tools journalists use to convey a broad, deep, complete story. Bird is concerned, too, that because of the narrower range of stories produced by tabloids — there are really only a handful of templates — stories containing significant socially valuable content, commonly the slower parts of a narrative, as journalists try to insert essential but often less than dramatic information, will dwindle. Thus, tabloid-style stories have the potential to swamp mainstream stories. The narrow range of narrative templates eventually could consume the meaningful story until it is dissolved into a tabloid story.

Mainstream journalists and their supporters argue that, by prioritizing the most exciting and emotional aspects of stories, tabloid journalism demotes or abandons aspects of a story that are essential to public awareness. By promoting awareness of trivial matters simply because they sell, it makes trivialities important to readers. Carolyn Kitch, in her chapter in Zelizer's *Changing Faces of Journalism*, said the tabloid practice of trying to make traumatic events understandable to the public through personal drama means favoring "certain explanatory narratives at the expense of others, masking or eliminating other lessons we might have learned from these stories."

For example, consider tabloid-style coverage of the massive damage and high death tolls from natural or man-made disasters. The anguish, the heroism, the fear, the raw emotion of victims and rescuers make for compelling stories. But when such tabloid-style stories dominate coverage and the victims are used exclusively to play on readers' emotions, coverage may pass over the causes and complexities involved in the public policy decisions surrounding the disaster. Tabloids may ignore less exciting or dramatic aspects of the event, Kitch suggests, or those aspects may make only a token appearance in a newspaper story or television report because audiences want exciting and emotionally involving news. Harrington, in his article "Popular News in the 21st Century," argued that, by tabloids' evoking either anger or empathy in readers, readers will ignore or discount the deeper and more complex aspects of the events.

Advocates of traditional journalism argue that reporters should limit or balance the emotional appeal of such stories and include elements that tabloids essentially ignore or give short shrift. Such a story would inform the public, tell readers what they need to do to stay safe and encourage them to join the public debate. But do mainstream reporters and editors always live up to this ideal, or are they sometimes also guilty of reporting almost exclusively in emotional terms and using heart-rending personal narratives?

In some coverage of such disasters, Kitch sees what she calls a commonness of narrative that "constructs an imaginary America in which feeling fixes everything. It promotes unearned self-satisfaction among people wholly unconnected with tragedy, while prematurely declaring the healing of wounds that remain, for the actual victims, quite raw." Emotion and feeling can make a story so much more compelling. But relying too much on emotion as the core of narrative, a common tabloid practice, can do disservice to the public, Kitch argued. Tabloids are prone to place common people and their emotions in the center of their stories. As Kitch said, "private emotions are turned into public ones." In this way, journalists "explain shocking news events by placing such characters into familiar narratives through which audiences recognize the meaning of those events."

Tabloidism Can Be a Good Thing

Supporters argue that tabs, or at least some of their practices, can be an asset to traditional journalism. Tabloid journalism expands the range of news topics and brings more news consumers into the social debate, whether the journalism is good or bad when compared to mainstream news media.

"There is ample evidence to suggest that a certain tabloidization of style, such as the emphasis on emotional storytelling that engages senses and emotions, actually enhances good journalism," wrote Sue Bird. So while there is criticism from traditional mainstream news media, she said in Colin Sparks and John Tulloch's 2000 book *Tabloid Tales,* there are "countervoices that see no harm, and even much good, particularly for the bottom line."

Just because news is popular or tabloidized doesn't automatically mean it's bad for readers. Pigeonholing tabloid style with a narrow definition and then labeling it all bad can limit discussions that could draw from tabloidism some valuable lessons for journalism. Henrik Ornebring and Anna-Maria Jönsson, in their 2004 study "Tabloid Journalism and the Public Sphere," said tabloid "emotionalism, sensation and simplification are not necessarily opposed to serving the public good."

Tabloids may allow people to recognize, feel, discuss and debate issues of importance to society on their own terms. That is, they may provide ordinary citizens with access to complicated stories by creating easy entry-points. They can provide simple ways of looking at stories that the mainstream news media have put out of reach by addressing them in terms that only relatively sophisticated readers could, or would, understand fully. That is, tabloid stories may be the only place some members of society go to read news stories about current issues. Without such stories, tabloid supporters argue, at least some people may never engage with some key social issues. For example, in the cases of political scandals or arguments about issues such as global warming or drugs in sports, tabloid stories may be some people's only news source, that is, the only one they access even if others are available.

If tabloid news media always are considered careless, money-making outlaws, the argument goes, then the only way for citizens to inform themselves about issue as good democratic citizens would be through untainted, serious, "quality news." The mainstream media's unchallenged monopoly is insulated from public need, however, and only those readers comfortable with mainstream style will consume this quality news media, leaving a lot of the public unengaged in debates about important community news.

"Abstract claims can become relevant and ring true only if authenticated through an individual's life experience," reasoned Harrington. News that reaches an individual but fails to connect viscerally may not be as useful as superior journalists think it should be. In other words, a tabloid story about people suffering from an economic recession — told with feeling, action and images — might educate the public more than traditional news stories.

Herbert Gans, a critic of modern news media, says tabloidization could be good for journalism. In his chapter, "Can Popularization Help the News Media?" in the Zelizer book, he said it could cure some of journalism's problems. What citizens need to know should not vary by taste, culture or class, he said. So the substance of news should be the same in tabloids and mainstream press. Only the presentation would differ. For example, simpler tabloid journalism may reach less educated people who do not consume mainstream news, delivering some information about the topic and bringing them into social discussions. Gans thus shares Bird's stance, but he also addresses the question of why tabloidism is often dismissed because it is considered low-class journalism.

Tabloid media, according to Kevin Glynn in his 2000 book *Tabloid Culture,* "express the growth of cultural multivocality." Tabloid stories using everyday

ing to explain dwindling audiences. Are they red herrings and convenient whipping boys for struggling mainstream journalism?

A number of critics say "yes." Catherine Lumby, quoted in Turner's article, argued that criticisms of tabloids and tabloidization can be interpreted as "aimed at protecting traditional definitions of what matters in public affairs — business, parliamentary politics, economics, the law and so on." It's not just the way stories are written; it's what they are written about that matters. Traditional news media, in this argument, see themselves being outflanked, while tabloid stories become popular, arguably denting the mainstream news media's influence. Critics of traditional media argue that there is narrowness about what tabloids cover and how they cover it. In Glynn's assessment, "The proliferation of tabloid programming, for example, challenges traditional journalism's narrowly constricted vision of what is allowed to count as a public issue." In other words, tabloids will often pursue, at length, stories that traditional news media may ignore, addressing subjects that audiences won't find in other news media, such as celebrity scandals and alternative medicine. Mainstream news is arguably more predictable, mostly covering topics they themselves have accepted over time as worthwhile news story topics — for example, the traditional court, police, politics and business beats that can dominate traditional news. Tabloids, on the other hand, regularly prioritize any story, or aspect of any story, that sells. They may do that solely because it sells, but, nevertheless, non-traditional news stories about non-traditional subjects reach the public.

Tabloids can also be of value, supporters say, because when they compete with mainstream journalists they challenge the mainstreamers to rethink what they consider important and useful and perhaps to popularize a story and make its reach broader. Tabloids may be able to push mainstream news media into broader subject coverage, flashier photos and graphics and brighter writing. Some critics argue that by hooking larger audiences into stories and holding their attention, tabloid news forms are democratizing news, putting news back in the hands of the people and creating a bigger public sphere.

This argument assumes that traditional media in the United States are rigid, hidebound and stuffy. Some observers see parallels in how news media are developing in China. In present-day China, tabloid-style news reporting is rapidly building an audience. Citizens are turning to the popular press as an alternative to mainstream media, which the Communist Party dominates. Sensational, entertainment-oriented tabloids also compete for advertising revenue with the officially supported press. Observers agree that Chinese tabloids offer an alternative to the mainstream news media, which is hemmed in by entrenched traditions and undue political influence. Michael Schudson, a news media scholar and critic, in his 2003 book *The Sociology of News,* asked this question of the Chinese examples, people and storytelling, rather than the more official, distant style of mainstream journalism, can help more subgroups within communities find a voice. Such stories include more subgroups in their coverage of communities. A subgroup may be a minority or simply sources whom the mainstream media generally don't use. Let's say tabloids commonly cater to, even pander to, a less educated audience than mainstream news, or at least produce less-than-thorough news reports. And let's say tabloid stories can be as shallow and flawed as their critics claim. Does that mean they can be dismissed as irrelevant or even harmful to journalism and its role in a democracy? Glynn wrote that "tabloid media matter because they constitute an important site of ongoing cultural politics." Parsing a story to judge its journalistic worth — how much it demonstrates basic, mainstream standards such as verification, transparency and accountability — is, in this argument, irrelevant. Readers have accessed it, assessed it, reacted to it and let it influence them, aware or not of "quality" problems. It is journalism, and it has done journalism's work.

Some research, such as the work of Yasuhiro Inoue and Yoshiro Kawakami in their 2004 study "Factors Influencing Tabloid News Diffusion," argued that readers evaluate tabloid stories much like mainstream stories — that is, they accept tabloid stories and process them in much the same way they do mainstream stories. Therefore, superficial differences may mean little. It is disingenuous to say that a story that is inaccurate and unfair can simply be dismissed. This argument assumes readers are aware of the inaccuracy and unfairness. "Cultural politics," said Glynn, "involves struggle over meaning that produces our understanding of ourselves, our 'others' and the place of ourselves and others in the world." Tabloid culture, he added, "is a product of the social amplification of popular knowledges [sic] that in one way or another question the capacity of more official ones to produce the authoritative truth of the experience of living in the contemporary United States" So, to their readers, tabloids stories can be as influential as stories in the *New York Times, Wall Street Journal* or major network news broadcasts. They can't be dismissed as politically, culturally or socially irrelevant just because they do not meet journalism's gold standards as described by critics and academics. Readers respond emotionally, not academically.

In response to criticism that tabloid journalism delivers cheap and tawdry stories, Graeme Turner, in his "Tabloidization, Journalism and the Possibility of Critique" article, asked whether notions of good taste mask a power motive and squelch debate. Is denying coverage, or self-censoring the style of coverage out of concerns for "good taste," a self-serving way for mainstream news to avoid stories or aspects of stories it would rather avoid? Are mainstream journalists saying, in effect, that "news is our ball and you have to play with it our way"? Turner essentially asks, Are tabloids scapegoats for mainstream news media try-

experience: "Sound familiar? A popular voice, an alternative voice, an oppositional voice, a cultural voice?" No, we are not China, but, as a model, this example warrants debate.

Finally, tabloidized stories may be the way to resolve the economic tensions in the media industry. Donald Matheson, in his 2007 article, "In Search of Popular Journalism in New Zealand," looking into the tabloid press in a Western parliamentary democracy, noted that a popular, personalized connection between news media and audience is absolutely necessary. Otherwise, he said, we get news consumers alienated from real democratic activity. He sees popular journalism as valuable because it conveys the political complexities of people's lives in terms of their own everyday experience.

It's Not Just Journalism — It's Culture

Except in their most stereotypical forms, tabloid journalism and mainstream journalism are not automatically polar opposites. Observers can see both tabloid and quality journalism as different sides of the same coin. Harrington, for example, has found "increasingly blurred boundaries of journalism." All media, he said, are "trivialized, commercialized and turned into a spectacle." He looked for middle ground between hard news and popular news. He also wanted to draw researchers away from "the sometimes too simplistic binary discourses that have tended to become characteristic of recent debates over 'tabloidization.'"

The debate has at times taken a cultural turn, approaching tabloidism not as good or bad but simply as journalism.

Cultural popularization is a common process. It takes higher culture and adapts it for a wider, less elite audience. Gans said that popularization is a common social process that occurs in many parts of society and is not limited to media. It makes anything from music to machinery user-friendly. Objects and ideas are made more salable by being available and understandable to a wider audience. The original users of the products usually disdain the dumbed-down version. Cadillac owners, for example, dismiss low-price Cadillac knock-offs from cheaper car makers as so much junk. Following that pattern, journalists will see nothing of value in the tabloids and their stripped-down approach. A knock-off handbag or cheap wine with a fancy label will do little harm, but, as Gans pointed out, news is judged not by taste but by its empirical accuracy. Inaccurate, incomplete or misleading news, created in the popularizing process, can hurt people and their society. It is even possible to argue that the use of emotion, so prevalent in tabloids, is part of a society-wide trend. As Kitch said, "Today, feeling is all around us, in public culture and in journalistic coverage of that culture."

The cultural discussion raises another issue, pointed out by Gans when he elaborated on his earlier argument that tabloids can deliver news to the less educated. He said that since "moderate and low-income people are the main consumers of tabloid news, tabloidization is a particularly handy verbal weapon used by more educated people to disparage the culture or less educated ones." So is an opposition to tabloidization and defense of more staid mainstream news production an elitist position?

Peter Dahlgren, in his chapter, "The Troubling Evolution of Journalism," in Zelizer's book, said increased tabloidization, as a form of popularization and a strategy to gain a larger audience, "is intrinsically neither good nor bad...." Democracy, he reasoned, can be nourished by news media if what is presented contains relevant information that is useful for citizens whatever form it takes.

Bird and Dahlgren, in their Zelizer chapters, argued that news stories fit into templates and procedures that determine their form and prioritize content. They also have ideological elements that reflect a way of seeing the world. Dahlgren said that stories not only fill a basic human need but "have an epistemological status: narrative constitutes a way of knowing the world. Stories serve as a device for conveying meaning, by structuring sequences, attributing motives, highlighting circumstances, and so forth." So rather than be concerned with tabloidization's use of sensational and emotional stories, he said, we should "focus instead on the ideological implications that the story frames offer — the moral of the story as it were." In other words, while the sensationalism of a news story, its visceral, emotional impact, is its most obvious first impression, audiences are also affected by less obvious aspects of the narrative. For example, in tabloidized coverage of the deaths of pop stars Michael Jackson and Whitney Houston, audiences reached behind screaming headlines to discern moral and cultural aspects of the story, to recognize, for example, relationships and social and cultural roles even though they were not the key parts of the story. In other words, these tabloid stories delivered more than a shallow sensational narrative.

If we place mainstream news at one end of a continuum and outlandish tabloid news at the other, and agree that both stray towards the middle at times, cultural critics say, we need to be able to identify when and where they commingle. Michael Schudson, in his book *The Sociology of News,* noted that soft news and infotainment — tabloid mainstays — are a "concoction governed by entertainment values more than news judgment." He asked a series of questions: "When is an interest in entertainment a legitimate effort to relate a complex situation as a compelling story? And when does the quest for sensation overtake the effort to tell a story?" Is the tabloidization process solely a cause for concern, or is it sometimes a potential opening to improved journalism? "Can the trend toward soft news be seen not as a submission to market forces but as an expansion of an overly narrow, rigid definition of news to encompass a wider range of important topics?"

Even before today's proliferation of news providers, traditional and tabloid media sometimes met on the same ground, according to cultural critics. In the cases of the car-crash death of Princess Diana, the Clinton sex scandal, the Casey Anthony trial and Whitney Houston's death in a Beverly Hills hotel bathtub, to cite just a few examples, coverage was startlingly similar on many occasions. For more modern examples of this coincidence at work look at coverage of natural disasters from mine collapses to hurricanes and tornadoes. It can be a valuable exercise to look at mainstream stories and try to find tabloid overtones.

Turner, in his article "Tabloidization, Journalism and the Possibility of Critique," said it doesn't much help our understanding of, say, Oprah Winfrey, to consider her long-running and extraordinary popular television talk show as representative of the cult of the personality and the trivialization of news values held to be consequences of tabloidization. It is more productive to see her appeal from a feminist perspective as a program that accesses modes of expression identified with sections of the community that were virtually unrepresented in the media. This argument suggests that traditional mainstream news media leave out a wide range of subjects when they rely on a time-proven formula of what is and isn't news. Shows such as Oprah Winfrey's, say her defenders, regularly brought issues beyond the regular mainstream fare — through intense personal narratives — to people who might otherwise not become part of the social debate on those issues.

The boundaries between tabloid journalism and quality journalism are still crystal clear if we compare supermarket tabloids and mainstream broadsheet dailies or network television news. But in terms of presentation style, tabloid-style stories aren't a bad way to present news, cultural critics say, even news stories about more complicated issues, by using photos, graphics and human interest angles to 'popularize' a story.

Assessment

The single biggest obstacle to assessing the role of tabloidism in journalism, of deciding how and where it can be of value and how its negative influences can be identified, may be its definition. One person's screaming tabloid journalism may be another's mainstream *tour de force.*

Sue Bird, in her Zelizer chapter, said of tabloidization that "the problem with the word is that, perhaps like 'obscenity,' everyone seems to recognize it when they see it but no one really agrees what it is." The word "has come to be understood as stylistic and content changes that represents a decline in traditional journalistic standards." And yet, Bird said emphatically, there is no clear, simple definition of tabloidization. Which raises an interesting problem: How do you address it and assess it if you can't clearly define it?

Ultimately, tabloid journalism is neither all bad nor all good. As Michael Serazio said in his chapter in Zelizer's 2009 book *The Changing Faces of Journalism*, there are "pitfalls and potential in tabloidization." And we are not in a situation where a compromising blending of tabloid and mainstream journalism can be conveniently assembled that will serve the public adequately. Any such blending would seem to be hard work on a story-by-story basis, perhaps resembling a decision-making process not unlike that used to determine ethical solutions to problems arising in a story.

"The big challenge, it would seem," said Dahlgren, "is to develop new popular forms that will both resonate with large audiences and also communicate in meaningful ways about important matters." Popularity of form is important. *The Washington Post's* famous Watergate journalist Carl Bernstein is on record as saying that "all journalism is popular or at least aspires to be at some level." Martin Conboy, a British tabloid observer, in his 2007 article "Permeation and Profusion: Popular Journalism in the New Millennium" in *Journalism Studies*, said that "all forms of contemporary journalism need to be able to develop strategies of popularization which allow them to maintain some form of authentic claim to represent the opinions and lifestyles of a broad section of the people."

Any new popular forms of news must arise in an era in which, as Bird noted, the criticism of tabloid reporters for using paid informants and gossip-mongers as sources is almost a quaint notion, now that anyone can post anything on the Internet and not bother to verify or follow ethical procedures. A virtually endless supply of free information, according to Bird, "gives license to its users to assemble their own versions of reality."

For the no-holds-barred Martin Conboy, boundaries are eroding between elite and popular cultures, including news media, but this erosion is not leading to a recognizable middle way or new set of standards of values. Inevitably there will be heated debates in newsrooms, story by story.

Sometimes tabloid-style popularization, even sensationalism, will serve the audiences. Other times, its use will fail them. Knowing when, and how, and why, to balance audience-and-rating-boosting tabloidism, shorn of its carelessness and thoughtless but loaded with its drama and passion, with more somber but essential information more calmly assembled and presented within the stories, is becoming an essential journalistic skill.

Perhaps the fact that both tabloid journalism and mainstream journalism are created by people from common backgrounds with surprisingly common goals is a starting point. Mark Deuze, in his 2008 paper "Understanding Journalism as Newswork: How It Changes, and How It Remains the Same," noted that both types of news are produced by similarly trained journalists who share characteristics and speak of similar values in their work. Bird has looked at how tabloids reported and wrote their stories and how tabloid writers related to such tenets as objectivity and credibility. Despite the fact that tabloids are "commonly regarded as deviant 'demons,'" she said, "a case is made that tabloid journalism belongs on the same storytelling continuum as daily newspaper journalism."

The evidence suggests that both remote end positions of the continuum are untenable, one far too unreliable and the other far too uninteresting. Journalists must negotiate some sort of fluid formula that allows them to call on both traditions to deliver news stories that the public can embrace while satisfying journalists that they are providing essential social information. The emergence of popular new media and social media, and the technology-based changes that will inevitably come, make this muddy middle ground unpredictable and increase the pressure on journalists to, in Dahlgren's words, "develop new popular forms that will both resonate with large audiences and also communicate in meaningful ways about important matters."

In the end, consider Schudson's understanding of the subject. He argues that it is possible that journalism serves the interest of free expression and democracy best when it least lives up to the demands of media critics for deep thought and analysis. Passion for the sensational event may be news at its democratically most powerful.

Points of View

Books

Bird, S. Elizabeth. *For Enquiring Minds: A Cultural Study of Supermarket Tabloids.* Knoxville: University of Tennessee Press, 1992. This analysis of contemporary supermarket tabloids examines the interplay among tabloid writer, text and audience.

Glynn, Kevin. *Tabloid Culture.* Durham, N.C.: Duke University Press, 2000. This study traces how tabloids relate to the debate over the meaning of social values and examines the cultural setting for the rise and popularity of tabloid news media, positioning the tabloids within society.

Morton, Paula. *Tabloid Valley: Supermarket News and American Culture.* Gainesville: University Press of Florida, 2009. This book examines the over-the-top supermarket tabloids, revealing their interior workings and their relationship to the mainstream news media.

Pelizzon, V. P., and N. M. West. *Tabloid, Inc.* Columbus: Ohio State University Press, 2010. The authors situate the tabloids alongside bloody gangster movies and hard-boiled pulp fiction, arguing that tabloids may be a literary art form.

Schudson, Michael. *Why Democracies Need an Unlovable Press.* Malden, Mass.: Polity Press, 2008. Coverage of sensational events may be modern news media at their best. This book puts tabloids within the context of news media as a whole.

Sparks Colin, and John Tulloch John, eds. *Tabloid Tales.* Lanham, Md.: Rowman & Littlefield, 2000. This collection of works by various authors examines some of the more dramatic tabloid stories, how they affect modern journalism and where tabloids may fit into the modern journalism landscape.

Zelizer, Barbie, ed. *The Changing Faces of Journalism: Tabloidization, Technology and Truthiness.* New York: Routledge, 2009. Scholars' essays consider how tabloidism affects the modern journalistic landscape.

Articles

Conboy, Martin. "Permeation and Profusion: Popular Journalism in the New Millennium." *Journalism Studies* 8 (2007): 1-12. Those fearful of the future of journalism see tabloidization as a threat to our social fabric, but the public sees it as a vehicle delivering more and more news choices.

Deuze, Mark. "Popular Journalism and professional ideology: tabloid reporters and editors speak out." *Media, Culture & Society* 27 (2005): 861-82. Deuze interviews journalists working for European tabloids and probes how they view their work and assess its professional value.

Harrington, Stephen. "Popular News in the 21st Century: Time for a New Critical Approach?" *Journalism* 9 (2008): 266-84. The way we see tabloidism is dated, and it is to our detriment if we do not change that approach.

Ktich, Carolyn. "Tears and Trauma in the News." Chapter 3 in Barbie Zelizer, ed. *The Changing Faces of Journalism: Tabloidization, Technology and Truthiness.* New York: Routledge, 2009. Sensational journalism is intended to "shock and provoke strong emotional responses among readers."

Matheson, Donald. "In Search of Popular Journalism in New Zealand." *Journalism Studies* 8 (2007): 28-41. Tabloidism can fit into modern democratic systems and not be a pariah.

Ornebring, Henrik, and Anna-Maria Jönsson. "Tabloid Journalism and the Public Sphere: Historical Perspective on Tabloid Journalism." *Journalism Studies* 5 (2004): 283-95. This article provides an account of the development of the genre.

Turner, Graeme. "Tabloidization, Journalism and the Possibility of Critique." *International Journal of Cultural Studies* 2 (2008): 59-76. Turner relies on a critical theory approach to examine tabloids in society.

16 Television News: Good or Bad?

"One of the basic troubles with radio and television news," wrote broadcaster Edward R. Murrow in 1958, "is that both instruments have grown up as an incompatible combination of show business, advertising and news. Each of the three is a rather bizarre and demanding profession. And when you get all three under one roof, the dust never settles."

Although television news has come a long way since its introduction in the late 1940s, television news still faces the challenge of walking a fine line between entertainment and serious content. Americans love to hate television. They love the entertainment it provides and hate it for the same reason. Television news is trapped somewhere between *I Love Lucy* and *The New York Times*. Was television journalism developed with the same integrity and dedication of its print forefathers? Or does its heart lie in entertainment and ratings, where sensationalism, action and drama determine what makes it onto the screen?

Despite our animosity toward it, almost all of us watch it. According to a March 1, 2010, report from the Pew Internet & American Life Project, "Understanding the Participatory News Consumer," most Americans still report getting their news primarily from television, with Internet sources coming in a close second. The country was watching when Neil Armstrong set foot on the moon, when President John F. Kennedy was shot, when the space shuttle Challenger exploded, when terrorists crashed two airplanes into the World Trade Center in New York, and when President Obama was elected. When anything happens in the news across the world, most people reach for the remote or whip out their smart phone. We want to know what's going on, and we want to know right now. And when the news is really momentous, nothing takes the place of a large television screen for watching events unfold before our eyes.

So, is television news good or bad?

Supporters argue that television news provides 24-hour coverage of stories we want to know about in a visual, entertaining and easy-to-understand format.

by Lisa M. Parcell
Wichita State University

Many of us make television news part of our daily routine, helping us become part of the "informed citizenry" essential for our democracy. In fact, supporters argue the television news format, with stories strung together into one program, discourages viewers from "cherry-picking" stories and gives viewers better exposure to a wider variety of news. Many also argue that television covers emotional stories such as riots, homecomings, celebrations and other special events better than print. In times of crisis, television news can give both information and comfort to concerned viewers in a format unlike any other mass medium.

Critics, however, charge that television news has a serious credibility problem. Television news distorts reality through reenactments, selection of shots for impact, a narrow range of story locations and coverage of pseudo-events like politicians' signing legislation, arriving, departing and walking about town to shake hands and kiss babies. In fact, many argue that television strays too far into the realm of sensationalism in a constant effort to improve ratings and increase profits. The often distracting and showy presentation of television news offers glitz, but takes away from substance. Critics also say that increasingly shorter news stories, dubbed "headline news," and shorter sound bites fail to give viewers a true understanding of the story. Live coverage, in particular, contributes to a lack of perspective and depth to news coverage. The 24-hour news cycle created by television is constantly in search of a story, critics argue, which often forces politicians, industry leaders and other officials to make decisions quickly with little time for reflection.

Origins of the Issue

CBS and NBC, building on their profits gained as radio networks and radio manufacturers, became the two major players in television after World War II. ABC, founded in 1943, later became a distant competitor. Although the Federal Communications Commission (FCC) licensed radio broadcast stations, the television networks avoided this regulation in their early days. Networks believed that if they provided a public service — such as a 15-minute news program — the FCC would not require them to be licensed, pleasing both the public and the networks. Beginning in 1941 the FCC did regulate network television stations and required some form of public service programming to be granted a license. The 1996 Telecommunications Act broadened the scope of regulation to include the Internet. While the goal of the law was to deregulate the broadcast business and allow for more competition in the industry, the industry instead has moved toward further consolidation and mergers of media companies.

Most of television's founding fathers began their careers in radio. Prominent radio journalists such as Edward R. Murrow, who covered World War II from his post in London, were at first reluctant to have anything to do with the new technology. Murrow feared a close association with television, especially because it had such a strong background in entertainment. Finally convinced that television could have a positive and profound impact, he adapted his popular radio show *Hear It Now* to a television version called *See It Now*, which first aired in 1951.

Early television news broadcasters were called "readers," men hired for their voice and presentation skills and not for any journalistic background. As television news departments grew in stature, "readers" were replaced with experienced newsmen, like Murrow, Cameron Swayze and Walter Cronkite. Before long, CBS and NBC began building up their televised news departments with reporters from their radio network and seasoned print journalists. By the middle of the 1950s, news "personalities" began to emerge with both a strong presentation style and a news background.

Although network evening news continued to improve in ratings, news programming remained less important than entertainment programming to the new television networks. In the 1950s, the networks only allotted 15 minutes to present the world's news. Not until 1963 for CBS and NBC and 1967 for ABC would television news finally break through the 15-minute time barrier and extend the evening news to half an hour.

In the 1960s and 1970s, the three networks continued to expand their news operations and increase the amount of news on television in various forms. Morning news shows, documentaries, news magazines, talk shows, political focus group programs, special reports, scheduled debates and other special public affairs programs were born during this period. Trustworthy news programs made the networks look good; but especially important, they began to make money, drawing in advertising dollars as they increased in popularity. Since news programming on average was less expensive to produce than entertainment programming, this added to their appeal to the networks at the time.

When CBS News anchor Walter Cronkite retired in the early 1980s, network news was facing new challenges and competition. In the past few decades the three networks have changed anchors many times in an effort to find a personality who could attract new viewers to a declining audience. Satellite technology made possible instant links around the world for breaking news. A combination of satellite technology and expanded cable operations enabled Ted Turner to launch the Cable News Network (CNN) in 1980. Critics initially scoffed at the idea that 24-hour news would appeal to the public, but when most Americans turned to CNN for coverage of the Persian Gulf War, critics conceded its place alongside the broadcast networks in news coverage. In 1979 C-SPAN, a cooperative service funded by cable systems around the country, was launched, which provides continuous political coverage; international media magnate Rupert Murdoch started

Fox News Channel in 1996, which provides a more conservative bent to news coverage; and NBC and Microsoft jointly launched MSNBC also in 1996, which provides viewers a more integrated news service between cable news and the Internet. Local television stations have used rapidly developing transmission technology and access to CNN and other networks to go beyond local news to cover national and international news. Running before network news, these local news programs now have the technology and ability to "scoop" the networks.

The Shortcomings of TV News

The stepchild status of television journalists to their older cousins in print has eased since television's birth. In the 1960s those in television news still looked to the wire services and newspapers for the full story. Barbara Matusow, in her 1983 book *The Evening Stars*, tells the following story that sums this up best.

When Tom Pettit was covering Alabama governor George Wallace's attempt to block the integration of the University of Alabama, an NBC editor in New York telephoned Pettit and told him he could get much of the material that he needed from the Associated Press' report. When Pettit replied that he did not have access to the AP, the editor told him to use the United Press International report instead. When Pettit explained that he didn't have UPI either, the exasperated editor declared, "Good Lord. Well, go out and get a copy of the *New York Times*. The story's on page twenty-three." Pettit then informed him that the *New York Times* was banned in Tuscaloosa. "After a pause," Matusow recounted, "the man in New York said, in disbelief, 'You don't have the AP? You don't have the UP? You don't have the *New York Times*? How in the hell do you know what's going on down there?'"

The oldest and most common criticism of television news revolves around its credibility. Charges of sensationalism bang an ever-growing dent into the credibility of television news. Sensational stories of fires, accidents and crime make much better television than stories on the economy, legislation and health care. Health care legislation and policy is often boring and difficult to personify on television. Murder trials, on the other hand, make great television. Television news programs covered O.J. Simpson's murder trial for weeks, yet unemployment and the bursting of the housing bubble remained difficult to explain on television. What makes good television also produces better ratings, which increases profits. This makes network owners happy. Unfortunately, these stories are not always the most important news pieces of the day. Often they just serve to boost ratings. Using these stories caters to what the viewers want and not to what they need to know, one of the oldest tenets of good journalism.

Another blow to television journalism's credibility, charges Av Westin in his

245

1982 book *Newswatch*, comes from the practice of reenactment. Reenactment can occur in many forms, but essentially involves recreating an action for the camera. While networks scorn blatant reenactment, some borderline practices continue. For example, some networks use the reverse question tactic in interviews. This involves reshooting the interviewer asking the questions once the subject has left. The journalist can now smoothly ask the questions and look more poised on camera. These shots are later edited into the interview. While this may create a more polished interview, it does not fully reflect the interview as it happened. A second and related technique, called the phony reaction shot, involves reshooting an interviewer's response to a subject's answer after the interview is over.

Other critics, like Carl Lowe in his 1981 book *Television and American Culture*, also accuse networks of distorting reality through camera shots and the locations of stories chosen. Since the networks are based in either New York or Washington, D.C., a disproportionate number of stories are done from that vantage point. For example, Lowe argues that a piece on gang violence will likely focus on the problems in one of these two cities and not stretch out to include "Hometown, USA." Similarly, a piece on the increasing use of crack cocaine would probably again center on New York and D.C., not a smaller American city. The problems that network executives and news people living in New York or Washington, D.C., run into every day become the problems of the nation. In other words, what is happening in New York and Washington is represented in the news as what is going on across the nation, and that is often a much darker and distorted reflection of America.

Lowe also criticizes how the particular shots the camera picks up, which are later used in the news piece, often distort the real situation. When covering a story, videographers (as well as still photographers) try to capture the moments of action in each story. If the president delivers a speech to Mothers Against Drunk Drivers, and he raises his fist once to show his anger at drunken drivers, that is the shot that will probably appear on the evening's news. This one outstanding gesture may upstage the outlining of his plan to stop the problem or reading off a list of names of young people killed on the road that year. Once this material hits the editing room, the distortion may become more pronounced. Video editors intensify the action by cutting out "dead," or inactive, scenes. In the typical murder story, the videographer generally arrives on the scene while the police are still questioning witnesses and looking for evidence. Hours may go by while the news crew waits for the police to finish their investigation at the scene. When the video finally arrives at the news station, this "boring" material is cut away. All that remains is a shot of the body being carried away and the suspect being stuffed into a police car. After the videographer and the video editors complete their jobs, the finished product little resembles the complete story that unfolded before the reporter's eyes.

What makes it on the news isn't always really news, explains Horace Newcomb in *Television: The Critical View* (1979). Pseudo-events like signing legislation, arrivals, departures, shaking hands and kissing babies are staged for the television camera. These non-news events offer a way to inject some excitement and visual drama into what is happening. For example, instead of a thorough explanation of how the new crime bill will affect the public, viewers get a great shot of the president signing the bill with a pen from a police officer killed in the line of duty. Crammed around the president stands every politician trying to form a connection to the bill, along with the widows and children of other officers recently killed. A touching picture full of patriotism and hope, but what does that really tell us? Not much.

No longer are we in the golden days of broadcast journalism when CBS President William S. Paley and his counterpart at NBC, David Sarnoff, allowed the profits from entertainment programming to help carry the news departments and, in return, meet the "public service" clause of broadcast license renewal. The 1980s, in particular, saw an increase in new network owners demanding cost-cutting measures designed to please stockholders but not necessarily news viewers. "Streamlining" became the buzz word. What resulted, charges Edwin Diamond in *The Media Show* (1991) and other critics, was an attack on expenses and staff cutbacks that crippled the news departments and limited news coverage. Networks added more videotaped packages prepared by affiliates to save the cost of sending video crews and correspondents. Straight pool footage transmitted directly to New York and voiced-over by the anchor was a cheaper substitute. In the end, many critics claim, cost saving resulted in news cutting.

In fact, the network television audience now gets only 22 1/2 minutes of network news per program. That's it. It's impossible to cram the news of the world into that short a time, according to many in the business, including former president of CBS News Fred W. Friendly in his chapter "The Nightly News: A Leap of Faith versus the Bottom Line" in Michael P. Beaubien and John S. Wyeth, Jr.'s book *Views on the News: The Media and Public Opinion* (1994). What we get instead is headline news — short blurbs of the top stories with video footage to back them up. News stories average only 90 seconds. An often repeated statistic says that the nightly newscast set in type would cover less than the front page of the *New York Times*. For crisis reporting or historic events short, up-to-the-minute news works well, but for more complex issues like civil rights, the economy, health care, or welfare, we are left with only part of the story, and even that is sometimes confusing. As Friendly put it, "what we don't know could kill us." And while 24-hour cable news stations have much larger news holes, they often still stick to the same formula of short, headline news coupled with video — just repeated as an endless news loop.

Not only do we get just headlines, but the ever-lamented sound bite is growing even shorter. According to Craig Fehrman in "The Incredible Shrinking Sound Bite" (2011) the average sound bite is now limited to about eight seconds. These little blips don't contribute much to explaining an issue. This is particularly a problem when covering an election. Short sound bites rob the candidates of enough time to define themselves and their platforms, according to Fehrman.

These abbreviated stories and short sound bites also cause a problem for viewers trying to absorb the news. When television material becomes confusing, the viewer cannot go back and re-read the story, unlike in a newspaper. What he or she missed is missed. And the short pieces are confusing, often not providing enough context and depth for understanding. Walter Cronkite recognized this in a speech he gave at the RTNDA Conference in 1976. He said there is "... inadvertent and perhaps inevitable distortion that results through the hypercompression we all are forced to exert to fit one hundred pounds of news into the one-pound sack that we are given to fill each night."

The length of news pieces is not the only thing making them confusing. The way television news is presented, viewers often pay more attention to the anchors, reporters, computer graphics and video tricks than to the news itself, according to Bonnie Anderson in her book *News Flash* (2004). The presentation distances the viewers from the news. Instead of concentrating on the words coming out of the reporter's mouth, we are noticing the color of her suit, the design of his tie, the graphics dancing across the screen and the colorful banners stretched along the bottom. The "news" gets lost somewhere in the presentation, says Anderson.

When Dan Rather took over the anchor position for CBS, he took over more than just the chair. His contract awarded him the title of managing editor. Whereas in the past the news producer had the final say in what made it onto the news, Rather insisted on an equal if not stronger voice. Some argue (in particular Barbara Matusow in her 1983 book *The Evening Stars*) that this "star" power (also given to managing editor Tom Brokaw and senior editor Peter Jennings), coupled with seven-digit salaries, gave these anchors and now their successors more power and control than is good for the television program or the country. In other words, for each television news program, one white, wealthy, middle-aged celebrity decides what is "news," Matusow contends.

The introduction of satellite technology, including the use of smart phones that provide instant news footage from almost anywhere on earth, opened up a new set of problems. As the "live" story becomes ever more popular, reporters are often thrust in front of the camera with the action behind them in order to bring viewers the exciting drama unfolding at that moment. But the problem is just that. The news is unfolding before them, and by reporting live we get coverage of only a select point in time and space. No longer do the viewers get the benefit of the story being shaped and edited to include background, analysis, predictions and consequences that help explain the story, explains critics Westin in *Newswatch* and Edwin Diamond in *The Media Show: The Changing Face of the News, 1985-1990* (1991). "Live" coverage may be exciting, but it doesn't always tell us very much. Many politicians have argued that the frantic, no-time-for-reflection pace of the 24-hour news cycle of television news has adversely influenced the way our government functions, often, according to Stephen Cushion and Justin Lewis in "Three Phases of 24-Hour News Television" (2010), forcing politicians to comment on unfolding news or make decisions without time for reflection and analysis.

The Strengths of TV News

Many of the major criticisms of television news are the same elements that form the basis for its benefits. Television provides news to the masses in an enjoyable and even entertaining way. When breaking news occurs, we all turn to television news. A story repeated in Robert J. Donovan and Ray Scherer's book *Unsilent Revolution* (1992) exemplifies the importance of television news to most Americans and even to newspapers.

As the late-edition deadline approached, Eugene Patterson, then managing editor of the *Washington Post*, sat with his staff watching the television screen for any last-minute developments in the Apollo Space Mission. A young employee entered the office, looked around and said, "I always wondered how a great American newspaper covered a space mission." "Well, you know," Patterson observed long afterward, "that is how we kept up with the story."

Newspapers, the medium television reporters turned to in the 1960s for information, now rely on television and other electronic news sources to keep abreast of breaking news. When it comes to breaking stories, electronic news coverage has a virtual monopoly, able to reach the public almost anywhere at any time through television, the Internet and hand-held devices.

Television is a universal medium. Almost everyone, even the nation's poor, has access to television news. You don't need to be literate to get your news from television, explains Gene F. Jankowski and David C. Fuchs in *Television Today and Tomorrow* (1995). People who never finished high school can generally watch and understand most television news. The combination of narration and video makes the news story relatively easy to understand. More importantly, most people enjoy watching television, probably because it is easy and designed to be entertaining, conclude Jankowski and Fuchs. Watching the network evening news is a relaxing way to push your own problems out of your mind and become wrapped up in the larger problems of the nation and world, claims Mark R. Levy in his research article, "The Audience Experience with Television News," in *Journalism Monographs* (1978). If you enjoy something, you will continue to use it. By increasing your use of television, you will increase the amount of news information to which you are exposed. More knowledge creates the desired "informed citizen" in a democracy. Since research shows people don't usually rely on only one source for information (including conversations with friends, listening to the radio in the car, chatting around the coffee pot at work, etc.), Levy says, any knowledge gleaned from television just adds more value to us as voting citizens.

Many people even make television news part of their daily routine for the information, entertainment and reassurance it offers each day, according to Alan Rubin and Elizabeth Perse in "Audience Activity and Television News Gratifications" in *Communication Research* (1987). Watching the news allows viewers to become a distant participant in ongoing history. Through the filter of a respected and trusted anchor, viewers are able to keep up with national and world events. Most serious news junkies prefer one news program more than others and organize their schedules around that program. Why people select one news program over another varies from person to person, but all seem to select a program based on its ability to help them find out what they want to know and then present it in an understandable, concise and entertaining way.

The way television presents the news often makes it easier for some of us to absorb the details. Television presents news pieces as illustrated stories. Each story includes a beginning, middle and end and is narrated by the anchor or one of a supporting group of correspondents who flesh out the details. The anchor ties together the individual news pieces to create a synopsis of the story of the world on that particular day. Ongoing news events like elections, crises and legislation in Congress become a continuing part of the overall story. As an election year progresses, for example, reporters give us a small amount of background information each day to help us find our place in the election coverage and then an update to keep the story line moving. By the end of this long interwoven story of the world's news, we believe we understand what is happening and maybe even where things are headed. Walter Cronkite even closed each CBS News broadcast with the words, "And that's the way it is...."

The old adage "a picture is worth a thousand words" is often applied to television. While the words of the correspondent or anchor may not add up to the amount of copy in a newspaper story, the accompanying video may tell the story just as well or even better. Watching video footage, the viewer gets a sense of "being there." Television covers certain news stories better than print, according to many critics, in particular Robert J. Donovan and Ray Scherer in *Unsilent Revolution* (1992). They explain that emotional stories with vivid images — riots, protests, homecomings, celebrations — make great television. The printed word was no competition for watching the East Germans spilling over the Berlin Wall to freedom, the victims of Hurricane Katrina clinging to their rooftops waiting for rescue, or shocked and terrified New Yorkers fleeing from the city on September 11, 2001. These scenes held so much conflicting emotion, that words could not describe them. Television took the audience to the scenes and showed what was happening.

Having the news stories strung together into a news program, either in a network evening newscast or a segment of CNN's *Headline News*, forces the audience to watch all the news pieces, explains Edwin Diamond in *The Tin Kazoo: Television, Politics, and the News* (1975). Unlike newspapers or online news sources, where readers can skip over articles or entire sections that do not interest them, the television format pulls the viewer through every news item. Viewers learn information that they probably need to know, even though they did not actively seek out the material, says Diamond.

Friendly and Dan Nimmo and James E. Combs in *Nightly Horrors: Crisis Coverage by Television Network News* (1985) agree that crisis situations are where television news excels. Television has the unique ability to make a continuous story easier to understand by simplifying the complex details around a few easily understood pictorial symbols. People turn to television during a crisis not only to keep abreast of the latest developments, but also for psychological reasons. Over the years viewers have grown to know and trust the network anchors, an advantage the networks have over cable and its ever changing roster of anchors. In times of crisis they turn to these men, as former president of ABC news Av Westin wrote in his book *Newswatch* (1982), to find out if the world is safe and if they are safe. They want to know the latest to judge their own security. Rather, Brokaw and Jennings understood this and remained on the air after the initial attacks on the morning of September 11th for over 15 hours straight, feeding America the news as it unfolded in an effort to both inform and provide comfort to viewers.

Breaking news is another area in which television shines, even in the face of some criticism. Twenty-four-hour cable news, news breaks and longer breaking-news specials give television news the opportunity to do what it does best — provide instant coverage at any time on any day from anywhere. When breaking news occurs, people tune in to see their favorite anchor present the latest footage and information as it is received. Although breaking news coverage opens the door to mistakes, the American public has come to expect, even demand, instant news coverage. And having time for fact-checking doesn't guarantee news will be free of errors. No matter how much time is allowed to check facts, mistakes can and will still be made. Americans have learned to expect a fair share of mistakes in return for fast news. Breaking news is one of the best services television provides — giving the country the news almost instantaneously.

Television news also receives high marks from some critics for covering special events. Inaugurations, celebrity funerals and weddings, political conventions, election days and the like all make great television coverage — and television makes the most of the opportunities, according to Westin. Long before the event, television news production staff and researchers collect and coordinate piles of background information, old footage, interesting tidbits, experts willing to be interviewed, analysts ready to explain the consequences and correspondents prepared to arrive on the scene. The day of the big event, members of the news team are so organized they are able to smoothly cover the story from beginning to end and even include extra information that makes the event more than just a giant photo opportunity.

One little known or recognized service that network television news provides is protection of the president. Through the system known as a "press pool," television news crews rotate covering the president every time he sets foot outside the White House, explains Judy Woodruff in *This Is Judy Woodruff at the White House* (1982). When the president leaves the security of that building, a camera crew and a news correspondent travel along with him. This not only gives the networks footage if anything newsworthy should happen, but it also provides video should any attack or other tragedy occur. For example, when President Ronald Reagan was shot outside the Hilton Hotel in Washington, D.C., the CBS news team captured the would-be assassin on video. Not only were CBS White House correspondent Judy Woodruff and her camera crew on the scene and able to broadcast the story almost immediately, but they were also able to supply the authorities with video of John Hinkley.

Television journalists play an important role during hostage situations in saving lives and keeping the issue in the public eye. When three young Americans were arrested in Iran in 2009 and charged with spying, the networks kept the situation in the forefront through continuous coverage. The same was true when missionaries Martin and Gracia Burnham were taken hostage in the Philippines in 2002. Constant reminders of their continued captivity in the news helped their families push for measures to bring them home.

Assessment

At its creation several decades ago, television fought charges of putting entertainment before serious news coverage, and today the industry still has serious credibility problems. Shrinking stories, shrinking staffs and shrinking sound bites has left television news viewers even less informed than before. Even with the addition of 24-hour cable news channels, television news still does a poor job of offering analysis, perspective and depth to what is covered. Americans who claim to get a majority of their news from television regularly "flunk" national polls on current events. Airing stories of a politician's infidelity and a Hollywood star's personal life over more serious pieces on the economy, national health care and unemployment further illustrate favoring sensationalism over substance.

Yet Craig Allen rightfully argues in his book *News Is People* (2001) that television news, local television news in particular, is actually designed to appeal to the overwhelming masses of Americans, not the intellectual elite who often criticize television news for "dumbing down" content. Many characteristics of local television news, the smiling and personable anchors, "eyewitness" news style, simplified stories and "news you can use" mentality, stemmed from the work of news consultants who spent decades asking average Americans what they want to see on their local news programs. Local news stations listened to their viewers and created news programs that allowed them to maintain a strong viewership, even as national network ratings declined. The gradual decrease of hard news and increase of softer, more human and entertaining news resulted from a need of news organizations to draw viewers and, in turn, advertisers to its product, Allen concludes.

In some capacity, television news programs will always do what they do best: cover breaking news, crises and pre-planned events. The public still trusts news anchors and relies on them in times of crisis. People will still turn to them for coverage of inaugurations, election days and other big media events. After all, what would Super Tuesday be without our news anchors to carry voters through the night and predict the results?

Geoffrey Baym explains in his book *From Cronkite to Colbert* (2010) that there have been, in fact, three distinct periods of television news: first, the "network age" of public service professional journalism of the Cronkite era; second, the "multichannel era" where news is a corporate product of commercial journalism; and finally our current era of the "post-network age," an unstable period of technological convergence and rapidly changing media forms and practices. With these changes the television news viewing audience becomes more fragmented every year as the public looks to alternative news sources, with many completely tuning out the news in favor of entertainment programming. Network evening news now maintains an undefined role sandwiched between local news programs and in constant competition with FOX, CNN and news sources on the Web. Many believe this is the end of network evening news. More realistically, the networks need to reexamine their mission. Just as newspapers redefined themselves after the advent of television, television must recreate its role. There are several ways this can be accomplished.

First, in relation to network local television news, the networks should continue to feed the local stations with national and international news. Local stations, in general, do not have the expertise or manpower to independently cover all national and international news. For this, networks provide a valuable service. Local stations, on the other hand, have what networks do not — time. Some local stations run newscasts both before and after the network news and another program later in the evening. By adding more national and international news to the local programs, the audience receives more of the news they need to know wrapped up in an entertaining style that appeals to their viewing public. While a mix of national and international news can always be found on cable, local news can tease out the relevance for their local audience.

Second, networks should adopt a more in-depth and analytical look at the news. Since "headline news" is available in multiple mediums 24-hours a day, network news should take advantage of its strengths, contacts, prestige and expertise, to go beyond the headlines. PBS has produced multiple in-depth, roundtable discussions of current events for years including a weekly segment that matches a representative from the Democratic and Republican parties to discuss issues, now represented by Mark Shields and David Brooks. The networks should produce their own expanded version within the nightly news program, not just on weekly shows like *Washington Week in Review* (PBS), *Face the Nation* (CBS), *This Week* (ABC) or *Meet the Press* (NBC). Instead of providing headlines of what is happening, correspondents should delve into the reasons behind what is happening. In the age of information-overload what the public needs is explanation and analysis.

Third, if more breaking news is left to cable and the Internet, networks should concentrate on, and cover more completely, a smaller number of stories. One five-minute news piece would replace five one-minute pieces. The "headline news" days would be over. Viewers wouldn't be left with just a taste of each story; they would have a richer understanding of the news of the day. If networks hand over the shorter, more routine news pieces to the affiliates, CBS, NBC and ABC will be free to do a more thorough examination of complex news events.

Fourth, we should recognize that there are some advantages to our current hybrid of news and entertainment media designed for a consumer society. As James Carey points out in his article "The Mass Media and Democracy: Between the Modern and Postmodern" in the *Journal of International Affairs* (1993), the network era style news left the citizens out of the discussion, speaking at them through the news, but not allowing them to enter the conversation. Also, in *From*

Cronkite to Colbert, Baym suggests that entertainment shows that successfully blend news information and entertainment, such as Jon Stewart's *The Daily Show* and its spin-off *The Colbert Report,* teach viewers how to think critically and go deeper into analysis of the real issues and current events than the traditional network or cable providers were able to do decades ago. Although not true news organizations, of course, Jon Stewart and Steven Colbert provide an entertaining and informative focus on news. Instead of mourning the loss of the dominant network era news, we should embrace the opportunity this new paradigm presents to create a more engaged and critical consumer public that can go beyond the reporters' unbiased objectivity to actively explore, discuss and shape issues in America.

Points of View

Books

Allen, Craig M. *News Is People: The Rise of Local TV News and the Fall of News from New York.* Ames: Iowa State University Press, 2001. Local television news successfully responds to public opinion in shaping news programs, creating entertaining and informative broadcasts to appeal to mass audiences.

Barkin, Steve M. *American Television News: The Media Marketplace and the Public Interest.* Armonk, N.Y.: M. E. Sharpe, 2003. Economic factors, fragmented audiences and regulatory laws have influenced television news content.

Baym, Geoffrey. *From Cronkite to Colbert.* Boulder, Colo.: Paradigm, 2010. Today's "fake news" shows have the potential to ignite political discussion among Americans and redefine television news.

Cushion, Stephen, and Justin Lewis. *The Rise of 24-Hour News Television.* New York: Peter Lang, 2010. The author provides a critical look at the strengths, weaknesses and challenges of the 24-hour news channels and their impact across the world.

Diamond, Edwin. *The Media Show: The Changing Face of the News, 1985-1990.* Cambridge, Mass.: MIT Press, 1991. Funding cutbacks in the 1980s crippled television news departments and limited news coverage.

Donovan, Robert J., and Ray Scherer. *Unsilent Revolution.* Cambridge: Cambridge University Press, 1992. Although television news has some disadvantages in covering news, it is particularly suited for covering emotional stories with vivid images.

Farnsworth, Stephen J., and Robert S. Lichter. *The Nightly News Nightmare: Media Coverage of U.S. Presidential Elections, 1988-2008,* 3rd ed. Boulder, Colo.: Rowman and Little-

field, 2010. During the elections from 1988 to 2008, television had "consistent problems in terms of fairness and focus on substantive matters rather than the horse-race reporting of the latest polls."

Iyengar, Shanton, and Donald R. Kinder. *News That Matters: Television and American Opinion*, Updated Edition. Chicago: University of Chicago Press, 2009. "Because of its wide reach and high credibility, television news obviously possesses the potential to shape American public opinion profoundly."

Jankowski, Gene F., and David C. Fuchs. *Television Today and Tomorrow*. New York and Oxford: Oxford University Press, 1995. CBS executives Jankowski and Fuchs cover the history of television, how programs are created, the role of advertisers, the impact of government regulations, the problem with television news and the future.

Kerbel, Matthew Robert. *If It Bleeds, It Leads: An Anatomy Of Television News*. Boulder, Colo.: Westview Press, 2001. "If something is graphic, if it is violent, if it catches your eye, it has to lead the local news. Because that is what local news is all about."

Lewis, Justin, Stephen Cushion, eds. *The Rise of 24-Hour News Television*. New York: Peter Lang, 2010. "24-hour news channels have reshaped the genre of news and [have had an] impact ... on democracy more generally."

Nimmo, Dan, and James E. Combs. *Nightly Horrors: Crisis Coverage by Television Network News*. Knoxville: University of Tennessee Press, 1985. Television news emphasizes crises, as illustrated by the coverage of People's Temple, Three Mile Island, Flight 191, Mount St. Helens and the Iran hostage crisis.

Articles

Blondheim, Menahem, and Tamar Liebes. "Television News and the Nation: The End?" *Annals of the American Academy of Political and Social Science* 625 (September 2009): 182-95. Unlike news broadcasts of the golden age of television news, modern TV news no longer gives the audience a reassuring sense of order to the world and the day's events.

Bock, Mary Angela. "You Really, Truly, Have to 'Be There': Video Journalism as a Social and Material Construction." *Journalism & Mass Communication Quarterly* 88:4 (2011): 705-18. Block describes and analyzes the daily work practices of video journalists in newspapers and television stations in this era of convergence.

Boyd-Barrett, Oliver. "The Nightly News Nightmare: Media Coverage of U.S. Presidential Elections, 1988-2008." *Journalism and Mass Communication Quarterly* 88:1 (2011): 222-24. U.S. television networks allow presidential candidates to speak in their own words on average one-quarter to one-third of the time of the average paid commercial, poorly serving American's citizenship and democracy.

Maier, Scott. "All the News Fit to Post? Comparing News Content on the Web to Newspapers, Television, and Radio." *Journalism & Mass Communication Quarterly* 87:3/4 (2010): 548-62. A content analysis of 3,900 news stories found that online news (compared to coverage from newspapers, network television, cable television and radio) maintained similar agenda-setting roles and story selection as traditional news media.

Painter, Chad, and Louis Hodges. "Mocking the News: How The Daily Show with Jon Stewart Holds Traditional Broadcast News Accountable." *Journal of Mass Media Ethics* 25:4 (2010): 257-74. Jon Stewart and his *Daily Show* colleagues hold traditional broadcast news media accountable to the public.

Quayle, Matt. "The Method of the Medium Is in Motion." *ETC: A Review of General Semantics* 67:3 (2010): 300-10. News is mainly for entertainment, not information; and new methods of electronic communication may facilitate productive public discourse.

Sagan, Paul, and Tom Leighton. "The Internet & the Future of News." *Daedalus* 139:2 (2010): 119-25, 154. Internet news has changed the way news is gathered and consumed, making news more personalized and interactive.

17

Conflict as a News Value

On October 23, 2004, Milwaukee police officer Andrew Spengler hosted a housewarming party for himself in the city's Bay View neighborhood. Liquor flowed freely. Many of his guests were fellow police officers. Two partygoers, college students Katie Brown and Kirsten Antonissen, showed up around 2:30 a.m. with two African-American men, Frank Jude and Lovell Harris. The quartet later reported that they immediately felt unwelcome because the women were white and the men were not. They tried to leave soon after arriving but were confronted outside the house by Spengler and at least nine others who accused the men of stealing Spengler's wallet and police badge.

The off-duty officers searched and then assaulted Harris and Jude. One of the men cut Harris' face with a knife before he was able to flee. At the same time, Spengler and a dozen or so of his cohorts were kicking and punching Jude mercilessly, jamming a pen into both of his ear canals, battering his face and breaking two of his fingers. Jude was arrested by the on-duty police officers called to the scene. He was then taken to a hospital with injuries so numerous that doctors could not record them all in their written report. Neither the wallet nor the badge was found. On February 6, 2005, the *Milwaukee Journal Sentinel* reported on the incident that had remained under wraps for several months while the police department conducted an internal inquiry. When the story broke, the Milwaukee County district attorney called the incident "horrendous" and "an abuse of power" and said some in the police department were obstructing his investigation. Word of the beating unleashed a long-running torrent of news coverage. State and federal prosecutions followed a grand jury investigation of the offending officers, and the parties filed multiple lawsuits.

This story, which documented racial and physical violence and police misconduct, was soaked in conflict, a perennial theme in the stories we tell one another. Humans are storytellers and always have been. Stories are the way we communicate with fellow humans. Embedded in stories is information about a

by Karen L. Slattery
Marquette University

culture's social structures, the ways we think that people should behave, how we should live and what we should value. Famed psychiatrist Carl Jung wrote that the stories that shape who we are and what we might become have always involved conflict, and events are understood in terms of opposites, for example, good and bad, dark and light, old and young and the like. So the stories journalists tell often will involve the drama that arises within conflicts between people, between people and the law and between people and society.

At the same time, journalists routinely come under fire for disseminating stories that revolve around conflict. How often do people ask: "Why is so much bad news reported?" Or, "When are they going to report some good news?" John McManus, in his 1994 book *Market-Driven Journalism: Let the Citizen Beware?* criticized the media for focusing on sensational, violent or even tasteless news stories. At the same time, scholar John Stevens, in his 1985 article "Social Utility of Sensational News: Murder and Divorce in the 1920s," argued that such news serves the purpose of helping to maintain and negotiate a community's moral boundaries.

When discussing the problem of conflict as a news value, it is important to note that while conflict has long been a topic associated with sensational news, stories about conflict are not necessarily sensational in and of themselves. In her 1994 article, "Sensationalism Versus News of the Moral Life: Making the Distinction," Karen Slattery noted that topics of stories that scholars and critics have long associated with sensationalism, including crime, natural disasters, sexual escapades and the like, all reflecting some form of conflict, do not always contain the markers of sensationalism. Those markers include, among other things, lurid headlines, loaded language and sensory details. Stories that emphasize the sensational are often packaged as isolated incidents and presented as matters lacking moral, political or social consequences. Journalists can and do present conflict-related stories that are important to citizens and self-governance in nonsensational ways. Those conflict-related stories can and do address issues of public interest and, thus, should not be confused with sensationalism as sensationalism. This chapter describes reports of news coverage of conflict-related issues and events in various studies but does not attempt to determine whether that coverage would count as sensationalism.

Origins of the Issue

To bring the definition of news into sharper focus, scholars distinguish between characteristics of an issue or event and the values of journalists who judge whether the story is worth covering. Some issues and events are marked by "news factors," or story characteristics that catch the journalist's attention. The

Jude incident, for example, had the news factors of immediacy, impact, unusualness and conflict, that is, the story was current, of interest to citizens concerned about public safety, out of the ordinary and laden with conflict.

The term "news values" reflects the journalist's professional values. The more an event's news factors match the journalist's news values, the more likely the story will be considered newsworthy. News values that predict which story becomes news include timeliness, novelty, conflict, human interest, significance and proximity. This standard list does not cover all journalistic values, including accuracy, completeness, deadlines, balance and the like.

Conflict, considered both a news factor and a news value, is an American news staple. Stories about disagreements between colonists and the British appeared in the colonial press. Press historians Michael and Edwin Emery, in their 1992 book *The Press and America: An Interpretative History of the Mass Media,* noted that when the press taps new markets, journalists choose stories that involve highly sensational or emotional conflict. For example, when the first penny newspaper, the *New York Sun,* appeared in 1833 it emphasized local events and violence. As newspapers drew a more educated audience, readers began to demand less sensationalized and more serious news stories. Despite the criticism, press emphasis on sensational news appeared again in the 1890s as yellow journalism and again in the 1920s with the emergence of tabloid journalism, marked by stories of crime, sex and movie stars.

Critics and journalists alike have long criticized the use of sensational stories to gain readership. Henry Raymond established the *New York Times* in 1851, for example, with a mission to inform readers and avoid the sensationalism his competitors offered . Nearly four decades later, the *Times* took a public swipe at its competition, which was then steeped in yellow journalism, when it adopted its famous slogan, "All the News That's Fit to Print." Criticism of the press for its heavy emphasis on conflict-related stories continues. For example, John Pauly, in his 2009 essay of the same title, asked, "Is journalism interested in resolution, or only in conflict?" He noted that journalists return "again and again to familiar stories of violence and human depravity."

Scholars, however, say that humans are drawn to stories involving conflict because conflict represents a threat to social and physical order. In her 1996 book, *Hardwired for News: Using Biological and Cultural Evolution to Explain the Surveillance Function,*" Pamela Shoemaker argued that humans constantly scan the environment for threats and naturally pause to examine stories about potential harms. Humans use the information to evaluate risks to themselves and to their communities.

Although most people see conflict as a sign of dysfunction, sociologists have argued that conflict serves social functions as well. German sociologist Georg

Simmel observed in his book, *Conflict: The Web of Group-Affiliations* (1955), that conflict "resolves the tension between contrasts," and its aim is unity even if "it be through the annihilation of one of the conflicting parties." Scholars who see conflict as socially useful have argued that, among other things, it binds groups together in the face of an external threat. Lewis Cosner wrote, in his 1997 book, *The Functions of Social Conflict,* that conflict stimulates new ways of thinking about solving problems and facilitates changes in social structures. Slattery likewise observed that conflict serves the purpose of reinforcing and renegotiating moral boundaries in the community. Thus, the goal of humankind should be to manage, rather than eliminate, conflict.

Conflict is a necessary feature of physical and social order, and it appears in the stories that a culture tells about itself. Journalists, whose job is to inform the public about the day's news, thus use conflict as a measure of a story's newsworthiness. How they should approach conflict, though, is a matter of serious debate. Critics, journalists and scholars offer contending views about the role of conflict-related news stories in hindering or advancing social progress, and they present arguments both for and against publishing such stories.

The Downside of Conflict as a News Value

Critics say that the major reason the press devotes so much attention to topics like crime and violence, i.e., conflict-related topics scholars associate historically with sensationalism, is to attract audiences for advertisers. Media critics have also pointed to the 1970s era of deregulation and the subsequent rise in shareholder interest for the decline in responsible news coverage. Since then, critics argue, communication companies have been bought, sold and resold in the interest of generating handsome revenue. If the leveraged properties failed to deliver profits to shareholders, they were sold or closed.

The resulting emphasis on the bottom line has shifted the focus of news away from public affairs reporting. In *Market-Driven Journalism: Let the Citizen Beware?* John McManus argued that the press is increasingly being driven by the corporate need to generate profits and, as a result, offers less quality public affairs reporting — that is, the type citizens need to self-govern effectively — and more news that emphasizes sensational news, that includes stories about conflict, for its own sake. McManus, who published his book in the mid-1990s, has said that with the rise of the Internet, new sources of information, including corporations and citizen journalists, have entered the market. In response, according to McManus, in a Web interview with UPUI.com's Eric Loo in 2010, the traditional news media have "amputated much of their reporting and editing staff and are more prone to cut corners than in the past.... Sensation is replacing substance, particularly investigative reporting." Part of the reason is that stories about crime and violence often demand fewer resources than investigative pieces that require more staff, time and money to prepare.

Like McManus, others have reported the upswing in sensationalism on television news in the United States and elsewhere. In addition to reporting stories of crime, violence and car wrecks, journalists now also routinely frame issues classified as public affairs in relation to conflict, according to Karen Slattery, Mark Doremus and Linda Marcus, in their 2001 study "Trends in Public Affairs Reporting on the Network Evening News: A Move Toward the Sensational." They cited, as one example, a televised interview with Texas Senator Kay Bailey Hutchinson about her frightening experiences with a stalker in a story that involved a bill related to tougher penalties for stalking. While the story was clearly about an action of a governmental body, and would be classified as public affairs, the element of conflict was foregrounded in the report.

James Stanyer, in his 2001 study "'A Right Seaside Bust Up': Television News Coverage of Internal Party Debates at the British Party Conferences," examined coverage of internal party debates in Britain and reported that the debates most likely to be covered by the press were those that featured "rancour" and "antagonism between clearly divergent sides." He blamed deregulation for weakening the broadcasters' commitment to public affairs reporting and an unwillingness to report the formal, "lackluster" debates. The journalists interviewed for his study told him that they were under pressure to attract the attention of viewers, suggesting that they may not have focused on the antagonism if they did not have to worry about attracting an audience.

According to McManus, the rise in sensational news, including conflict-related stories, at the cost of stories related to civic affairs has serious implications for a democracy. In his Web interview with Eric Loo in 2010, McManus likened the news media to the "nation's central nervous system," saying that it "connects us with each other's pain and progress." Informed and intelligent collective decision-making is not possible without the media to help us make sense of what goes on around us.

In addition to crowding out stories about civic affairs, critics say, the news media's overemphasis on conflict-related stories in an attempt to attract an audience creates other problems. A heavy emphasis on stories related to violent conflict, including stories of tragedy, crime and the like, that are often treated in a sensational fashion, suggests that the world is a "mean" place. Viewing that kind of content, according to scholars, shapes our perceptions about the environment in which we live and the people who inhabit it. In her study of television news visuals, "Seeing is Remembering: How Visuals Contribute to Learning from Television News" (1990), Doris Graber argued that news photos that depict the negative or violent aspects of events can attract attention to stories and contribute to learning from news. It follows that the use of visuals that focus on the violent aspects of a story may influence the way an audience thinks about people involved in the stories. For example, Timothy Meyer, in his article "Some Effects of Real Newsfilm Violence on the Behavior of Viewers" (1971) examined the relationship between visual and verbal information in television news. He reported that changing the verbal explanation in a news clip that visually depicted a man being shot in the head by another man determined how audience members said they perceived the victim.

Most studies have centered on pictures in newspapers and television, but it should be noted that audience members may not attend to pictures in a Web news environment in the same way they do in TV and print news environments. Laura Arpan and Firat Tuzunkan examined the effects of browsing through news stories on the Web in their 2008 study "Conflict Photos in News about Protests." They had subjects look through stories on a fictitious news website. Five of the six stories were "distracter" stories, while the sixth featured information about students protesting university budget cuts. One of the accompanying photos depicted a student kicking another student in the stomach. The researchers reported that the photo of physical violence did not necessarily attract attention to the story, but study subjects who saw it evaluated the protesters more negatively than subjects who did not see it.

In addition to shaping audience perceptions of the world, the "others" in it and the social and political processes that move it along, new concerns have been raised of late. New Zealander Alison McCulloch is a freelance journalist who worked on the foreign desk at the *New York Times* for more than five years following the attack on New York's Twin Towers. She has argued that news stories in one country are influenced by the way that narratives take shape in another. She pointed out specific ways that the terrorism coverage following 9/11 influenced the way the New Zealand government thought about terrorism in that country.

Terrorism was not a regular feature of New Zealand's news landscape before 9/11, McCulloch wrote in her 2008 essay "'Maori Terror Threat': The Dangers of the Post-9/11 Narrative." Yet since then, that nation has enacted the Terrorism Suppression Act. She linked the law and its application to the way that the international news media framed the story of the aftermath of the attack on the United States, basing her observations on her work, as well as journalistic and academic sources.

According to McCulloch, the larger 9/11 news narrative follows a classic good-versus-evil paradigm and plays on fears of other cultures, particularly Arab and Muslim. She argued that dividing people into groups and pitting them against one another misses the nuances and complexities that shade life and can lead to loss of rights and protections that a civil society normally provides. She said, for instance, that New Zealand authorities invoked the Terrorism Suppression Act in 2007 to execute warrants in raids against Maori activists. She argued that the international press in particular framed the story as "terrorism," thus imposing on New Zealander Maori another version of a "fear-filled us vs. them story." She argued that labeling someone a terrorist is a powerful accusation because the term is a stereotype and is open to multiple interpretations.

McCulloch also noted the effects that the overarching terrorist narrative, in play following 9/11, has had on journalism practices. News stories, she has argued, refer to "vague" reports regarding people's possible links to terrorism, often with little regard for whether publishing information related to investigations will jeopardize a fair trial. McCulloch also pointed out that the relationship between the government and the press has been strengthened in the wake of the 9/11 attacks, in part because the media are now driven by 24-hour news cycles and depend on the government for information. Further, fast-tracking terrorism stories to the front page attracts attention but also paves the way for strengthening the state apparatus and shaping legislation and foreign policy in ways they might not otherwise be shaped. These possibilities, already realities in other countries, according to McCulloch, should serve as a caution to New Zealand's journalists.

A third problem arises, according to news critics, because the implications of embracing conflict as a news value are not fully appreciated. A 2009 study pointed to the news genre that actually builds conflict into the presentation format. The genre is anchored to the practice of impoliteness and aims to reaffirm a particular worldview. In the study, titled "Impoliteness and Identity in the American News Media: The 'Culture Wars,'" Pilar Garces-Conejos Blitvich called the emerging genre "news as confrontation" and cited cable programs featuring hosts Bill O'Reilly, Glen Beck, Nancy Grace and Sean Hannity as examples. These hosts, she argued, engage in incivility because it attracts attention and infuses programming with "the drama and the tension that go along with impoliteness."

Garces-Conejos Blitvich noted that traditional interviewing assumes a neutral stance by the interviewer who is eliciting information for an "overhearing audience." The interviewer must judge when to engage in tough questioning. Alternatively, cable hosts who practice "news as confrontation" use incivility to strategically construct an identity that distinguishes them from other journalists. The main purpose of the interview is to reaffirm a particular worldview rather than inform the public. While they ask questions, the interviewers who use the tactic of impoliteness often "monopolize the floor, answering their own questions and engaging in debate." The incivility reflects an effort to marginalize the point of view and the speaker with whom the interviewer disagrees. Further, Garces-Conejos Blitvich noted that the strategy is useful in creating a rapport with viewers.

The emergence of "news as confrontation," according to Garces-Conejos Blitvich, is linked to the growing number of voices of minorities and women in the public sphere. Cable hosts, she argued, generally cater to the white, middle-class male sector of the audience that has lost power in the public arena, and they draw on impoliteness to establish a perceived relationship with those who share the same values. Not wanting to be seen as biased, the hosts invite guests with alternative viewpoints onto their programs and then draw on the tactics of impoliteness and incivility to undermine the ideas offered by the guests. Hosts defend incivility by aligning themselves with the "watchdog" role of the press, suggesting that such behavior is needed to protect themselves and the audience from the ideologies of the liberal press.

Political scientist Diana Mutz also studied impoliteness in her 2007 study "Effects of 'In-Your-Face' Television Discourse on Perceptions of a Legitimate Opposition." She reported that incivility in the media furthers negative perceptions of political candidates and exacerbates the perceived differences between the viewers and the candidates. This tactic implies that negotiation, common ground and compromise are not possible and polarizes individuals with differing opinions.

The increased dependence on stories that relate to conflict in the media play a role in the way that citizens perceive the culture in which they live. When the media focus on stories that involve conflict or generate artificial, impolite conflict to boost ratings, audience members are likely to perceive the world as nasty and brutish, peopled with "others" with whom one cannot reason or civilly engage. Such perceptions, scholars say, color how we, and the rest of humanity, live our lives.

The Upside of Conflict as a News Value

Other researchers point out that stories centered on conflict can reflect legitimate threats to physical and social order. They note that stories related to murder, theft, prostitution, droughts, executions, war, piracy, suicide, rape, revenge, the evils of alcohol and the like appeared in newspapers and broadsides in the 16th through 19th centuries. Scholars of 20th and 21st century journalism have documented the continued trend in both television and broadcast news. While they have linked these conflict-related topics to the problem of sensationalism, these topics are also, arguably, related to issues that society cannot afford to ignore. Knowledge of such threats, regardless of story treatment, draws readers' attention to pressing problems and allows them to take action as more-informed citizens.

In his 1959 study, *Class and Class Conflict in Industrial Society,* sociologist Ralf Dahrendorf pointed out that conflict is "an essential feature of [social] structure and process" in that it stimulates new ways to think about solving problems and facilitate change. The first reason to embrace the concept of conflict as a news value is because, as scholars have suggested, the mass media can effect social change, depending on the historical circumstances. David Demers and Kasisomayajula Viswanath argued in their 1999 work, *Mass Media, Social Control & Social Change: A Macrosocial Perspective,* that conflict-related stories that hold the promise of social change are routinely found in news coverage in papers, on television and radio and on the Web.

George Sylvie's 1991 study of the coverage of civil unrest, "A Study of Civil Disorder: The Effect of News Values and Competition on Coverage by Two Competing Daily Newspapers," offers an example of how the press chronicles and the community follows up on a conflict. He examined coverage of civil disorder in two daily newspapers in Louisiana in the 1980s. Violence broke out on September 20, 1988, in a parking lot at a grocery store in Shreveport. The store was in an area of Shreveport called Cedar Grove, home to a largely black population. The incident began when two white women drove into the store parking lot with the intention, according to police, to buy drugs. After one was robbed in the process, she fired a gun into a crowd of people standing nearby, striking and killing 20-year-old David McKinney, a black man. As word got out about the incident, angry African Americans gathered in the parking and threw bricks through the store windows and at whites who were passing by.

In turn, according to Sylvie, business owners armed themselves for protection, fearing what might happen next. Tensions escalated, with angry residents burning and looting businesses, firing guns and throwing bricks at police and firefighters. The papers, the *Shreveport Journal* and the *Times,* reported on the riot and the fact that black leaders criticized the city's mayor "for his reluctance to cite racism as the root of the violence." For the next couple of days, area residents met with city officials in an effort to work through the problem. The *Times* began printing a series of stories about racial relations called "In Black and White," and the *Journal* ran stories in a similar vein during the next two years. While Sylvie drew comparisons and outlined differences in the coverage, he stopped short of speculating on the effect that the coverage might have had on race relations. His study offers evidence, however, that the press moved beyond the events as they unfolded to offer perspective on the problem of race relations in that area.

David Sumner's 1995 work focused on the media's role in bringing about social change during the sit-ins in the South in 1960. Sumner interviewed participants in the sit-ins for his study, "Nashville, Nonviolence, and the Newspapers: The Convergence of Social Goals with News Values," as well as journalists who covered the story. His goal was to find out about the role of the news media from the perspective of those who were involved the movement and those who covered it.

In February 1960, four black students quietly took seats at a store lunch counter that refused to serve black customers. The students, who were attending four Nashville universities, planned the protest in advance. They had spent time at workshops learning the practice of nonviolence, which involved both discipline and self-protection. Sumner reported that the students recognized that they needed the news media as an ally because they "wanted to show the wider public that they were not the ones who caused violence or confrontations." Former student John Lewis told Sumner that he and his colleagues were aware of the power of the media, particularly television, to convey the nonviolent nature of the movement. When violence at the lunch counter did erupt, the public saw that the perpetrators were "young White 'thugs' and onlookers." Another student, also involved in the sit-in, said that the news coverage made a difference in the support from the larger community. "We realized that the eyes of the world were on us, and we wanted to put on our very best conduct," said participant Bernard Lafayette. A local pastor told Sumner that the demonstration's purpose was to make a statement to "the entire community. In the sense that the press covers it and it gets out there, it's tremendously important." Those involved in the sit-in said that they had good relationships with *Tennessean* reporter David Halberstam, telling him that they thought that his coverage was fair and accurate and allowed them to continue their protest. "That's the most important thing anybody ever said to me as a journalist," Halberstam said. As news of the sit-ins spread, others began participating in similar protests across the South. By May 10, Nashville store owners agreed to open their lunch counters to African-American customers. According to the students, not all of the press was instrumental in advancing social change. They said they viewed the *Tennessean* as vital to their cause, but they did not view the coverage of the competing newspaper, the *Banner*, in the same light.

Sumner's study is noteworthy in that it identifies, from the participants' perspective, the power of the media in furthering their social agenda. Sumner argued that the press played an important role in advancing the students' cause because the story lent itself to a natural narrative account of conflict. He pointed out that as the civil rights movement expanded to include less obvious heroes and villains, the news coverage became, overall, less sympathetic.

The phenomenon of conflict, according to sociologists, also pushes a culture forward in the process of reinforcing or renegotiating its moral boundaries. The news media facilitate that push by reporting conflict-related stories. In his 1985 study, "Social Utility of Sensational News: Murder and Divorce in the 1920s," John Stevens examined the moral dimension of news, arguing that coverage of stories related to social deviance allows society to reaffirm its moral standards. Social deviance reflects a conflict between actors and the social and moral norms of the community.

According to Stevens, the news media publicized moral problems and citizens respond by weighing in with opinions and judgments in the public arena. In doing so, a line is established over which one must not step. Stevens pointed out that "the clarification of that line helps establish what is and is not acceptable in the society." He further argued in his study that much of the work of defining and redefining moral boundaries is done through court trials, adding that the news media "increase the range of the vicarious participation to those far beyond the courtroom walls."

Stevens detailed a crime story that was one of the most heavily publicized during the 1920s, the Hall-Mills case. The Rev. Edward Hall was an Episcopalian minister in New Brunswick, New Jersey, whose wife was from a prominent family. He had an affair with Eleanor Mills, a singer in the church choir and the wife of the church sexton. The entwined bodies of Hall and Mills were discovered in a local lover's lane one night, and their love notes were sprinkled over the corpses. A neighbor who lived on a nearby pig farm reported that on the night of the murders she thought someone was in her field stealing corn. When she checked it out, she said she saw four people silhouetted against the sky. She said she heard the shots that killed the couple. Stevens noted that the overarching news narrative that played out, sensationally, in the press included, among others, conflicts involving the "ill-starred lovers," "the wronged wife" and the "pathetic husband of the choir singer."

The news coverage of the story was extensive but trailed off when no arrests were made. Four years later, in 1926, the authorities got a break in the case and arrested a number of people, including the minister's wife and her brothers. Again, the newspapers widely reported the events, including the trial. The case became the most publicized trial in American history up to that point. One New York newspaper, the sensational *Evening Graphic*, offered thousands of readers the chance to participate in the story by "sending in their solutions to the case, in 50 words or less." After weeks of testimony, the jury deliberated five hours before acquitting all of the suspects. According to Stevens, writers at the time said the story attracted so much attention "because everyone loves to see a minister caught in sin." The coverage served to reaffirm the public's belief that ministers should "practice what they preach" and murderers should be caught and tried. Stevens concludes that the press performs "a useful service in forcing society to reconsider its values. This is no less true, even if profit is the primary motive for publishing."

Stevens would be likely to say that the story of the police beating of Frank Jude, told at the beginning of the chapter, also fits into the category of coverage that forces members of a community to reconsider or recommit to moral boundaries. The story, reflecting physical and racial conflict, forced community members to confront issues related to violence, racial tensions and the violations of expectations by people hired to protect citizens and punishment. Seven police officers were tried for civil rights violations, found guilty and sentenced to prison. The citizen outrage reaffirmed moral boundaries that also were observed by the chief judge in a 2009 7th Circuit appellate court opinion, *United States v. Bartlett et. al.* He wrote, "The distance between civilization and barbarity, and the time needed to pass from one state to another, is depressingly short. Police officers in Milwaukee proved this the morning of October 24, 2004." The case sent the message that those who are hired to protect citizens are expected to do so.

Because conflict, in the words of German sociologist Ralf Dahrendorf, is a "stubborn fact of social life," humans spend part of each day making themselves aware of potential harms or reacting to harmful situations. Conflict helps serve the social process of organizing people into groups around those perceived or real threats to their ways of life. Since humans cannot be everywhere at once, they depend on the news media to operate as informants.

Dahrendorf's observation was reflected in a study of the behavior that emerged among the people involved in Hurricane Katrina, an event that pitted humans against the environment. Havidan Rodriguez, Joseph Trainor and Enrico Quarantelli examined government documents, fieldwork data for the University of Delaware's Disaster Research Center and news media reports for their 2006 study "Rising to the Challenges of a Catastrophe: The Emergent and Prosocial Behavior Following Hurricane Katrina." They argued that the records indicate that, contrary to media reports during the early days of the storm, victims, rescuers and local agencies improvised in ways that suggested a serious effort to cooperate with one another in order to cope with the catastrophe.

Yao Qingjiang, Liu Zhaoxi and Lowndes Stephens examined one year's worth of disaster reporting by the *New York Times*, *Los Angeles Times* and *New Orleans Times Picayune* for their 2007 study, "Hurricane Katrina Recorded." They noted that the initial coverage focused on looting and violence, but pointed out that, after the initial crisis passed, the coverage shifted in tone. Using moral theory to guide the analysis, they reported that stories reflected outside support for recovery as well as community efforts to rebuild, noting that many of the stories told of the efforts of victims and rescue teams to work together to clean up and

recreate the city and to aid the residents. Their findings lend support to sociologists' claim that conflict can serve as a social force and has the potential to bring people together to fight for a common cause. The stories of the events arguably rose to the level of news, at least in part, on the basis of the underlying conflicts and response to those conflicts by the humans involved.

Conflict, researchers say, serves important functions in social life. Conflict pushes people to rethink or reaffirm moral boundaries and leads people to organize themselves to respond to harm or threats of harm. Conflict is certain to be reflected in at least some of the events that occur in social life of the community and, as a result, ought to be considered as legitimate news in the eyes of journalists.

Assessment

Conflict is a natural part of our everyday lives, and it often poses serious threats to our well-being. Because individuals cannot be everywhere at once, we depend on the media to alert us to possible physical dangers and social or moral misdeeds. That way, we can make informed decisions about what, if any, actions are necessary. The scholarship suggests that conflict as a news value for journalists makes sense.

Other studies, however, suggest that conflict as a news value can be problematic for a democracy. In particular, the news media often rely on conflict-related news stories to attract audiences who are naturally inclined to attend to stories about threats. Coverage of conflict generates income for news corporations. This type of coverage often creates false impressions about the world and the people in it. The misimpressions can lead to bad policy making.

Taken together, research studies suggest that conflict as a news value is a complex phenomenon. Conflict-related stories serve to enhance the social good in some instances and detract in others. One serious concern is the news media's overemphasis on conflict as a news value in an attempt to draw an audience. At the heart of this concern is the concept of manipulation. Media manipulation frames stories to show conflict where none may exist. Manipulation is harmful to audience members because the media fail to treat audiences as rational, responsible human beings. Instead, they are treated as a means to an end, which is profit-making. The harm is compounded when the public makes irrational decisions based on misinformation.

Reporting conflict is not always problematic. But because the news media's practice of overemphasizing conflict-related stories, in sensational ways to earn a profit, can be harmful, the practice is a moral problem that requires a moral solution. Solving the problem requires a two-pronged approach. The first involves journalists; the second involves citizens who consume the news.

Journalists as moral agents are required to decide responsibly which stories they wish to tell and how to cover them responsibly. When deciding whether to publish a story, the journalist has to ask questions related to intent. What is the purpose of publishing the story? Is it to draw lines of conflict to attract reader interest? Or does the story present an issue that requires the community's attention? Codes of ethics for journalists are based on the idea that the profession's primary consideration is the public's interest. The codes assume that news users need accurate, fair and complete information to function in a democracy.

Sissela Bok, in her 1989 book *Lying*, offered a useful way to think about moral decision-making when choosing whether to publish stories involving conflict and how to cover them. She proposed a "Test of Publicity." Her test is designed to examine the "excuses advanced for disputed choices." The test requires that the moral agent be able to defend the reason for choosing to do one thing and not another, in this case, reporting a story about a particular conflict. The test assumes that the journalist would be able to defend his or her choice to a broad audience of reasonable people who are able to think critically. Bok said that no one can be excluded from the audience on principle and all are assumed to be able to understand the process of weighing and balancing conflicting moral principles to make a reasoned choice.

Would the Frank Jude coverage described at the start of this chapter pass Bok's Test of Publicity? Only the journalists who reported it can know their true intentions, but on its face, it would appear that it would. The story reflected a conflict of major proportions. The police beating had implications not only for Jude personally but for everyone else living in the community whom those police served. To suggest that these kinds of stories be toned down or not reported at all because they are "bad news," and the media already spend far too much time on stories involving conflict, would only deny community members the opportunity to weigh in on a matter in which they clearly have a stake. Replacing stories in which citizens have a legitimate interest with prescribed "good news" for the sake of taste or propriety, that is, conflict-free stories, would only create another form of misimpression.

Putting choices about covering conflict-related stories to the Test of Publicity forces journalists to think through what they are doing and why. They must ask themselves if the event or issue involving conflict is the result of a public policy that begs to be reconsidered. Is community action required? Or, is generating profit the overarching reason for covering a conflict-related story in sensational detail? The Test of Publicity requires journalists to ask and honestly answer questions related to conflict-related stories and the notion of the public good.

In summary, the problem of drawing on conflict as a news value, as the arguments show, is a complicated issue, one that is intertwined with the problem of sensationalism. Stories related to conflict reflect a natural part of the human condition. Deciding how and when to cover those stories is the task of the responsible journalist.

Points of View

Books

Cohen, Akiba A., Hanna Adoni, and Charles R. Bantz. *Social Conflict and Television News.* Newbury Park, Calif.: Sage, 1990. The authors examine the relationship between social conflict as presented on TV news and how people perceive social conflicts.

Gans, Herbert. *Deciding What's News: A Study of CBS Evening News, NBC Nightly News, Newsweek and Time.* New York: Random House, 1979. Gans' key finding in this influential content analysis of print and broadcast news is that conflict, in all of its forms, dominated the news agenda.

McManus, John H. *Market-Driven Journalism: Let the Citizen Beware?* Thousand Oaks, Calif.: Sage Publications, 1994. Sensationalism, which includes conflict and controversy, is a driving force behind market-driven journalism.

Pelizzon, V. Penelope, and Nancy M. West. *Tabloid, Inc.: Crimes, Newspapers, Narratives.* Columbus: Ohio University Press, 2010. Crime films in the first half of the 20th century were influenced by tabloid news coverage of crime.

Seaton, Jean. *Carnage and the Media: The Making and Breaking of News about Violence.* London: Penguin Books, 2005. From earlier eras to the present day, the press has presented stories of crime and violence because the audience wanted it to do so.

Stevens, John. *Sensationalism and the New York Press.* New York: Columbia University Press, 1991. Sensational stories, including conflict-related stories, played a major role in competition between early 20th century newspapers.

Wykes, Maggie. *News, Crime and Culture.* Sterling, Va.: Pluto Press, 2001. Conflict metaphors in news satisfy narrative demands for heroes and villains and for good and evil.

Articles

Bonde, Bent Noerby. "Mass Media and Journalism on the Edge in Violent Conflicts." (2006). Available at http://web32.bornholm-web.dk/downloads/Note%20on%20Mass%20Media%20and%20Journalism%20on%20the%20Edge%20in%20conflicts1.pdf. "[C]hanges in the media behaviour and journalism in a conflict situation can be crucial for transforming the conflict into a sustainable peace.... [However,] it is necessary to find a balance between media freedom and social responsibility, which also will remain valid and desirable in a post-conflict democratic development."

Garces-Conejos Blitvich, Pilar. "Impoliteness and Identity in the American News Media: The 'Culture Wars.'" *Journal of Politeness Research* 5 (2009): 273-303. The emerging news genre of "news as confrontation" reflects an insertion of the news value of conflict into the news presentation format.

Hindman, Douglas Blanks. "Community Newspapers, Community Structural Pluralism, and Local Conflict with Nonlocal Groups." *Journalism & Mass Communication Quarterly* 73 (1996): 708-21. In periods of change, media reports of both internal conflict and conflict with outside groups contribute to the maintenance of community stability and adjustment to change in the larger social environment.

Puddephatt, Andrew. "Voices of War: Conflict and the Role of the Media." *International Media Support Report* (2006). Available at http://www.i-m-s.dk/files/publications/Voices%20of%20war.pdf. "Mass media often play a key role in today's conflict. Basically, their role can take two different and opposed forms. Either the media take an active part in the conflict and have responsibility for increased violence, or stay independent and out of the conflict, thereby contributing to the resolution of conflict and alleviation of violence."

Shoemaker, Pamela. "Hardwired for News: Using Biological and Cultural Evolution to Explain the Surveillance Function. *Journal of Communication* 46 (1996): 32-47. The news value of conflict dovetails with the human need to monitor the environment for potential threats.

Singletary, Michael W., and Chris Lamb. "News Values in Award-winning Photos." *Journalism Quarterly* 61:1 (1984): 104-08. Content analysis of NPPA award-winning news photographs determined that four out of five photographs reflected the news value of conflict (accidents, disaster, crime, and violence).

Slattery, Karen L. "Sensationalism Versus News of the Moral Life: Making the Distinction." *Journal of Mass Media Ethics* 9:1 (1994): 5-15. Sensational topics in news, including those related to conflict, can be read as topics that are associated with threats to our moral lives.

Stevens, John. "Social Utility of Sensational News: Murder and Divorce in the 1920s." *Journalism Quarterly* 62:1 (1985): 53-58. News stories of deviance put the audience in the position of confronting their own values.

Sylvie, George. "A Study of Civil Disorder: The Effect of News Values and Competition on Coverage by Two Competing Daily Newspapers." *Newspaper Research Journal* 12:1 (1991): 98-113. The news coverage by two local newspapers of a riot in Tennessee emphasized manifestation of conflict rather than the cause of the conflict.

18 Coverage of Crime

He was a bright journalism student with an infectious passion for news. He could persuade other students to work well past midnight, after the labs had closed, to continue refining work he knew was not yet good enough for air later that day. But one day, the graduating senior went to class and declared that he had wasted four years of college. He was serious and shaking when he declared he was done with news. He would never go into the business. What happened? A crime story had left him disillusioned and angry. His friends were angry. They were all angry about a story that had hit too close to home. They claimed media coverage had blown it out of proportion and indicted his entire — and beloved — fraternity.

One of his fraternity brothers, in what was described and accepted as an accident and not hazing, had used toilet paper to wrap another member head to toe like a mummy. The details of what happened next still are disputed, but somehow the toilet paper caught fire. Police said the fraternity brother ignited the toilet paper with a match. The police report says the victim was in flames up to his shoulders before he realized he was on fire. He dropped and rolled to extinguish the fire. That, according to the police report, set the carpet on fire.

The victim was not injured and did not need medical attention. Police say he only had singed pants and first-degree burns on his hand. But the fraternity brother suspected of setting him on fire was charged with first-degree arson, first-degree wanton endangerment and tampering with physical evidence because he had tried to clean up the fire damage. Police also cited alcohol violations in the house. The house was shut down, and the chapter on campus was suspended for two years because of the alcohol violations, according to reports and the president of the fraternity's state alumni association. The suspect eventually pleaded guilty to wanton endangerment and criminal mischief in the incident and was sentenced to two years' probation.

The star journalism student swore off news because, in his words, he had

by Melvin Coffee
University of Kentucky

gotten a first-hand look at how news can distort the "truth." He also feared that distorted news could, by association, turn an entire community of innocent people — in this case, he argued, every member of his fraternity — into criminals.

Eventually, the young reporter reined in his emotions. Within weeks of graduation, he had landed a job as a reporter at a television news station in a small market. Reflecting on the news coverage of the "Flaming Mummy," he swore he was never going to be "that reporter." Yet four weeks into his job, he was reporting the lead story for the station. He was pumped. The "awesome" story was about a man who had been gunned down at a local bar and pool hall. The man was engaged to the mother of his infant child. He was not widely known in the community — just an average citizen. And the newbie reporter had the story. Its focus when the story aired was on what happened and where the investigation stood. In addition to talking with investigators and bar patrons, he had, in terms of television news, "the goods" — emotional interviews with family members.

"I felt bad because they cried, but it was awesome," he said. "Man, with all the crime that happens here, there is no shortage of news in this town. It's sad, but it makes my job a little easier."

A little easier. Why? The abundance of crime meant he had lots of news to cover. He didn't have to think about it. In school, he expressed frustration with crime news; now on the job, he relished it. In that short transition between student and professional, he had struggled with both sides of the dilemma of covering crime: what makes a crime incident newsworthy, and what makes it an isolated incident that does not pertain to a broader audience in the community where it happens? In just four weeks on the job, he had embraced the newsroom cliché, "If it bleeds, it leads." And he had embraced the notion that the more salacious or outrageous the crime incident, the more newsworthy it is. Was he, then, admitting the "Flaming Mummy" reporting about his fraternity brother that had so angered him, was indeed news, and if so, what determines newsworthiness when it comes to covering crime? This chapter will attempt to address these ongoing questions of covering crime: why do news organizations cover crime? When is it really necessary, and when is it really just superfluous?

Origins of the Issue

Reporting on crime has served an important purpose in society. Crime coverage can help make individuals more aware of what is happening in their communities and how to live safer or more secure lives. It can help authorities apprehend suspects and investigate and solve cases. Reporting on the consequences of criminal activities can dissuade others in a society from committing the same or similar crimes. As psychologist Erik H. Erikson wrote in his classic book, *Childhood and Society* (1963), publicizing crime and punishment can help clarify the lines of acceptable behavior within a society.

Although most crimes have little direct impact on readers or viewers or listeners who are taking in those reports, they do tend to appeal to news consumers if only for the elements of human drama or salacious behavior. According to Mitchell Stephens in his book *A History of News* (2007), crimes that intrigue news consumers have four things in common: a woman or child as victim or suspect; a high-ranking or well-known person as a victim or suspect; some doubt about the guilt of the suspect; and hints of promiscuous behavior by either the victim or the suspect. He cites such widely reported crimes as the Lindbergh kidnapping in 1932, the Patty Hearst kidnapping in 1974 and the murder of O.J. Simpson's former wife, Nicole Brown Simpson, in 1994. A more recent example might include the trial of Casey Anthony, the 22-year-old Florida woman who was acquitted in her 2011 trial on charges she murdered her two-year-old daughter Caylee Anthony who was reported missing in July 2008 and whose remains were found in a wooded area near her home in December 2008.

Stephens also contends crimes that spread fear through a community because of their brutality and randomness also draw widespread attention. These cases include such serial-killer cases as the Boston Strangler in the early 1960s; the Son of Sam attacks in New York City during 1976 and 1977; the Atlanta child slayings from 1979 to 1981; the Washington, D.C., sniper attacks that lasted three weeks in October 2002 in Washington, Maryland, and Virginia; the September 11, 2001, terrorist attacks on the World Trade Center in New York City and the Pentagon in Washington, D.C.; and the mass killing of twelve people at a theater in Aurora, Colorado, in 2012.

The intrigue with crime coverage is not new. The penny press capitalized on it in the 1830s. The *New York Sun* was one of the first papers to feature a daily crime news column in 1833. However, it seems to be heightened now because of the proliferation of print, online and electronic news outlets. It is impossible to discuss coverage of crime without noting the vast amounts of news inventory available in 24/7 news operations online and on the air. And there appears to be an appetite for crime reporting. A September 2011 study from the Pew Research Center's Project for Excellence in Journalism and Internet & American Life Project shows across platforms — newspaper, television, radio and online — crime reporting is the fourth most popular topic people look for (66%) in local news, behind weather, breaking news, and politics.

To be sure, television changed the landscape of covering crime around the time of the assassination of President John F. Kennedy in 1963. With its coverage of the shooting, television news developed a protocol for what is now called breaking news. It had all the elements that news organizations depend on so much today: continuous and unpredictable deadlines; competition; the challenge of constantly updating stories often with little or no new information; and the speed of disseminating information with previously untested challenges to accuracy, fairness, and balance. Television also was being tested, knowingly or not, on its ability to cover a breaking crime story without inflaming fear. Journalists deliberately focused on not sensationalizing a sensational story. But reporters themselves became witnesses to a sensational crime, and witnesses by definition play significant roles in the reporting of breaking news and crime stories. And when TV cameras caught live the slaying of suspect Lee Harvey Oswald on November 24, Americans throughout the country became witnesses. What normally would have played out months later in a courtroom was now being seen in real time on television. These events were too important and too gripping to leave to the morning paper.

So breaking news of crime became a mainstay of American television news coverage. In fact, in his book *We Interrupt this Newscast: How to Improve Local News and Win Ratings Too* (2007), Tom Rosenstiel and his co-authors write about the heavy concentration of crime news in local television and its prominent placement. Their surveys include interviews with more than 2,000 journalists working for 154 local stations. Of the 2,400 newscasts they analyzed, 61%, almost two-thirds, led with a crime, accident, or disaster story.

Covering Crime: It's Too Much

An overarching criticism of crime coverage is that there is so much of it that it distorts the way people view and react to the communities they live in, and that crime on television in particular shapes and distorts viewers' concept of reality. Media critic George Gerbner is one of many scholars whose research draws that conclusion. His often-cited study, "Cultural Indicators," involved years of research that began in the 1960s. He wanted to know if watching television influences how people see the world. He concluded that violence on TV has a tremendous influence: people were afraid of their own community, and exposure to violence on TV often led them to overestimate the number of people who actually committed serious crimes. Gerbner called this view the "mean world syndrome."

Walter Lippmann noted as early as the 1920s in his book *Public Opinion* that because we cannot understand everything that happens in our society through direct experience, we depend on "pictures in our heads," many of them violent images delivered by the news media, to tell us about our world and community.

Lori Dorfman wrote in "Off Balance: Youth, Race and Crime in the News," a study commissioned by Building Blocks for Youth and prepared by the Berkeley Media Studies Group and the Justice Policy Institute (2001), that crime coverage has an even more damaging impact — that the *way* crimes are reported distorts citizens' perceptions of society and actually *promotes* some types of crime. What's more, crime coverage disproportionately implicates and stereotypes minorities, paints an inaccurate picture of youth, inspires copycat crime and warps citizens' perception of their community.

Youth crime

Dorfman suggested media coverage of youth crimes is unbalanced. The result of the skewed coverage, she wrote, is a public that believes youth violence is on the rise and that something must be done about it. Dorfman says the danger of this is that the public then supports policies based on the notion that youth crime is a more serious threat than it is.

Dorfman continues that when it comes to covering crime involving youth and people of color, news consumers are getting "confusion rather than clarity — part of the story, not the whole story," because, she argues, those news reports reflect an imbalance of what is actually happening statistically. The report cites the number of homicides committed by youth as reported in network news increased 62% from 1993 to 1999. In fact, the number of such homicides actually declined during that time period.

In a study of three of the largest newspapers in California, the *Los Angeles Times*, *San Francisco Chronicle* and *Sacramento Bee*, the Berkeley Media Group shows coverage of violence routinely at the top among youth topics: 25%, compared with 26% for K-12 education coverage. All other topics scored 8% or less, including recreation, entertainment, health, sports, fashion, drugs, alcohol, and sex. The problem, the authors note, is that the high percentage of coverage on youth violence means readers are not getting the whole picture. They are left to infer that youth crime is rampant, which reinforces their stereotypes and biases.

Crime and race

Several studies have shown imbalances when it comes to race and crime coverage. Black victims, for example, are less likely to be covered in newspapers than are white victims, and stories are considered more newsworthy when the victims are white. Blacks and Latinos are more likely to be portrayed as perpetrators of crime than other groups.

Susan B. Sorenson, writing for the *American Journal of Public Health* (1998), notes a dramatic disparity. She and other authors in the article found, during five years of reporting (1990-1994) in the *Los Angeles Times*, murders of blacks and Latinos were grossly underreported. In that period, 80% of homicide victims in

Los Angeles were black or Latino, but blacks were half as likely to be reported as victims as whites were. Latinos were two-thirds as likely to be reported as victims compared with whites. The article notes that, when a white person was a victim, the story received greater play. The victims typically were women, were very young or very old, held high socioeconomic status and were killed by strangers.

Rather than portrayed as victims, blacks more often were reported as suspects, notes Robert Entman in "Blacks in the news: Television, modern racism, and cultural change," a 1992 article in *Journalism Quarterly*. Black suspects, he wrote, are routinely depicted as poor, dangerous and no different from other blacks who did not commit crimes. He also found that blacks are more frequently reported in connection with violent crimes. His research also shows blacks were more likely to be shown (and not identified) in mug shots and in police custody and to be perpetrators more often than victims. As a result, the public develops social images of blacks and other minorities either as instigators of crime or as people who do little to prevent it. They are not portrayed as positive role models or leaders in a community that is trying to reduce or cope with crime.

Copycat effect

One of the strongest arguments against some crime coverage is that the copycat effect could put more people at risk than the original crime. Researchers have found numerous examples of possible copycat crimes. Loren Coleman points out several in the book, *The Copycat Effect: How the Media and Popular Culture Trigger the Mayhem in Tomorrow's Headlines* (2004). For example, in September 1994, a pilot named Frank Eugene Corder crashed a stolen plane into the South Lawn of the White House. No one on the ground was injured, and Corder died. It was never made clear what his motive was. Within four months of that incident, news organizations reported on what seemed like a flurry of attacks or attempted attacks on the White House. Martin Duran fired twenty-nine shots at the White House in October before a bystander tackled him. He was convicted of attempting to assassinate President Bill Clinton and was sentenced to forty years in prison. In December a homeless man charged across Pennsylvania Avenue waving a knife that was taped to his arm. U.S. Park Police shot him in the leg and abdomen. The man died of cardiac arrest at a hospital where he was being treated. Coleman cites other incidents, including school shootings, suicides and workplace violence, in which the perpetrators said media attention to the earlier, "original" crime spurred them to action. Although not all the crimes are attributed to news coverage, Coleman does suggest that some language in news reporting, such as "successful" suicides, etc., sheds a positive light on crime and glorifies it in the eyes of the would-be copycat criminal. He also suggests repeated and saturated coverage of the criminal event, without contextual reporting, could contribute to copycat crimes.

News organizations often have been criticized for reporting too many details in a crime, particularly concerning "how-to" types of stories, as when reporters describe how a person was able to acquire materials to build a bomb illegally. Although the point of such a story may be to show lax security or law enforcement, critics say it encourages others to take advantage of weak links in systems that are supposed to protect citizens. Even more banal information can lead to copycat crimes: Burglars may learn how to bypass security systems by going through rooftop vents, or parents may learn to use small children to steal for them because children generally aren't suspected of wrongdoing.

Covering Crime: It's Essential

Proponents of crime coverage argue that stories about criminal activity do have positive effects on society, if they are reported correctly. They say that proper coverage becomes an issue of public health and in that regard should be reported aggressively, even when the crimes involved youth, minorities or potential "copycat crimes." What's more, they argue, crime happens, and reporters need to tell people what's happening no matter what perception it creates. They also argue stereotyping exists mostly because crime reporting focuses on the aggressors rather than the victims and, they argue, most reporting on aggressors happens to be about minority aggressors. They also support coverage on youth crime because, some say, media have gone too far in trying to conceal the identities of young offenders — protecting them encourages youth violence and other crimes; media cannot be blamed for copycat crimes; statistical "reality" is hard to measure as not all crimes are actually reported anyway.

Youth crime

In covering crime involving youth and minorities, for example, the Berkeley Media Studies Group looks at crime coverage in two different categories: thematic versus episodic. Should news organizations report on the episode itself — simply what happened — or should they look for a theme or context for reporting the crime? Lori Dorfman and others wrote in "Off Balance: Youth, Race and Crime in the News," a study commissioned by Building Blocks for Youth and prepared by the Berkeley Media Studies Group and the Justice Policy Institute (2001): "Thematic reporting looks at the big picture, examining connections between similar events, looking for trends, emphasizing the questions 'why' and 'how.'

Thematic coverage also includes efforts to curb violence, such as the politics of gun control or sentencing reform. In this analysis, any story in which one-third or more of the content is focused on issues or a pattern of events is labeled thematic. Episodic reporting, in contrast, focuses on a single event. It is a snapshot of 'what' happened. It is reporting at the micro level."

The authors also say that thematic reporting does not need to be investigative or in depth. They say it should, however, look at every story in a greater context, including some historical or social perspective which, the authors note, could provide more basis for citizens to judge whether what they have learned from watching or reading a crime story merits action to challenge current public policy. They cite the 1999 shooting at Columbine High School in Colorado, where two seniors killed twelve students and a teacher before killing themselves. The reporting covered the shootings and the fear that settled into the community, but it also focused on high school cliques, social outcasts, bullying, the roles of violent movies and video games in American society and gun control laws.

Dorfman, writing for the Berkeley Media Studies Group, would argue that focusing on these issues has a direct effect on anyone watching this story. The group further argues it doesn't take a story of that magnitude to illuminate greater social issues that might have a direct impact on a greater society. For example, when covering a domestic-violence shooting, reporters also could include current, proposed or even rejected laws to help protect victims. In many jurisdictions, for example, victims of domestic abuse have no legal recourse until they have been assaulted. Dorfman argues if news organizations would devote more resources to the most likely kinds of violence then they could incorporate some contextual reporting so their viewers, listeners or readers can be better informed and take action for the greater good of their community or society.

In the winter 1998 issue of *Nieman Reports*, Jane Ellen Stevens in her article, "The Violence Reporting Project: A New Approach to Covering Crime," expanded on that argument, specifically to focus on reporting on violent crime from the perspective of public health. It cited the Berkeley Media Studies Group and others who were brought into the project. Researchers cited 1977 findings from a group of physicians in the U.S. Public Health Service. They said violence in this country at the time was an epidemic. They found at the time violent injuries, homicides and suicides were in the top five causes of death before age 65 in this country, and that the highest rates of violent death and injury occur among children and adolescents. The U.S. Centers for Disease Control and Prevention cited several causes, including availability of firearms and alcohol, racial discrimination, and unemployment. (To be sure, those numbers were unusually high, according to the FBI's Supplementary Homicide Reports, 1976-1997. The FBI reports cite serious crimes, including violent ones, committed by young people increased at a fast rate in the 1960s and reached epidemic proportions by the late 1980s. The report says those figures were tied in part to "a growing market for cocaine and especially its derivative, crack, in the 1980s and by the easy availability of guns. Young people in some quarters joined gangs, worked as the street soldiers in drug distribution networks, armed themselves, and killed one another with rising frequency. Fortunately, this began to subside in the mid-1990s." The FBI reports show overall crime numbers still are trending down.) Stevens argued in her article that even with what might appear to be exhaustive reporting on crime, news organizations traditionally report many fewer violent incidents than actually happen in their communities. Crime, therefore, was under-reported, not over-reported; and, as a result, news consumers were led to believe crime had no direct impact on them. She argued each incident also has economic consequences on the community (cost of medical treatment, incarceration, trial, etc.) and long-term consequences. Crimes, she said, should be covered more extensively to include a public health and prevention perspective.

In that same 1998 winter issue of *Nieman Reports*, David Doi expanded on how to write about public health issues by using "good media practices" that are in place in some news organizations. Such practices can make coverage of crime beneficial rather than simply sensational. The practices ask the following questions:

- Does action need to be taken?
- Is there an immediate threat to safety?
- Is there a threat to children?
- Does the crime have community impact?
- Does the story lend itself to crime-prevention efforts?

The news organizations don't report violent crime prominently without accompanying in-depth analysis, setting it in a broader human and policy context. When reporting a homicide or violent crime, for example, the following questions will be addressed in the story:

- Did the victim and perpetrator know each other or were they related?
- Was there a history of domestic violence related to this crime?
- Was alcohol or other substances involved?
- If a shooting involves a young person, can the gun used be traced back to its point of origin and intermediate transfers?

On the smallest level, crime coverage proponents say it is important to know what is happening, even if sometimes it is difficult to hear. On a larger scale, they argue crime coverage is important and essential when a news organization reports crime facts but also provides context in its reporting.

Assessment

Some newsroom managers argue that crime sells. People are voyeurs. They say they may *say* they don't want to see it, but they watch it anyway even with one eye open. News programs devoted almost entirely to crime, like *Dateline NBC*, proliferate, as do blocks of cable programming that resurrect forgotten murders. Covering crime is easy. It often doesn't need deep research or enterprise to satisfy the "daily beast" or fill the news hole left gaping by 24-7 cable news channels and the Internet. Crime stories come to newsrooms through press releases, scanners and even reader and viewer phone calls, emails and social media. Crime stories, if not actually newsworthy, have the appearance of news. They forever have been a staple of news organizations as Mitchell Stephens pointed out in *A History of News* (2007).

Ratings and subscriptions drive coverage, and so does competition, especially when a story has a high profile. Financially strapped newsrooms allow little time for reporters to investigate enterprise stories that take longer than a day. As deadlines approach, stories that are not turning out so well get shelved for easy "gets," or doable stories, and many newsroom managers argue that crime is one of those types of stories. For example, a fraternity brother set afire after being rolled up in toilet paper is just too good a story to bury.

But research by the Pew Research Center's Project for Excellence in Journalism, News Director Survey (2002), shows that television news directors and news managers get it wrong when it comes to covering crime because they misunderstand what the public says it wants in crime coverage. The survey says no natural hunger for crime coverage exists. It says people are fed up with the way stories are covered. The study says news consumers want more of what is known as viewer benefit. That is, "what's in it for me?" News viewers want to know how each story relates to their lives. The study concludes this is true in all coverage, but especially in crime coverage. The survey goes on to show support for the argument made by Dorfman, et al, that crime reporting should be thematic and not episodic. The report says viewers don't mind crime reporting as much when it is reported with context and community relevance rather than for the purpose of sensationalism, as most viewers currently judge the majority of crime reporting.

At a seminar, "New Tech Creates New Pressures," held in Cincinnati in August 2010 and sponsored by the Radio Television Digital News Foundation in association with the Ohio Association of Broadcasters, a focus group addressed crime coverage in their communities in and around Cincinnati. Parents in the focus group expressed a fear that letting their children watch the news would corrupt their view of their community and even terrorize them. They worried that exposing their children to news will traumatize them because of what they described as excessive, irrelevant and gratuitous crime coverage. They essentially were giving credence to George Gerbner's "Mean World Syndrome" theory. Consequently, some parents turned away from television news entirely. They said they avoid most crime reporting even in the newspapers. They made it clear that they've lost their trust in news organizations. Others said they want to know, but they can't bear to watch or read so much of it, so they often ignore the news.

What newsrooms have sometimes failed to use as guiding principles in orchestrating crime coverage, are the same standards of ethics that apply to so many other sensitive issues in newsrooms. Professional organizations like the Radio Television Digital News Association and the Society of Professional Journalists constantly tweak their standards to make sure they are current and reflect upon contemporary media issues. Al Tompkins with the Poynter Institute for Media Studies in the online article "Smarter Crime Coverage" advises when it comes to covering crime, journalists should keep stories in context and report *context* as well as facts and truth.

As newsrooms debate coverage of crime, editors and news directors might consider adhering to the rules of basic journalism over ratings or circulation, because research such as the Pew Research Center's Project for Excellence in Journalism shows that solid journalism is much more likely to retain news consumers rather than turn them off. Does the public have a right or need to know? How important is the information? What can newsrooms do to minimize harm... to the subjects in the story as well as to their readers, listeners or viewers? How will reporting the story provide the community with information that allows them to act and make a difference in their communities? Are news organizations reporting crime news because it's sensational, or because it matters? As part of their public duty, newsroom leaders need to apply their knowledge about what their audience concerns are. Then they need to combine those concerns with journalism ethics in order to make decisions about how they cover crime. In short, when it comes to covering crime, the focus of a story cannot solely or predominantly be on what happens. It should be on what matters.

Points of View

Books

Coleman, Loren. *The Copycat Effect: How the Media and Popular Culture Trigger the Mayhem in Tomorrow's Headlines*. New York: Paraview Pocket Books/Simon and Schuster, 2004. Highly publicized acts influence others in society to copy them.

Jewkes, Yvonne. *Media and Crime*, 2nd ed. Thousand Oaks, Calif.: Sage, 2010. This comprehensive "explores the complex interactions between media and crime from a critical and authoritative standpoint."

Robinson, Matthew B. *Media Coverage of Crime and Criminal Justice*. Durham, N.C.: Carolina Academic Press, 2011. The author examines "how crime and criminal justice are treated in the news and entertainment media ... [and corrects] major misconceptions created by coverage of crime and criminal justice." Corporate ownership of the mass media is partly to blame for the problems.

Rosenstiel, Tom, Marion Just, Todd Belt, Atiba Pertilla, Walter Dean, and Dante Chinni. *We Interrupt this Newscast: How to Improve Local News and Win Ratings Too*. New York: Cambridge University Press, 2007. Local television news can attract viewers without the "if it bleeds it leads" approach. How stories are reported is more important than simply which stories are reported.

Surette, Ray. *Media, Crime, and Criminal Justice: Images, Realities, and Policies*, 4th ed. Belmont, Calif.: Cengage Learning, 2010. The author "corrects common misconceptions regarding the mass media's effects on crime and justice."

Articles

Brzostowski, Marie, and Catherine Leidemer. "Crime Coverage in the Media: The People Get What the People Want." http://unbound.intrasun.tcnj.edu/archives/opinions/old/opins98/media/index.html. Media coverage exaggerates the amount of crime that actually happens.

Entman, R. M. "Blacks in the news: Television, modern racism, and cultural change." *Journalism Quarterly* 69 (1992): 341-61. Black people more often are reported as suspects. Black suspects are routinely depicted as poor, dangerous, and no different from other blacks who did not commit crimes.

"Practicing Responsible Journalism when Covering Crime." Society of Professional Journalists, http://www.spj.org/ethicscrime.asp. Felisa Cardona, a crime reporter for the *Denver Post*, "has found ethical and profoundly effective ways to report and write about matters requiring tremendous fairness and sensitivity." This article summarizes "some of the things she considers when writing about crime, crime fighters and crime victims."

Sorenson, Susan B., J. G. Manz, and R.A. Berk. "News media coverage and the epidemiology of homicide." *American Journal of Public Health* 88:10 (1998): 1510-14. During five years of reporting (1990-1994), the *Los Angeles Times* underreported the numbers of murders of blacks and Latinos.

19

Media and Politicians' Privacy

Democratic candidate Jeff Greene filed a libel suit against the *St. Petersburg Times* and *Miami Herald* in 2010 after he lost his primary bid for a U.S. Senate seat. The lawsuit accused the newspapers of "a coordinated and agreed-upon plan to assassinate Greene's character, to diminish his chances of winning ... and to impair the future earning capacity of an extremely successful businessman," according to an Associated Press story posted on the First Amendment Center's website. One article and a follow-up editorial focused on a Greene condominium deal with a California businessman who was later indicted for mortgage fraud in a case unrelated to Greene. Another story covered boxer Mike Tyson's allegations of illegal drug use and partying on Greene's yacht. Greene repeatedly said that both stories were false and that he gave the newspapers evidence of that before publication.

Greene's lawsuit involved the publication of information that many would consider private — personal business dealings, drug use, and activities at a private party. In the past few decades, however, such topics have become a staple of media reporting on political candidates and office-holders. Are such topics legitimate news stories that shed light on the character of candidates and public officials, or does this type of coverage deflect debate from pressing political issues? Answers to that question will vary, but the media's preoccupation with private information regarding politicians is likely to continue in today's heated partisan climate.

J. Patrick Dobel, in an article in *Administration and Society* in 1998, outlined four reasons for the media's focus on the private lives of public officials. The first reason discussed in the article, "Judging the Private Lives of Public Officials," is that the "self-imposed restraint of the media to avert their eyes from private lives of officials [has] ended," and court decisions have limited the ability of public officials to sue for libel. Second, Dobel wrote, the decline of political parties has given the media more influence as gatekeepers. Third, "candidates and interest

by Sherrie L. Wilson
University of Nebraska at Omaha

groups exploit the new media standards and use private scandals to discredit competitors and their positions." Fourth, groups have questioned the distinction between public and private lives.

Privacy issues on a range of topics have generated media attention in recent years. Here are some examples:

• During the 2008 presidential election, media outlets had to determine the newsworthiness of the pregnancy of vice presidential candidate Sarah Palin's unwed teenage daughter. Eventually, most organizations carried stories, particularly after the information had already been widely disseminated.

• When Eliot Spitzer was attorney general of New York, he aggressively prosecuted prostitution organizations. When he was governor of New York, he signed into law a bill that "severely penalized those who patronize prostitutes, rather than penalizing the prostitutes themselves," wrote Candace Cummins Gauthier in a chapter in 2010's *Journalism Ethics: A Philosophical Approach*. He was forced to resign after his involvement with an international prostitution organization became known. Most argued that releasing information about Spitzer's relations with prostitutes was justified because of the hypocrisy of his public stand on the issue in relation to his personal actions.

• Aides to South Carolina Gov. Mark Sanford in 2009 told the public that the governor was hiking on the Appalachian Trail. Eventually, the public learned that he was actually in Argentina visiting a woman with whom he was having an affair. The incident raised questions about who was in charge of the state government during his absence.

This chapter focuses on the debate over media coverage of politicians' private lives. Critics of such coverage argue that even public officials deserve some privacy and that excessive coverage is not necessary to the proper functioning of a democracy. Those who defend coverage argue that private matters do play a role in the qualifications of public officials and politicians and that many citizens consider such matters important as they make voting decisions.

Origins of the Issue

Media ethical standards concerning private information about politicians have changed over the years. During the presidency of Franklin Roosevelt, the media began a tradition of news coverage regarding politicians' private lives that lasted for forty years, according to Larry Sabato in his 1991 book *Feeding Frenzy: How Attack Journalism Has Transformed American Politics*. The view was that the "private life of a public figure should stay private and undisclosed unless it seriously infringed on his or her public performance," he wrote. Even if reporters wanted to report on personal information regarding politicians, their supervisors typically did not approve. In the mid-1960s, Eileen Shanahan of the *New York Times* tried to report that Russell Long, a Democratic senator, was drunk on the Senate floor. Her editors rejected the story.

When John F. Kennedy was president, reporters who covered the White House knew about his promiscuity, but they never wrote about it and apparently did not consider it relevant. Journalists treated similar allegations about President Lyndon Johnson the same way. The rules began to change in 1974, wrote Alicia Shepard in her 1999 article "Gatekeepers without Gates" in *American Journalism Review.* The turning point, she recounts, was when stripper Fanne Foxe and U.S. Rep. Wilbur Mills of Arkansas, chair of the House Ways and Means Committee, went carousing in Washington, D.C. After police stopped Mills on traffic violations, Foxe ran from the car and jumped into the Tidal Basin in front of the Jefferson Memorial. Because the incident was so public, voters soon became aware of Mills' problems with alcohol.

Another key turning point came in 1987 when Gary Hart, a Democratic presidential contender, took Donna Rice, an aspiring actress, to his townhouse overnight. Some reporters had heard that Hart was a womanizer, but most did not write about his escapades until he challenged suspicious journalists to follow him. Two reporters from the *Miami Herald* took up the challenge, staked out Hart's townhouse and learned of his relationship with Rice. Hart eventually withdrew from the presidential race. One of the reporters, Tom Fiedler, defended the relevance of the Hart story because it demonstrated Hart's hypocrisy, according to Shepard in her 1999 article.

Shepard also wrote of Bill Clinton facing accusations of affairs and improper conduct during his campaigns for the presidency and when he occupied the office in the 1990s. In early 1998, details began to emerge about his encounters with one-time White House intern Monica Lewinsky. *The Drudge Report,* a conservative gossip blog, reported that *Newsweek* was holding a story involving the affair. Soon after, mainstream media began repeating the allegations, a pattern that continued throughout the controversy. Clinton initially denied the allegations, but in August 1998 he acknowledged to a grand jury that he had a sexual relationship with Lewinsky. He then went on television to admit the deception.

In his 2004 book *Voyeur Nation: Media, Privacy, and Peering in Modern Culture,* Clay Calvert discussed the "voyeurism" of the Clinton-Lewinsky affair, including discussions of semen-stained dresses and oral sex. Calvert argued that the media "perpetuated politics as voyeurism even after President Clinton was acquitted by the U.S. Senate of perjury and obstruction charges" by continuing to cover other women's allegations against Clinton. In the wake of the Clinton-Lewinsky scandal, *Hustler* magazine publisher Larry Flynt, a Clinton supporter, bought a full-page advertisement in the *Washington Post* offering $1 million to anyone who could provide evidence of having an affair with members of Congress or other top government officials. Eventually, according to Calvert, Bob Livingston, a Republican congressman from Louisiana and House speaker-designate, admitted adultery and resigned.

In a time before the Internet and 24-hour cable news channels, the mainstream media functioned as gatekeepers that decided what the public needed to know. Former *Washington Post* Executive Editor Ben Bradlee said that, at times, the editors of major newspapers conferred with each other about whether to publish sensitive stories. "In their paternalistic fashion," Shepard wrote in her 1999 article, "they were apt to hold stories about a politician's sex life, unless the peccadilloes were deemed to affect his or her job performance." The modern media landscape, however, offers many ways beyond the mainstream media for salacious stories to gain public attention.

Private Affairs Are Not Newsworthy

Journalists need to exercise caution, argue critics of media coverage of politicians' and public officials' private affairs, when revealing private information.

In his 2010 book *The Ethical Journalist: Making Responsible Decisions in the Pursuit of News*, Gene Foreman framed the issue as a debate between two guiding principles in the Society or Professional Journalists' ethical code: "seek truth and report it" and "minimize harm." In evaluating whether a politician's extramarital affairs, for example, deserve news coverage, some journalists argue that such topics reveal a politician's true character. Such accusations also may reveal hypocrisy if the politician has campaigned on a "family values" platform. Other journalists, however, contend that extramarital affairs are not newsworthy unless they represent a pattern of sexual harassment or affect the politician's performance in public office.

The public has mixed views about media coverage of officials' private lives, Daniel Riffe concluded in a 2003 article in the *Journal of Mass Media Ethics.* About three-fourths of the Ohio residents Riffe surveyed thought that a public leader's personal life can affect job performance. "Despite believing what a public leader does in private is important, and despite the perceived interest in such matters among most people, only 37 [%] believed 'the news media have a responsibility to examine leaders' private lives.'" Two-thirds of respondents disagreed that the media are "generally fair" in covering public leaders' private lives, and 84% thought the media "pay too much attention" to leaders' private lives.

The results of Riffe's survey show that, even in an age dominated by the Internet, many people object when media reveal what they see as excessive private information about politicians. In her chapter in the 2010 book *Journalism Ethics*,

Candace Cummins Gauthier defined privacy as "control over access to oneself and to certain kinds of information about oneself." When people are in public locations, photographs and audio and video recordings do not ordinarily invade their privacy. An invasion of privacy, however, may result from photographs taken or recordings made in situations where people may ordinarily expect a zone of privacy — for example, a doctor's office or a drug treatment center. A similar distinction occurs with information about people. Information such as our birth date, arrest records and, in the case of public employees, annual salaries is considered public information. Most information about us, however, is not a matter of public record, and dissemination of such information may result in invasion of privacy. "Privacy is essential for our sense of ourselves as persons and as self-determining moral agents," Gauthier wrote, arguing that recognizing our own privacy rights and respecting those of others are part of what helps us develop as individuals.

People desire certain levels of privacy. Even politicians who seek public attention set limits on access to themselves and their families. "While they may be willing to give up some privacy in order to have successful careers, they often also attempt to reserve some areas of privacy, particularly regarding their emotional attachments and personal relationships," Gauthier wrote. People show respect for each other by not invading others' privacy. For journalists, this societal expectation comes into conflict with their professional obligation to provide information to the public. Gauthier distinguishes between information that the public needs to know and information that the public wants to know. For example, the public may need information about government and public officials, which may justify the invasion of privacy in some circumstances. Yet the public also criticizes media organizations that cross boundaries in invading privacy. The challenge for journalists, Gauthier wrote, is providing important information in a way that satisfies the public, advances news organizations' financial interests and meets professional ethical standards.

In the 2010 book *Outrageous Invasions: Celebrities' Private Lives, Media and the Law*, Robin D. Barnes wrote that, in the United States, "privacy is recognized as significant for autonomous feats and essential for relaxation, solitude and shared intimacy. Moreover, privacy is a prerequisite for the adequate formation of personal, political and spiritual identities." The social norm of privacy sometimes may clash with the ideals of freedom of speech and freedom of press. The release of private information raises concerns about the motive and context for publication, Barnes argued. Although Barnes' book focused on invasion of privacy for celebrities, some of the concepts apply to politicians, who are often regarded as celebrities, particularly during elections. Barnes wrote:

"By giving the media wholesale license to look for and expose celebrity scandals, inconsistency, perversions, and neuroses, media moguls were given free rein to create, perpetuate, and manipulate the public's voyeuristic tendencies. Even those who refuse to buy sleazy tabloid magazines fail to object to their pervasive presence.... We witness the media raids on the private lives of individuals, yet we rarely speak out. It is as though we have lost our sense of where to draw the line."

The lines have blurred between "news and entertainment, mainstream and tabloid journalism, and celebrities and political figures," producing a society "bedazzled by show business and dizzying celebrity worship," Barnes contends. As more and more people turn to television comedic sources for debating the qualifications of candidates, the "rules of political engagement" have changed. Stand-up comedians now influence the outcomes of political elections.

Calvert, in his 2004 book, discussed what he called "mediated voyeurism," which he defined as "the consumption of revealing images of and information about others' apparently real and unguarded lives, often yet not always for purposes of entertainment but frequently at the expense of privacy and discourse through the means of the mass media and Internet." Social, political, technological and legal forces have converged to allow this type of media content to proliferate. These forces also influence our conceptions about privacy, newsworthiness, public interest and freedom of speech. Society has seen the emergence of what he called the "voyeurism value of free expression" — "a modern-day rationale for protecting expression under the First Amendment." Calvert used the word "value" because he contends that mediated voyeurism is valued by many, from the audiences who watch it to the media corporations that produce it. Traditional First Amendment goals of free speech, such as "truth, better government, self-realization," are replaced with the "voyeur value." Media organizations use the First Amendment to protect their right to use hidden cameras and to enter places where they were once prohibited — all in the name of serving the public. With regard to politics, the "voyeurism value" leads to "politics as spectacle — a politics in which we watch mediated images of candidates, without interaction with them," Calvert wrote. Voyeurism may further erode political participation.

Yet another concern is that constant media coverage of the private lives of politicians will deter many qualified candidates from seeking public office. A 2010 column by Andrew Coyne in *Maclean's* noted that some think politicians are held to an "impossible standard, as puritanical as it is archaic," with regard to their behavior. In 1991's *Feeding Frenzy,* Sabato argued that the media coverage of politicians has raised the "price of public life," deterring some from entering public service. Journalists exacerbate this phenomenon by defining their role as that of "gatekeeper," enabling them "to substitute for party leaders in deciding which characters are virtuous enough to merit consideration for high office."

Journalists often defend their treatment of politicians and candidates by noting the need to counteract the influence of political consultants and image makers who surround today's candidates. Since Watergate, Sabato argues, political scandals have become a staple of media coverage, sometimes at the expense of covering more important issues.

Media coverage of the private lives of politicians has been called harmful to family members and associates, even though they may deserve a broader zone of privacy than the politicians. In their 2010 book *Making Hard Choices in Journalism Ethics: Cases and Practice*, David Boeyink and Sandra Borden use Monica Lewinsky as an example of how those connected with public officials can be harmed. Months of media coverage of Lewinsky's affair with President Clinton oversimplified who she was. ABC's Barbara Walters interviewed Lewinsky and said she found the young woman to be more intelligent and well-spoken than coverage had suggested. Boeyink and Borden borrowed the term "quasar" from film scholar James Monaco "to describe 'silent' celebrities who are thrust into the limelight by news events and have no control over their stories and images." The coverage of those around politicians robs people of their privacy and dignity, the authors contend, and journalists need to weigh the harm of invading privacy against the principle of truth telling.

Private Affairs Are Newsworthy

In today's society, the mass media have become the major source of information about political candidates and office holders. As a result, say those who defend media coverage of politicians' and public officials' private affairs, such coverage sometimes becomes necessary as part of informing the public.

Coyne's 2010 column in *Maclean's* noted that the public and private lives of politicians cannot easily be separated. He wrote: "If a public official were discovered robbing banks in his spare time, I doubt anyone would say it was strictly a private matter. I can't help wondering if those who claim to be unmoved that a politician cheats on his wife would feel the same way if someone were to cheat on them." If politicians lie to their spouses, Coyne argues, they may treat their constituents the same way. Some people think a politician's private life demonstrates his or her character and judgment. Politicians want the public to know about their private lives when the story is positive. So shouldn't public and private aspects of their lives also be linked when the story is negative? Coyne urges journalists to exercise judgment and ask whether the information is true, fair and relevant before publishing any story.

Dobel, in his 1998 article, noted that, morally, public officials exercise authority because they act on behalf of the public. The public affords officials legitimacy and pays for the operations of their offices. As an official's responsibility and power increase, so does public scrutiny. For those holding public office, two traditionally private areas immediately become subject to public scrutiny. The first is a public official's health because mental and physical well-being can influence his or her performance in office. In addition, an official's personal finances come under scrutiny because economic conflicts of interest can endanger the appearance of fairness and impartiality in the job.

Because of this need for public scrutiny, the media become the means by which the public obtains information to evaluate the character of politicians and officials. In addition to providing information about government, the media also provide a framework for understanding those facts, according to Philip Patterson and Lee Wilkins in 2011's edition of *Media Ethics: Issues and Cases*. Politicians try to control their images projected through media coverage, they wrote, and "often it is sexual scandal or financial wrongdoing that brings down the carefully crafted veil that major politicians erect." Journalists cover what Patterson and Wilkins called "political character" — "the intersection of personality and public performance within the cultural and historical context." Journalists who explore politicians' character issues risk invading the privacy of those covered. Paraphrasing ethicist Sissela Bok, Patterson and Wilkins wrote that investigating the private character of public people is justified if the people are in a position to do harm. If so, invasions of privacy to reduce that threat are justified. When doing such investigations, they wrote, journalists must weigh the harm done to others, including family members of the politicians, and exercise discretion in what information they use.

In a 1994 article in the *Journal of Mass Media Ethics*, L. Paul Husselbee discussed the journalist's role as an information provider against people's right to a zone of privacy. The public relies on the media for access to information, and a democracy cannot function without an informed electorate. Journalists have a "moral obligation to distribute information as a means of leveling the playing field of society," Husselbee contends. Journalists accomplish this goal through their efforts "to redistribute the power that information provides." Because they gather information and provide it to the public, thus limiting the power of institutions that might otherwise exercise too much control, journalists also must act ethically. The privacy rights of individuals and groups need to be considered. The balance between the right to inform and the right of privacy tilts toward journalists because the First Amendment protects press freedom. First Amendment power, however, does not, Husselbee wrote, diminish the need for journalists to act responsibly when weighing decisions about invasion of privacy.

News organizations, Sissela Bok argued in her 1989 book *Secrets: On the Ethics of Concealment and Revelation,* need to be free to probe private matters as a check on both government and business. Journalists have a "much clearer public mandate to probe and to expose than do, for instance, social scientists and private detectives," Bok wrote. Journalists cannot confine their news coverage to people who have given consent, but no clear line defines what areas of private life journalists should avoid exploring. For example, "the serious illness of a political candidate or the paranoia of a government leader are surely matters for legitimate public concern" and should be shared with audiences, Bok wrote.

In a 2003 *Journal of Health Communication* article, Sam N. Lehman-Wilzig also emphasized that those who enter politics should realize that their private lives will come under scrutiny. The ethical issues regarding medical privacy will become more problematic in the future, Lehman-Wilzig argues, because of the Internet and digital delivery of information. The potential has increased for obtaining and disclosing personal medical information. Also, the science of genomics will allow increased predictions about what diseases will attack a person.

People in public positions surely realize that they face a level of scrutiny higher than what is appropriate for private individuals. In the United States, the idea of the "public's right to know" is linked to the First Amendment guarantees of free speech and free press. Bok contends that the "government has the duty to reveal that which the public has a right to know," which requires a free press and media access to governmental information. She wrote:

"The public has a legitimate interest, however, in all information about matters that might affect its welfare, quite apart from whether a right to this information can be established. If the press is to fulfill its public mandate, it should provide the greatest possible access to this broad range of information. In addition, journalists also report on much that is of interest to the public, not because of any need for information, but rather to satisfy curiosity. Such reporting is equally legitimate, but it requires attention to individual privacy."

Even though the public tends to criticize the media for invading privacy, one survey indicated that many do understand the benefits of media coverage of certain types of private information. In a 1992 *Journal of Mass Media Ethics* article, James Glen Stovall and Patrick Cotter found that respondents expressed support for publishing information including an elected official receiving gifts from those trying to influence the government and an elected official having a serious drinking or drug problem. In contrast, respondents showed less support for publishing more personal items such as an official's family member having a substance abuse problem and a family member's annual salary.

Two surveys found that journalists do exercise ethical judgment about what private information to disclose. In a 2000 issue of the *Journal of Mass Media Ethics*, Sigman Splichal and Bruce Garrison reported on 1993 and 1999 surveys of daily newspaper editors' views on covering politicians' private lives. In general, journalists were more cautious about covering politicians' private lives in 1999 than in 1993. For example, journalists in 1999 felt less strongly about covering extramarital affairs than those surveyed in 1993. Also in 1999, more editors thought the media paid too much attention to public officials' private lives. Overall, in 1999, more journalists said they would not cover news about a candidate having an affair unless other issues were involved.

Splichal and Garrison also wrote about the surveys in a 2003 *Newspaper Research Journal* article, noting that editors in both surveys cited "linkage" as a major factor in whether they would report about a public official's or candidate's private behavior. The researchers defined "linkage" as "a relationship between the particular private information and a person's public position with respect to that information, such as an anti-abortion candidate who has used or had a family member use abortion services." Splichal and Garrison concluded that journalists will continue to cover the private lives of politicians, often because other media are already publishing the information. Editors also realize that private information interests many people, even though providing this information may harm media credibility. Journalists are left with the ethical dilemma that "readers want the private information but deplore the messenger."

Assessment

Journalists, ethicists, political scientists and public officials have all offered suggestions for determining the proper balance between the public's right to know about public officials' private lives and the privacy rights of public officials. Many have presented theories, tests or principles for balancing the two areas.

Sabato suggested a type of "fairness doctrine" that gives voters sufficient information to use in judging candidates and office holders but that is also fair to politicians. His list of private information appropriate for media use includes "all money matters (investments, transactions, earnings, taxes, and so on)," "all health matters that may affect the candidate's performance in office," "any incident or charge that reaches a police blotter or a civil or criminal court" and "sexual activity where there is a clear intersection between an official's public and private roles." His list of private information inappropriate for media use includes "non-legal matters involving the candidate's underage children and also other family members, except to the extent that the relatives seek the limelight or influence the official," "current extramarital sexual activity as long as it is discreet, non-compulsive, and official's partner(s) are not connected to his or her public responsibilities and are not minors," and "sexual orientation per se, unless compulsive behavior or minors are involved."

Taking another approach, Foreman, in *The Ethical Journalist*, offers a three-step template for deciding whether publishing private information is an intrusion into a politician's privacy. The first step is to analyze how much information and which details the public needs to know. Journalists should ask whether the information assists people with their daily lives and with decisions about governance of the community. The second step is to analyze the likely harm that publishing the information may inflict on the subjects of the news story. The journalist also should consider the degree of privacy the subjects should reasonably expect. The final step is to weigh the importance of the information against the harm to the subjects resulting from the breach of privacy. The journalist also should consider whether some harmful details can be omitted from the news coverage and still provide the information necessary for the public.

Gauthier made similar arguments in her 2010 book chapter, suggesting that journalists weighing publication of private information consider the ethical principle of respect for persons. This "requires that persons be treated with respect for their self-determination, their relationships and emotions, their reasonable goals and their privacy." Self-determination includes the right of people to control access to themselves and information about themselves. Respecting relations and emotions limits journalistic access to the family members and friends of public officials. The utilitarian principle in ethics also comes in to play for journalists wrestling with privacy issues. This principle requires that "benefits be maximized and harms minimized." Gauthier contends that journalists need to weigh potential harms of revealing private information about public officials against the expected benefits. Further, news organizations must examine the harm and benefit to all people who could be affected, not just the public official or politician. The person whose privacy is being intruded upon, his or her family members and friends, and journalists and their news organizations all enter the equation. Publication of sensitive private information can be justified only if the benefits outweigh the harm.

Revealing private information could cause "loss of self-determination and self-respect, loss of reputation and political office, emotional damage, and the destruction of important relationships," Gauthier wrote. With the publication of private information, journalists and their news organizations may benefit from financial success, promotions and awards. The public and the democratic process both benefit by being more informed about the character of public officials. Voters are in a better position to choose their leaders with full information. Before using information that infringes on public officials' private lives, journalists must consider the relevance of the information. A connection should exist between the information and the candidate's role as a public official. The connection may relate to the official's character and whether he or she deserves the public's trust. Information about such issues as sexual conduct or drug use also may raise questions about the public official's character. The situation becomes even more compelling, Gauthier noted, if the candidate lied about the activities or if the activities are illegal. In the case of drug or alcohol abuse, the relevance of the infraction may depend on whether it occurred recently or many years ago. Journalists also need to consider whether the private information they are considering for release relates to the stated values or positions of the politician or public official.

Overall, most of the solutions offered by experts involve ethical balancing, calling for journalists to respect both the public's right to know and a concern for public officials' privacy. Journalists need to start by asking whether the information is true and accurate. Too often in today's fast-paced digital media environment, journalists quote from other news sources, including some that are not reliable, and do not verify the information. The result can be shoddy journalism that puts ethical standards at risk. Once journalists are sure that the information is true and accurate, they need to evaluate each bit of private information on a case-by-case basis, using applicable ethical principles and the considerations suggested above. Only then will a fair decision result.

Points of View

Books

Barnes, Robin D. *Outrageous Invasions: Celebrities' Private Lives, Media, and the Law*. New York: Oxford University Press, 2010. The book examines the role and nature of privacy in Western democracies and chronicles the legal battles waged by celebrities in both the United States and Europe against a press corps that invades their private lives.

Boeyink, David E., and Sandra L. Borden. *Making Hard Choices in Journalism Ethics: Cases and Practice*. New York: Routledge, 2010. Journalists should minimize harm when writing about private issues involving politicians.

Bok, Sissela. *Secrets: On the Ethics of Concealment and Revelation*. New York: Vintage Books, 1989. News organizations need to be free to probe private matters as a check on both government and business.

Calvert, Clay. *Voyeur Nation: Media, Privacy, and Peering in Modern Culture*. Boulder, Colo.: Westview Press, 2004. Media organizations use the First Amendment to protect their right to invade people's privacy, all in the name of giving the public what it wants.

Foreman, Gene. *The Ethical Journalist: Making Responsible Decisions in the Pursuit of News*. Malden, Mass.: Wiley-Blackwell, 2010. Journalists should examine how much information the public needs to know when deciding how much private information to publish.

Patterson, Philip, and Lee Wilkins. *Media Ethics: Issues and Cases*, 7th ed. New York: McGraw Hill, 2011. When journalists consider violating politicians' privacy rights, they should weigh the harm done to others and exercise discretion.

Sabato, Larry J. *Feeding Frenzy: How Attack Journalism Has Transformed American Politics.* New York: Free Press, 1991. Starting with the presidential administration of Franklin Roosevelt, the media kept the private lives of politicians private. That began to change in the 1960s and 1970s.

Articles and Book Chapters

Coyne, Andrew. "Private Lives and the Public Interest." *Maclean's* 123 (March 1, 2010): 9-10. The personal actions of politicians reflect their character and leadership style.

Dobel, J. Patrick. "Judging the Private Lives of Public Officials." *Administration and Society* 30 (1998): 115-42. With today's media environment, few boundaries exist between public officials' public and private lives. The public legitimately wants to know about the personal lives of politicians as a way of evaluating politicians' character.

Gauthier, Candace Cummins. "The Ethics of Privacy," pp. 215-230 in *Journalism Ethics: A Philosophical Approach*, Christopher Meyers, ed. New York: Oxford University Press, 2010. This essay addresses the practical conflicts for journalists, their employers, the owners of news organizations and the public regarding issues of privacy in reporting the news.

Husselbee, L. Paul. "Respecting Privacy in an Information Society: A Journalist's Dilemma." *Journal of Mass Media Ethics* 9 (1994): 145-56. When journalists want to use private information from database research, they should ask why the information is important and whether they have alternatives.

Lehman-Wilzig, Sam N. "Political Ill-Health Coverage: Professional-Ethical Questions Regarding News Reporting of Leaders' Ailments." *Journal of Health Communication* 8 (2003): 59-77. Those who enter politics should realize that their private lives will come under scrutiny, particularly in an Internet age.

Riffe, Daniel. "Public Opinion About News Coverage of Leaders' Private Lives." *Journal of Mass Media Ethics* 18 (2003): 98-110. Most Ohio residents believe job performance can be affected by what goes on in private lives, but most don't believe scrutiny of private matters is a media responsibility and find such coverage excessive and unfair.

Shepard, Alicia. "Gatekeepers Without Gates." *American Journalism Review* 21 (March 1999): 22-9. Mainstream media no longer serve as gatekeepers with regard to publishing information about the private lives of politicians.

Splichal, Sigman, and Bruce Garrison. "Covering Public Officials: Gender and Privacy Issue Differences." *Journal of Mass Media Ethics* 15 (2000): 167-79. In general, based on the results of two studies, journalists were more cautious about covering politicians' private lives in 1999 than in 1993.

Splichal, Sigman, and Bruce Garrison. "News Editors Show Concern for Privacy of Public Officials." *Newspaper Research Journal* 24 (Fall 2003): 77-87. Readers want private information about politicians, but publishing it hurts news media credibility.

Stovall, James Glen, and Patrick R. Cotter. "The Public Plays Reporter: Attitudes toward Reporting on Public Officials." *Journal of Mass Media Ethics* 7 (1992): 97-106. The public supports publishing some private information about elected officials.

Wojdynski, Bartosz W., and Daniel Riffe. "What Kind of Media, and When? Public Opinion about Press Coverage of Politicians' Private Lives." *Journal of Mass Media Ethics* 26 (2011): 206-23. The study found a public increasingly accepting of media coverage of politicians' private lives.

Anonymous Sources

Officials say, and spokesmen confirm. Experts, aides and authorities reveal. Specialists report, and insiders admit.

Who are these anonymous providers of much of the news presented to Americans today? They are the unnamed sources, the off-the-record newsmakers who occasionally request, and often demand, the promise of confidentiality from the media in exchange for information of public interest.

Don't tell anyone I told you so. It's on deep background. And not for attribution.

Journalists sometimes rely on blind sources, especially when covering news in Washington, D.C. Some studies have shown that as many as 55% of all network television news stories and 80% of national news magazine stories contain at least one anonymous source. In a 1993 study of national and large regional newspapers published in *Journalism Quarterly*, Daniel Hallin and his colleagues found that about half of the executive branch sources in stories involving national security were anonymous. Yet nearly all news organizations have policies discouraging the use of unnamed sources.

When and under what conditions should a journalist use anonymous sources? Reporters argue that granting anonymity to a source can help them gain access to information that would otherwise remain unobtainable. But one of the criticisms against giving the protection of confidentiality to a news source is that it often undermines the public's trust and confidence in the accuracy and veracity of the reporter's information. The public's ability to judge the believability of a story is compromised when the source is unknown. And damage can be done by unsubstantiated accusations made by people unwilling to be identified.

What are the rules governing the use of unnamed sources? Who decides that it's appropriate to grant anonymity — reporters or their editors? Who should initiate confidentiality — journalists or their sources? Is the reporter obligated to protect the identity of a source when circumstances change?

by Matt Carlson, Saint Louis University
and Lori Bergen, Marquette University

The stakes are high: More than one reporter has gone to jail to keep a promise of confidentiality. And more than once, the veil of anonymity has been lifted to reveal less-than-ideal news practices and even fakery. The use of unnamed sources has created journalism's heroes as well as its goats — and the line between these positions appears less defined than one may think.

Given the crisis of credibility for journalism today, it's time to examine journalists' routine use of unnamed sources in the news. First, this chapter examines the role that anonymous sources have played in the American media over the past several decades. Then, the chapter turns to arguments both for and against the practice of source confidentiality.

Origins of the Issue

Confrontations over unnamed sources are by no means a modern phenomenon. Since the founding of the republic, officials bent on protecting secrecy have clashed with reporters whose goal is to bring to light secret governmental actions. Although we may think that journalists and officials don't always get along today, it was much worse for 19th century *New York Herald* reporter John Nugent. As Donald Ritchie recounts in his 1991 book *Press Gallery*, after writing about the secret Senate treaty to end the Mexican-American War in 1848, Nugent was called before the Senate to reveal his source. He declined, and an exasperated Senate decided to keep him locked up in a committee room in the U.S. Capitol. The *Herald* backed its correspondent by doubling his pay and continuing to print dispatches from his imprisonment. After a month, with no imminent disclosure, the Senate released Nugent and the question of who leaked the story remains a mystery.

Throughout the 20th century, the use of unnamed sources continued at all levels of the government. A famous example in the 1970s was Deep Throat, the anonymous source who played a central role in the Watergate political scandal during the Nixon administration. Deep Throat was the nickname given to a key unnamed source of *Washington Post* reporters Bob Woodward and Carl Bernstein in their quest to unravel the mystery behind the 1972 break-in at the Democratic National Committee's headquarters in the Watergate complex. Although not mentioned in the original reporting, Deep Throat became a household name after his portrayal in Woodward and Bernstein's 1974 best-seller *All the President's Men* and the hit movie based on the book two years later. Woodward had met with Deep Throat several times, including clandestine middle-of-the-night encounters in parking garages, where he received tips driving the reporting forward. Deep Throat's identity remained the subject of intense speculation for decades, until 2005, when former FBI executive W. Mark Felt admitted to being the secret source. Felt's revelation fueled a debate over the ethics of leaking to the press. Supporters praised Felt for helping expose rampant White House corruption resulting in the resignation of President Nixon and the criminal conviction of several staff members. Yet others denigrated Felt by suggesting his main motive to be nothing more than revenge for being passed over for FBI director. As Matt Carlson argues in his 2011 book *On the Condition of Anonymity*, the split in opinion points to a larger dispute over the value of officials secretly becoming unnamed sources.

After Watergate, journalists used anonymous sources with increasing frequency, but without the corresponding caution required to prevent criticism. As historian Alan Brinkley of Columbia University observed in a *New York Times* article in June 2005, Watergate "created generations of people trying to replicate that role by digging in more and more unsavory ways. As much as Watergate is a model of the journalism that we admire, you can also see in it the origins of the distrust we have today."

A new standard was set for reporting about everything from government to gardening. Some reporters considered it "sexier" to use an unnamed source than one on the record. Disguising source identities could add prestige to some reporters' stories. Sources came to expect anonymity, and reporters were quick to offer it. Anonymous sources were used as a matter of style as opposed to a matter of content.

Around the same time as the Watergate scandal, the U.S. Supreme Court waded into the issue of unnamed sources and the question of whether journalists had special rights to protect their sources' identities from prosecutors. The 1972 *Branzburg v. Hayes* case joined the efforts of three reporters trying to avoid answering subpoenas seeking the identity of their sources. In a 5-4 decision, the court ruled that while the First Amendment did extend to journalists a right to protect the identity of their sources, reporters did have something of a "qualified privilege" offering limited protection. This ambiguous ruling has remained in place ever since, leading many prosecutors to avoid coercing reporters to give up their sources. Some members of Congress responded by calling for a federal shield law—a set of legal conditions that would protect journalistic confidentiality. Meanwhile, both before and after the *Branzburg* ruling, states enacted their own shield laws. According to the summer 2011 issue of *The News Media and the Law*, published by the Reporters Committee for the Freedom of the Press, 40 states have shield laws protecting journalists' privilege to maintain secrecy in shielding their sources, and many other states have extended similar protections to journalists through case law. Meanwhile, congressional bills establishing a shield law have come and gone, but by early 2012 none had passed.

These examples show how journalists, elected officials and justices have been in conflict over the need to keep some sources anonymous. Now, this chapter will consider the major criticisms directed against the use of unnamed sources and the evidence to support those concerns. Later, it will turn to arguments made to support their use. Finally, the chapter will address those who support unnamed sources, but only under strict conditions.

Criticizing Anonymous Sources

Many critics of anonymous sources argue that the costs of using them are so great that journalists and their news organizations should abandon them. Writing in a 1995 *Washington Post* column titled "The Cost of Anonymity," newspaper editor Geneva Overholser warned that "the use of unnamed sources is among American newspapers' most damaging habits." Overholser's word choice — habit — is telling. It describes a behavior that one engages in without thought — a generalized, automatic reaction to a specific situation. With unnamed sources appearing in story after news story, reporters and editors need to consider what the regular use of anonymity does to the credibility of journalism.

In a 2005 *Quill* magazine column, Fred Brown wrote that veiled sources "make a lot of readers, viewers and listeners suspicious. Secrecy raises questions about the motives of both reporter and source. It hurts the credibility and accountability of media outlets." This idea appears to be more than merely speculation. Research by journalism professors Miglena Mantcheva Sternadori and Esther Thorson in a 2009 *Newspaper Research Journal* article has shown that news audiences consider stories with unnamed sources to be less credible than those with full attribution. Although anonymity may make life easier for reporters chasing a story, its widespread use threatens the delicate trust that journalists work so hard to establish.

What are the concerns that critics have about this "habit" of granting anonymity? At the very least, they include the notion that reporters are too lazy to find on-the-record sources or fail to work hard enough to persuade a source to allow attribution. But more insidious deficiencies also lurk behind anonymity. Too many sources use anonymity to hide their self-serving agendas and escape reprisal. Some journalists are also self-serving, making unseen deals with sources not necessarily in the public interest.

A lack of named sources may allow reporters to hide uncertainties or, in extreme cases, make things up. This is not as far-fetched as it may seem. In 1980, *Washington Post* reporter Janet Cooke was stripped of a Pulitzer Prize for her series "Jimmy's World" chronicling the life of an 8-year-old heroin addict. Cooke used anonymous sources to tell the story of "Jimmy," a pseudonym that veiled the identity of the child. But later, the newspaper found out that Cooke had fab-

ricated "Jimmy." Two decades later, in 2004, *USA Today* foreign correspondent Jack Kelley was fired after editors discovered he had hidden outright fabrications behind the use of anonymous sources. Such high-profile incidents further erode the trust in journalism.

To understand more mundane problems with unnamed sources, consider the problem of leaks. With nearly any government entity, it is not unusual for seemingly private information to wind up in the hands of a journalist. Stephen Hess, who researches the interaction of the press and the government, provides many reasons for officials to leak information to the press in his 1996 book *News and Newsmaking*. With the "Whistle-Blower Leak," heroic, unnamed sources risk their jobs or even their safety to expose dangerous or illegal conduct of their employers. But, as Hess points out, leaks can occur for many less heroic reasons. A source may offer a reporter a "Policy Leak" to alert the public to an issue. The "Trail-Balloon Leak" allows officials to float a possible action without having to take responsibility for the idea in case it's a dud. An "Ego Leak" refers to a source who may leak unattributed information just to feel important, or a source may offer a "Goodwill Leak" to a reporter to get a future favor. Finally, the dreaded "Animus Leak" allows a source to attack others publicly without retribution. What these leaks reveal is that unnamed sources often fail to live up to the romantic cliché of brave whistle-blowers working with journalists to bring wrongdoing to light.

The problem of leaks can be understood best by looking closely at how journalists covered allegations of Iraq's weapons of mass destruction in the buildup to the March 2003 invasion. For many months, top officials in the Bush administration actively touted Iraq's weapons capabilities in on-the-record speeches and interviews as the nation moved closer and closer to war. Many citizens became convinced, too, of the necessity of a military intervention, especially as these public claims of the administration were corroborated by news reports — citing mostly unnamed-sources — in many of the nation's top media outlets. In front page stories in both the *New York Times* and *Washington Post*, "senior officials" across the government seemed to confirm the evidence for Iraq's hidden arsenal. Even Bob Woodward, perhaps the reporter best known for his insider connections, said on CNN's *Larry King Live* on February 5, 2003, just weeks before the war: "Suppose we go to war and go into Iraq and there are no weapons of mass destruction. I think the chance of that happening is about zero. There's just too much there." As the Bush administration struggled to account for its mistakes, the press was called to account for how it had gotten its own investigative work so wrong. In the May 26, 2004, edition of the *New York Times*, editor Bill Keller took the unusual step of addressing how it had consistently erred in its pages. In a special note to readers, Keller wrote: "In some cases, information that was controversial then, and seems questionable now, was insufficiently qualified or allowed to stand unchallenged. Looking back, we wish we had been more aggressive in re-examining the claims as new evidence emerged — or failed to emerge." Much of this reporting relied on unnamed sources, from both the U.S. government and Iraqi exiles.

Reporters who covered the WMD beat, especially Judith Miller of the *Times,* defended their work by placing the onus on officials who had promulgated erroneous intelligence reports. The reporters considered their reporting accurate insofar as it reflected accurately what these officials thought. The problem with anonymous sources, however, is that audiences cannot know who is speaking and have no recourse for examining their claims. It is up to the reporter, as Jack Shafer wrote in his February 12, 2004, *Slate* column, to judge the merit of information being provided. "The job of a good reporter — investigative or otherwise — is more like that of an intelligence analyst than a stenographer," Shafer wrote. "A good reporter is supposed to dig for the truth, no matter what 'people inside the governments' with 'very high security clearances' might say." Critics such as Shafer chided reporters for merely *recording* source statements instead of *scrutinizing* their veracity and potential for problems.

The weapons of mass destruction episode illustrates the danger of unnamed sources. Critics charged journalists with showering too much attention on top officials in step with the government's official line. Once the war began and the WMDs failed to materialize, this reporting helped undermine the already shaky credibility of journalism. The public is less likely to trust the accuracy of news reports and more likely to question the ethics of reporters. Because anonymous sources mask the true motive or agendas of the source, the public is less likely to know how reliable the information may be.

There is one important final argument against using anonymous sources to consider — the difficult legal and ethical situations that can result. As a purely practical matter, journalists should be cautious in using anonymous sources because of potentially disastrous consequences. Anyone who's heard a secret knows how difficult it is to keep it. Journalists should be aware that in granting anonymity, they create both a moral and legal obligation to maintain that trust. Yet doing so is not always easy.

Several visible cases where the press used unnamed sources illustrate this dilemma: What happens if the journalist is compelled to break the promise? As Stephen Klaidman and Tom L. Beauchamp wrote in their 1987 book *The Virtuous Journalist,* competing values may at times override the obligation of confidentiality. The risk of disclosure is present in any such promise. But, in general, journalists break promises of confidentiality under two circumstances. The first is when a judge orders them or their news organizations to provide confidential informa-

tion that may be relevant to a criminal or libel case. The second is when reporters and editors decide to break the promise themselves because of the overriding news value of the source's identity to a story. In the 2011 book *Communication and the Law*, Cathy Packer wrote that courts are now insisting that journalists offer evidence to show that their relationship with a source was, in fact, confidential. And recently, courts have begun to treat these agreements like contracts.

The Supreme Court's 1991 decision in the case of *Cohen v. Cowles Media Co.* emphasized journalists' obligation to keep their promises of confidentiality. The case involved the *Minneapolis Star Tribune*, the *St. Paul Dispatch* and a political party worker, Dan Cohen, who provided documents to reporters at both newspapers with information damaging to the opposing party's candidate for lieutenant governor. Cohen's information disclosed that, over a decade before, the candidate had been charged with unlawful assembly when she protested on behalf of minority workers and had once been convicted of shoplifting $6 worth of sewing materials. Cohen received promises of confidentiality from the reporters, but editors at the two newspapers decided that his identity and the political "dirty trick" he was playing on the opposing candidate was itself newsworthy. They ignored the reporters' promises of confidentiality and identified Cohen as the source in the subsequent stories.

Cohen sued the two newspapers for breach of contract and misrepresentation after he lost his job on the day the stories were published. Although the Minnesota Supreme Court refused to find that contract law protected the promise of confidentiality to a news source, the U.S. Supreme Court held that under Minnesota's common law of *promissory estoppel* (which protects people from injustice when they rely and act on a promise), a source could sue for damages against a news medium that broke its promise of confidentiality. The court said publishers of a newspaper "have no special immunity from the application of general laws." The case was sent back to the state court, where a $200,000 damage award was upheld.

In their 1996 book *Fundamentals of Mass Communication Law*, Donald Gillmor, Jerome Barron, Todd Simon and Herb Terry suggest that this case gives journalists reason for concern. "[T]he Court has opened the door to alternative theories of liability, and the decision is likely to encourage other sources who have been 'burned' to consider suing," they wrote. These authors also identify the key point to remember: "In many ways, however, the newspapers have no one but themselves to blame in *Cohen*," they wrote. "If the editors had honored the promises of confidentiality and chided the reporters later in private, there would have been no case."

The *Cohen* case emphasizes the responsibilities journalists should assume when promising confidentiality and underscores the seriousness of such a pledge. The promise of confidentiality, once granted, cannot be easily violated by the media. Such a constraint provides a compelling argument for avoiding the use of anonymous sources.

Meanwhile, the changing nature of news has added more complications to unnamed sources due to the evolving notion of just who qualifies as a journalist. In 2005, a young journalist who shot video of a protest that turned violent was asked by investigators to hand in his footage and testify about what he saw. Normally, such a request would never reach a journalist, except that prosecutors did not consider 23-year-old blogger Josh Wolf to be a professional journalist worthy of any protections. Wolf refused to give up footage or the names of protesters and wound up in federal prison for over seven months before a compromise was reached. If the future of journalism is unclear, uncertainty also reigns around the questions of legal protections and obligations surrounding unnamed sources.

Defending Anonymous Sources

In the early 1970s, right before Watergate, the *Washington Post* tried an experiment: Reporters would no longer use unnamed sources or even listen to a source insisting on anonymity. This policy shift, radical as it was, was designed to curb the flood of unattributed information flowing through the pages of the *Post* each day. Editor Ben Bradlee decided that someone had to interrupt the cycle in which anonymity had become expected and normal, rather than a special case. Often, high-level sources gathered reporters together for background briefings with the condition that the source's name would not be mentioned in stories. If *Post* reporters started refusing to grant anonymity, the reasoning went, sources would have no recourse but to offer their assertions on the record for the world to see. The problems of anonymous sources, listed above, would then be history.

The policy change lasted two days.

Media scholar Ben Bagdikian, then an editor at the *Post*, explained the problem in a 2005 *Columbia Journalism Review* commentary, where he wrote that "unnamed sources will not be vanishing anytime soon. They serve too many purposes for both the news media and officialdom." The *Post* simply could not cover the government fully without allowing sources to speak confidentially. Thus, if the readers of the *Post* — both ordinary citizens and policy-makers — wanted to know what was really going on, then they had to accept that not all sources would be named. Clearly, using anonymous sources may not be ideal, yet no one would choose the alternative either: being kept in the dark about what public institutions were doing.

Although we should not ignore the problems of unnamed sources, or should

ignore their potential benefits, granting anonymity allows journalists to provide information that otherwise would go unreported. As Philip Taubman, Washington bureau chief of the *New York Times*, described the situation to *Television Week* in June 2005: "The day we outlaw the use of anonymous sources in the coverage of the CIA, the Pentagon, the White House, the State Department and other national security agencies is the day we cease to cover them effectively." Journalists cannot adequately account for the actions of secretive institutions purely through press conferences and prepared materials.

We can find reminders about the importance of unnamed sources in news stories that expose secret government doings. For example, the actions of the CIA remain closely guarded secrets that the agency keeps out of public view. So when *Washington Post* reporter Dana Priest broke the story of prisoner rendition to covert prisons called "black sites" in November 2005, her reporting necessarily relied on unnamed sources. Very little was known about these sources, but by protecting their identities, Priest brought to light the existence of what some labeled "enhanced interrogation techniques" and what others flatly called torture. The story garnered Priest print journalism's top commendation, a Pulitzer Prize, for her "persistent, painstaking reports" on the secret prisons.

Priest's reporting on black sites touched off a larger debate about the type of reporting made possible by unnamed sources. After her story appeared, the White House and others argued that the press should never expose secret government activities used for national defense. Doing so only renders such activities useless. Others, however, believed that it's better for U.S. citizens to know what their government was up to, particularly when such activities might be illegal. Proponents of this view support the mission of journalists as providing "a conduit of information" to the public. And the flow of information would be diminished if reporters were prohibited from writing anything that they could not attribute by name and title.

Former CBS News reporter Daniel Schorr was no stranger to unnamed sources. His reporting for CBS earned him multiple Emmys for covering the Watergate scandal as well as the wrath of Congress for not revealing his source of a leaked secret report detailing illegal FBI and CIA activities in the 1970s. Schorr stood by his principles, even when let go by CBS. On the May 31, 2005, program of NPR's *All Things Considered*, he offered an impassioned defense of the practice: "I think this republic has been saved by leaks at various times. For example, would Clinton have been impeached had it not been for an original leak? Would Reagan have not been in trouble with the Iran Contra affair were it not for a big leak? And then Nixon, of course. The presidents and the White Houses and the governments have all kinds of ways of hiding things, and the only way that you can penetrate that is if somebody, as a kind of a whistle-blower, is willing to leak. And I think that's very valuable for our republic."

In the end, using anonymous sources is often the only way to uncover questionable — or even illegal — activities taking place within the government of a democratic nation. If the press is to live up to its self-defined role of acting as a watchdog, it must be given the tools to do its job properly.

For a final defense of unnamed sources, let's return to the reporting on WMDs in the lead-up to the Iraq War in 2003. Although much of the reporting had been wrong, not every reporter botched the story. Warren Strobel and Jonathan Landay, two reporters working for the Washington Bureau of the Knight Ridder newspaper chain, also used unnamed sources in pursuing the WMD story, but produced much different stories. In the week in which the *New York Times* published a front page story headlined "U.S. Says Hussein Intensified Quest for A-Bomb Parts," Strobel and Landay's story ran as "Lack of hard evidence of Iraqi weapons worries top U.S. officials."

How did they arrive at findings so different from their peers? They bypassed the top officials and instead went after other, less-glamorous sources lacking the same political agenda. As Strobel explained in a profile in the August 2004 issue of the *American Journalism Review*, "People at the [*New York*] *Times* were mainly talking to senior administration officials, who were mostly pushing the administration line. We were mostly talking to the lower-level people or dissidents, who didn't necessarily repeat the party line." These two reporters faced pressure from the White House for their critical reporting that deviated so much from other news organizations, but continued to pursue the weapons story. After the war had started and much of the predominant reporting was shown to be flawed, the pair was heralded for their work.

It's impossible to second-guess what may have happened had other reporters followed the same practices as Strobel and Landay during the confusing time following the September 11, 2001, terrorist attacks, or during the period before the start of the war in Afghanistan, and later with the eventual invasion of Iraq. But the lesson is clear that effective journalistic vigilance is essential, even when it involves talking to sources off-the-record.

Allowing Unnamed Sources ... on Conditions

Amid high-profile controversies involving unnamed sources, the *Boston Globe* offered an editorial on June 2, 2005, hoping to explore the problems of using anonymous sources without banning them entirely. "[T]he sourcing of news stories," it wrote, "is again a hot topic, largely because unnamed sources have hurt press credibility. Some outlets use them far too carelessly, to allow cheap shots or to supply information that could be put on the record by better reporting.

Others fail to follow the *Post's* general rule in Watergate that every story needs at least two independent sources. Too many sourced stories have turned out to be wrong. The current trend toward stating the reason for anonymity is healthy."

As this quote makes clear, even advocates of source anonymity support it with reservations and limits on the circumstances and conditions under which such anonymity should be granted to a source. One of the best pieces of evidence for that concern is the preponderance of newsroom policies and ethical guidelines that specify when and where unnamed sources should be used.

The *New York Times* offers a good example of guidelines governing unnamed sources, one it makes public on its corporate website, www.nytco.com. After the newspaper's much criticized reporting on Iraq's WMDs, its top leadership revised the policies on unnamed sources. This was a much needed attempt to think through the significance of unnamed sources, as well as the underlying mechanics, to avoid future incidents that would weaken the newspaper's credibility or drive away readers.

The resulting document begins with a call to curtail source anonymity by specifying conditions under which it is acceptable. Rather than routine use, unnamed sources should appear only in "highly sensitive stories, when it is we who have sought out a source who may face legal jeopardy or loss of livelihood for speaking with us." This is a high bar, and one not met by many unnamed sources cropping up in the news. In recognition of this new standard, the *Times* policy also accounted for sources coming to the newspaper with information but demanding anonymity: "If the impetus for anonymity has originated with the source, further reporting is essential to satisfy the reporter and the reader that the paper has sought the whole story." That is, reporters start from a position of doubt rather than trust. The source may be used only after the reporter has worked to verify the source's information.

The *Times* policy also confronts the thornier question about those officials who demand anonymity in nearly every interaction with a reporter. Here, the newspaper stresses that "the reporter should press the source, after the conversation, to go on the record with the newsworthy information that has emerged." This statement reiterates the overarching desire to cut down on anonymity when it is unnecessary.

A number of other provisions are spelled out in the policy, particularly with regard to the type of information that a source provides anonymously:

- "Confidential sources must have direct knowledge of the information they are giving us."
- "We do not grant anonymity to people who are engaged in speculation."
- "We do not grant anonymity to people who use it as cover for a personal or

partisan attack."

• "Anonymity should not be invoked for a trivial comment, or to make an unremarkable comment appear portentous."

• "We do not promise sources that we will refrain from additional reporting or efforts to verify the information being reported."

Thus, it is not only the source's circumstances that matter, but *what is being said* that matters. Ideally, unnamed sources should *only* provide facts they can substantiate, not opinions or speculation or — worst of all — attacks for which they use anonymity to escape accountability.

Finally, the *Times* policy on unnamed sources stresses the need to disclose as much information as possible while still maintaining confidentiality. Of particular importance is explaining *why* a source has chosen to remain unidentified. "We accept an obligation not only to convince a reader of their reliability but also to convey what we can learn of their motivation," states the policy. Instead of merely identifying a "senior official," reporters should explain their position more fully and specify their reasons for avoiding being named. Again, the point is to be as transparent as possible instead of assuming that the credibility of the newspaper or the reporter will be enough to convince readers of a story's truth.

Journalism ethics scholar and Indiana University professor David Boeyink provided seven guidelines for using anonymous sources in an article on the abuses of anonymous sources that appeared in the *Journal of Mass Media Ethics* in 1990. His position is that, although journalists routinely use unnamed sources, the standard should be for full attribution. "The source of the information is critical to understanding the meaning and significance of the message," he wrote. Exceptions to the standard should only occur with ample justification to limit abuse of the practice. Boeyink's guidelines are these:

Promises of anonymity must be authorized by the editor. Journalists learned their lesson after Janet Cooke's deceptive story about "Little Jimmy," the nonexistent 8-year-old heroin addict. Benjamin Bradlee, her editor at the *Washington Post,* has said it's impossible to catch a deceiver like Cooke. But if the newspaper had required that at least one editor know the identity of Jimmy, Cooke's deception would have been exposed and the story stopped before publication. Boeyink argues that "involving a second person is a crucial check within the system to ensure that the story is accurate and fair in the face of the potential for error or abuse."

Anonymous sources should be used only for a just cause. Boeyink argues that one of the fundamental operating principles of journalism is the attribution of sources. So overriding is that principle that anonymity should be used only if the alternative has significant value: exposing public corruption or publishing information needed for citizen involvement in democratic government. "The burden of proof rests with those who want to use anonymous sources to demonstrate why a story is important enough to allow the use of unattributed information to override the preferred standard of attribution," Boeyink wrote. Using anonymous sources in unexceptional stories — cases where the risk of distortion is low or the story is simply interesting and not really important — sets a worrisome precedent. For an example of a mundane use of unnamed sources, despite the newspaper's provisions above, the front page of the *New York Times* Arts section based an October 27, 2009, story about the possibility of a director taking on a rumored new film project on sources speaking "on condition of anonymity." Using an unnamed source in an arts story about a movie trivializes the entire concept and undercuts the credibility of stories where shielding the identity of sources is crucial.

Anonymous sources should be used only as a last resort. Meeting this criterion means working harder to get information on the record. It also means, often, spending more time and more money. But reporters should turn to reasonable alternatives to get the information, such as shifting the emphasis from human sources to documents, and include the cost of damage to the media's credibility and the public's knowledge of the issues in the calculation, Boeyink suggests.

Identify sources as fully as possible, with reasons for anonymity explained in the story. News stories should provide the reasons for granting anonymity so that audiences can judge the credibility of the source, the possible motives for not wanting a name used and whether the source is a low- or high-level official.

Balance potential harms and benefits of anonymous sources. The possible harm that may occur to an individual or institution should not outweigh the importance that a story has to the community. It won't always be easy to measure the benefit to society against the harm that might be done to one individual, but Boeyink's argument is that journalists are obliged to consider those competing outcomes whenever a story involves anonymous sources.

The reporter, media and source should have just intentions. Journalists shouldn't use anonymous sources to "win prizes, sell newspapers, or to be the first to get a news story," Boeyink wrote. Nor should sources be allowed to hide their identities in the media simply to advance their own ends. Journalists must be cautious of serving a source's agenda when granting anonymity, and they have the added obligation of needing to know enough about the source and the circumstances to be capable of making that judgment.

Get independent verification. Confirmation of information from a second, independent source makes good journalistic sense — even when journalists don't use anonymous sources. Journalists need to be even more certain of the accuracy and completeness of information when they provide anonymity to a source, because publishing something that's untrue is an even greater sin when the source is unnamed.

Newsweek magazine experienced this pain in 2005 when it printed a small item alleging that an upcoming military report would contain charges of abuse of Guantanamo Bay terrorism suspects, including that a Koran was flushed down a toilet. The reporters learned this information from an unnamed source, and then treated a lack of comment from the Department of Defense as a corroborating source. In fact, there was no report. Had the reporters really checked it out, they would have saved the magazine from an embarrassing retraction.

Ultimately, Boeyink argues that the consequence of using anonymous sources is that readers and viewers are denied a critical prerogative: the ability to judge for themselves the validity of the information they are given. They have no way of knowing if the source of the speculation is a low-level bureaucrat or the defense secretary. The risks of manipulation grow, the risks to credibility and accountability are real, and the value of the news is diminished.

Assessment

Should the use of unnamed sources continue as a legitimate journalistic tool? Probably so, but with caution and care. Given that American journalists rely heavily on the practice, it would be unreasonable to suggest that it simply be abandoned. For the press to act as a watchdog, anonymity is a necessary tool. But it is not without its dangers, as any journalist should admit.

For a glimpse at this balance between usefulness and hazardousness, look at public opinion about unnamed sources. On the one hand, it seems the overriding argument that legitimate stories would remain in obscurity without some measure of confidentiality between reporters and sources has struck a chord with the public. Although Americans continue to criticize the press for inaccuracy, lack of fairness and sensationalism, they also endorse the practice of unnamed sources — at least in principle.

According to a 2005 report put out by the Pew Research Center for the People and the Press, 76% of Americans approved of the news media's practice of uncovering and reporting corruption and fraud in business, government agencies and other organizations. This endorsement, however, is no free pass for journalists to use unnamed sources as often as they want. When presented with a question weighing the benefits of unnamed source-aided disclosure against the negative of potential inaccurate reporting, 54% of people found the practice to be too risky. It seems the public expects the press to be a watchdog, but a careful one. Maintaining this delicate balance is a challenge that should not escape journalists.

One solution to the problem of unnamed sources is simple: follow the rules. Most news organizations have rules about the use of unnamed sources, although those rules may not always be followed. From reviews of newsroom policies, we know that most maintain certain conditions for granting anonymity. These conditions generally include that an editor have knowledge of the source, that the story is important, that anonymity was used only as a last resort, and that reasons for granting anonymity are included in the story. Most newsroom policies and ethical guidelines concur that the standard should be to avoid anonymous attribution. When used responsibly, in moderation, when circumstances require them, journalists can be confident that they haven't fallen into the trap of habitual use.

David Johnston's 1987 *Columbia Journalism Review* article with techniques from some of the best reporters in the nation remains relevant today for helping journalists think through how to avoid the habit of unnamed sources. The first technique is to use documents. Reporters can find both online and offline written materials that can be used either to confirm information provided by a source who wants anonymity or as a starting point to keep sources from requesting it in the first place. Sources are more inclined to go on the record when they know a reporter already has substantial information that's verified. Another approach Johnston raises is at first to promise sources not to quote them by name. Then, after gathering important information, the reporter can suggest that if the sources want to see such information in a news story, they must help the reporter document the assertions, or go on the record themselves. Another technique is to read back quotes to sources. This reassures sources that a reporter wants to be fair and accurate and can help establish a rapport based on trust with the source. A final technique is to bounce one side against the other: Get sources on one side of a story to talk off the record and then use that information to verify the other side's materials.

Critics point out that thorough investigative reporters don't have to cite anonymous sources in the stories that are ultimately published. The trend for good investigative reporting has been toward use of unnamed sources as a beginning point for covering a story. An investigative reporter initially may receive information from a source who requires confidentiality as a condition for providing the information, but the reporter proceeds to confirm that information independently through other sources. Once the story is published, all sources are attributed.

But all reporters do not enjoy the luxury of many months and other resources to conduct such extensive investigations and multiple source confirmation. More often than not, the use of anonymous sources occurs when reporters are, as some have charged, simply lazy. Or they are working on deadline, feeling competitive pressure and the need to get the story before somebody else publishes it first. Those situations may prompt reporters to sidestep the rules that might otherwise have required more careful and full verification of facts.

In the end, remember that rules and ethics are not quite the same thing. Reporters may follow guidelines but still deceive their editor or, worse, their audience. One test, then, that a journalist should ask is this: who ultimately benefits when a source is allowed to speak without being named — the source, the journalist, or the public?

The trick to kicking the habit may be in weighing the relative costs associated with using unnamed sources. News organizations need to balance the economics of more thorough and conscientious reporting with the risk of losing credibility. We may not see the end of anonymous sources, but a more responsible approach by journalists who are aware of the costs of using them.

Points of View

Books

Bok, Sissela. *Secrets: On the Ethics of Concealment and Revelation*. New York: Pantheon Books, 1982. This philosophical approach features the moral and ethical issues associated with secrecy in society and includes several chapters relevant to the use of secret sources, whistle blowers, and investigative journalism. Bok defends secrecy as morally desirable in many cases, but also comments on its potentially destructive side.

Carlson, Matt. *On the Condition of Anonymity: Unnamed Sources and the Battle for Journalism*. Champaign: University of Illinois Press, 2011. This book tracks public debates about journalism in a series of recent controversies involving unnamed sources at the *New York Times, Washington Post, Time, Newsweek,* and CBS News. It argues for the need to preserve the use of anonymity, but only when firmly grounded in the public interest.

Goodwin, Gene, and Ron F. Smith. *Groping for Ethics in Journalism*, 3rd ed. Ames: Iowa State University Press, 1994. The authors argue for a prescriptive ethical code for journalists and deal with several issues related to secret sources, including arguments for and against their use, the rituals of confidentiality, and the legal problems related to protecting sources.

Hess, Stephen. *News and Newsmaking*. Washington, D.C.: The Brookings Institution, 1996. This book carefully reveals how news in Washington gets made beyond what the public sees in the finished news product. It contains an interesting examination of the self-interestedness lying at the heart of many unnamed sources that goes against the idealistic image of the altruistic whistleblower.

Pearlstine, Norman. *Off the Record: The Press, the Government, and the War over Anony-*

mous Sources. New York: Farrar, Straus and Giroux, 2007. "Confidentiality has become a weapon in the White House's war on the press, a war fought with the unwitting complicity of the press itself."

Articles and Book Chapters

Bagdikian, Ben H. "When the Post banned anonymous sources." *American Journalism Review* August/September 2005. "[A] ban on unnamed sources is impractical. That anonymity is granted far too frequently is abundantly clear. But there are times when using anonymous sources makes sense. Whistleblowers who report misdeeds or illegal activity by their companies or agencies face retaliation if they do so on the record. They could be demoted, fired or worse."

Boeyink, David E. "Anonymous Sources in News Stories: Justifying Exceptions and Limiting Abuses." *Journal of Mass Media Ethics* 5:4 (1990): 233-46. The author considers current practices and policies on anonymous sources, as well as the justification for and danger of using them. He offers seven guidelines for editors and reporters that suggest when and under what conditions such sources should be used.

Hallock, Steve. "The 'anonymous' lessons of the Libby trial." *St. Louis Journalism Review* March 1, 2007. "When even staunch advocates of First Amendment protection for the media raise legal doubts about journalists' uses of anonymous sources, it is time for journalists to pause and rethink their increasing, unabated use of these sources."

Hood, Lucy. "Naming names." *American Journalism Review* May 2006. "Newsrooms are struggling with the dilemma of whether to use the names of illegal immigrants. Anonymous sources are under fire as threats to credibility. Yet identifying undocumented immigrants could lead to their deportation."

Kirtly, Jane. "Striving to unmask anonymous sources." *American Journalism Review* September 1995. "Aggressive efforts by companies such as Philip Morris make it harder to protect sources' confidentiality."

Klaidman, Stephen, and Tom L. Beauchamp. *The Virtuous Journalist.* New York: Oxford University Press, 1987. Chapter 6, "Maintaining Trust," pp. 154-79, discusses the relationship of reciprocity between journalists and their sources, including examples of cases involving confidentiality. The authors blend philosophy with concrete examples to argue for minimal legal constraints on journalism.

Packer, Cathy. "Confidential Sources and Information," chapter 14 in W. Wat Hopkins, ed., *Communication and the Law*. Northport, Ala.: Vision Press, 2012. This chapter provides a good primer on the legal aspects of confidential sources.

Ritea, Steve. "Going It Alone." *American Journalism Review*, August 2004, 16-17. Two reporters used unnamed sources to get the story of Iraq's "Weapons of Mass Destruction" correct when nearly all other reporters had gotten it wrong.

Shepard, Alicia. A. "Anonymous Sources." *American Journalism Review* December 1994. "A flurry of inaccurate stories about O.J. Simpson based on unnamed sources has rekindled the debate over their use. Detractors say they hurt the media's credibility. Defenders say without them important stories would never be told."

Son, Taegyu. "Leaks: How Do Codes of Ethics Address Them?" *Journal of Mass Media Ethics* 17 (2002): 155-173. This content analysis finds that many news organizations' codes of ethics offer little guidance on what to do with leaked information, which leaves the journalist in a precarious situation of lacking predefined rules for dealing with confidential sources and information.

Sternadori, Miglena Mantcheva, and Esther Thorson. "Anonymous Sources Harm Credibility of All Stories." *Newspaper Research Journal* 30:4 (2009): 54-66. In this experiment, the presence of unnamed sources negatively affected readers' perceptions of a story's credibility.

21 Checkbook Journalism

Public relations practitioners talk to journalists because it's their job. Whistleblowers talk because they see it as the right thing to do, or they've got an ax to grind. Politicians talk when it's in their best interest. Movie stars talk when they have a new film to hype. Victims of crime or other disasters talk because it's cathartic or because they want the world to know their story. Others talk simply because a journalist asks.

And then there's another reason why sources provide information to journalists: Because news organizations pay.

"Checkbook journalism" is the practice of compensating sources who provide information. Sources who possess a marketable commodity of information, access, images or insight are willing to sell what news organizations want, and some news organizations are willing buyers. In exchange for payment — cash, travel expenses or other consideration — journalists receive a competitive advantage through access to the information they need for stories. News organizations usually demand exclusivity to the information, which they hope brings larger audiences and the ability to charge higher rates to advertisers. For those reasons, some news organizations let money talk in the quest to win what they call "the get" — the interview and images they want to tell the day's hot story.

The term "checkbook journalism" has neither a clear-cut definition nor an exhaustive list of what it constitutes. Any list begins with direct payment to sources in exchange for interviews or information. A distinction that some say has little difference is a "licensing fee," the term some news organizations use when they buy rights to photos or videos while noting that the interview with the images' owner is free. Some ethicists say any remuneration constitutes checkbook journalism, regardless of the journalist's motive, because it hinders objectivity and blurs the traditional source-reporter relationship. Nicholas Von Hoffman (famous for losing his commentary job on CBS's *60 Minutes* after calling Watergate-plagued President Richard Nixon a "dead mouse on America's kitchen

by Chris Roberts
University of Alabama

floor") argued that it occurs when news organizations buy public opinion polling, because the poll results are manufactured news. Some purists argue that having "experts" on retainer, ready to offer their insight when news breaks, is a form of checkbook journalism. The business of buying book and broadcast rights from people caught up in newsworthy events may constitute checkbook journalism, too, especially when news organizations that are part of media conglomerates make deals that include access to the conglomerates' non-news divisions.

With checkbook journalism, there is a fine line between legitimacy and criminality. In some instances, prosecutors have filed bribery charges against public officials and other sources. The Society of Professional Journalists' 2011 *Journalism Ethics* book flatly states that checkbook journalism is "something serious journalists say is wrong." The Radio Television Digital News Association's code of ethics is similar, stating that "electronic journalists should not pay news sources who have a vested interest in the story."

In some nations, paying for information is merely a cost of doing business, and politicians and athletes routinely expect money before helping journalists. Most American mainstream news organizations forbid the practice. Local broadcasters and newspapers rarely pay, usually for reasons of ethics, economics and a lesser need for exclusivity. But some television networks, national news organizations and book publishers leap in and out of bidding wars in the chase for celebrity, crime, court and political stories. And it is common among tabloid and entertainment-focused media.

Some see the practice as a non-moral issue, others as a hold-your-nose-but-do-it necessity in a competitive media environment, and others as a journalistic sin.

Checkbook journalism is legal in the United States, despite attempts to ban it. As a response to checkbook-wielding news organizations scoring scoops (occasionally at the expense of truth) in the O.J. Simpson murder trial, the California Legislature forbade witnesses to criminal acts from receiving any "benefit" for their information. A court quickly tossed that law on First Amendment grounds in 1995, but courts have ruled it legal for governments to forbid criminals from cashing in on their crimes. Regardless of the law, remember that it's a mistake to conflate what is legal with what is ethical.

Origins of the Issue

It is unknown who wrote the first check to a source. An early instance came with the *Titanic's* 1912 sinking, when the *New York World* promised to pay the wireless operator of the nearby *Olympic* for news, with journalistic reminders to be quick and "mention prominent persons." It is unclear whether a deal was made, but the *New York Times* paid $1,000 (or $20,000 in current dollars) to a *Titanic* wireless operator.

An early practitioner of checkbook journalism was William Bradford Huie, a Southern journalist who paid three racist killers for their stories. His 1956 *Look* story included interviews with the two killers of Emmett Till, a black teenager they claim flirted with a white woman. Each killer received $2,000 (about $16,000 today), safe from double jeopardy after an all-white jury found them innocent. In 1968, Huie paid James Earl Ray $40,000 (nearly $250,000 today) to tell about assassinating Martin Luther King. In an afterward to Huie's *Three Lives for Mississippi*, author Juan Williams said Huie "seems to have inadvertently invented 'checkbook journalism.' "

Time magazine first noticed checkbook journalism in 1962, when it showed how British tabloids paid for access to killers and jurors. As a tabloid editor lamented, "It's getting to the point that when you ask anyone the color of his hat, he says, 'Six quid and I'll start talking.'" A year later, *Time's* parent began buying news. Time-Life Inc. paid Henry Zapruder $150,000 (more than $1 million today) to give *Life* stills from the home movie showing bullets striking President John F. Kennedy. Zapruder's family later sold rights to CBS before the U.S. government bought all film rights in 1999 for $16 million. In the 1960s, Time-Life paid $500,000 to the seven *Mercury* astronauts for access.

Payments continued throughout the next decades. In a 1972 *Columbia Journalism Review* article, *McCall's* editor Robert Stein spat at those who would pay for information: "[W]e are anxious to enrich any witness to a great media event as long as he promises to tell us 'the real truth' behind the outpouring of news that we have been consuming so avidly: James Earl Ray, Charles Manson, Lt. Calley, Sirhan Sirhan, Jacqueline Kennedy's dressmaker ... Judy Garland's last husband — we want to hear them all."

Stein could have added politicians to that list. In early 1975, CBS News paid $100,000 (or $400,000 today) to H.R. Halderman, the Nixon aide who later that year began an 18-month prison sentence for Watergate crimes. Nixon struck it richer in 1977, when British talk-show host David Frost paid Nixon roughly $600,000 (or $2 million in today's dollars) for his first post-Watergate interview. NBC was among the losing bidders for the interviews, which 45 million people watched during five syndicated broadcasts. In both instances, buyers said they were buying "memoirs," not news. Critics demurred, noting that the sellers' comments were newsworthy regardless of the newsmaker's current job title.

Checkbook journalism drew its first admonition in journalism textbooks during the 1970s. The Society of Professional Journalists' code of ethics first mentioned it in its fifth revision in 1996, when, in the wake of multiple news organizations bidding for news in the O.J. Simpson trial, the SPJ advised members to be "wary of sources offering information for favors or money; avoid bidding for news." Still, the practice continues.

Arguments for Checkbook Journalism

John Cook said he once was like most American journalists, believing that buying information is "in the same moral category as paying for sex." The former *Brill's Content* reporter, writing in 2011 in *Columbia Journalism Review*, said he's changed his mind now that he works for the Gawker media group, a 2003 Web startup with nearly a dozen sites that have made money and lured millions of viewers after buying news content.

Money and audience views are about the economics, which is the least-common denominator in most arguments that see checkbook journalism as ethically appropriate or at least ethically neutral. Supporters of checkbook journalism offer both practical and ethical arguments.

Cook argued that legitimate news organizations that won't pay for information miss out on important stories, such as the British parliament scandal or the *National Enquirer's* 2007 scoop that former presidential candidate John Edwards lied about fathering a child out of wedlock.

Cook's sister websites have opened their checkbook in at least three notable occasions. Jezebel.com paid $10,000 for original photos from a 2007 *Redbook* cover that Cook said showed "just how radically and creepily women's magazines use Photoshop to digitally hack away at their subjects." Sister site Gizmo do.com paid $5,000 in 2010 for an iPhone 4 prototype, revealing its details months before the notoriously private Apple planned to debut it. (The site's former editor apologized to Apple co-founder Steve Jobs weeks before Jobs' death.) And the head of a third sister site, Deadspin.com chief Nick Denton, called it "a great investment" after buying indecent pictures and explicit voicemail messages that former Jets quarterback Brett Favre apparently sent to a woman who worked for the NFL team. "All of the above stories were true and important," Cook wrote. "None of them are less correct, or less pure, because filthy lucre was involved. And it's not certain that any of them would have come to light absent a monetary inducement. Ethical squeamishness aside, if paying for evidence of massive and systemic abuses of the public trust is wrong, then I don't want to be right."

New York University professor Robert S. Boynton says payments sometimes may be appropriate, since "we owe our sources everything." Deadspin's Denton was more succinct about the changes that the Internet has brought to journalism. Paying for information, he said at a December 2010 media conference, "gets the traditional media contorted. They're envious, but they're disapproving, and it's a

beautiful thing to watch."

The unstated question is what Denton meant by "traditional media." In reality, practitioners of checkbook journalism include many "traditional" media organizations, or at least newsgatherers owned by traditional media organizations. Although tabloid publications such as the *National Enquirer* are known for buying news, some of the nation's most prestigious news organizations (or subsidiaries of conglomerates with prestigious news organizations) have engaged in the practice. Take, for example, the 2008 example from the gossip news organization TMZ, which paid $165,000 to Thomas Riccio for audio of the confrontation between two memorabilia dealers and a group of men that included Simpson. Riccio, who apparently arranged the confrontation, also scored payments from ABC and the syndicated *Entertainment Tonight* tabloid show, which is distributed by CBS Television. The website thesmokinggun.com, a Time Warner subsidiary that reported on the deal, noted that TMZ was "apparently the only Time Warner entity that is allowed to pay for stories or tips." (Time Warner divested itself of TMZ when it spun off its AOL subsidiary into a separate company.)

Although major television networks are now trying to steer clear of the practice, they have long been in the business of paying for information to beat competitors. ABC News has presented multiple examples during the past few years. Three months before Casey Anthony was charged with killing her daughter in 2008, ABC paid her $200,000 for rights to video of 2-year-old Caylee. The payment became public in 2010, two years after the deal was struck, when a judge ordered that information be revealed in open court. Anthony was found not guilty in 2011. Less than month after the verdict, *Forbes* magazine questioned whether she was paid for photos of her posted on several tabloid websites. "She has to capitalize now," *Forbes* quoted an anonymous "insider" as saying. "In a couple of months, people won't give a sh*t."

Anthony was among several involved in her trial who received compensation from ABC. Her parents received three nights in a Ritz-Carlton hotel. The utility worker who found Caylee's body testified that ABC paid him $15,000 as a licensing fee for photos of a snake that may or may not have been near where the body was found. Roy Kronk told the court that, while ABC paid him only for the photo, "I knew there would probably be an interview involved."

ABC also paid a woman who was caught up in sex and politics. It paid $15,000 for photos sent to Megan Broussard, who was among several women receiving lewd photos by U.S. Rep. Anthony Weiner, D-N.Y. He originally denied sending such images, but in 2011 he quit Congress and confessed to lying. The network's Chris Cuomo said ABC had little choice but to open its wallet. "I wish money was not in the game, but you know ... someone else is going to pay for the same things," he said on CNN's *Reliable Sources*. "I wish it were not. You do, too.

But it is the state of play, and to say otherwise I think is false."

The Weiner and Anthony examples each had some degree of serious news value. But stories involving celebrities, which rarely have news values that would vault them to the front page or the top of an evening newscast, are more likely to include a checkbook than traditional news stories. This chapter could list hundreds of examples of celebrities who are paid for interviews or pictures. As this chapter was being written, it was reported that *People* magazine (a Time Warner publication) paid $1.5 million in 2011 for the wedding photos of the 72-day marriage of NBA player Kris Humphries and Kim Kardashian, who is famous for being famous. *People* paid another $300,000 for photos of their engagement party. At the Cannes Film Festival in 2012, a film company listed "participation fees" of up to $3,900 for journalists who wanted to interview movie stars. And if the celebrities aren't the ones paid, then someone "close" to them might be. Much of the fodder for gossip-focused publications comes from anonymous insiders — usually family, friends, workers or hangers-on — who will dish for dirt. Celebrities often require their employees to sign non-disclosure agreements to limit what is leaked (or sold) to tabloid papers, TV shows and websites — and enforce it, unless the celebrity seeks to stay in the public spotlight.

Another reason for paying is to save time and effort while scooping the competition. The *Daily Telegraph*, a British newspaper, in 2009 paid an undisclosed amount to someone (likely a government worker) for documents revealing how members of Parliament misspent hundreds of thousands of pounds on personal expenses. The stories led to resignations, investigations, criminal charges and changes to parliamentary procedures. Writing in the *Guardian* newspaper, journalist Heather Brooke expressed her disappointment that she spent five years battling government for access to the records, only to see the *Daily Telegraph* scoop her at the last minute by buying the data before its official release. "I asked myself — what is the point of doing all that work, going to court, setting a legal precedent, dealing in facts, when every part of the government conspires to reward the hacks who do none of these things?" she wrote.

Another reason news organizations pay for stories is to generate news that they otherwise would not be able to create on their own. In the past decade, NBC's *Dateline* paid a group to find trouble when it wrote checks to Perverted Justice, an advocacy group whose members pose as teenagers online to catch adults who solicit sexual conversations. The network paid the group for its help in at least 10 episodes of *To Catch a Predator*, which ran from 2004 to 2007. Some praised the show for bringing attention to the crime, and it drew solid ratings. But an ex-producer sued the network, claiming she was fired after telling her bosses that the show violated journalistic principles and NBC's own rules. Two courts agreed that Marsha Bartel lost her job as part of a round of job cuts

across the news division, not because she raised ethical objections about the arrangement. *Predator* host Chris Hansen said payments to Perverted Justice were ethical, calling them similar to contracts the network has with retired generals who offer commentary. NewsLab President Deborah Potter, writing in the 2009 book *Media Ethics*, dismissed his analogy as a stretch of logic: "The generals aren't setting up the wars for NBC to cover."

Not every deal is so controversial. Some organizations will pay for newsworthy information they were not in a position to collect on their own. For example, CNN paid a licensing fee in 2011 to a Florida man who used his cell phone to record a police shooting in Miami. CNN's broadcast and print versions of the story acknowledged payment but not the price for the video, which the man later turned over to prosecutors. This was a rare instance when news organizations mentioned payment as part of the news story; some ethicists say transparency plays a role in determining the morality of making payments.

Other reasons for buying access are about practicality. Worldwide, journalists tell of the need to bribe people to cross borders or to navigate bureaucracies in nations where corruption runs rampant. Journalists who work in those countries say they simply won't get the story if they don't pay.

Media conglomeration may be another reason in favor of the practice, or at least a reason for its proliferation. News organizations often are just one division of a story-telling organization, and some media companies make deals with newsmakers in both news and non-news settings. The synergy comes by deals that pay the newsmaker in exchange for getting the news story and offering other money-making possibilities with non-news divisions.

Viacom sought such synergy in 2003, when it sought exclusive rights to the stories of a pair of previously unknown people, Army Pvt. Jessica Lynch and rock climber Aron Ralston. The *New York Times* said Viacom offered "stardom" to Lynch, who was rescued while a prisoner of war in Iraq, through partnerships with subsidiaries CBS News, CBS Entertainment, MTV and publisher Simon & Schuster. She made deals with other organizations instead, including a book contract with Random House, a division of the Bertelsmann media corporation. In the case of Ralston, who cut off his arm to free himself after falling during a hike in Utah, Viacom's CBS News division offered a deal that would let it film Ralston's rehabilitation as part of its news coverage and to help him contact Viacom's entertainment divisions. Eventually, he appeared on CBS' *Late Show with David Letterman* and published his 2004 autobiography, *Between a Rock and a Hard Place*, with Viacom's Simon & Schuster. A News Corp. subsidiary, not Viacom's Paramount Pictures, financed *127 Hours*, the 2010 movie that was nominated for six Academy Awards. A Viacom official told the *New York Times* that the offers were ethical, because its letters to Lynch and Ralston plainly stated that CBS News is independent and that "there's no quid pro quo stated or implied."

Once a deal is made, the relationship changes between a news organization and its source. That may not be a bad thing, especially for journalists struggling with difficult stories. In instances including written contracts that spell out what is expected for the payment, the deal may require that sources provide the "full truth" as they know it. Liars wouldn't be paid. That would help journalists dig more deeply into stories and perhaps require a little less effort in comparing the information they bought against information from other sources.

Media ethicist A. David Gordon, writing in the 2011 edition of *Controversies in Media Ethics*, said that regardless of whether a deal is made, the battles "between news and infotainment outlets will ensure that at least one version of the material reaches the public." He noted that other news organizations eventually can use the information for their own reporting. Moreover, the exclusivity required in such deals gives the journalist more time to report the story — and to "sell it" with promotions.

The sellers have reasons for making deals that go beyond a fatter bank account. People who find themselves in the spotlight quickly learn that it's not "the media" calling for an interview — it's individual calls from each of the dozens of individual newspapers, wire services, magazines, local TV stations and international broadcast news organizations, TV networks, websites and other news organizations. Taking media calls quickly becomes bothersome, as does repeating the story. By making a deal with a single news organization, the source can be spared talking to all the others.

Moreover, since media are essentially making money by reporting the story, why should the source be the only one who doesn't cash in? This argument assumes that information is a commodity, an argument that can be disconcerting to some journalists but nonetheless rings increasingly true in today's society.

Ethicist Gordon offered both utility- and duty-based ethical arguments for paying some sources. A payment "provides benefits to most people in the society (i.e., information for the public, and both control and cash for the people selling the information,)" which might produce more good than harm. Moreover, paying sources is a tangible way to treat them "as ends in themselves rather than merely as means to be exploited toward the end of providing information or titillation for the public." Gordon draws a line, though, when it comes to public officials: They have no right to sell public information for their own gain.

The title of a 1994 *Columbia Journalism Review* article about the topic — "When Checkbook Journalism Does God's Work" — offers another justification for payments. Writer Louise Mengelkoch said payments can bring a better life to "the powerless in our culture," using the example of how *Hard Copy's* $3,000 payment for an exclusive interview helped a poor family that had made national news because of a rape trial. Such payments touch upon the ethical imperative of altruism, a notion that journalists in some circumstances should drop the façade of detachment and help people from whom they receive information. The late comedian Sam Kinison explained the hard-hearted nature of mass communication this way: "I'm very moved by world hunger. I see the same commercials, with those little kids, starving and very depressed. I watch those kids and I go ... 'I know the film crew could give this kid a sandwich.'"

Many journalists see more good than harm in providing food, clothing or shelter to story subjects who simply need help to live. While a journalist covering a famine or disaster cannot help everyone, being able to make an immediate, tangible difference in someone's life can boost the recipients' spirits and ease the guilt that journalists sometimes feel when covering such difficult stories. Many journalists would say that is acceptable, especially if the aid is not linked to the source's decision to provide information. Rachel Smolkin, writing in 2009's *Media Ethics*, said journalists should first do their jobs of bearing witness before following their conscience about whether to help.

Dart Center for Journalism and Trauma executive director Bruce Shapiro, whose organization focuses on the ethical reporting of violence and tragedy, said he knows of cases where reporters have helped by adopting refugees or providing other aid. "After the Haiti earthquake, some foreign reporters quietly volunteered at food stations on their off-hours," he said in an email interview for this chapter. "I don't think of this as checkbook journalism so much as an expression of social solidarity."

Arguments Against Checkbook Journalism

Most journalism textbooks, ethics codes and mainstream journalists oppose checkbook journalism. Their concerns fall into categories of ethics, the law and practical journalistic considerations.

The main ethical concern is that paying for information lessens access to and quality of the discourse that is fundamental in the marketplace of ideas. Democracy and self-determination thrive when individuals have access to useful information, and the fear is that some necessary information may not become public if knowledge-holders will not contribute without payment. "As a noble ideal, the relationship between community and media is bonded not by financial gain, but by the sharing of knowledge and experience," wrote the Poynter Institute's Kenneth Irby in response to a 9/11 survivor who wanted $911 for interviews on the first anniversary of the attack on the World Trade Center. Checkbook journalism, Irby wrote, cheapens the First Amendment's call for a free press.

A second concern is credibility. The public, already leery of news organizations and other institutions, may be less likely to believe the message and messenger in cases of checkbook journalism. John Michael Kittross, in the 2011 version of *Controversies in Media Ethics*, said it leads important news available only to the highest bidder, while free information comes from public relations practitioners, advertisers and others with ulterior motives. The result: "Bias will be more likely and we all will lose," Kittross wrote, because the balancing information was sold to a higher bidder. Gordon was less worried, saying that no direct correlation between checkbook journalism and credibility has been established and is beside the point anyway "in view of all the more likely problems that also might diminish the media's credibility."

The credibility of the seller also comes into question when deals are made. Plenty of people are willing to invent stories, or to sweeten a true story with fiction, in hopes of making money. Shelley Ross, a former *Good Morning America* producer, wrote on her blog that offering payments for interviews or licensing fees for images is "little more than an invitation to lie.... If your story, ahem, 'photo or video' is worth only a couple hundred dollars, what might you do or say to make it worth thousands more?"

Sheena Upton might know the answer. The California woman claimed in newspapers and on television (including a planned payment from ABC's *Good Morning America*) that she injected her 8-year-old daughter with Botox. She later said a British reporter paid her to invent the story, a claim the reporter denied while acknowledging she paid Upton $6,000. A 2011 Associated Press story noted that accounts from both Upton and the reporter "appear murky and are filled with dubious details."

Concerns about truth and payments run in multiple directions. In some cases, a source may feel external pressure or an internal obligation to give the journalist a "better" story, regardless of the facts. In other instances, the journalist may feel an added burden to develop a terrific story to justify payment, leading news organizations to not actively pursue information that may cast doubt on the story. Or they may overhype a story, through promotion or by giving the story more prominence than its news value would otherwise dictate, because the story came with an investment that must be recovered.

A related but more insidious concern is that news organizations might strike deals that intentionally hamstring their reporting efforts. The late Don Hewitt, who created CBS' *60 Minutes,* is quoted in 2003's edition of *Groping for Ethics in Journalism* as saying that newsmakers sometimes seek to "negotiate what will and will not be asked during an interview," or that news organizations will "promise that they will only ask soft questions" to land the interview. Or some publicists will make "bundling" deals with news organizations — you can have access to the celebrity you want only if you publicize lesser-known celebrities also in the publicist's stable. When this happens, journalists have traded their independence for exclusivity. Journalists on the outside, meanwhile, face another roadblock in their search for a harder truth. They will have to rely on second- or third-hand information, leading to biased or incomplete stories.

The Associated Press story about the "Botox mom" also hinted at another problem with checkbook journalism. The story said that a potential source approached for the story asked to be paid, a practice forbidden by AP rules. The problem is the slippery slope where more sources demand money before talking, which can slow the reporting process while the deal is struck and also force journalists to "shell out a constant stream of cash," as *Groping for Ethics in Journalism* author Ron F. Smith wrote in its 2003 edition. *Australian Journalism Review* authors Nicola Goc and Jason Bainbridge said the shift to information-as-commodity reached Australia's public eye in 2006, after a reporter asked Todd Russell on live TV for an exclusive interview about the fourteen days that Russell and another man were trapped in a Tasmanian mine. Russell's reply: "Tell me how big your chequebook is and we'll talk." Australian media giant Publishing and Broadcasting Limited paid $3 million to the men. It is telling that Russell first appeared not on a news broadcast but on the *Footy Show*, a sports show, an act that further blurs the line between news and entertainment.

Critics of checkbook journalism say that when a source asks "how big your chequebook is," that source becomes a commodity. Journalism becomes a business in which the information, the buyer and the seller become products to be bought or sold. One goal of journalism ethics training is to help newsgatherers develop empathy toward sources, and checkbook journalism leads news organizations to treat people as a means to an end, not as ends unto themselves. Goc and Bainbridge said the question is "what is actually being commodified — the 'suffering' (the story)" or the people who sell their stories. Sources who seek money become commodities to use and to be used. In a society where many members of the public believe journalists don't respect them, audiences may think that paying sources turns what should be an interpersonal bond into an impersonal business transaction. The journalist may still treat the source with respect, but the money taints the relationship.

Critics also argue that checkbook journalism can turn news organizations and individual journalists into items that can be bought and sold, too. If the quality of the news organization matters less than its willingness to write the largest check, journalists may feel less need to use their knowledge, skills and ethics to persuade a potential source to grant the interview. It can cheapen the journalist and hurt the quality of the story. As Kittross wrote, if journalists believe that information is a mere commodity, then "how long will it be before we, ourselves, also are on the block? What will be *our* price? Who will pimp for *us*?"

Another ethical concern is precisely whom to pay. As mentioned previously, Gordon noted that it is wrong to pay public officials for information, because they have access to information as a result of their jobs and because public information should be just that.

Critics also point out legal concerns. At what point does checkbook journalism become a bribe? Great Britain confronted that question after several Metropolitan Police officials were arrested on charges of taking money to provide information to *News of the World*, the News Corp. tabloid shut down in 2011 after it improperly tapped into voicemails of hundreds of people. A former director of public prosecutions said it was "blindingly obvious" that News Corp. officials made corrupt payments to police officers. While public officials have many legitimate justifications for deciding which news organizations deserve their assistance, personal gain is not one of them.

Critics are concerned that, while laws forbid criminals from making money off their crimes, journalists sometimes pay people who may have committed crimes. Sixteen months after Gizmodo paid for access to an iPhone prototype, a California prosecutor filed theft charges against two men who found and sold the device. Authorities executed a search warrant in the home of a Gizmodo editor, but no charges were filed. The *New York Times* noted a 2010 effort by the U.S. Justice Department to find and prosecute people who have sold celebrity health records and other documents to tabloid journalists. Some health workers have been prosecuted, but not news organizations. The question for journalists is one of ethics, not law, as they struggle with deciding whether to use information gleaned by real or apparent illegal means.

A lack of transparency is another concern of critics. News organizations, they argue, usually don't tell news consumers that a story included payment to sources. Critics say the public deserves complete information when evaluating the credibility of a news source. News organizations occasionally reveal that they paid for information, but most news about payments is revealed by competing news organizations. Jill Geisler said in a 2011 Poynter Institute post that news organizations that hide payments are wrong. In the "rare event" that a news organization buys information, she wrote, then it should reveal to the public "what you paid, for what items and why, including indirect costs such as travel, hotel and meals. If use of the material is exclusive, say that." Poynter's Al Tomkins said news groups that won't reveal the price for competitive reasons, or because they are worried it might lead the public to expect payment if they ever become news sources, are wrong because they are "paying too much." His bottom line: "Disclosure mitigates harm but doesn't erase it."

A final concern of critics is that checkbook journalism doesn't do what it's supposed to do. A key reason for buying news is to gain exclusivity that leads to larger audiences and advertising. A former ABC News president, however, said that economic justification often falls short. "If you could prove that by spending $20,000 you would make $70,000, OK, I can justify that," David Westin told the *New York Times* in 2011. "But I'll be doggone if you could go through any of those payments, trace them through and see if it made any sense." The direct payoff may further be limited by competitors who work other sources to find similar information and will quickly repurpose exclusive content as soon as they can. Exclusives have a short shelf life. Also, the money spent on sources is money not spent to support the thin budgets for newsgathering and staff. The $75,000 spent on a single piece of video is $75,000 not spent to pay a year's salary for a journalist who would report many more stories.

Assessment

Few mainstream journalists are comfortable entering the marketplace of ideas with a checkbook in hand — even when they do. It is telling that ABC News recently decided to stop paying news subjects for exclusive interviews. The *Daily Beast's* Howard Kurtz noted in 2011 that the network did not vow an absolute ban and made its decision with "no public announcement or fanfare." ABC spokesman Jeffrey Schneider said licensing deals had "become a crutch, and an unnecessary one." Critics noted that ABC's decision came only after outsiders reported that it paid $200,000 to Casey Anthony and $10,000 in the apparent "Botox mom" hoax, which tarnished the network's credibility and reputation.

An outright ban on paying news sources is both contrary to the First Amendment freedoms and not likely in today's fierce competition for hot stories. The best that journalists can do is to clarify when checkbook journalism might be appropriate, which would require drawing distinctions between news and entertainment; pursue a de-escalation in the practice by media organizations that report "hard" news; and be transparent when it occurs.

Clarifying when checkbook journalism might be appropriate is the first step, which would aid news organizations, journalists and the public. Some conglomerates have malleable ethics, in which "hard" news property cannot use a checkbook but a sister property focused on entertainment news can. Except for the number of zeroes on a check, or the relative "hotness" of the news, is there an ethical difference between paying $50 and $50,000? Duty-based ethicists would say no, but most conglomerates take a more teleological approach to their business and draw distinctions among properties.

Conglomerates with both hard news and entertainment news properties may well work against themselves and the public by reinforcing the notion that some newsmakers can become dealmakers and others cannot. This distinction is difficult in a world where the *National Enquirer* breaks news of political scandals, serious newspapers publish celebrity news, and *Time* and *People* are part of the same corporation. The result is a public that is unclear where the boundaries lie, and a single brush that tars the entire operation.

Even individual journalists are confused. The *New York Times* noted that while NBC occasionally pays for news, the network once "rebuked" a staffer who bought clothes for a kidnapping victim who was interviewed on *Today* in 2002. Other journalists are confused by conflicts between ethics codes and their consciences, especially in instances where helping a source seems morally right regardless of what a corporate policy says.

The second step would be a unilateral decision by competitors to holster their checkbooks. Economics is at work here: If there are no buyers, then people with information cannot sell. The Poynter Institute says news organizations should pay licensing fees "only to information providers who are not involved in the story documented by their material," such as free-lancers or other third-party witnesses. The unintended consequence is that sources might go to lesser news organizations that are willing to buy, driving more consumers to tabloid-style papers, TV shows and websites. It would mean journalists in higher-quality news organizations, which would be more likely to check information and provide context, would chase more stories instead of break them.

A final step would be revealing details in the rare instances when payments occur, so that consumers can use that information in gauging credibility. The public deserves to know when news organizations made deals that could give the public less access to information — including having less information available from other news organizations because of exclusivity deals. Also, news organizations can work harder to keep each other honest, by reporting when competitors make deals. The SPJ Code of Ethics says journalists should "[e]xpose unethical practices of journalists and the news media," and the SPJ counts checkbook journalism among those unethical practices.

Can the practice of checkbook journalism be ended? Probably not, given the fuzzy lines between news and entertainment, the widening ethical standards among news organizations fighting for the same story and the First Amendment freedoms that give individual journalists the right and responsibility to be independent in pursuing news. The only solution may be for individual journalists to police themselves and to call out competitors who don't play fair.

Points of View

Articles and Book Chapters

Boynton, Robert S. "Checkbook Journalism Revisited." *Columbia Journalism Review* (January/February 2006): 12-14. While reporters should not "go around handling out twenty-dollar bills to everyone they interview," there are times when journalists ought to be willing to pay for information.

Cook, John. "Pay Up: Sources Have Their Agendas. Why Can't Money be One?" *Columbia Journalism Review* (May/June 2011): 55. News organizations that refuse to pay for information are not necessarily morally superior to those that do.

France, David. "Saving Justin Berry." *New York* (October 28, 2007). http://nymag.com/guides/money/2007/39957. *New York Times* reporter Kurt Eichenwald, who sought to rescue a teenager from the Internet sex business and later wrote about it, gave money to the teen before deciding to turn it into a news story. The reaction to the story, and the pushback, made for difficult times for the reporter.

Goc, Nicola, and Bainbridge, Jason. "The Beaconsfield Mine Disaster and the Evolution of Chequebook Journalism." *Australian Journalism Review* 30:1 (2008): 99-112. The authors use the example of two men who survived two weeks trapped in a Tasmanian mine to show what happens when a battle over checkbook journalism plays out in the open. The result, they say, shows the shift toward news (and people) as commodities and the shift from news to entertainment.

Gordon, A. David, John Michael Kittross, John C. Merrill, William Babcock, and Michael Dorsher. *Controversies in Media Ethics*, 3rd ed. New York: Routledge, 2011. In point-counterpoint style on pages 493-496, Kittross offers reasons why treating news as a commodity will destroy journalism's public benefit, and Gordon reminds readers that news already is a commodity and "journalism is surviving quite well, thank you."

Mengelkoch, Louise. "When Checkbook Journalism Does God's Work." *Columbia Journalism Review* 33:4 (1994): 35-38. A small payment from *Hard Copy* helped a Minnesota family besieged by media organizations after a horrible crime.

Moos, Julie. "5 Reasons Broadcasters Pay Licensing Fees for Stories and Why it Corrupts Journalism." The Poynter Institute (June 9, 2011). www.poynter.org/ latest-news/top-stories/135226. Experts from the Florida-based journalism think tank describe the problems with "licensing fees" that are really examples of checkbook journalism, and they provide broadcasters with ethical and practical reasons for exiting the morass.

Rutenberg, Jim. "The Gossip Machine, Churning Out Cash." *New York Times*, May 21, 2011, A1. The tabloid print, broadcast and Web industry acquires news with cash, including payments to sources later charged with stealing private information.

Society of Professional Journalists. *Journalism Ethics: A Casebook of Professional Conduct for News Media.* Portland, Ore.: Marion Street Press, 2011. The national organization's explication of its journalistic ethical standards includes a checkbook journalism case study under its "conflicts of interest" section.

Stein, Robert. "The Excesses of Checkbook Journalism." *Columbia Journalism Review* (September 1, 1972), 42-48. The editor of *McCall's* magazine looks at how news organizations and book publishers began paying criminals and other villains for the rights to interviews and memoirs. He reminds readers that "exclusive" does not mean "worthwhile," a distinction still missing nearly four decades later.

Stelter, Brian, and Bill Carter. "For Instant Ratings, Interviews With a Checkbook." *New York Times* (June 12, 2011), B1. Checkbook journalism wound its way into major broadcast networks in the days before ABC said it would stop the practice.

Thornton, Brian. "The Murder of Emmett Till." *Journalism History* 36:2 (2010): 96-104. While investigating the Mississippi murder, William Bradford Huie paid the killers for their stories.

Van Hoffman, Nicholas. "Public Opinion Polls: Newspapers Making Their Own News?" *The Public Opinion Quarterly* 44:4 (1980): 572-73. Paying for public opinion polling is an exercise in checkbook journalism.

22 Narrative in News Writing

A front-page article in the *Los Angeles Times* in 2010 began this way: "The searchers carved skid row into quadrants and advanced in small groups, aiming flashlights into the cold."

Consider all the things we do not know after having read this sentence: We know neither who or where the searchers are, nor who or what they are searching for. And we certainly don't know why they are doing whatever they're doing. In other words, we know none of the five W's.

In paragraph 5, we learn a little about who and where: The searchers are unnamed volunteers and Los Angeles County workers. In paragraph 6, we meet our first named character. In paragraph 8, we learn for whom the searchers are searching — "the 50 people likeliest to die on skid row's streets" — and why they're looking for them: so they can house them.

The story, by reporter Christopher Goffard, was more than 2,500 words long. It was the first installment of a four-part series that appeared in the paper every other day for a week. The series was about 11,000 words.

"Project 50: Four Walls and a Bed" represents a departure from standard newspaper writing practice. Instead of summarizing the important developments in the first paragraph and then filling in some of the background, detail and explanation in subsequent paragraphs, as most news stories do, Goffard's story opens like a play: The lights come up on a scene already in progress. As the action unfolds, the audience begins to understand who and where these people are and what the situation is. Seven main characters enter: the director of the housing program and six skid-row denizens. We get to know them. By the end of the story, we have developed a rooting interest: We want this housing experiment to work. And it does, but not for everyone. One client has landed in prison. One is about to return to the streets. The others have begun the one-step-forward, two-steps-back climb out of the abyss. Goffard tracked the Project 50 participants for two years.

by Russell Frank
Pennsylvania State University

Stories like Goffard's usually are referred to as narrative journalism. The term can be confusing. Most of a newspaper's textual content is narrative in the sense that information is presented in story form, as opposed to lists or charts. The distinction between conventional news writing and narrative news writing is a matter of emphasis: Writers of conventional news stories focus on providing important information; writers of narrative stories focus on telling good stories. Or as journalism professor Thomas Berner argued in a 1986 paper presented to journalism educators: "Story journalism entertains and interprets while information journalism provides data."

Proponents of narrative journalism argue that good storytelling is exactly what newspapers need to compete with the other news media. Quick snippets of information are available everywhere — on television, on radio, on cell phones, on computers. Newspapers are for *readers.* Maybe readers are turning to other media not because they don't have time but because they're bored. And maybe what is boring them is not the news itself, but the way the news is told. "Not that many newspaper articles," wrote Steve Weinberg in a 1998 *Columbia Journalism Review* article, "are really stories." Give readers flesh-and-blood characters confronting the great and terrible possibilities of life rather than dry statistics and disembodied voices, and they'll keep reading, even if the stories are long.

Defenders of the traditional style of news writing say the just-the-facts approach is more important than ever. In a hectic age, people want their news the way they want their workday breakfast — in quick gulps, hold the frills. Even if they had the leisure to settle in with a long story, in an age of shrinking newsroom budgets, editors feel like the time-consuming, in-depth reporting that goes into a narrative piece is a luxury they can no longer afford. They also worry that when telling a compelling tale takes precedence over providing information, reporters will be tempted to embellish the facts with touches of fiction.

Origins of the Issue

Narrative journalism is nothing new. John Hartsock, in his book *A History of American Literary Journalism* (2000), wrote that it is "part of an ancient enterprise as venerable as poetry and drama." In other words, all tellers of true stories might be considered narrative journalists. The newcomer, rather, is the practitioner of objective, inverted-pyramid journalism. After all, it seems only natural that in every age, the teller of any story, whether true or imagined, will want to be as artful as possible. The anomaly was the introduction of a style of storytelling that was deliberately "artless." Such an approach could have arisen only at a time when art and science were thought to be antithetical — when people began to conceive of a science of journalism that should be capable of describing the social and political world much as biology describes the physical world. A scientific journalism, so the thinking went, entailed an unadorned rhetoric. Anything beyond the basic facts would introduce the taint of the writer's interpretation or perspective. "A man who doesn't make his language ornate cannot be deceiving us," literary critic Hugh Kenner wrote in an essay in Norman Sims' *Literary Journalism in the 20th Century* (1990) on the triumph of "the plain style."

In addition to becoming "plainer," newspaper writing became more formulaic, for two practical reasons. In the days before news pages were designed on computers, reporters and editors did not know exactly how much space a story would take up on the page or whether there was going to be room for all of it. If a story, laid out in a column of newsprint, was twelve inches long but the person composing the page of metal type had room for only ten inches, he was going to slice off the bottom two inches. The way to avoid lopping off any crucial information was for the reporter to arrange facts in the order of their importance, from top to bottom. Thus the inverted pyramid was born.

A second reason for the inverted pyramid is that it accommodates readers who may not have time to read the paper from cover to cover. It allows busy readers to be at least minimally informed of the news of the day just by scanning the headlines and first few paragraphs of each story.

Meanwhile, the older style of journalism, which took the form of the "sketch," or short human-interest story, in the 19th and early 20th centuries — when Mark Twain, Charles Dickens and Stephen Crane all wrote sketches — appeared less and less frequently in daily papers, finding a home instead in magazines and what would come to be known as alternative newspapers. It wasn't until the 1960s that a growing number of writers began to feel that conventional journalism, preoccupied as ever by the doings of powerful people and institutions, was not up to the task of documenting the social upheavals of the era.

Hunter S. Thompson, Tom Wolfe, Joan Didion, Norman Mailer, Truman Capote, Gay Talese and others began writing about the colliding worlds of sex, drugs, rock 'n' roll, celebrity and politics as if they were cultural anthropologists. But instead of writing in the detached, fly-on-the-wall style that had long held sway at the *New Yorker* magazine, the New Journalists, as Tom Wolfe called them, included what it felt like to them, as observers, to be strangers in a strange land. Or they wrote in a fragmented style that attempted to reflect the chaos they were trying to describe. Or they howled and hooted in a way that let you know exactly what they thought about the people and scenes they were observing.

This kind of writing may be entertaining, the traditionalists said, but it is not journalism. The perceived excesses of the new journalism continue to cast a shadow over the newspaper world today. Editors know readers like good storytelling. They worry about good storytelling taking precedence over truth-telling.

Newspapers' Last, Best Hope

Practitioners of narrative journalism and the editors they work with believe that narrative stories are more than valuable additions to the mix of newspaper content. They may be crucial to the industry's survival. Their criticisms of conventional hard news stories center on both the subject matter of those stories and the style in which they are written. The problem with the subject matter of so many news stories, they contend, is that their focus on powerful people and institutions can feel remote from readers' everyday lives. The stylistic problem with these stories is that their structure and tone can come across as a dry, impersonal recitation of facts rather than as a dramatic tale told by a fellow human being. Narrative stories, proponents argue, can forge a more personal connection between readers and newspapers, keeping print journalism relevant in an age of electronic alternatives.

In his 1997 book *Intimate Journalism*, Walt Harrington, a former *Washington Post* reporter and a leading exponent of narrative journalism, contended that the story of our time is not just what the president did yesterday, or what happened on Wall Street, or the latest fire, flood, tornado, hurricane, earthquake, murder or war. It is the stuff of daily life: how we work, play, eat, dress, celebrate and grieve. Yet these aspects of life were usually given short shrift in the newspaper. To a great extent, the news, like history, was a man's world of male politicians, male generals and male captains of industry. Stories about these movers and shakers were "hard" news. "Soft" news was consigned to the features section, which was once mainly the women's pages. In an industry that prized scoops above all things, the star reporters covered the scoop-generating hard news beats as a matter of course. As important as these stories are, they often seem to be about people and events that are peripheral to our concerns. Taxes and governments rise and fall, but barring catastrophic reversals of fortune that hit us where we live, we are mostly preoccupied with the people, places, things and doings that comprise the daily and yearly round. And because many of us are at least occasionally restless or curious, we can also become interested in other people, places, things and doings, especially if we put ourselves in the hands of a good guide. The restless and curious reporters at newspapers began to petition their editors to let them try to be that sort of guide.

These reporters, who practice what Harrington refers to as "the journalism of everyday life," are often said to seek the extraordinary in the ordinary. But when storytellers bring readers news of people whose lives are nothing like their own — such as when they're profiling celebrities — they may also be said to be finding the ordinary in the extraordinary, as journalism professor Robert Boynton put it in his 2005 book, *The New New Journalism*. Reporters who introduce readers to communities they know little or nothing about could also be said to be finding the ordinary in the extraordinary. Proponents of narrative writing say that such stories show readers that people who appear to be quite different from them are not that different after all. Both kinds of stories, they say, benefit readers. Stories that find the extraordinary in the ordinary can freshen readers' appreciation of the taken-for-granted routines and rituals that fill their days. Stories that find the ordinary in the extraordinary can foster intercultural understanding and expand readers' sense of life's possibilities. The importance of both kinds of awareness begins to answer the question of why these kinds of stories began to find a place alongside the hard news stories about government, politics, crime, catastrophe, business and so on.

Nevertheless, it's worth noting how long it took for editors and writers who favored narrative journalism to overcome bias against this style and gain status and prestige commensurate with that accorded to hard news reporting. The first Pulitzer Prize in feature writing was not awarded until 1979 — more than sixty years after the awarding of the first prize for reporting. That first winning feature, significantly, was a work of narrative journalism by *Baltimore Sun* reporter Jon Franklin. "Mrs. Kelley's Monster" begins: "In the cold hours of a winter morning Dr. Thomas Barbee Ducker, chief brain surgeon at the University of Maryland Hospital, rises before dawn. His wife serves him waffles but no coffee. Coffee makes his hands shake." The story chronicles Ducker's attempt to remove a tumor — the monster — from the brain of a 57-year-old woman named Edna Kelly. He does not succeed. Mrs. Kelly dies.

What, then, is the difference between Franklin's masterful narrative and standard newspaper features, derided by Tom Wolfe as "long and hideously sentimental accounts of hitherto unknown souls beset by tragedy or unusual hobbies"? The best answer might be the depth of the reporting. Like the narrative story, a feature may begin the way "Mrs. Kelly's Monster" and Christopher Goffard's story about homelessness do, with a scene rather than a summary. It may include snippets of conversation between or among characters in addition to sources' answers to the reporter's questions. It may also include detailed descriptions of people and places. But the characters in a feature story often serve a different function from the characters in a work of narrative journalism. The feature writer may be less intent on readers getting to know this or that individual than on using those individuals as examples of a group.

If "Mrs. Kelly's Monster" were a conventional feature story, we would probably meet Ducker and Kelly, learn in a "nut graf" that Ducker is one of many neurosurgeons attempting to save the Mrs. Kellys of the world from their agony, or that Kelly is one of many brain tumor sufferers who are seeking relief through neurosurgery. Then we would be introduced to some of those other doctors or patients. In other words, the story would turn out not to be about Ducker or Kelly at all. It would just use the tried-and-true technique of using the particular to get at the general. Franklin stays with Ducker and Kelly the whole way. To use a cinematic analogy, instead of zooming in on participants in newsworthy events, then zooming out to a wide shot of the "big picture," writers of narrative stories maintain a tight focus on the actors in a drama. If Franklin does his job well, by the end of the story readers will grieve for Kelly and share Ducker's frustration that he could not save her.

In narrative journalism, wrote Roy Peter Clark of the Poynter Institute in a 2001 article in *Nieman Reports, what* becomes plot, *who* becomes character, *where* becomes setting, *when* becomes chronology and *why* becomes motive. Proponents believe each of these storytelling elements can contribute to a revival of interest in newspapers.

Plot: The conventional news story may be about a dramatic event, but it is rarely written in a dramatic style. As we have seen, the idea is to spring the biggest news on the reader at the very beginning, not lead up to it slowly to build suspense. Reading the lead of a news story is like watching a play backwards: First we have the climax, and then we find out what led up to it. A contributing factor in the development of a more narrative style may have been the recognition that the conventional approach is an efficient way of delivering information, but as journalism scholars S. Elizabeth Bird and Robert Dardenne point out, it doesn't make for a satisfying reading experience. In one notable narrative experiment, Tom French, a reporter at the *St. Petersburg Times*, wrote a story about a murder trial in which he withheld the verdict until the 112th paragraph. Readers got to experience the conclusion of the trial the way people in the courtroom did — as a chronological sequence whose outcome could not be foretold.

Character: One of the criticisms proponents of narrative journalism level at traditional news stories is that they are populated by "talking heads" — disembodied voices that are not situated in time or space. The reader is rarely told what these characters are wearing or doing. Indeed, they lack personalities altogether.

"People want to read about people," writes Mike D'Orso. "More than anything else, we are fascinated — appalled, amused, delighted, dismayed, inspired, entranced — by the men and women who stand up and breathe on the pages of a well-crafted story." As discussed earlier, the focus on character is what distinguishes narrative journalism not just from the conventional hard news story, but from the conventional feature. We get to know characters in two ways: from what they do and from what they say. Most of the quotes in a news story are either responses to a reporter's question or excerpts from public remarks such as a speech or a news conference. Writers of narrative stories do interviews, of course, but they also like to listen in on conversations between or among the people they're writing about. Ted Conover, who has gotten his stories by laboring in the fields with Mexican farm workers, riding the rails with hobos and working as a prison guard, instructs those who would try their hand at literary journalism to "participate and immerse, rather than simply interview and observe."

Such dialogue gives narrative journalism a more naturalistic feel than most conventional news stories have. Even when an interview is more like a relaxed conversation than a prosecutorial grilling, it is still a highly unnatural situation: Few of us reveal much about our backgrounds, beliefs or inner lives to strangers. The kind of reporting that narrative journalists do is often referred to as fly-on-the-wall journalism because sometimes, instead of interacting with their sources, the narrative journalists are watching and listening as their sources interact with each other. On the page it appears as if the speakers are oblivious to the presence of the reporter — and to the future inspection of their words and deeds by the readers — just as the characters the actors play in a stage play usually appear to be oblivious to the presence of the audience. The audience gets an inside look at events and meets people as if they were in the same room. Thus the narrative style adds word-by-word excitement and immediacy to the news.

Setting: Another weakness of traditional news accounts, according to advocates of narrative journalism, is that they fail to engage the senses. Readers want to know how it felt to be in a particular place at a particular time. Michael Gartner, a former reporter, editor, publisher and network news president, likes to tell a story about his first journalism job at a small newspaper in rural North Carolina. His editor was blind. "Make me see what you saw," he told Gartner when he sent him out on assignments. That is exactly what narrative journalists try to do for their readers. The writer is the eyes — and ears and even the nose — of the reader, reporting back on how places looked, sounded and smelled. "I have to know what your sweat smells like," reporter Joe McGinniss told a source to convey what allowing him into his life was going to entail. Janet Malcolm recounted this story in her 1990 book *The Journalist and the Murderer*.

When narrative writers drive somewhere with one of their characters, they don't just say he got in his car. They tell us the make, model, color and condition of the car. If the source goes out for a meal at midday, they don't say she ate lunch. They say she had the tuna melt on a toasted English muffin with a glass of iced tea, no sugar. Is what the character ate for lunch important? Only to the extent that the details make the scene more vivid, easier to imagine. The best narrative writers are always on the lookout for what we might call the revealing detail — the bit of description of clothing or home décor or mannerism that adds to our understanding of who this person is.

In 1997, Ken Fuson, a *Baltimore Sun* reporter, tracked a high school production of *West Side Story* from auditions to casting through rehearsal to opening night. The story starts this way:

> Spellbound she sits, her mother on one side, her boyfriend on the other, as another young woman performs the role that will someday be hers.
>
> Since she was little, Angie Guido has dreamed of standing on stage, playing the Puerto Rican girl who falls in love with the Polish boy named Tony.
>
> Maria.
>
> She will be Maria in West Side Story.

Demand for Fuson's six-part series was so great that the *Sun* reprinted 20,000 copies — and sold them all. The lesson: People who like to read will stay with a long story if a good writer gets them to care enough about the characters to want to know what happens to them. The writer Paul Many says this kind of writing is print journalism's "last, best hope." Before the Internet, the argument for narrative journalism went like this: Television and radio have seriously undermined the primacy of newspapers when it comes to reporting breaking news. And no matter how big and flashy and colorful newspaper graphics become, they will never move, the way video images do. So what is the one thing newspapers can do better than their competitors? Tell stories. Journalistic narrative storytelling works for reporters, editors, publishers — and readers. It can differentiate exemplary news organizations from their competitors.

Practical and Ethical Misgivings

Those who resist the call for more narrative writing in newspapers raise concerns on two fronts: the practical and the ethical. Practical concerns have to do with the amount of time it takes to report an in-depth story and the amount of space such stories consume in newspapers looking to reduce their number of pages in response to declining advertising revenues. Ethical concerns center on worries about fabrication, invasion of privacy and the conflicts of interest that can arise when reporters get too involved in the lives of their sources.

In-depth reporting that underpins a work of narrative journalism cannot be done over the telephone or via e-mail. It requires immersion in the lives of the people one is writing about, or what Gay Talese in his 2003 book simply calls "the art of hanging around." Capturing all the sensory detail is the least of it. A writer who hopes to get at the inner life of her subjects — their hopes and fears as they grapple with the challenges of life — needs to earn their trust. That takes time. A source might not even begin to feel comfortable with a reporter hanging around the place or feel convinced that she is genuinely interested until the reporter comes back again and again. "They're guarded the first time and second time and the first 10 times," says Mark Kramer, former director of the Nieman Foundation Program on Narrative Journalism at Harvard University. "Then you get boring. They forget you're there," he told Norman Sims in the 1984 book *The Literary Journalists*. Clearly, this is not the kind of journalism where the reporter gets the assignment in the morning, spends an hour or two with the people she is writing about, dashes back to the newsroom and cranks out a story for the next day's paper. Fuson, for example, followed the high school musical for four months.

Nor is this the kind of storytelling that can be done in a few hundred words. As editor Maria Carillo of the *Virginian-Pilot* acknowledges, in an age of newsroom budget cuts, not many editors feel they can spare a reporter for the week or month or even several months that might be needed to get to know the sources well enough to presume to write about them. In an age when we are all said to lead such busy lives and have such short attention spans, not many editors feel like it makes sense to devote the space to narrative journalism.

Narrative journalism also gives rise to ethical concerns. The goal of narrative journalists is to tell a story with enough details to bring plot, character and setting to life in the imagination of readers. They obtain the information they need in two ways: by immersing themselves in the lives of their characters and by conducting extensive interviews with their subjects to reconstruct scenes where they could not be present. Both approaches — immersion and reconstruction — have ethical pitfalls.

Immersion. Reporters have a hard time remaining detached when they spend a lot of time with a source and want to encourage the source to reveal aspects of his or her private life. But what are the limits of that friendship? The journalist's job is not to glorify the people he writes about, but to portray them in all their complexity, "warts and all," as the saying goes. As Janet Malcolm made abundantly clear in *The Journalist and the Murderer*, an honest portrait could be a hurtful portrait. The source could feel shamed and, therefore, betrayed.

Problems can also arise when a crisis occurs in the source's life. A friend would step in and lend a hand. A reporter may want to help but feels constrained: The reporter's responsibility, wrote Isabel Wilkerson in a chapter in *Telling True Stories*, is to report what happens in people's lives, not to influence what happens. For a story for the *Washington Post* about how welfare reform would affect people barely getting by, even with government money, Anne Hull spent time with a family in Kentucky. At one point, the couple didn't have enough gas money to take their feverish baby to a doctor. Hull's car was parked outside, as the family well knew. "I wanted to throw the notebook down, stop being the reporter, and take care of the baby," she wrote in her chapter in *Telling True Sto-*

ries. But she resisted. "If I, an accidental visitor, solved their problem, then it would no longer be a true story." Fortunately for all concerned, Hull had to compromise neither her story nor the health of the child: The father pawned his shotgun for the gas. Had the baby's life been in danger, Hull said she would have intervened.

Sonia Nazario had a similar rule when she was reporting two searing stories for the *Los Angeles Times.* One was about the perilous journey children take from Central America to find their parents in the United States. The other was about children of addicted parents. The ground rules for both projects were that she would intervene "only if I felt that a child was in imminent danger," she explained in a 2006 article for *Nieman Reports,* recounting her ethical dilemmas about the reporting. She would — and did — watch them suffer.

Not intervening when suffering is occurring is hard to defend. Saying that reporters should not change the course of events, as Nazario and Hull do, probably does not satisfy most readers. The heck with the story, readers are apt to say. Help the child. In their defense, Hull and Nazario write that the story's purpose is to make the public aware of a problem. The hope is that awareness leads to calls for action and, then, action. But proponents of narrative writing claim that "systemic problems" don't hit the reader right between the eyes. Tales of suffering do. However, as Martin J. Smith pointed out in a 1993 *Quill* article, alleviating the suffering of one person might be good in the short term for that individual, but not so good in the long term for building awareness of the systemic problem.

Reconstruction. Reporters who immerse themselves in their sources' lives rely on their own powers of observation, made keen by years of practice. Reporters who want to reconstruct events that happened when they were not present must rely on the incomplete observations and faulty memories of their sources. Crime narratives in particular, a hugely popular sub-genre of narrative journalism since the publication of Truman Capote's *In Cold Blood* in 1965, invariably reconstruct a crime scene because, as Mark Kramer pointed out, "murderers usually try not to do their work in front of writers." But when reporters tell readers exactly what people were wearing and doing and saying on some occasion that happened weeks, months or even years ago, they may arouse suspicions: How do they know all this? Might they fill in the gaps in their sources' memories with what they suppose must have happened? This opening scene from a 1997 story written by Associated Press reporter Julia Prodis, illustrates the problem:

The trooper's blue lights flashed in the rearview mirror. Peck floored it, Josh grabbed the revolver and Jenny, curled up beside him in the back seat, looked frantically out the back window.

They were far from home on this desolate Arkansas highway. It was the middle of the night and the time had come for the best friends to fulfill their pact: If caught by police, the boys, just 15, and Jenny, 12, would commit suicide.

They had it all planned—or so they thought—days ago. Josh would shoot Jenny first. (She didn't have the guts to do it herself and, if she was going to die, she wanted Josh to do it.) He would shoot Peck next, then kill himself.

They were rocketing faster than 100 mph in their stolen Grand Prix and the trooper was closing in. Just ahead, Peck saw a big rig blocking the only open lane in a construction zone.

They were trapped. It was time.

Peck slowed to a stop 20 feet behind the truck.

Josh cocked the gun, turned to Jenny and looked deep into her green eyes.

"I love you," he said and kissed her.

"Close your eyes."

Obviously, Prodis was not in the stolen car with Peck, Josh and Jenny as they were about to carry out their suicide pact. Yet she knows what Jenny was thinking, what Josh said and that Josh "looked deep into her green eyes." Had the three teens carried out their suicide pact, Prodis wouldn't have known exactly what was said and done in that car. As it turned out, though, the boys killed themselves, but before 12-year-old Jenny could follow suit, the state troopers intervened. The story of what happened in the car came from Jenny's taped interview with a police investigator.

Prodis said she was amazed at Jenny's recall of the details. It does seem to be the case that extraordinary events can burn themselves into people's memories to an extraordinary degree. But the reporter plays a crucial role as well. For example, when former U.S. Sen. George McGovern agreed to talk to *Washington Post* reporter Laura Blumenfeld about the death of his daughter due to alcoholism for a 1995 article, Blumenfeld asked him what he was doing before he got the news and to show her exactly where he was when the police came to the door. All told, Blumenfeld spent six hours interviewing McGovern. Together, she and McGovern walked through the scene "gesture by gesture," she said.

If Blumenfeld's style of reporting is typical, it suggests that narrative journalists may be victims of their own thoroughness as information gatherers and their descriptive powers as writers. "'This can't be right,'" Tom Wolfe wrote in a parody aimed at his detractors and included in his book *The New Journalism.* "'These people must be piping it, winging it, making up the dialogue.... Christ, maybe they're making up whole scenes, the unscrupulous geeks....'" He contends that the New Journalists were merging the reporting techniques of investigative journalism with the writing techniques of novelists. The idea was, first, to immerse oneself so deeply in one's subject that one acquired the authority to describe even the minutest details, and, second, to structure the writing as a series of scenes, complete with dialogue, action and description of the setting. Such writing reads like fiction, Wolfe said, but is grounded in fact.

Or is it? Two excerpts, both originally published in 1970, will convey the flavor of some of the New Journalism. The first is from Wolfe's "Radical Chic," which is about the embrace of the Black Panthers by New York writers and artists:

At 2 or 3 or 4 a.m., somewhere along in there, on Aug. 25, 1966, his 48th birthday, in fact, Leonard Bernstein woke up in the dark in a state of wild alarm. That had happened before. It was one of the forms his insomnia took. So he did the usual. He got up and walked around a bit. He felt groggy. Suddenly he had a vision, an inspiration. He could see himself, Leonard Bernstein, the egregio maestro, walking out on stage in white tie and tails in front of a full orchestra.

This next excerpt is from Hunter S. Thompson's "The Kentucky Derby is Decadent and Depraved":

Moments after the race was over, the crowd surged wildly for the exits, rushing for cabs and buses. The next day's Courier told of violence in the parking lot; people were punched and trampled, pockets were picked, children lost, bottles hurled. But we missed all this, having retired to the press box for a bit of post-race drinking. By this time we were both half-crazy from too much whiskey, sun fatigue, culture shock, lack of sleep and general dissolution.

Critics complained that Wolfe not only takes us inside Bernstein's bedroom; he takes us inside Bernstein's head. Thompson's piece is less about the Kentucky Derby than it is about Thompson's drunken experience (or non-experience) of the Kentucky Derby. Both techniques — writing about what is going on in someone else's head and writing about what is going on in one's own head — were significant departures from conventional journalism. And they made many conventional journalists and critics, notably novelist and journalist John Hersey and novelist Herbert Gold, uncomfortable. Since the thoughts in other people's heads are unknowable unless they reveal them to us, Wolfe's piece veers dangerously close to fiction. Because the thoughts in one's own head were not considered the proper object of journalistic investigation, Thompson's piece veers too close to memoir or personal essay.

After reading works by Wolfe and other New Journalists, John Hersey, best known for his book *Hiroshima* about the experiences of six survivors of the first of the atomic bombs dropped on Japan in 1945, declared that "the time has come to redraw the line between journalism and fiction." John McPhee, one of the most prolific and influential narrative journalists, took to task those New Journalists and their followers who combined the experiences of multiple sources into one made-up character. "Where I came from," he said, "a composite character was a fiction."

Lingering doubts about the creep of fiction into the nonfiction of the New Journalists have contributed to the reluctance of today's editors to give free rein to reporters who want to try their hand at narrative writing. Though major fabrication scandals at the *New York Times, Washington Post* and *Boston Globe* in the late 1990s and early 2000s did not involve narrative writing, they heightened public skepticism about *all* journalism, as David Craig noted in *The Ethics of the Story*, which probably added to editors' skittishness about a style of news writing that has been the most prone to playing fast and loose with the truth. As Anthony DeCurtis of *Rolling Stone* noted, the more awards narrative journalists win and the more copies that book-length works of nonfiction sell, the more tempting it becomes for reporters "to give that scene the manufactured oomph that lifts it from the dreary realm of mere reporting into the shimmering world of artistic expression."

Overuse. A third concern about narrative writing is that a more literary style has become so appealing to reporters and some editors that an increasing number of hard news stories are topped by narrative or feature leads. Such introductory passages, wrote David Craig, can "simplify issues and shed light on how they affect people." But an over-reliance on anecdotal leads, he said, can become monotonous and trigger complaints from readers who would prefer not to wade through a lot of window dressing before they get to the five W's. Former *New York Times* editor Max Frankel passed along a made-up example composed by a colleague named J. Russell King:

> Elvira Brown's aging face seems almost to be a map of the parched, weather-beaten Texas countryside that has been her home for eighty-three years. Through the eyes that squint in the harsh sunlight, she has seen Dallas grow from a tiny cowtown into a midland capital. The street outside of her tiny house used to be nothing more than a dust trail in summer and a mudhole in winter.
>
> Years ago, she would sit on this porch and watch cattle drives pass. Today, a procession of quite a different sort passed along the now-paved course.
>
> It was a motorcade. It flew by at top speed on its way to Parkland Memorial Hospital. Top speed because, it seems, the President of the United States was inside. And he was dead.

Sometimes, Frankel reminds us, the old summary lead is the best way to get across information that people need to know. Furthermore, cautioned Richard Read, a reporter at the *Oregonian,* in a 2001 *Neiman Reports* article, "the narrative approach doesn't fit every story.... By seeing events through the eyes of a main character, are we shortchanging other viewpoints? By arranging plot points and scenes, are we bending reality to fit a preconceived narrative structure?"

Assessment

Most of the New Journalists wrote for magazines and alternative publications rather than for mainstream newspapers. Narrative writers such as Jon Franklin, Ken Fuson, Tom French, Sonia Nazario and Anne Hull, all of whom work or have worked for newspapers, employ a style that hews much more closely to the detached, third-person tradition characteristic of hard news reports. Most would agree with Mark Kramer's rules for literary journalists: "no composite scenes, no misstated chronology, no falsification of the discernible drift or proportion of events, no invention of quotes, no attribution of thoughts to sources unless they'd had those very thoughts, and no unacknowledged deals with subjects involving payment or editorial control." John Hersey put it more succinctly: The "one sacred rule of journalism," he wrote, is that "the writer must not invent." Roy Peter Clark seconded the motion: "Clear lines can be (and should be) drawn between fiction and nonfiction."

The substantial body of narrative writing that has appeared in newspapers and magazines since the 1970s has largely allayed concerns that the writers of these kinds of stories were blurring the boundary between fiction and nonfiction. One way an increasing number of narrative writers have begun vouching for the factuality of reconstructed scenes without interrupting the flow of the story is to include "About This Story" boxes that list the sources of all unattributed and unwitnessed information. Mark Kramer and Wendy Call note that Sonia Nazario's endnotes came to 7,000 words, and reader reaction suggests that the notes were read and appreciated. "Unsourced information," wrote Berner, "leaves a gap through which a dishonest reporter intent on drama can weasel false information."

What remains is the concern about the cost of in-depth reporting and the doubt that readers have the patience for long-form journalism. At a time when reporting staffs and news holes are shrinking, the resource issue has become particularly vexing. But narrative journalists contend that pitting short inverted-pyramid stories against long narratives sets up what Clark calls "a false dichotomy." As even the most ardent promoters and practitioners of narrative journalism acknowledge, readers will continue to look to newspapers, whether printed or electronic, for the nuts-and-bolts stories about civic life — no-nonsense accounts of what the city council, the police department and the fire department did last night. The inverted pyramid form, says Fuson, remains "a great form to use in getting information out to people quickly." Walt Harrington says he has "no quarrel with that tradition. I revere it."

At the same time, not all narrative stories require weeks of reporting or columns and columns of newsprint. And as Kramer notes, "Almost any news story can benefit from a morsel of narrative because sensory reports engage readers, drawing them into the pleasurable illusion of immediacy." *New York Times* reporter Rick Bragg took a narrative approach to covering the Oklahoma City bombing in 1995. He wrote the story in two hours.

Meanwhile, in the world of online journalism, space is no object — not to mention the storytelling possibilities offered by the addition of audio and video. The online version of "Blackhawk Down," *Philadelphia Inquirer* reporter Mark Bowden's account of America's ill-fated peacekeeping mission in Somalia in 1993, became "part illustrated book, part documentary film, part radio program." Putting the story online also offered a solution to the problem of sourcing reconstructed events by allowing for the use of hyperlinks.

Editors have always tried to offer readers a balance between the hard-hitting and the light-hearted, between stories they need to know and stories they might be interested in knowing. While not every reader wants to settle in with a 3,000-word magnum opus every day, and not many editors can afford to allow reporters to spend weeks or months on such a story, the popularity of Fuson's "West Side Story" piece, Bowden's "Blackhawk Down" and others like them clearly indicates that there is enough of an audience for narrative writing to make it part of the mix at least occasionally. Dispatches from what Harrington calls "the everyday worlds in which we and all our readers live" are what can make people excited about dipping into their morning newspaper.

Points of View

Books

Craig, David. *The Ethics of the Story.* Lanham, Md.: Rowman & Littlefield, 2006. Narrative journalists need to consider the ethical implications of the choices they make in reporting and writing their stories.

Harrington, Walt. *Intimate Journalism.* Thousand Oaks, Calif.: Sage Publications, 1997. This collection includes Harrington's essay on the importance of storytelling in journalism and work by Susan Orlean, Madeleine Blais and others.

Kramer, Mark, and Wendy Call. *Telling True Stories.* New York: Plume, 2007. Narrative journalists write about their craft.

Sims, Norman, and Mark Kramer, eds. *Literary Journalism.* New York: Ballantine, 1995. This anthology features essays on narrative journalism by the book's editors and work by John McPhee, Tracy Kidder, Joseph Mitchell and others.

Wolfe, Tom. *The New Journalism.* New York: Harper & Row, 1973. This book includes Wolfe's famous manifesto for a "new journalism," as well as examples of the genre from Hunter Thompson, Truman Capote, Norman Mailer and others.

Articles and Book Chapters

Bird, S. Elizabeth, and Robert Dardenne. "Myth, Chronicle and Story: Exploring the Narrative Qualities of News," 67-87 in *Media, Myths and Narratives.,* James Carey, ed. Newbury Park, Calif.: Sage, 1988. The most engaging news stories are written in a narrative style.

Frank, Russell. "'About This Story': Making Narrative Journalism Accountable." *Nieman Reports* (September 2002): 49-52. An increasing number of newspapers are running information boxes that list the sources for the unattributed facts in a narrative story.

Frank, Russell. "'You Had to Be There' (And They Weren't): The Problem With Reporter Reconstructions." *Journal of Mass Media Ethics* (Autumn 1999): 146-58. Journalists who reconstruct events that they did not observe need to tell readers how they know what they know.

Hershey, John. "The Legend on the License." Originally published in *Yale Review* (Autumn 1980); reprinted in *Killing the Messenger*, Tom Goldstein, ed. New York: Columbia University Press, 1989: 248-67. Hersey issues a stern rebuke to those who blur the boundary between fiction and nonfiction. The reporter, he writes, must not invent.

"Narrative Journalism." *Nieman Reports* (2001). In this special issue of *Nieman Reports,* practitioners discuss the craft of narrative journalism.

Talese, Gay. "Origins of a Nonfiction Writer," 227-57 in *The Gay Talese Reader.* New York: Walker, 2003. Talese traces his development as a narrative journalist.

Weinberg, Steve. "Tell It Long, Take Your Time, Go in Depth." *Columbia Journalism Review* (January-February 1998). Immersion journalism attracts readers.

23

The Techno-Savvy Journalist

Wielding cell phones, digital cameras, laptops, and audio recorders, reporters have plunged into the electrifying and sometimes terrifying world of journalism 2.0. It's a land othf hyperlinks, photo slideshows and partnerships. It's a place where former rivals learn to play nice as television anchors promote the stories written in the local newspaper and formerly anonymous newspaper journalists become celebrity interviewees on live television. This isn't your grandma's old fashioned pen and paper news. This is journalism dosed with technological steroids.

As one of the most memorable presidential elections in history unfolded, CNN News unveiled a technological marvel that was stripped straight out of a scene from *Star Wars*. Just as a hologram of Princess Leia appeared to Luke Skywalker, news correspondent Jessica Yellin "popped" into the CNN newsroom to discuss the 2008 election. A semi-creepy white light outlined her body. Yellin appeared to stand in front of Wolf Blitzer on the CNN set as a sort of hologram. She actually was standing in a tent surrounded by twenty-five high-definition cameras in Chicago's Grant Park. That same night, CNN journalists displayed a virtual U.S. Capitol. As explained by David Bauder in "CNN Adds Holograms to Election Coverage" on the *New York Times* website, plenty of people weren't impressed by all of CNN's bells and whistles. Nonetheless, if publicity was what CNN was looking for, the network executives certainly got what they wanted.

For better or worse, technology is transforming the news industry. Audiences have changed, and the media have been forced to step up their game to accommodate them. Philip Meyer stated in *The Vanishing Newspaper: Saving Journalism in the Information Age* (2004) that his statistical analysis of circulation trends suggests that the last newspaper will appear in April 2040. Magazines have attempted to re-invent themselves by changing their content emphasis, such as *Newsweek*, which began emphasizing analysis rather than traditional news. News outlets have moved their content online to satisfy the lifestyles of

by Jenn Burleson Mackay
Virginia Tech

their readers, yet "The State of the News Media 2010 Annual Report on American Journalism" found that audiences resist reading advertisements online. Some 79% of those readers surveyed said they rarely, if ever, click on an online advertisement.

The journalist's day-to-day work schedule also has changed to accommodate technology. As Henrik Ornebring suggested in his *Journalism* article "Technology and Journalism-as-labor: Historical Perspectives," technology has allowed journalists to acquire many of the skills that once were in the domain of production workers. Jane Singer in the *Journalism and Mass Communication* article "More Than Ink-Stained Wretches: The Resocialization of Print Journalists in Converged Newsrooms" suggested that some journalists feel as though they are performing more tasks on top of the work that they already do. At the same time, as suggested by Amy Schmitz Weiss and Vanessa de Macedo Higgins Joyce in their *Journalism* article "Compressed Dimensions in Digital Media Occupations: Journalists in Transformation," technology has provided audiences with new ways to interact with the media. John V. Pavlik wrote in his *New Media & Society* piece, "New Media and News: Implications for the Future of Journalism," that new technology allows readers to become fact checkers. He also suggested that journalists now have new tools that can add additional dimensions to news stories.

Media professionals are struggling to find a successful model of journalism for the 21st century. That situation has led mainstream newsrooms to shrink in size as tiny start-up news entities pepper the Internet. Converged news relationships have emerged, and journalists learned new skills. This chapter will consider how technology has allowed journalists to serve readers through hyperlocal news sites as well as the quality news that have developed through converged newsrooms. It also will ponder the devastating effects that technology has had on newsrooms as journalism practitioners struggle for survival.

Origins of the Issue

The life of journalism always has been intertwined with the technology that allows it to exist. As new media forms have come to the forefront, critics have quickly questioned whether the older, traditional media could survive the onslaught. On one hand, the traditional advertising-based model that journalism relied on from its glory days has been challenged as new technologies split audiences and forced media to compete for profits. On the other hand, former competitors have united in the hopes of capturing larger audiences.

The influence of technology on journalism can be seen from the early days of radio. As Philip Meyer explained in his 2009 *Quill* article, "Journalism History is

Merely a List of Surprises," radio technology gave audiences a sense of immediacy. Herb Morrison's passionate account of the *Hindenburg* explosion on May 6, 1937, illustrated that truism. Joe Garner's book *We Interrupt This Broadcast* recounts Morrison's experience. The Chicago radio reporter was at a Naval air station in New Jersey to provide listeners with a live account of the German hydrogen-borne passenger airship's flight when chaos erupted. With a trembling voice, Morrison described what he witnessed to his live audience: "It's crashing! It's crashing terrible! Oh my! Get out of the way, please.... Oh the humanity!" It was impossible for newspapers to give audiences a live experience like that. As time progressed, television joined the immediacy game as Telecom satellites were established. That process has continued with the Internet providing instantaneous communication.

Besides the immediacy of broadcast and later electronic media, newspapers found many challenges to their supreme status as the outlet of choice for advertisers. By the late 1940s, Meyer explains, radio was earning 16% of national advertising revenue. Next, newspapers had to face the growth of network television and the eventual evolution of popular cable and satellite television channels. The new media outlets gave advertisers a variety of places to spend their money. Magazines responded to the saturated market by developing content that targeted specialized audiences. Specialization continued as the online media evolved. Google developed a method for providing Internet users advertising that was tailored to their interests. Advertisers now could track whether anyone clicked on their advertisement. Furthermore, advertisers could pay for who really read the advertisement rather than paying for people who merely might glance at the ad. Newspapers also faced an online advertising challenge from Craigslist. As sociologist Michael Schudson explained in his *Journalism* article "Ten Years Backwards and Forwards," the website began cutting into daily newspaper classified revenue in 2000.

As new media forms evolved, interest in cross-ownership followed. As described by Stephen Quinn in his *Journalism Studies* article "Convergence's Fundamental Questions," digital technology has made convergence possible. Historically, regulations were a major influence in the evolution of convergence. Mickie Edwardson wrote in the *Journalism History* article "Convergence, Issues, and Attitudes in the Fight Over Newspaper-Broadcast Cross-Ownership" that the Federal Communication Commission sent media owners mixed messages for several years regarding cross-ownership. On one hand, a court of appeals stated in 1938 that no rule prevented a newspaper from broadcasting. That same year, however, the FCC gave preference to broadcasting license applicants who didn't own a newspaper. The U.S. Supreme Court ruled in 1940 that anyone could broadcast as long as the frequency was available, but the next year, the FCC decided that the *South Bend Tribune* could not possess licenses for two radio stations in a single city. With time, the rules were relaxed. In the summer of 2003, the FCC determined that a single corporation could own both a newspaper and a broadcast station in the same market under some circumstances. As the rules evolved, several cross-ownership relationships have developed such as Media General's ownership of the *Tampa Tribune* as well as the local television station WFLA-TV. Not everyone has been pleased with the development of convergence, however. Critics have suggested that shared ownership would diminish story diversity. Regardless of the criticism, other convergence relationships have emerged. Rich Gordon discussed several types of convergence existing in the United States in his book chapter in Kevin Kawamoto's *Digital Journalism: Emerging Media and the Changing Horizons of Journalism*. He cited partnerships between news organizations and internal organizational changes as convergence forms.

The emergence of digital technology has lead to a plethora of other changes in the way news is gathered and delivered. An Nguyen wrote in the *Journalism Studies* article "Facing 'The Fabulous Monster': The Traditional Media's Fear-driven Innovation Culture in the Development of Online News," the media have two traditional responses to the development of new media: "kill them or join them." Nguyen, Liz Ferrier, Mark Western and Susan McKay reported in the *Australian Studies in Journalism* piece "Online News in Australia: Patterns of Use and Gratification" that there were few, if any, online newspapers in 1993. By 1998, there were 3,112 online newspapers and 3,900 online magazines in addition to a variety of radio and television sites. More and more new organizations have adopted an online presence, but the news media have been criticized by multiple authors for failing to make an original online product that was better than their traditional news medium.

The Blessings of Technology

Joshua Bell, a renowned classical violinist stood in a subway with his instrument. As his bow glided across the strings to produce complex melodies, his would-be audience walked away. An occasional passer-by paused to listen, but most people barely glanced his way. A video camera taped to the ceiling recorded the apathy of an audience who had no idea that they were listening to a famous musician. The news story was the brainchild of *Washington Post* journalist Gene Weingarten. The print version of the story ran in the paper's Sunday magazine, but perhaps the online version was the most notable. It allowed audiences to

view clips of the subway performance as they read through the text. As Charles Layton explained in the *American Journalism Review* article "The Video Explosion," the violin piece became one of the most viewed stories on the newspaper's website.

Technology has allowed audiences to become part of the storytelling process. It has led journalists to develop new skills that make them more marketable and has led former competitors to develop a newfound respect for one other. In simplest terms, it has led to journalistic progress. This section will highlight the ways that technology has left a positive imprint on journalists and the media as a whole.

Online technology has given journalists a newfound freedom in their reporting, as suggested by Sue Robinson in the *Journalism Practice* piece "Someone's Gotta Be in Control Here." Her study of thirty-five journalists suggested that media practitioners feel that new media give them the opportunity to experiment by adding video and audio to stories. One journalist said, "I take (readers) along in sounds and visuals as well as with my words and give readers a chance to experience what I am experiencing in the field, alongside me."

John Pavlik wrote in his book *Journalism and New Media* (2001) that access to new media technology "represents a potentially better form of journalism because it can re-engage an increasingly distrusting and alienated audience." The technology has many advantages, Pavilk said, such as the ability for journalists to search for diverse sources and new ways to double-check facts. He argued that a new form of news is developing as a result of new technology. He called this news style "contextualized journalism" and explained that it has five elements. First, journalists have access to a variety of storytelling tools including text, audio, animation and even 360-degree video. Those options allow journalists to select the best way to tell a story, rather than restricting themselves to the confines of traditional media. The second element of contextualized journalism is hypermedia, or the use of links to connect a story to related information or other relevant Web pages. The next element is the audience involvement that is inherent to the new media. Unlike more passive media such as newspapers and television, new technology permits audiences the opportunity to immerse themselves in a story. Dynamic or fluid content is the fourth element. The Internet allows audiences the ability to experience the news in real time, as updates are filed the second they are made available by journalists. Finally, customization is a piece of contextualized journalism. Pavlik argued that personalization allows audiences to craft their news so that it fits their lifestyles. For example, readers might choose to get sports news related to their favorite teams or stock news related to their personal investments. The new formula for journalism has the potential to give audiences news in a way that the traditional media cannot. As Pavlik explained, "The space and time limitations of analog print and broadcast media have foreshortened the news and led to a newsroom culture in which most stories are reported in truncated form, telling each story from a single point of view and providing the audience with reports that purport to be the truth." New media also have the potential to free journalists from the deadline limitations of traditional media. Journalists have the flexibility to update stories and add more details as they confirm facts. Traditional technology forces the journalist to stick with the single story that was confirmed by a specific deadline. With new media, however, journalists "might post the story that they were able to confirm early in the day.... Hours later, they can post updated stories." Pavlik argues that this flexibility could help journalists to focus more on getting the facts right rather than meeting a tight deadline.

Pavlik also said that newsroom organization structure has been transformed in response to new technological developments. Rather than maintaining the militaristic pyramid of command that traditional newsrooms relied on, online newsrooms tend to embrace a "more experimental and adaptable entrepreneurial culture." This structure allows journalists to work in a more flexible, decentralized environment, which may include a variety of free-lance reporters.

Many critics suggest that technology is responsible for some of the less pleasant aspects of the media today, such as the emphasis on celebrity news rather than public service information. Bonnie Brennen wrote in her *Journalism* article "The Future of Journalism," however, that new technology has led to some impressive new public service journalism through the development of nonprofit media, such as voiceofSanDiego.org and MinnPost. She argued that nonprofit journalists "consider information an important public service rather than solely a commodity." The new ventures are funded through grants and donations from audiences. Although these media typically rely on free-lancers or less experienced journalists, the nonprofit media have scooped the traditional press with stories on local corruption. Their reports have even led to government investigations.

Hyperlocal news also has grown through the use of new technology. The idea of hyperlocal journalism is to report stories that are relevant to small neighborhoods and communities. Hyperlocal media provide audiences with news that is more relevant to their small communities than the news that they typically would have received from the mainstream media. How these sites operate varies greatly. David Kurpius, Emily Metzgar, and Karen Rowley explained in their *Journalism Studies* article "Sustaining Hyperlocal Media" that hyperlocal media organizations are found in larger cities. What separates them from traditional media is the emphasis on narrow topics that are relevant to small communities. Residents might add commentary to the sites through blogs or by submitting their own content. Hyperlocal efforts often are funded through nonprofit foundation grants. Funding is available to these media because they are filling a gap that has been left in the traditional media. But mainstream media outlets are trying hyperlocal news, too. The journalists at the Gannett's *New-Press* in Fort Myers, Florida, explored this journalistic technique by using what Kate Marymont described as microsites in her *Quill* article "MoJo a Go-Go." Mobile journalists, which she refers to as mojos, were given laptops and sent into communities to find local stories that would be published on the newspaper's microsites. "No story was too small to cover," Marymont said. "If a wreck was blocking an intersection, the neighborhood residents could learn about it online." The *Chicago Tribune* took a different approach to its hyperlocal journalism, as Kyle Leonard explained in the *Nieman Reports* article "Going Hyperlocal at the *Chicago Tribune*." The organization launched TribLocal.com. Rather than relying on trained journalists to cover the neighborhood news, it is relying heavily on community residents to upload content. He referred to the approach as citizen journalism. He said the content is similar to what you might expect to hear in "barbershop" discussions. "It's stories about you, your neighbors, your friends, sometimes your town leaders, and what's happening in your life and in the place you call home," Leonard said.

New technological challenges have led many newsrooms to venture into the world of convergence. Newsrooms have developed different types of convergence relationships as discussed by Rich Gordon in his 2003 book chapter in Kevin Kawamoto's *Digital Journalism: Emerging Media and the Changing Horizons of Journalism*. Gordon explained five types of convergence existing in the United States. The first is ownership convergence, where different types of news media, such as a newspaper and a television station, are owned by the same corporation and work together. Tactical convergence refers to the partnerships between media that are owned by different companies. Structural convergence occurs when new positions are created within a newsroom. Re-organization occurs and newsgathering methods evolve in those newsrooms. Information-gathering convergence refers to newsrooms that rely on multi-skilled journalists. Storytelling convergence refers to the new formats for telling stories. Media companies across the world have delved into convergence, as explained by Stephen Quinn in the *Journalism Studies* article "Convergence's Fundamental Question." Convergence puts new tools in the hands of journalists. It gives them the opportunity to select which medium is the best for a given story. Convergence also allows media owners to cast a wider coverage net over an area, increasing the size of their audience. One of the biggest assets of convergence comes from the advertising sector. The system can allow business owners to develop advertising campaigns that stretch across media. A once competitive relationship between different media becomes a partnership when it is beneficial to both parties.

Convergence has had its critics. Some suggest it will lead to weaker reporting. Edgar Huang, Lisa Rademakers, Moshood A. Fayemiwo and Lillian Dunlap conducted a case study of the well-publicized convergence operation at the *Tampa Tribune.* Until March 2000, the *Tribune,* WFLA-TV and TBO.com operated as three separate entities. After that time, the three news organizations were moved into a single office building. Employees of the three organizations began meeting together and working together on news stories. The study's authors looked at the quality of journalism at the news organization before the converged relationship began, at the beginning of convergence and three years into the relationship. Their *Convergence* article "Converged Journalism and Quality: A Case Study of the Tampa Tribune News Story" found that the *Tampa Tribune* worked with its converged television station to share news tips across media platforms. They found that articles published in the *Tribune* remained fair and balanced. The number of locally produced stories has remained stable over time, but the newspaper has increased its publication of national and international stories.

The changing face of journalism is leading journalists to develop a host of new skills that make them more marketable, as described by Jane B. Singer in the *Journalism and Mass Communication Quarterly* article "More than Ink-Stained Wretches: The Resocialization of Print Journalists in Converged Newsrooms." Singer surveyed journalists working in several different types of converged newsrooms. She found that newspaper journalists are developing a deeper respect for broadcasters and tend to view convergence as something that is beneficial to themselves as well as their employers. The journalists suggested that they enjoy working with people who have different talents from themselves. Singer's study also suggested that newspaper journalists find that Web updates could be useful to their work; updates help them to focus before they write longer stories.

New media also have given journalists immediate access to their audience and sources. Pavlik noted in his *New Media and Society* article "New Media and News: Implications for the Future of Journalism" that journalists have instantaneous access to reader feedback. If they make a mistake, reporters will hear about it in droves of e-mail messages. The Internet also has given journalists new access to sources. Journalists can search for experts from around the world sim-

ply by surfing the Web. He also suggested that new technology, such as laptop computers, has provided journalists with tools that make it quicker for them to write stories.

The Curse of Technology

Technology can be seductive, but it also can lure journalists to misuse or abuse their power. Consider Jayson Blair. On May 11, 2003, the *New York Times* ran a lengthy front-page article that outlined a series of factual errors and accounts of plagiarism that Blair perpetrated during his career at the paper. The article "Correcting the Record: Times Reporter Who Resigned Leaves Long Trail of Deception" by Dan Barry, David Barstow, Jonathan D. Glater, Adam Liptak and Jacques Steinberg, reported that the 27-year-old reporter filed expense reports suggesting that he had traveled across the country, when he had never left New York. He sent e-mails to his editors to tell them about the progress he was making on a story in Maryland while he was still in New York. "His tools of deceit were a cell phone and a laptop computer — which allowed him to blur his true whereabouts — as well as round-the-clock access to databases of news articles from which he stole." Blair's tenure at the *Times* was nearing its end when the *San Antonio Express-News* accused him of plagiarism. In his own book, *Burning Down My Master's House,* Blair recounted lying to his colleagues about the reasons why his story about a Marine who died in Iraq was strikingly similar to a story that was published in the Texas paper. He told them that he confused his own notes with the story from the paper. He also recounted how he lied to them flying to Texas for the story, a trip he had never made.

Technology can be an indispensible instrument for journalists. It can empower them to excel at reporting. However, it also can be a damaging device that propels advertisers to many venues, taints journalistic credibility, and deteriorates the credibility of the profession.

One of the most damaging effects of technology has come from advertising. The Internet has opened a vast number of options for advertisers. *Washington Post* reporter Paul Farhi explained the situation in his *American Journalism Review* article "Don't Blame the Journalism." He discussed the prosperity that newspapers once enjoyed as they operated in one-newspaper-towns. For several decades, many papers had no true competitors. The corporations yielded massive profits. Then classified advertisers stopped paying for newspaper ads. They could easily go to online sites such as Craigslist and eBay for free or for a nominal fee. Furthermore, local retailers who had once advertised in the paper disappeared. Newspaper owners may have hoped that online advertising would be their saving grace, but "online readers tend to dart in and out, spending far less time on a newspaper site than a subscriber spends with a paper," Farhi wrote. Online ads are therefore less valuable to advertisers than traditional advertisements.

Many scholars are calling for the media to find a new business model to support the industry. For example, Joel Kramer reported in the *Nieman Reports* article "The New Front Page: The Digital Revolution" that his publication, a nonprofit website called MinnPost, lures advertisers by "providing ... a high-quality environment and excellent service and asking them to pay accordingly." He said that local competitors charge less for their advertising and Google Ads offers to sell advertising on the news organization's own site for a 10th less than what MinnPost charges. The result is that a limited number of advertisers are willing to pay MinnPost for advertising. The publication also is encouraging advertisers to sponsor a section of the site, rather than buying individual ads. They have had some success with sponsorship. MinnPost journalists also have learned to write shorter stories to fill the site. Kramer said the news organization gets more site visitors when they publish several shorter stories than if they publish a single longer story. Journalists still write longer pieces, but they publish fewer investigative pieces than they might if more funding were available. To be fair, the news is not all bad for MinnPost. The site may have reduced the amount of money that it spends on news gathering, but it has also more than doubled visits to the site, while proudly proclaiming that it doesn't publish stories about Paris Hilton and Lindsay Lohan. The site's staff members are striving to make a new model work at a time when journalists aren't sure what their next step should be.

News organizations have moved toward a higher level of hyperlocal news in the pursuit of a new business model. David Kurpius, Emily Metzgar and Karen Rowley wrote in the *Journalism Studies* article "Sustaining Hyperlocal Media" that it has been difficult for journalists to find a profitable model for this journalism reform. Their case study of ten hyperlocal media providers found that the media organizations had developed projects that may not be able to survive long-term. It also may be difficult for media in other communities to replicate their funding models. New media executives also have discussed charging audiences for online content. As previously mentioned, however, the "State of the News Media" study found that only 35% of online consumers specified that they had a favorite news site. Most of those people suggested that they would no longer visit the site if they were asked to pay for the content.

Technology and the need to publish information quickly also may be leaving a nasty bruise on journalistic credibility. Paul Farhi wrote in the *American Journalism Review* article "Lost in the Woods" that the modern news cycle has become so competitive that journalists may be more concerned with posting information quickly rather than focusing on the accuracy of their reports. As an example, Farhi cited the coverage of professional golfer Tiger Woods' sex scandal. Rather than digging for facts and searching for legitimate news sources, Farhi said the mainstream news media "piggybacked on aggressive but not always accurate reporting." In many cases, the journalists cited reports from other news media in their accounts, such as the entertainment gossip website TMZ. Pavlik also noted in "New Media and News: Implications for the Future of Journalism" that new technology may lead journalists to make more news judgments without adequately checking the facts. As an example, he mentioned the *Dallas Morning News*' decision to publish a report regarding a Secret Service officer's knowledge about the affair between President Bill Clinton and Monica Lewinsky. Story inaccuracies led the news organization to retract the report that same day it was published.

Journalists may feel other pressures that come from working in the new media environment. Jane Singer wrote in her *Journalism and Mass Communication Quarterly* article "More Than Ink-Stained Wretches: The Resocialization of Print Journalists in Converged Newsrooms" that journalists are essentially being asked to do more work on top of their traditional jobs to accommodate the demands of new technology, including posting Web updates in addition to writing their news stories. Her study found that some journalists don't feel they have the training that they need to operate in converged newsrooms, although some journalists noted that the training issue wasn't as difficult as they initially feared. Sue Robinson's interviews with journalists as discussed in her *Journalism Practice* article "Someone's Gotta Be in Control Here" found that multimedia journalists in some newsrooms felt that they were losing their journalistic creativity as they became "computer coders" rather than journalists. Headlines are selected on the basis of words that will be search-engine friendly. Robinson also wrote about the news industry's struggle to manage online commentary. Newsrooms have struggled to develop rules to govern online discussions. Her paper also stated that NYTimes.com had closed down some of its message boards because of profanity.

Technology has the potential to raise a host of new ethical issues for journalism as well. *Time* magazine was criticized after its 1994 cover depicted a digitally manipulated image of O.J. Simpson with darker skin than his natural complexion. Deirdre Carmody wrote in the *New York Times* article "Time Responds to Criticism Over Simpson Cover" that critics accused the magazine of giving Simpson a "more sinister appearance and was thus guilty of racism." The photo, which was originally a mug shot taken by the Los Angeles Police Department, also appeared in its original form on the cover of *Newsweek* magazine. Magazine staff denied that there was a racial intention behind the image. *Time's* managing editor, James R. Gaines, explained that the image was a photo illustration, which was completed under a tight deadline. Edwin Martin wrote in the *Journalism and Mass Media Ethics* article "On Photographic Manipulation" that photo manipulation was available to photographers long before digital technology was available. Photographers could use the same sorts of cropping and dodging tools in the darkroom that they can now use on the computer. That said, Martin wrote that the ease of digital technology could lead to more and more manipulation. Digitally altering an image to change the way the sky looks or to remove items in the background is deceptive. "In such cases," he said, "some viewers are undeniably deceived, because they will draw false conclusions about how the scene actually was at the time of the photographing." He argued that photo manipulation can lead to credibility issues for photographers.

Digital technology can be used to alter reality in many other ways. CBS News got overly creative with its use of graphics during its 1999 coverage of New Year's Eve. During broadcasts, the staff digitally inserted the CBS logo behind anchor Dan Rather to cover NBC's promotions, which were displayed on a massive screen in Time Square. Gail Shister wrote in the *Philadelphia Inquirer* article "Rather Criticizes CBS News' Use of A Digital Alteration" that the network was criticized by multiple sources, including its own anchor. Rather said the network needed to do something to block its competitor's promotions during the broadcasts, but that it should have found another method or at least told viewers what it was doing. Andrew Heyward, CBS News president, told the paper that he "didn't see this as a big controversial decision." John Pavlik wrote in "Journalism and New Media" that the ability to manipulate images has made it more important than ever for individuals to verify news content through multiple sources. It's even possible to fabricate video, as was demonstrated by an advertising consultant whom Sen. John W. Warner hired to create a negative political advertisement during Virginia's 1996 senatorial campaign. The synthetic video showed competitor Mark Warner shaking hands with former governor L. Douglas Wilder. The handshake never occurred. Mark Warner's head was placed on the body of another person.

New technology has already created an environment where anybody, regardless of journalistic training, can publish her or his own account of news events. Traditional journalists serve the public by making responsible choices, Pavlik wrote. He suggested that bloggers and new media publishers should uphold the same standards, but history has shown that they don't. As an example, he cited Matt Drudge's account of Bill Clinton's affair with intern Monica Lewinsky. Drudge broke the story on his website, the *Drudge Report,* by relying on rumors rather than factual evidence. *Newsweek* magazine had the same information, but it opted to hold on to the story until its reporters could check the facts. Pavlik wrote, "Authenticity of content, source verification, accuracy and truth are all suspect in a medium where anyone with a computer and a modem can become a global publisher."

Assessment

Technology is journalism's gift and its poison. Technology lies at the core of journalism, from the most basic newspaper story to the most sophisticated multimedia journalism presentation. Technology has empowered journalists with new methods for gathering information and structuring stories. As Sue Robinson stated in the *Journalism Practice* piece "Someone's Gotta Be in Control Here," technology has given journalists new, creative storytelling methods. Add to that the audience members' new opportunities to become part of stories by submitting their own content to hyperlocal news sites or by interacting directly with journalists by posting feedback. It's easy to see the potent effect that technology has on journalism.

But it's also created new media that drain revenues. With advertisers spreading their money across a wider variety of media, the traditional media are struggling to survive. "The State of the New Media 2010" report suggested that newspaper circulation is dropping along with the audience for network television news. The news media are caught in a transition period, which has led to many new start-up journalism outlets. Some of these outlets are publishing important stories, but even those new outlets are struggling to find a financially stable way to survive. Research suggests that audiences aren't willing to pay for content, so journalists seem to be in an impossible situation. Advertisers don't want to pay them, and audiences don't want to, either. Is anyone willing to fund journalism?

Furthermore, technology has created a 24-hour news environment. Journalists can publish information quickly and update stories as the facts become available. Audiences have become accustomed to receiving information quickly. Yet, that opportunity for instant information has been marred with credibility problems. Journalists may publish unconfirmed details or rumors because they want to meet the audience's expectation for instant information. In June 2010, rumors swirled that renowned guitarist Eric Clapton was going to perform at the Down by the River Festival in Roanoke, Va. He was not listed on the schedule, but he reportedly has a music touring relationship with a band that was on the schedule, the Derek Trucks and Susan Tedeschi Band. According to a blog post by *Roanoke*

Times Managing Editor Michael's Stowe, "Incorrect Clapton Post an Unfortunate Mistake," the day of the concert, a musician posted on his Twitter account that Clapton would play. A reporter for the *Roanoke Times* sought out a promoter for the show to confirm the story. The promoter told the journalist that Clapton had checked into a local hotel. Minutes later, the journalist posted an update online announcing that Clapton was going to be on stage. Shortly after the posting, the journalist heard from a band manager who told him that Clapton wasn't performing. The news organization corrected the post within two and a half hours, but the damage already was done. After the incident occurred, the promoter who initially confirmed that Clapton was in town told the paper that he meant for his comment to be a joke. The reporter and Clapton's fans probably didn't think it was funny.

Other ethical issues accompany technology, such as the ease of digital photo manipulation. New technology also has given the media more reasons to write shorter, less-detailed stories. Those stories are less expensive to write, and in the current climate, saving money is important to a struggling industry.

Convergence has developed as a possible solution to journalism's financial woes. Partnerships among outlets have allowed the media to share story tips. Convergence also has allowed the media to cross promote one another. Television and newspaper journalists have different news-gathering routines, but they are expected to work side by side in many cases. Journalists also are being forced to publish website updates in addition to their traditional news stories. Journalists have admitted that the updates can help them to focus before they write longer stories, but the updates require more work for no extra pay. Although some journalists embrace the opportunity to select the method for telling a story such as text, video, or audio, others are struggling with technological training. Some simply don't feel like they are prepared to work in this new environment, or they fear that their creativity is being stripped away as they become technicians rather than journalists.

It seems that nearly all of the advantages that come with new technology also come with a host of disadvantages. Journalists must rely on new technology and change their practices to accommodate it. At this point, though, it seems that technology is damaging journalism more than it is helping it. With time, the news media probably will find a way to grow and prosper with technology as it has in the past. Just as general interest magazines evolved and strengthened their market position by seeking out special interest audiences, the news media must find a way to survive and thrive in journalism 2.0. Perhaps in time, technology will lead to a healthier news industry. The promises of creative storytelling already are beginning to be fulfilled and audiences seem intrigued by the interactivity

and customization opportunities online. For now, we're all waiting to see which news organizations will survive new media and which will vanish.

Points of View

Books

Dooley, Patricia L. *The Technology of Journalism*. Evanston, Ill.: Northwestern University Press, 2007. Technology has influenced journalism throughout history.

Pavlik, John V. *Journalism and New Media*. New York: Columbia University Press, 2001. New media are changing journalistic content, journalistic routines, newsroom structure and the relationships between journalists and other people, such as audience members and sources.

Pavlik, John V. *Media in the Digital Age*. New York: Columbia University Press, 2008. New technology has the potential to allow journalists to encourage public discussions about issues that are important to society.

Sturgis, Ingrid, ed. *Are Traditional Media Dead? Can Journalism Survive in the Digital World?* New York: International Debate Education Association, 2012. Several chapters explore the influence of digital technology on journalism.

Zelizer, Barbie, ed. *Then Changing Faces of Journalism: Tabloidization, Technology and Truthiness*. New York: Routledge, 2009. Several chapters explore how technology influences our understanding of the media.

Articles and Book Chapters

Boczkowski, Pablo. "Technology, Monitoring, and Imitation in Contemporary News Work." *Communication, Culture & Critique* 2:1 (2009): 39-59. Using an ethnographic study of news organizations in Argentina, Boczkowski considers how technology influences news gathering.

Edwardson, Mickie. "Convergence, Issues, and Attitudes in the Fight Over Newspaper-Broadcast Cross Ownership." *Journalism History* 33 (2007): 79-92. Regulations and other issues have influenced the development of converged media.

Flew, Terry, Christina Spurgeon, Anna Daniel, and Adam Swift. "The Promise of Computational Journalism." *Journalism Practice* 6 (2012): 157-71. The use of technology and the influence of computer science can lead to new investigative journalism.

Gordon, Rich. "The Meanings and Implications of Convergence, " 53-73 in Kevin Kawamoto, ed., *Digital Journalism: Emerging Media and the Changing Horizons of Journalism*.

Lanham, Md.: Roman & Littlefield, 2003. Gordon's chapter describes the various types of convergence existing in the United States.

Hermida, Alfred. "Twittering The News." *Journalism Practice* 4 (2010): 297-308. The use of social media is influencing journalism.

Huang, Edgar, Lisa Rademakers, Moshood A. Fayemiwo, and Lillian Dunlap. "Converged Journalism and Quality: A Case Study of *The Tampa Tribune* News Stories." *Convergence* 10 (2004): 73-91. The *Tampa* has maintained quality reporting while operating in a converged setting.

Kurpius, David D., Emily T. Metzgar, and Karen M. Rowley. "Sustaining Hyperlocal Media: In search of funding models." *Journalism Studies* 11(2010): 359-76. Various types of hyperlocal newsrooms have developed, and some have the potential to survive.

Nguyen, An. "Facing 'The Fabulous Monster': The Traditional Media's Fear-driven Innovation Culture in the Development of Online News." *Journalism Studies* 9 (2008): 91-104. Traditional media journalists feel threatened by new media, but they are working actively to develop the next stage of online news.

Ornebring, Henrik. "Technology and Journalism-as-labour: Historical Perspectives." *Journalism* 11 (2010): 57-74. There has been a historical relationship between the journalism workforce and technology.

Quinn, Stephen. "Convergence's Fundamental Question." *Journalism Studies* 6 (2005): 29-38. If managers and journalists work together, convergence can be a tool for creating outstanding journalism.

Robinson, Sue. "Someone's Gotta Be in Control Here." *Journalism Practice* 1:3 (2007): 305-21. Interviews with journalists describe how technology is transforming newspaper journalism's purpose with journalists exploring new ways to engage audiences.

Singer, Jane B. "More Than Ink-Stained Wretches: The Resocialization of Print Journalists in Converged Newsrooms." *Journalism and Mass Communication Quarterly* 81 (2004): 838-56. Convergence is leading print journalists to have a broader view of their profession.

Usher, Nikki. "Service Journalism As Community Experience." *Journalism Practice* 6 (2012): 107-21. New technology has changed the relationship between readers and journalists.

Weiss, Amy Schmitz, and Vanessa de Macedo Higgins Joyce. "Compressed Dimensions in Digital Media Occupations: Journalists in Transformation." *Journalism* 10 (2009): 587-603. Globalization is influencing online journalism.

24 Social Media and the News

Within one week of its posting in early March 2012, filmmaker Jason Russell's YouTube video condemning the human rights abuses of Uganda warlord Joseph Kony became the most watched viral video, attracting more than 75 million views. The success came "thanks in no small part to an army of young supporters who flexed their power by using social media to drive celebrities and friends to watch and share the video.... 'Kony 2012' is undeniably a social media phenomenon made possible by support from celebrities," wrote Jacob Soboroff on MTV.com on March 12.

Although traditional news outlets had been reporting on Kony's army for years, few people took notice until celebrities started spreading the word through Twitter, Facebook and other social media platforms. For example, pop star Rihanna shared the link with her 15.9 million Twitter followers. On March 12, Comedy Central's *The Daily Show* with Jon Stewart showed clips of the traditional news outlets (ABC News) and journalists (Anderson Cooper) touting their past Kony coverage and lamenting how audiences ignored their work. Host Stewart took the media to task. "Mainly the media just seems annoyed that it took this guy [Russell] to get people to listen...'I mean we're handsome. We're on TV. Why won't Rihanna retweet our Kony stories?' "

The Kony example shows the shifting patterns of news delivery in a new era where social media platforms drive audiences to websites, alert them to issues and even help mobilize groups into action. The good news for journalists and traditional news outlets is that social media have allowed their work to reach larger audiences, as viral sensations blow up the Internet. Social media also allow journalists to connect with existing audiences in new ways and engage in conversations with opinion leaders and average citizens in their communities. Finally, these platforms have greatly expanded news gathering and reporting capabilities and have allowed journalists to break news instantly and cover events live.

Social media have a downside for the industry, however. As with the Kony

by Jennifer Greer
University of Alabama

story, traditional journalists are no longer solely setting the agenda for their audiences. In a social media environment, everyone with a sufficiently large following, even Rihanna, can alert the public to "important" topics. As a result, the community agenda and the national agenda become increasingly fragmented. From the business side, news organizations are realizing that everyone on the planet, or at least everyone with a smart phone, is a potential reporter. As social media and other digital delivery forms siphon advertisers away from traditional news outlets, media companies seeking to do more with less are shedding traditional journalistic work forces and relying more on citizen reporters who submit free, but often low-quality, copy, video and images. Finally, the rush to be first and to compete with the millions who are "breaking news" on social media has compromised journalistic norms and ethics in multiple cases.

This chapter examines the origins of digital delivery in the news industry and then explores how social media have both enhanced and hurt traditional U.S. journalism.

Origins of the Issue

Digital delivery of news content was fueled, many argue, by the fear that traditional delivery forms would become irrelevant in the Internet age. U.S. newspapers started moving online in various formats more than 25 years ago. By the end of 1995, more than 330 U.S. newspapers had some type of online service, and the industry had settled on the World Wide Web as the electronic platform of choice. Broadcast and cable outlets got into the online news delivery game a bit later, but virtually all had at least a basic website by 2000. Newspaper and broadcast executives who once viewed digital delivery as a threat to their core print and on-air revenue base began to embrace these tools as a means of long-term industry survival. Sites grew in content, interactivity and sophistication throughout the 2000s, according to Xigen Li's 2006 book *Internet Newspapers.*

Social media build on the ideological and technological foundations of the interactivity-driven Web 2.0, promoting the exchange of user-generated content. The first major U.S. social network, MySpace.com, went online in August 2003, allowing members to post pictures, videos and personal details. By 2008, it was the nation's largest social network with more than 200 million users. Rival site Facebook was created in 2004 for college students and opened to the public in 2006. Facebook rapidly overtook MySpace as the dominant U.S. social network. It counted more than 500 million users worldwide by 2011.

Microblogging emerged in the 2000s from the Web phenomenon of blogging, where people share news, opinions or digests online through a personalized forum. Twitter, the leading microblogging site, launched in 2006, allowing

individuals and organizations to blast brief bursts of information in 140-character posts. Twitter counted more than 200 million users worldwide in 2012, and eMarkerter.com estimated that unique monthly U.S. visitors to Twitter averaged between 20 million to 26 million for the year. A January 2010 Nielsenwire report found a year-to-year increase of 82% in global time spent on Facebook, Twitter and other social media sites. In the United States alone, the average citizen spent six hours and nine minutes on social network sites during December 2009, up 143% from December 2008. The figures have continued to increase since then.

Because of the reach of sites like Twitter and Facebook and because of the time audiences devote to these platforms, U.S. news organizations have been establishing social media presences of their own since the mid-2000s. In 2007, *The Oregonian* in Portland became the first major newspaper with a Twitter feed. One blogger, Graphicdesignr.net, found that by 2009, about 1,300 Twitter accounts were affiliated with U.S. newspapers. A 2009 study of the largest 100 newspapers, conducted by Allen Rindfuss for *The Bivings Report*, found that 62% had at least one Twitter feed. On average, newspaper feeds had 17,717 users and tweeted eleven times daily, Rindfuss found. Even the smallest U.S. newspapers were promoting Twitter feeds on their websites by 2010. Jennifer Greer and Yan Yan, examining U.S. newspapers' sites in a December 2010 *Grassroots Editor* article, found links to newspaper Twitter feeds present on 31.4% of the sites and links to newspaper Facebook pages present on 17.1% of the sites. Larger papers were more likely to link to Facebook and Twitter sites from their websites than were the smaller papers, the researchers found.

A Pew Internet & American Life Project survey released in March 2010 noted that, despite these efforts by news organizations, a subtle shift was occurring in how readers were getting news in a digital delivery environment. The report, *Understanding the Participatory News Consumer*, found that online news audiences, rather than going straight to websites produced by news organizations and journalists, were shifting to using their "social networks *and* social networking technology to filter, assess and react to news." The survey found that 75% of U.S. online news users get news through forwarded e-mail and social media, and 52% share news links through social media. Rather than going directly to the websites, or even the social media pages, of traditional news organizations, audiences were getting news recommended by friends and members of their social networks.

How Social Media Benefit Traditional News Organizations

The changing digital landscape, with social media taking an increasingly larger role each year, has clear benefits for traditional news outlets. The phenomenon is broadening the reach of these organizations, allowing them to connect with new audiences, build stronger relationships with their communities and reach sources and cover news in new ways. Each is explored below.

Reaching New Audiences

Traditional news organizations are launching and promoting affiliated social media feeds on YouTube, Facebook, Twitter, Pinterest and other social sites. But they're not content to let audiences stumble upon the information. Many have teamed up with marketing firms to push news content through social networks to new audiences. Industry insiders say these efforts are paying off, benefitting content producers and audiences alike. News outlets are reaching different audiences, and readers are able to access quality journalism and great storytelling from sources around the globe.

In the social media universe, not all communities are geographically defined. Although local news typically is of interest to readers in a certain area, a heartfelt story (complete with cute photos) about a puppy plays the same in Birmingham, Ala., as it does in Tucson, Ariz., St. Louis, Mo., or Nome, Alaska. The *Birmingham News* found this out in January 2010 when a reporter wrote a brief blog post about a puppy rescued by a railroad worker after its paws were frozen to a track where a train was due within the hour. The puppy, later named Track, was taken to a shelter and eventually found a family. The post on al.com was promoted by a social media marketing firm that al.com employs. That effort generated hundreds of thousands of page views from readers around the country and beyond. The story became the most viewed post on al.com for the first quarter of 2010, attracting more readers than stories about the University of Alabama winning its thirteenth football championship and a professor killing three colleagues during a meeting in Huntsville, Ala. (Want proof of the viral nature of the puppy story? Google "puppy on track," and it's the first link that pops up.)

News outlets also use social media to reach younger audiences not in the habit of turning on the evening news or picking up a print newspaper. The 2010 Pew Internet study, *Understanding the Participatory News Consumer,* found younger people significantly more likely to use Twitter and other social media at least periodically for news (36% of those younger than 30 reported doing so) than older adults (6% of those 50 and older). On cell phones, a platform upon which people increasingly access social media, 13% of those ages 18 to 24 reported accessing news regularly, compared with just 5% of those 50 to 64. Pew also found news sharing through social media to be on the rise, especially with younger adults. For example, the survey found 13% sharing information about the 2010 Haitian earthquake through social media. For adults ages 18 to 29, about 24% said they shared news about the event through social media, compared with only 7% of those 50 to 64.

Chuck Lenatti offered reasons for these trends in a 2009 *Seybold Report* article, "Missing the Mark: Why Online Newspapers Fall Flat with Younger Readers." Lenatti stressed that young adults gravitate toward social media for news because they feel more engaged by the reciprocal form of communication social media offer. Traditional news content doesn't offer this interactivity, and newspapers have been slow to embrace social media as a news delivery tool, he argued.

Jennifer Greer and Yan Yan, in a December 2011 *Grassroots Editor* study titled "Connecting with Younger Readers," found significant changes in the way younger audiences accessed their local newspaper. Comparing college students' use of newspaper content between April 2010 and April 2011, the researchers found that readers' reported frequency of going directly to their preferred local newspaper's website significantly decreased. In contrast, accessing content from the paper's site through a Facebook post significantly increased. Further, the preferred way of connecting with that newspaper changed. About half as many students in 2011 as in 2010 said they preferred to go directly to their local paper's website. Over the same time, four times as many students said they preferred to get the content and links delivered though Facebook posts. This same pattern was found for all news sites, not just the local newspaper. In just one year, frequency of use of all news websites dropped, but use of news delivered through Facebook and Twitter significantly increased.

Although links into newspaper and broadcast and cable news sites from Facebook and Twitter still account only for a small portion of traffic into newspapers' websites, traffic is increasing rapidly. For example, the *New York Times* saw its referrals into nytimes.com from Twitter quadruple between December 2008 and December 2009, according to a January 2010 *Venture Beat* article, "Will the *New York Times* Meter Kill Traffic from Social Media?" Further, in November 2011, CNN's feed had slightly more than 4 million followers, but by July 2012, the feed had grown to 5.01 million, a 25% increase in just seven months. The feed had climbed to 79 on the list of the 100 most followed Twitter feeds. Vivian Schiller, then general manager of NYTimes.com, told ajr.com in a January 2009 article, "Networking News," that social media marketing was just one of several essential strategies for disseminating news online — and surviving economically. "We're an equal opportunity disseminator," Schiller said. "The point here is to disseminate our feeds because they drive traffic."

Building Connections with Communities

At the July 2012 five-state Southeastern Press Convention, *Tallahassee (Fla.)*

Democrat and tallahassee.com Executive Editor Bob Gabordi told publishers that if they were just using social media to boost audience numbers online, they were missing the mark. "Everyone thinks that social media is about driving traffic to the website. That's not what it's about. It's about building relationships with the community."

Gabordi said editors at his paper use Facebook and Twitter to send out breaking news and promote upcoming special sections and projects, but the key is "building that affinity with the brand." The paper's Web content is protected by a pay wall, meaning only paid print or online subscribers have full access to content. But to promote the brand and help audiences see tallahassee.com as the place for community news, editors offer exclusive content and other special features only to the paper's friends and followers on social media. "The main use is to try and build bridges and have our staff there to interact with readers and engage readers in a conversation. It's key that there's that back and forth."

These active and engaged members of a digital community can help build content and enhance media information in ways unheard of in the one-to-many mass communication era of the past. Social networking provides convenient tools for news composing, editing, commenting and sharing, which facilitates widespread news delivery beyond traditional channels, a further boon to news organizations. Aaron Smith and Lee Rainie, in a December 2010 Pew Internet report, *8 Percent of Online Americans Use Twitter*, investigated the content shared by active posters on Twitter. They found that although updates on users' personal or professional lives were the most popular content, 55% of active users shared links to news stories.

Frequent posting on Twitter helps a news organization develop relationships with audiences. *Slate's* John Dickerson argued in a summer 2008 *Neiman Reports* article, "Don't Fear Twitter," that Twitter builds "a community of readers who find their way to longer articles because they are lured by these moment-by-moment observations." Paul Farhi in a 2009 article, "The Twitter Explosion," on ajr.com, wrote that "Twitter attracts the sort of people that media people should love — those who are interested in, and engaged with, the news." He cited one estimate that the average Twitter user is up to three times more likely to visit a leading news website than the average person.

Building ties with active members of social networks can help newspapers enlist them as recruiters. These opinion leaders online can refer their own followers to the papers' content, leading to increased readership of news stories. As many researchers have argued, social media bridge the gap between mass communication and interpersonal communication, with audiences using sites for both purposes. The ability to connect media outlets and readers in new ways relies on social media's self-designed group ties, which bring the advantages of

offline interpersonal and group relationships into a mass communication setting.

In a January 2009 ajr.com article, "Networking News," washingtonpost.com Executive Editor James Brady summed up this trend. "The one thing that gets lost in all the automation and search engine gaming algorithms is that people want to know what their friends think and what people respect. One way to get content in front of you is to have your friends recommend it; that's a social filtering of news."

Covering News in New Ways

Interactivity with users and the growing numbers on social networks have transformed the newsgathering and news dissemination routines in many positive ways, some argue. Journalists can reach new sources and can break news faster than their peers of even a decade ago could have imagined.

Editors of the *Tuscaloosa* (Ala.) *News* harnessed the power of Twitter and Facebook for both news gathering and news delivery on April 27, 2011, when an EF-4 tornado ripped through the town, killing 53 people. Many cited the newspaper's Twitter feed as a deciding factor in the paper winning the 2012 Pulitzer Prize for breaking news. City Editor Katherine Lee wrote in the summer 2012 *Neiman Reports*:

"We discovered that a disaster is ready-made for social media tools, which provide the immediacy needed for reporting breaking news. Our reporters and photographers were on the street within minutes of the storm, tweeting and posting photos of the devastation.... Reporters' tweets and photos were aggregated to the paper's website and Facebook page so people could see a continuous stream of information in the minutes immediately after the storm hit."

These social media posts helped the public know where the destruction was, what areas to avoid and where to go for help. National Guard officials later told the paper the Tweets helped first responders know where to deploy resources. Further, the paper used social media to allow the community to share stories and post queries about people they were trying to locate.

The *Tuscaloosa News'* experience is a vivid example of changes taking place in newsrooms — big and small — throughout the country. Reporters now find sources and stories by being integrated in numerous social networks. For example, the *Tallahassee Democrat* routinely uses these networks to find and advance stories for its community. After the 2012 death of a Florida A&M University marching band member in a reported hazing incident, reporters found inside angles and new leads through comments posted through Facebook, Gabordi said. "It makes it more two-way, and you are able to get feedback," the executive editor said.

Increasingly, legacy news media find themselves not only breaking stories, but taking information swirling on social networks, verifying it, adding context and publishing coherent stories to help audiences. In the aftermath of the 2011 tornado, the *Tuscaloosa News* started a blog to clear up dozens of rumors bubbling up on social networks, Lee said. The Poynter Institute's Craig Silverman, writing in a 2012 summer *Neiman Reports* article titled "A New Age for Truth," documents an emerging specialty area of journalism focused on "verifying photos, videos, tweets, status updates, blog posts and other digital ephemera," a practice he terms "the New Verification." Journalists and non-journalists alike use social media both to gather information and to check the accuracy of that information. Silverman writes: "Never has it been so easy to expose an error, check a fact, crowdsource and bring technology to bear in service of verification." Lila King, participation director for CNN Digital, explained in the same issue of *Neiman Reports* that the network goes beyond simple verification when using social media content. "At CNN, we see it as our responsibility to add context and analysis to what we use from iReport and other social media platforms."

Social media also allow news organizations to break news to their communities in new ways. Twitter, especially, is ideal for delivering breaking news. Print outlets at best can rely on a special print edition when breaking news occurs (for example, on September 11, 2001). Local broadcasters rarely break into regularly scheduled programming, unless a story is huge. Online editions help newspapers and local broadcasters break news in real time, but the immediacy and format of information delivered by social media have given journalists the power to break news instantaneously.

Twitter, which allows for quick blasts of information in real time, has been the go-to format for newspapers delivering breaking news. Greer and Yan, in a 2011 *Newspaper Research Journal* article, found newspapers adopting Twitter more quickly and widely than Facebook. Further, newspapers update their Twitter feeds more frequently than their Facebook pages. On average, newspapers' Twitter communities were twice the size of their Facebook communities, and the largest Twitter feed had six times as many followers as the largest Facebook page, the study found.

One year after the tornado, Lee observed that the *Tuscaloosa News* actively and routinely incorporates Twitter and Facebook into its coverage. Reporters tweet from city hall meetings, link to stories from readers and follow up on comments on Facebook. "We have been confronted with stark evidence of how useful (social media) can be to the newsgathering process and to readers who are increasingly ingesting news in untraditional ways."

How Social Media Hurt Traditional News Organizations

The speed with which news organizations can deliver breaking news through social media — incorrectly — was demonstrated on June 12, 2012. Within minutes of the release of an historic court opinion, the CNN Breaking News' Twitter feed read: "Supreme Court strikes down individual mandate portion of health care law." CNN delivered the news quickly — but it was wrong. The Supreme Court actually upheld that part of President Barack Obama's health care law. The feed from Fox News contained the same error.

Although both news organizations corrected their mistake within minutes, the gaffe was fodder for jokes by late-night comedians and online communities. The example shows one downside of the social media phenomenon — journalistic credibility can suffer. Other downsides include a shift in the traditional agenda-setting role of the news media, which could lead to a fracturing of the public's knowledge on issues. Further, newsroom staffing has been slashed as organizations rely more heavily on citizen-supplied content delivered via social networks.

Shift in Agenda-Setting Functions

On May 1, 2011, President Obama asked the broadcast networks for airtime to make a dramatic and historic announcement. When television outlets broke into programming about 10:50 p.m. Eastern time, many journalists already knew what was breaking. Anchors, however, held the story in deference to the president. Twitter and Facebook users didn't offer the same courtesy — they were blasting out the news: U.S. Special Forces had killed Osama bin Laden. At 10:25 p.m., Keith Urbahn, former Defense Secretary Donald Rumsfeld's chief of staff, was the first credible tweeter to leak the news. "By 11 p.m. ... news was spreading virally around the world. At that time, there were more than a dozen Facebook posts with the word 'bin Laden' every single second," the *New York Times* reported two days later. TV anchors and newspaper Web editors gave up trying to hold the story; the social media chatter had forced them to steal the president's thunder. Obama's announcement at the podium at 11:30 p.m. Eastern time was historic, but it was hardly a surprise, thanks to social media.

Dominant news forces like longtime CBS News anchor Walter Cronkite or the *New York Times* once chose what to cover and what to emphasize, setting the news agenda for a nation. Although traditional news outlets still provide much of the news in a social media era, the way people access that content is in flux. In today's environment, this agenda-setting function is shifting to hundreds or even thousands of social media opinion leaders.

In 1963, Bernard Cohen, in his book *The Press and Foreign Policy,* famously asserted that the press "may not be successful much of the time in telling people what to think, but it is stunningly successful in telling its readers what to think about." A decade later, Maxwell McCombs and Donald Shaw tested this assertion through a series of studies on how audiences learned about political news. In what they termed "the agenda-setting function of the mass media" in a 1972 *Public Opinion Quarterly* article, McCombs and Shaw asserted that the public's judgments of issue salience can be influenced by the frequency and prominence of coverage media give an issue.

In recent history, those agendas have been shaped by leading community or national news outlets. In a digital communication environment, however, anyone with a large following has the potential to shape the agenda. That includes pop singer Lady Gaga, who produces the top feed on Twitter with nearly 28 million followers as of August 2012. In contrast, only three traditional news organizations had Twitter feeds ranked in the top 100 by followers (see twitaholic.com): CNN Breaking News, the *New York Times* and CNN's main feed. Most of the other top 100 Twitter feeds were linked to entertainers (Justin Bieber), reality stars (Kim Kardashian), entertainment programs (*The Ellen Show*), politicians (Barack Obama) and sports entities (the NBA). It's clear that, at least in the Twitterverse, mainstream news media face stiff competition for the public's attention.

Why are these opinion leaders important? In early mass communication research, they were identified as key intermediaries between media and large audiences — a concept termed the "two-step flow of communication" by Elihu Katz in 1957. Katz argued that community members, rather than getting information directly from mass media, relied on opinion leaders to share and filter information from professional communicators. Although the theory fell out of favor not long after it was proposed as average citizens had more ready access to media content and literacy in the United States soared, researchers are reviving it today for its explanatory value in communication on social networks.

Some contend that in a digital democracy, people want to go to trusted sources to which they feel connected. "Not only are audiences fragmented and difficult to reach, but they are also increasingly distrustful of both news and advertising, preferring instead recommendations from friends, family," argued Matthew Nisbet and John Kotcher in a March 2009 *Science Communication* article. Opinion leaders on the Internet can become trusted sources within their communities of interest: They can attract a massive audience while simulating the kind of personal, friendly conversation that builds trust among followers. A study titled "Who Says What to Whom on Twitter" and presented at the WWW 2011 conference in Hyderabad, India, found that 46% of media tweets pass these elite intermediaries to ordinary users. Of all the tweets received by ordinary users, only about 15% come directly from the media.

A research team examining top Twitter feeds in 2011 and 2012 found that nearly 30% of the posts containing links to or re-tweets of outside information came from traditional news organizations and journalists, suggesting that these sources still can have strong voices in shaping the agenda. The study, "Do Traditional News Outlets Matter in the Twitterverse?" presented at the national 2012 AEJMC convention in Chicago, found, however, that traditional news content was significantly more likely to be used by feeds produced by journalists and news organizations than it was for any other type of Twitter feed. Other Twitter leaders, including politicians, entertainers and business people, rarely used traditional news content as a source for their posts. By topic, traditional news sources were likely to be used for tweets about politics and economics; traditional sources were rarely used when people posted about entertainment, general news and personal topics.

These studies collectively suggest an increasingly fragmented news agenda, with many voices weighing in on what's important. As a result, audiences now hear a cacophony of voices, some expert and some amateur, squawking about the news, with no clear idea of who really knows what. In one infamous example, actor Ashton Kutcher tweeted his shock at the firing of Penn State football coach Joe Paterno. At the time, Kutcher was oblivious to the fact that Paterno was embroiled in a scandal over the cover-up of accusations involving assistant coach Jerry Sandusky and child molestation. Audiences receive different information based on the delivery environment they choose. Audiences reliant on social media for news might have different knowledge from those who read a daily print newspaper or watch a television news program. The result may be fewer common frameworks and knowledge, limiting deliberation on public issues.

Economic Shifts and Layoffs

Social media challenge not only the agenda-setting role of traditional news media but also the news media's profitability. Many researchers have linked these new delivery formats to cutbacks in traditional delivery forms — for example, print editions of newspapers — and to mass layoffs at legacy organizations.

Since the penny press era in the 1830s, U.S. newspapers have relied on an advertiser-supported economic model. The concept is simple. Instead of charging audiences the full price of the content, newspapers and, later, broadcast news operations sold audiences to advertisers, who paid for space in print or on air to reach mass audiences. In contrast, in the subscription model, audiences pay full cost for the content. In the early 1990s, the first online newspapers relied on a subscription model, limiting access to print subscribers or those paying a monthly fee. As search engines began driving online traffic, publishers saw the growing digital audience as a specialty cohort that might attract advertisers. Besides, the Web provided just a sliver of the companies' profits, as the traditional delivery form (print or broadcast) supported all newsgathering operations. As a result, the online pay walls came off and banner ads, buttons and rotating display ads started to crowd newspapers' homepages.

As audience preferences shifted from print and broadcast to online and mobile in the 2000s, print circulation and TV ratings dropped — and ad revenue dropped right along with them. Social media played a dual role in the massive economic shift that hit the news industry in the late 2000s. First, as companies had the same tools at their disposal as newspapers and broadcasters, reliance on legacy media to reach mass audiences diminished. Advertisers built websites and hired social media directors to reach audiences directly and spent less of their budgets on traditional media buys. Second, these same tools available to advertisers became available to other non-journalists, who could compete with news organizations in providing news with very low overhead. Start-ups relied on one or two editors supervising teams of community free-lancers. Third, although social media drive traffic to news websites, these outlets have shifted the advertising rate structure online. Once, sites charged premium prices for banner ads and ads on their homepage as the main entry page. But social media referrals link to specific stories rather than the homepage, shifting entry into websites from the homepage to internal pages. Sites no longer can charge premium prices for certain spots online.

At the 2012 Southeastern Press Association Conference, some publishers and editors like the *Tallahassee Democrat's* Gabordi argued that the industry had erred in removing pay walls. Sessions at the conference focused on maximizing mobile revenue and introducing digital subscription models. Executives pondered how to retrain audiences accustomed to getting free content to pay for information online, a move many saw as key to economic survival. Gabordi argued that credibility is the key for news organizations competing in a digital delivery environment where non-journalists have the same tools at their disposal as journalists. "The quality of journalism is our competitive advantage when we are competing against free," he told those at the July 2012 conference. "People still come to us, because we have to be better."

Journalists and newsroom leaders, however, say they have found being better than non-journalists increasingly difficult in an era of newsroom budget cuts and mass layoffs. Layoffs in news, like all industries, happen. But news layoffs accelerated in the late 2000s, a nationwide economic downturn coupled with the loss of print subscription and ad revenue, in part due to social media. Multiple websites have sprung up to watch these trends. One, newspaperdeathwatch

.com, tracks papers that have closed or cut back on the days they print. Another, newspaperlayoffs.com, tracks newspaper layoffs and buyouts across the nation.

In June 2012, Advance Publications announced cuts of about 600 jobs at four newspapers: the New Orleans *Times-Picayune* and its papers in Birmingham, Mobile and Huntsville, Ala. The move, which cut the four newsroom staffs at least in half, was coupled with an announcement that the papers would print only on Wednesday, Friday and Sunday as the company shifted its focus to the websites. Chuck Dean, a political reporter at the *Birmingham News*, was told his job didn't fit company's "template." He told Steve Meyers at pointer.org in a June 12, 2012, article that he understands that the business is shifting to the Web but that news must be the top priority. "I think it's most likely they want to hear me commit to a digital-first philosophy," Dean said. "I don't have a print-first philosophy. I have a journalism-first philosophy. If you can do journalism on carved stone, I'm all for that."

Changes to News Content and Challenges to Credibility

The layoffs and shrinking newsgathering forces present multiple challenges to journalism, challenges that many argue will hurt the lifeblood of the news industry — its credibility. Critics of the changes brought on by social media contend that the most talented and seasoned journalists have been discarded, leaving too few inexperienced reporters to cover growing and increasingly complex communities.

One laid-off reporter from the *Times-Picayune* was working until her September 30, 2012, severance date set by Advance gave an example of these effects in Jim Romenesko's July 8, 2012, blog. New Orleans had three homicides (including a murder-suicide) in short succession over one July weekend. Without a Saturday night metro reporter, Kari Dequine Harden said she ended up staying after her shift to get the news out — but only one story was carried online, and it was buried deep in the site. "And yet we are focused on digital now? Enhanced? Who is buying this?" she wrote to her supervisors in an angry email after the weekend. "Our product is suffering. Big time. And you all should be aware of that because it means losing respect in the community and losing readers."

Critics contend that news organizations have replaced trained and committed journalists like Harden in the name of profits while relying too heavily on amateur citizen content delivered via social media. One CNN executive said social media sites were indeed a factor in the network's decision to lay off more than fifty photojournalists, technicians and librarians in November 2011. Jack Womack, CNN's senior vice president of domestic news operations, in an email to staff, wrote: "We looked at the impact of user-generated content and social media, CNN iReporters and of course our affiliate contributions in breaking news.

Consumer and pro-sumer technologies are simpler and more accessible. Small cameras are now high broadcast quality. More of this technology is in the hands of more people."

The challenge for news organizations in using citizen content, CNN's King wrote in her 2012 *Neiman Reports* article, is not only verifying that it's accurate but also providing context. Those working with this content must shed a light on the fact that citizen journalists aren't trained in objectivity and news values. "Most of the video we see ... comes from someone in the heart of the story, with a very subjective view of events. No surprise, of course, because iReport and most social media platforms are built for sharing the moments of your life."

Silverman in his 2012 *Neiman Reports* article argues that relying too much on citizen-produced content can open up news organizations to "fraudulent messages and images engineered by hoaxers, manipulators and propagandists, putting pressure on the verifiers to be even more vigilant. "The price for inaccuracy has never been higher. The new world of information abundance, of real-time dissemination, of smartphones and digital cameras and social networks has brought the discipline of verification back into fashion as the primary practice and value of journalists."

Social media also pressure traditional news organizations to break stories before they've undergone full verification. Broadcasters and online news providers have long had the ability to cover news in real time, but journalists traditionally have worked to verify rumors before sharing them with audiences. Howard Finberg and Martha Stone in the Online News Association's 2002 *Digital Journalism Credibility Study* observed that while traditional news outlets and their online counterparts are restricted by professional standards and social pressures to provide accurate and unbiased messages in their coverage, other online producers can deliver messages without these constraints. Online messages are not restricted by news gatekeepers' verification of the facts, analysis of content or editorial review. Finberg and Stone's work was done before social media emerged and further magnified this difference.

Obama's announcement of the killing of bin Laden is just one example of this change. But at least the news turned out to be true. This was not the case in January 2012, when legendary Penn State football coach Joe Paterno lay dying of cancer. On the Saturday night before Paterno's death, an independent student publication at the university, Onward State, posted an article stating that Paterno had died. It promoted its story on Twitter, and CBSSports.com picked up the story. "Links to the reports were shared online by hundreds of journalists, athletes and others; most linked to CBS," Brian Stelter of the *New York Times* reported on Januaury 22, 2012. CBS did admit failure "to verify the original report." The Associated Press, in contrast, published a Twitter message debunking the false reports and later posted a story on how the mistake had occurred. "The lesson for everyone should be that accuracy still matters," Lou Ferrara, the AP's managing editor for sports, entertainment and multimedia, told Stelter. Social media tools should not cause news outlets to compromise their standards, he said. "If anything, this is when news organizations need them most."

Assessment

The trend is clear: Audiences are getting their news in new ways. Increasingly, that means turning to social networks and referrals that may or may not rely on content from traditional news outlets. In September 2010, the Pew Research Center for the People & the Press in a report titled *Americans Spending More Time Following the News* found that although use of traditional delivery platforms (broadcasting and print) was declining slightly, news consumption across digital platforms — websites, cell phones, email, social networks and podcasts — is increasing. Thus, news consumption is at its highest levels since the 1990s. That's good news for journalists who have worked to hone their craft and news companies built on providing credible information. What is unclear is the role traditional news organizations and journalistic values will play in this new environment.

Neiman Reports Publisher Ann Marie Lipinkski, writing in the summer 2012 issue, asserted that journalists and core values must play a strong role given the challenges the new delivery modes pose to the profession — and to society. "The journalism of verification and the immediacy enabled by social media can sometimes collide. The hidden hand of an editor methodically confirming or correcting is not a value hardwired into the mobile phone outfitted with Twitter."

Even critics of the new information environment cannot deny that social media present many advantages for news gathering and dissemination. More people read content, and journalists can reach more sources and access more raw information than ever before. Further, news organizations can provide news in real time and can interact with communities, finding and telling stories that had been invisible in the past. Evidence suggests that social media could offer a true turning point for the profession both in the role it plays in U.S. democracy and in the methods journalist use to play that role.

But these advantages are not without risk. Journalists and news organizations face an uphill battle at trying to present news that matters to audiences inundated with millions of publishers and broadcasters via social media. They face pressure to publish information before it has been verified, and they are having to do more with less as advertisers have found new ways to reach consumers. The biggest challenge for the industry is to make its voice heard in the cacophony that is the social media environment. News leaders must put their credibility first, as it is what will ring true for audiences. They must educate readers and viewers about why they can be trusted by making their processes and values transparent. Ironically, social media offer the perfect delivery format for transparency.

While many decry social media as the death knell for traditional journalism, others contend that the opportunities these networks bring outweigh the risks. The challenge, then, is for the news industry to not only embrace social media but to figure out how to use it to full advantage. The good news is that traditional news media appear to be well poised to continue their role as the chief source of information by reaching audiences in places they're congregating digitally. The fact that news outlets have adopted such a wide array of social tools in a relatively short time bodes well for the spirit of innovation necessary for them to thrive in the 21st century. But traditional media outlets can no longer be just adopters in the social media era. They must become leaders. Finding new ways to use social media to enhance their role is not only the key for their survival, it is the key for the survival of a system of government built on a strong and independent press.

Lipinkski sums up this issue succinctly, writing in *Neiman Reports* that "human obstacles to truth are now aided by increasingly sophisticated co-conspirators. One of the great challenges for reporters and editors is to harness technological tools and put them to work responsibly on behalf of news verification and dissemination."

Points of View

Books

Finberg, Howard, and Martha Stone. *Digital Journalism Credibility Study.* Washington, D.C.: Online News Association, 2002. In one of the earliest studies of shifting news consumption, the authors found that audiences rated online news as credible as news from traditional news sources. Further, data showed that younger people were more likely to get news digitally and that consumers were using online news to enhance rather than fully replace traditional news delivery formats (print and broadcast).

Li, Xigen, editor. *Internet Newspapers: The Making of a Mainstream Medium.* Mahway, N.J.: Lawrence Erlbaum Associates, 2006. This book contains multiple chapters exploring how newspapers developed a digital presence and the implications the shift has on journalism and on U.S. society. The book explores how news is presented online and interactivity, comparing newspapers with other media.

Neiman Reports: Truth in the age of social media. Ann Marie Lipinkski, publisher. Cam-

bridge, Mass.: The Neiman Foundation for Journalism at Harvard University, Summer 2012. This issue is devoted to how journalists expose manipulations, provide credible information and find reliable voices in the social media era. It features multiple articles from news executives and industry experts arguing that social media can be a positive force if journalists continue to focus on core values.

Purcell, Kristen, Lee Rainie, Amy Mitchell, Tom Rosenstiel, and Kenny Olmstead. *Understanding the Participatory News Consumer.* Washington, D.C.: Pew Internet & American Life Project, March 1, 2010. Available online at http://pewinternet.org/~/media//Files/Reports/2010/PIP_Understanding_the_Participatory_News_Consumer.pdf. This report presents data of a national survey conducted in 2009 and 2010 showing that news consumers are increasingly getting news from a variety of sources, including mobile devices. News has become more portable, personalized and participatory, the study found.

Smith, Aaron, and Lee Rainie. *8 Percent of Online Americans Use Twitter.* Washington, D.C.: Pew Internet & American Life Project, Dec. 9, 2010. Available online at http://pewinternet.org/~/media//Files/Reports/2010/PIP-Twitter-Update-2010.pdf. This report presents data from the first ever nationwide survey aimed exclusively at Twitter users. Data show that urbanites, young adults, African-Americans and Latinos use Twitter more than the average American. Twitter also is used as a news source by a growing segment of the population, the report found.

Articles and Research Papers

Craig, David. "In the New Network, Old Values Bend But Don't Break." *Journal Of Mass Media Ethics* 27 (2012): 66-68. In this essay, the author reminds current and future journalists to maintain their ethical standards even as social media and social networks may make it easier to overlook them.

Emmett, Arielle. "Networking News." Ajr.com (December/January 2009). Available online at http://www.ajr.org/article.asp?id=4646. Traditional news outlets are embracing social media as a way to reach new audiences, drive traffic to their websites and survive economically.

Farhi, Paul. "The Twitter Explosion." Ajr.com (April/May 2009). Available online at http://www.ajr.org/article.asp?id=4756. Journalists are embracing Twitter as a newsgathering and news dissemination tool. The author, though, questions how long Twitter will be the social media platform of choice for journalists.

Greer, Jennifer, and Yan Yan. "New Ways of Connecting with Readers: How Community Newspapers are Using Facebook, Twitter and Other Tools to Deliver the News." *The Grassroots Editor* 51:4 (2010): 1-7. Community newspapers are adopting, at a surprisingly quick pace, social networking sites like Facebook and Twitter to reach news consumers. Newspapers that embrace these tools may have an advantage in adapting to the Web 2.0 and digital delivery environments, the authors conclude.

Greer, Jennifer, Justin Blankenship, and Yan Yan. "Do Traditional News Outlets Matter in the Twitterverse? Agenda-setting and the two-step flow on top microblogs." Association for Education in Journalism and Mass Communication, August 10, 2012, Chicago, Ill. This study examined top Twitter feeds' reliance on established news sources for information shared in posts. News outlets and journalists were the most heavily relied upon outside source for content. Traditional news providers still play an agenda-setting role in the social-media environment, perhaps through the two-step flow of communication.

Lenatti, Chuck. "Missing the Mark: Why Online Newspapers Fall Flat with Younger Readers." *Seybold Report: Analyzing Publishing Technologies* 9:3 (February 5, 2009): 5. This article reports on a study that examined how younger and older newspaper readers from the United States and other countries were connecting with newspapers. Younger readers are looking for more interactivity than print papers — or even their online editions — can provide. Increasingly, younger readers turn to social networks for information.

Murthy, Dhiraj. "Twitter: Microphone for the Masses?" *Media, Culture & Society* 33 (2011): 779-789. Journalism can and should use social media sites such as Twitter to gather breaking news but should be cautious in assuming that a majority of the audience is using these sites with regularity.

Index